Vanishing for the vote

MANCHESTER
1824

Manchester University Press

Vanishing for the vote

Suffrage, citizenship and the battle for the census

JILL LIDDINGTON

with
Gazetteer of campaigners

compiled by
Elizabeth Crawford and Jill Liddington

Manchester University Press
Manchester and New York

distributed in the United States exclusively
by PALGRAVE MACMILLAN

The right of Jill Liddington to be identified as the author of this work has been asserted by her in accordance with the Copyright, Designs and Patents Act 1988.

Published by Manchester University Press
Oxford Road, Manchester M13 9NR, UK
and Room 400, 175 Fifth Avenue, New York, NY 10010, USA
www.manchesteruniversitypress.co.uk

Distributed in the United States exclusively by
Palgrave Macmillan, 175 Fifth Avenue, New York,
NY 10010, USA

Distributed in Canada exclusively by
UBC Press, University of British Columbia, 2029 West Mall,
Vancouver, BC, Canada V6T 1Z2

British Library Cataloguing-in-Publication Data
A catalogue record for this book is available from the British Library

Library of Congress Cataloging-in-Publication Data applied for

ISBN 978 0 7190 8748 6 hardback
ISBN 978 0 7190 8749 3 paperback

First published 2014

The publisher has no responsibility for the persistence or accuracy of URLs for any external or third-party internet websites referred to in this book, and does not guarantee that any content on such websites is, or will remain, accurate or appropriate.

Typeset by Servis Filmsetting Ltd, Stockport, Cheshire
Printed in Great Britain by Bell & Bain Ltd, Glasgow

Contents

Maps

List of figures

Acknowledgements

To a greater degree than in my previous writing, this is a collaborative book – and so the span of names of all those I would like to acknowledge is fuller than usual. Foremost, I thank Elizabeth Crawford for her considerable contribution to the research: we embarked on the census project together five years ago, and then collaborated again last year in compiling the Gazetteer. Elizabeth not only contributed her unrivalled familiarity with suffrage biographies, but also married this with her considerable electronic search skills.

As this book is broad in its ambition, drawing together so many individual campaigners, my debts to suffrage historians are particularly extensive. I am extremely grateful to Angela John for generously sharing with me her knowledge of Henry Nevinson and his manuscript diary; to Tara Morton for her Suffrage Atelier expertise, and for devising our Kensington and Chelsea history walks together; to Elizabeth Oakley of the Housman Society for so open-handedly sharing her detailed knowledge on Laurence and Clemence Housman; to Anne Summers for our sunny suffrage walk-and-talk down from Hampstead Heath to Belsize Park; Frances Bedford of the Muriel Matters Society for so enthusiastically guiding me round Muriel's Adelaide; plus Gemma Edwards at Manchester University for assistance with the Helen Watts manuscript, and her father Barry Edwards in Bristol for regaling me with the manuscript's dramatic transmission story.

As my research journeys have criss-crossed so many communities up and down England, I have enjoyed the hospitality and expertise of local suffrage historians, and I warmly thank: Joy Bounds for introducing me to Constance Andrews and her fellow evaders in Ipswich; Kathleen Bradley for exploring Bath and Batheaston with me; Irene Cockroft for guiding me around Wimbledon and Richmond; Sarah Ryan for taking me down to Clemence's street in Swanage; Annie Moseley for our visit out to Lowestoft's windswept house of mass evasion; Colin Cartwright for discussion on Buckinghamshire; and Alison Ronan and Mike Herbert for sharing their knowledge of Manchester history.

Public libraries and record offices have had a rough time of it recently, so I am particularly grateful to librarians and archivists, notably in Manchester, Bristol, Nottingham, Gloucester, Portsmouth, Kensington, Battersea and Street in Somerset. The staff of the Women's Library, despite reorganizing for the move to LSE, have been unfailingly helpful, as has Beverley Cook at the Museum of London. Along with Colin Harris at the Bodleian Library, they have made my many research visits a real pleasure.

For all their help with the book's illustrations, I thank in particular: Hugh Alexander at TNA; Inderbir Bhullar at the Women's Library; Daniel Brown of Bath in Time; Beverley Cook at the Museum of London; John Brock, descendant of Mabel Capper; and staff at Wandsworth Heritage Service.

For kind permission to quote, I am most grateful to the Bodleian Libraries, University of Oxford for the Nevinson diary; the National Trust and Gloucestershire Archives for the Blathwayt diaries; the Museum of London Suffragette Collections, for the Jessie Stephenson memoir; the British Library for John Burns's diaries; and the Trustees of Street Library for the Housman letters.

For their expert reading and commenting on chapters in draft, I am particularly indebted to: Pat Thane for her generous help on the Edwardian roots of the welfare state; Eddy Higgs, the census historian, for his scholarly suggestions; June Hannam, historian of Bristol and the Blathwayt diaries; June Purvis, biographer of Emmeline Pankhurst; Elizabeth Crawford; Elizabeth Oakley of the Housman Society; and most especially Angela V. John for so generously reading and commenting on the entire draft.

The publication of this book has been assisted by a grant to Manchester University Press from The Scouloudi Foundation in association with the Institute for Historical Research (2011); additionally, my research costs were facilitated by a grant, also from The Scouloudi Foundation in association with the Institute for Historical Research (2012). These two awards have helped with the book's design and illustrations; and I am also extremely grateful to Paul Grove for his professional map design.

Finally I would like to thank Emma Brennan, my editor at Manchester University Press, who has carefully guided this book right through from original idea to publication; and all the MUP staff who saw it through production. I also appreciate the friends who kept me going when hypothyroidism slowed the writing down to snail's pace. And as ever, my greatest debt of gratitude is to Julian Harber, not only for helping with some of the more elusive census searches, but also for enthusiastically believing in the project over the last four years – from early start to final finish.

Abbreviations used in the text

General

ILP   Independent Labour Party; the ILP had joined with the trade unions to form the Labour Party.

LGB   Local Government Board, the Whitehall department responsible for planning and administering the 1911 census. Rt Hon John Burns MP was LGB President.

TNA   The National Archives, Kew.

Suffrage

LSWS   London Society for Women's Suffrage. The influential LSWS was run by Pippa Strachey.

NUWSS   National Union of Women's Suffrage Societies, formed 1897. NUWSS president was Mrs Fawcett. Suffragists campaigned using constitutional tactics.

WFL   Women's Freedom League, formed 1907 as a break-away from WSPU, mainly over internal democracy. Charlotte Despard was president. WFL suffragettes also deployed militancy, increasingly using tactics of non-violent civil disobedience.

WSPU   Women's Social and Political Union, formed 1903 by Emmeline Pankhurst. WSPU suffragettes soon initiated militant tactics, master-minded by Emmeline's daughter Christabel.

WTRL   Women's Tax Resistance League, formed Oct 1909.

Adult suffrage wanted the vote for all men and women by abolishing the property qualification. The People's Suffrage Federation was formed in 1909.

Chronology

1908

Apr   Asquith becomes Prime Minister, Lloyd George is Chancellor.

May   WFL caravan departs for tour of Surrey, Sussex and Kent.

Jun   NUWSS procession and WSPU rally. Stone-throwing starts.

Aug   Lloyd George visits Germany to investigate social welfare provision.

Oct   WSPU 'rush the House of Commons'. Muriel Matters (WFL) chained to the grille.

1909

Feb   Muriel Matters flies over London in a balloon, distributing handbills.

Apr   Lloyd George announces his 'People's Budget'.

Jul   First suffragette prisoner refuses food. WFL begins its vigil at Westminster.

Sep   Asquith's meeting in Birmingham interrupted by suffragettes.
Forcible feeding introduced in Winson Green prison, Birmingham.

Oct   First meetings of the Census Committee and of Women's Tax Resistance League.

1910

Jan   General Election: Liberals confirmed in power, though with reduced majority.

Jun   Census Bill: second reading.

Jul   Conciliation Bill: passed.

Aug   Lloyd George polishes his National Insurance Bill.

Nov   WSPU's 'Black Friday' at Westminster.

Dec   General Election: Liberals confirmed in power again, though still with reduced majority.

1911

Feb	The King's Speech read to the Commons: women's suffrage omitted.
Apr	Census night – Sunday 2 April.
Apr – May	Constance Andrews and Emma Sproson imprisoned: non-payment dog licence.
Jun	Coronation Procession: forty thousand women from all suffrage societies march together.
Aug	The House of Lords, threatened by creation of new peers, passes the Parliament Bill.
Sep	Clemence Housman imprisoned in Holloway for tax resistance.
Nov	Asquith announces manhood suffrage bill.
Dec	Lloyd George's National Insurance Bill passed and becomes law.

1912

Spring	NUWSS's labour-suffrage pact; WSPU window-smashing across London.

1918, 1928

Women over thirty win the right to vote, followed by women over twenty-one.

1946

National Health Service Act passed; the NHS was finally created in 1948.

Introduction

This book tells the story of what happened on one single night, Sunday 2 April 1911. It tracks the increasingly hostile relationship between the Liberal government and the suffragettes, neither side willing to concede an inch. Both flanks in this battle clashed at one moment of heightened political drama: census night. Yet this narrative is little known. The documentary evidence of the 'battle for the census' lay forgotten for generations. Released only recently, it can now at last be read, a century later – long after the political dust has settled, with no participants still alive.

By April 1911, 'Votes for Women' campaigning was nearing its height. For eighteen months, hunger-striking suffragettes had been subjected to forcible feeding in prison. Meanwhile, suffragists, preferring campaigns using constitutional tactics, had developed a dense network of local branches and regional federations.[1] Alongside, professional suffrage groups mushroomed – artists and actresses, writers and men's leagues. All shared the same aim: votes for women on the same terms as they were given to men. And this impressively rich tapestry of large organizations and smaller ginger groups grew ever more adept at lobbying Asquith's government.

By then, the Liberals had been confirmed in power by two 1910 general elections. Theirs might be a fragile majority in the Commons; but at least the elections had given Chancellor David Lloyd George an electoral mandate to pursue daringly ambitious reforms, notably his keystone National Insurance scheme. Less flamboyantly and heading the Local Government Board, John Burns continued his crusade against slum housing and appalling infant mortality levels. And, overarching all, the electoral mandate lent Herbert Asquith at Number 10 renewed vigour in his battle for parliamentary supremacy over the reactionary House of Lords, so helping clear the way for the government's extensive health and welfare reforms.

The antagonism between the government and suffrage campaigners had by 1911 grown so bitter that observers outside Britain were amazed. The international suffrage movement looked across the English Channel aghast: Britain, the world's first industrial nation, could boast well-educated wage-earning professional women, indeed even tax-paying woman; yet it had become 'the storm-centre of the women's rebellion'. One German suffragist wrote dramatically of those years:

> The storm-centre of the warfare which waged ... from Lapland to Italy, from Canada to South Africa, was England ... Delicate women ... allowed themselves to be thrown into prison, went on hunger-strike to the verge of death. They suffered for their principles as no other women in any other country have done.[2]

Now, in spring 1911, suffragette organizations urged women, all still unenfranchised, to defy the law and boycott the census. This census rebellion would not be a violent confrontation, like forcible feeding in prison or street battles with the police. Rather, it would be peaceful civil disobedience to challenge the very meaning of citizenship. What *did* it mean, in an otherwise supposedly mature democracy like Edwardian Britain, to be a grown woman, yet to be treated politically like a child, a criminal or a lunatic?

The state required everyone to comply with the census law: suffragettes announced they would refuse. As Sunday 2 April neared, this grew into a contest of minds, of intellects, a battle for the constitutional high-ground, as each side – suffragettes versus Liberal ministers and their civil servants – tried to out-argue, out-wit and out-organize the other. Thus raged the battle for the census. The government evoked the imperative of reliable census data upon which to base future welfare reforms. Suffragettes drew upon distinctive traditions of resistance to an undemocratic state by the disenfranchised. Quiet rebellion, particularly of tax resistance, looked back to ancient roots in English constitutional history. Some had been overtly political – as John Hampden's refusal to pay ship money in the in 1630s. Others drew upon nonconformist heritage – notably Quaker; or inspired by the civil disobedience campaigns of Mohandas Gandhi in South Africa.[3]

The full historical significance of census night, virtually forgotten for almost a century, can only now be recounted – with the opening up of 1911 census schedules. This brand new documentary evidence was publicly released by the National Archives from its vaults only in January 2009.

Most suffrage histories adopt a broad time-frame, from Emmeline Pankhurst's founding of the Women's Social and Political Union (WSPU) in 1903, to the outbreak of war in 1914; or from the 1860s' movement beginnings up to 1928 when all women over twenty-one finally won the right to vote.[4] More rarely have such histories selected a narrower framework. This book, unusually, has a particularly tight focus: one night, well into the campaign, and the months leading up to it.

Similarly, suffrage histories predominantly focus on the campaigners themselves – their petitions and deputations, arrests and trials, their giant processions and delicately embroidered banners. Thus their political opponents – Cabinet members and vote-denying diehards – are relegated to bit-part caricatures who failed to recognize that women had the march of history firmly on their side. Likewise, histories of the Edwardian political turmoil largely focus on key Liberal ministers themselves – notably Prime Minister Asquith and his Chancellor Lloyd George; and on broader sites of conflict – Irish Home Rule, the armaments race with Germany, trade union and industrial militancy. In histories of this hubbub, Votes for Women is routinely relegated to irresponsibly irksome noises off. In such accounts, women (usually just suffragettes) might merit a few pages, at best a single chapter.[5]

Alongside this, census literature has offered scant acknowledgement of the persistent refusal by the Liberal government to enfranchise women: reference to the suffrage boycott remains notably absent. Demographic historians have been keen to celebrate the impeccable professionalism of elite civil servants and 1911's technological achievements (counting machines powered by electricity). It was as if such men had no wives and daughters back home, raising pesky queries about citizenship over the breakfast table. The upshot is: suffrage historians and political (especially census) historians created two distinct historiographies.[6]

This book brings together these two separate narratives, at one sharp point of intersection: census night 1911. It is an account of that conflict – between suffragettes and their supporters on one hand, and on the other the government and Liberal intelligentsia. It was a night when every single resident in every single home the length and breadth of Britain was to be documented in vivid and unprecedented detail.

The public release of the evidence of suffragettes' defiant census boycott had been expected in 2012. But a surprise was in store. On Tuesday 13 January 2009, under a Freedom of Information ruling, the National Archives made individual 1911 census schedules for selected counties accessible – three years early. Gradually during 2009, all English counties became fully searchable by the public, along with the census enumerators' summary pages which offer vivid pen-portraits of individual neighbourhoods.

Excitement was palpable, particularly among family historians keen to trace their ancestors, and among those whose interest had been whetted by *Who Do You Think You Are?* For this census was indeed special. Unlike its predecessors, a 1911 schedule can be read exactly as it was written, usually in the head of family's own hand (rather than transcribed into a book by the enumerator, sometimes standardizing information in the copying process). Here therefore we can glimpse into each Edwardian family's distinctive life. We can read the defiant statements certain suffragettes wrote right across their schedules; we can see any smudging, scribbling and even doodling. Thus the 1911 census offers for the

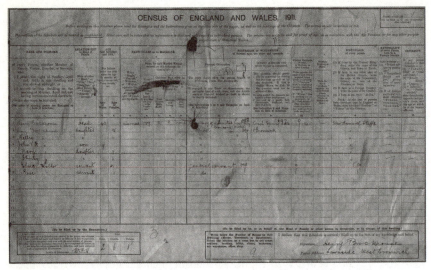

1 The census schedule of Henry Brockhouse, West Bromwich, the Black Country. His wife, a WSPU member, is mysteriously absent – unlike his children.

very first time a unique opportunity to eavesdrop right into the heart of Votes for Women homes.

When fellow suffrage historian Elizabeth Crawford and I heard of the census's imminent release, we quickly re-jigged our research agendas and set to work. Among all the thousands of suffrage campaigners, we looked particularly for boycotters: both census *evaders*, determined to hide from the enumerator, whom we expected to be very tricky to find; and *resisters* who stayed put, returning defiant schedules, though often with very incomplete data. As we needed to be armed with as much biographical information as possible, our initial search was of names listed in Elizabeth's *The Women's Suffrage Movement: a reference guide*.[7] However, this produced such a daunting number of census searches that we soon decided we would have to focus just on England, reluctantly omitting Wales and Scotland. So we looked for those resident in England in spring 1911, gradually adding less prominent campaigners involved in local suffrage activity or just little known; eventually our database totalled 572 campaigners right across England and we began to analyse this data.[8]

All our suffrage reading had led us initially to believe that boycotting had been very widespread; but our findings now suggested considerably lower levels of activity, and we began to assess possible reasons behind this. We retained however our strong sense of the significance of this census rebellion. Faced by such stiff odds, it demanded considerable personal courage to boycott. So, when our research was published in 2011 as '"Women do not count: neither shall they be counted"', it was subtitled 'suffrage, citizenship and the battle for the 1911 Census'.[9]

During 2010, Elizabeth moved across to work on another research project.[10] However, I remained mesmerized by the 1911 census's potential for historians. I was conscious that our article had had to be hedged around with 'Provisional Findings' and 'Preliminary Conclusion'.[11] Further searches remained compelling. I could not let go. Hence this book.

Elizabeth and I had conducted detailed investigations across two counties: her home city London, and for me Yorkshire, site of my *Rebel Girls: their fight for the vote*.[12] These two regions had rapidly thrown up stark contrasts. Was the rest of England more like London, the suffrage mecca, or more like the industrial and rural vastness of Yorkshire, with boycotters few and far betweeen? Were there indeed 'two Englands'?

To find out, I set out on journeys. During 2010–11 my research trips, usually by train, sometimes by road, criss-crossed England, visiting key boycotting communities, then re-visiting them, until I almost met myself coming back. Luckily, I was already familiar with 'suffrage city' Manchester, site of *One Hand Tied Behind Us* (1978);[13] and with residential Kensington, west London home of suffrage writers and artists, notably the 'census siblings' Laurence and Clemence Housman. Other newer adventures beckoned: the Black Country towns of the West Midlands; East Anglian coastal communities like Ipswich; the seaside resorts of Southsea and Torquay. Other cities – Birmingham, Bristol, Nottingham – I now found myself approaching from an unfamiliar angle, pacing their streets with a newly focused research agenda: a suffrage census-night detective chase.[14]

For each city, town or suburb, I drilled deeper down into the rich archival and printed sources, often widely dispersed after a century. I worked forwards and backwards, from individual schedules, across to local histories, Edwardian street directories and the local press – then sideways, to the enumerator's summary page of a neighbourhood. With community networks thus reconstructed, local suffrage clusters suddenly became visible. Alongside, I read more deeply into the competing 1909–11 political narratives, notably John Burns's diaries to see how *he* viewed suffragettes; Lloyd George's awe-inspiring championing of National Insurance provision – and the waves the two men created among many women, all disenfranchised.

Here, then, is the first full-length account of the 1911 suffragette census rebellion, featuring portraits of the boycotters themselves. Academic historians have often preferred aggregated census data rather than reading the handwritten original documents in their own right.[15] However, rather than the wisdom of hindsight, household schedules here are read just *as they were written* – completed on census night itself, 2 April 1911. This book returns the suffrage boycotters to their firesides, to their own communities, right across England. With forensic precision, it aims to pin down campaigners at one key moment, the night each woman *had* to decide whether to comply, to evade, or to resist. They are each seen on the site, and at the moment, of their census decision.

This history swerves away from the well-known protagonists. Rather than urbanely patrician Asquith or 'Welsh wizard' Lloyd George, the key minister tracked here is necessarily John Burns, 'The colossus of Battersea'. Burns's Cinderella Whitehall ministry, the Local Government Board (LGB), was responsible for the census operation. Similarly, the key suffragette group high-lighted initially is not so much the well-known Pankhursts' WSPU, but rather the less celebrated Women's Freedom League (WFL), led by mildly eccentric Charlotte Despard, also from Battersea. So the book draws these hitherto some-what over-shadowed figures into the limelight.

The WFL had broken away from the WSPU in 1907, largely over the Pankhursts' perceived lack of internal democracy. Indeed, the rebel WFL remained painstakingly democratic – though, like the WSPU, it too had its kamikaze moments of spiky militancy. Nevertheless, it built a distinctive style of civil disobedience, especially after Charlotte Despard met Gandhi in 1909. Central to this lay the right, and indeed the obligation, to resist a tyrannical state which withheld political citizenship from women. From this conviction sprang the WFL initiative of organized tax resistance; from this it was but a small and logical step to resist the state's far more universal demand: to comply with the census requirements.[16]

The census aimed for a comprehensive recording of every inhabitant, of the 34 million people across England. So this book takes as its premise: Votes for Women *everywhere*. Good stories of 'celebrity suffrage' are not omitted: suffra-gette martyr Emily Wilding Davison, two years before her death, is discovered hiding overnight from the enumerator in a small Westminster cupboard; and, not far away and equally unintentionally, Emmeline Pankhurst is found listed on the census of a Holborn hotel. Alongside, and recorded on identically printed schedules, are however women hitherto 'hidden from history'. As might be expected, some are branch secretaries in towns with a strong suffragette presence. Others pop up unexpectedly: flat-dwellers in city centres, women living at the end of suburban tube lines, or in remote market towns. Thus in West Bromwich, Mr Brockhouse's mysteriously missing wife surfaces here, though little known to suffrage historians.[17] All were equally disenfranchised, yet all were counted – or at least, so census officials intended. 'The lowliest she in England' trying to make ends meet in over-crowded housing was of as keen interest to census statisticians as a woman surgeon or suffrage dowager with half-a-dozen servants.

In the grander Edwardian houses, the unbending egalitarianism of the census schedule, with its impertinently probing questions and nasty little columns, irked not a few heads of family. Husbands such as Henry Brockhouse were asked about the length of the marriage, how many children had been born and how many had died. However, the advantage of this state surveillance is that – apart from a few of the most determined evaders – almost everyone *was* counted some-how, even if the enumerator had to rely on information from a neighbour or police.[18] Everyone – however humble – counted. This comprehensive documen-tation now permits suffrage historians to reposition 'Votes for Women', to take them from a disembodied existence in the histories, back where women actually lived, in their homes, in their streets, right across England, on census night.

Finally, this book aims to address key questions. It analyses how widespread was the 1911 suffragette boycott – and where. What patterns can historians detect to map spatial patterns across the great English regions and their myriad communities? What numbers were involved in the boycott; and, behind these numbers, what were individual motives for responding on census night as each did – evading, resisting, complying? This returns attention to the Edwardians' broader political agenda: the tensions between suffrage militancy and constitu-tional tactics to achieve a shared aim; and the conflict between prioritizing two different political goals: welfare reform and women's citizenship.

*

From these aims flows the structure of this book. It opens with four prelude sections, introducing key people and their Edwardian politics. Then the chrono-logical narrative covering eighteen months (October 1909 – April 1911) moves towards the census night climax. Most of the story unfolds in public places: at Westminster, in meeting rooms where committees plotted, in public halls with platform speakers urging their audiences on. This narrative peels the layers back to a more optimistic era when dignified civil disobedience seemed successful at chipping away at the Government, back to *before* the arson campaign began.

There then follows a shift in tone and focus, in Part III, 'Places and Spaces'. The pace now slows right down, from chronological briskness to a generous pause of time: just one weekend, one night, merely a few hours. It would of course be impossible to tell the census night story across the whole of England. Selection criteria would have to be identified.[19] From my research journeys, I selected four main areas where the census boycott was particularly widespread: London's bohemian suburbs (Hampstead, plus Kensington and Chelsea); and two major urban areas, the Bristol – Bath and Manchester regions. Not only did these four areas reveal many boycotters, but crucially I could also supplement campaigners' bare schedules with individual vivid personal testimonies.

Daily diaries are of course a magnificent source, allowing eye to be pressed to keyhole. The journals selected here record conscious personal defiance of the enumerator (or, much more rarely, a willingness to comply). Of these, the diary of Hampstead journalist Henry Nevinson illuminates both the boycotts near his home and the entertainments in central London that weekend. Second, Annie Kenney, WSPU organizer for the Bristol region, stayed with the Blathwayts near

Bath; and the diaries of the Blathwayt family, a regular trove for suffrage historians, record census happenings in the Bath area.[20] The boycott in Kensington is
illuminated by a rich cache of letters exchanged between two loving Housman
siblings – Laurence at home and Clemence hiding away in Dorset; their correspondence offers as intimate an hour-by-hour testimony as any diary. For
Manchester, the WSPU organizer was Jessie Stephenson; and her unpublished
memoirs, a little-known typescript, offer a wonderfully vivid blow-by-blow
account of census night across the city.

Then, in the final 'Places and Spaces' chapter, I spread my gaze more widely to
reflect a broader England, with its population of 34 million. This north-to-south
'English Journey' glances briefly at selected local communities, both those where
the boycott was widespread and those where – often surprisingly – it was not.

This geographical mapping of census night in key communities is followed
by a brisker Afterwards chapter taking the story into the final peacetime years.
The historiography chapter then reviews those earlier texts, both suffrage and
census titles, that particularly helped shape this history. The final Analysis chapter dissects this new evidence to assess the boycott's significance, and to look
at correlations with particularly women's occupations. The book ends with the
Gazetteer of Campaigners compiled jointly; arranged geographically, it records
five hundred household schedules.[21]

The logic of this book's structure and sequencing does I think work best,
to help make sense of the complex maelstrom of Edwardian political history.
Here, then, is the battleground for democracy laid bare, a conflict for competing meanings of citizenship, between two rival concepts of democracy and the
state, battling it out up and down England. Government 'by the people' versus
government 'for the people'; with Emmeline Pankhurst and Charlotte Despard
championing one model, and John Burns and Lloyd George the other. For one,
democracy worked, offering vital reform outcomes *for* welfare recipients; for
the other, a tyrannical state denied women full citizenship, excluded them from
participating in the political process, and did *not* work.[22] Alongside also ran a
sharp collision over the effectiveness of tactics to woo politicians and the public:
for suffragettes in the WSPU and WFL, boycotting the census (and so breaking
the law) would be effective propaganda; for suffragists in the extensive National
Union of Women's Suffrage Societies (NUWSS), constitutional tactics were less
likely to alienate key politicians and the public, and so would be more effective.
Many a committed campaigner found herself caught in between – and had to
make an unenviable decision on census night. It was a close call.

This book is about these complex conflicts, the results of which were so well
documented across the country on census night that, a century later, virtually no
household escapes the historian's gaze. So let battle commence!

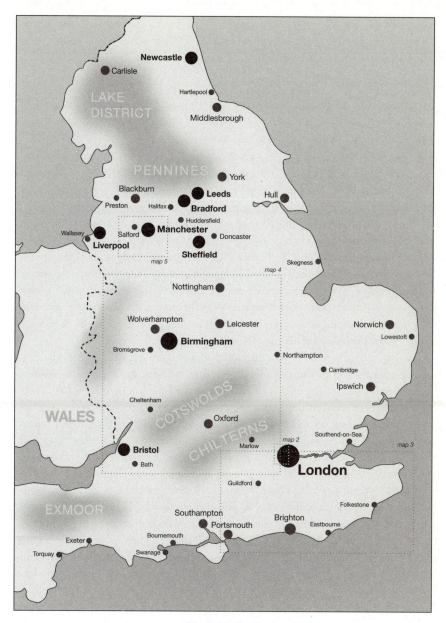

Map 1 England.

PART I

Prelude: people and their politics

1

Charlotte Despard and John Burns, the Colossus of Battersea

It was a confrontation waiting to happen. Both shared a crimson socialist past and an impoverished south-London neighbourhood. Yet amid volatile Edwardian politics, what distinguished the two drove them apart into increasingly warring camps. Charlotte Despard, well-to-do eccentric widow, had chosen to leave her spacious home in the Surrey heathlands. She re-located to Battersea, selecting not just to any part of the borough, but the cramped noisy streets of Nine Elms. Here, down by the Thames wharves, shunting-yards jostled for space with gas works and pumping stations. By contrast, Battersea *chose* John Burns. One of eighteen children, he grew up competing for limited space in a cellar-dwelling near Charlotte Despard's newly adopted home.

Both also shared a similar passionate late-Victorian Marxist socialism, well before the founding of the Labour Party; both immersed themselves idealistically in local practical politics of bringing urgently needed housing reform to Battersea. And both shared a deep belief in the right to vote, in the power of the ballot box, Burns even becoming MP for Battersea. All adults should be enfranchised – to help curb such cruel social inequalities.

But there the similarities ended. Their political priorities diverged dramatically, especially from 1906. Charlotte Despard, one-time socialist, shifted whole-heartedly to women's suffrage – and never looked back. Meanwhile, John Burns became the first working-class man to enter the Cabinet. Thereafter, their political antagonism sharpened bitterly – democracy *by* equal citizenship, or democracy *for* welfare reforms; achieving desired aims using civil disobedience tactics, *or* by working lawfully through the parliamentary processes.

Burns was not only the sole Cabinet minister with impeccably proletarian credentials; he alone also had the misfortune to represent a central London constituency, almost visible from suffrage headquarters. And Charlotte Despard, rising through the suffragette ranks to become Women's Freedom League (WFL) president, soon had her sights trained on the Member for Battersea. Burns, preoccupied with pushing reforms through his ministry, swatted off such irritating hecklers as so many small buzzing flies. Yet neither WFL nor WSPU suffragettes let opportunity slip to harass Burns. As the Liberal government's battle with the House of Lords grew fiercer, and with it the likelihood of elections, the more personal became the mortal combat between Despard's suffragettes and Burns's Battersea loyalists.

*

Their two back-stories could not contrast more dramatically. Charlotte French was born in 1844 into a well-connected naval family. This however offered scant protection either from a mid-Victorian ramblingly inadequate education, or from family misfortune: her father died when she was ten, and her mother was committed to a lunatic asylum shortly after. Still rather unworldly, Charlotte in 1870 married Maximilian Despard. A successful businessman and a rationalist, Max allowed his bride new freedoms. But it was, her biographer suggests, a chilly liberty; and for Charlotte it proved a disappointing marriage, not least because it remained childless.[1]

The prosperous Despards moved into an imposing mansion standing in fifteen acres of tranquil Surrey heathland at Oxshott. Since the opening of the Waterloo–Guildford rail line in the 1880s, their village had become a desirable retreat for well-to-do Londoners. Here, Charlotte wrote, 'I soothed my disappointment and expended my superfluous energies in taking up all sorts of causes' – of which particularly significant was the Nine Elms Flower Mission whereby ladies with country gardens distributed flowers in London slums. For her, this spelled Thames-side Battersea.

Max died in 1890. Charlotte became something of a recluse, shutting herself up at home. It was an aristocratic Oxshott neighbour who came to her rescue. Hearing of the widow's grieving seclusion, she suggested taking up her Battersea philanthropy again. Charlotte seized on this with uncompromising vigour – and her *own* life now began. 'It was only after my husband's death', she said, 'that I was able to give full expression to my ideals.'[2]

She was soon unstoppable. Within months, she had bought a house on Wandsworth Road near Nine Elms. This morphed into the Despard Club, a nurse was hired, toys provided for needy back-street children, and trips organized out to Oxshott. Indeed, Charlotte's brother John French, already Lieutenant-Colonel, moved *his* family into Max's mansion. So, although she retained a small cottage on the estate, Charlotte severed her last link to married life and went to live in Battersea.

Meanwhile, she remedied her woefully deficient schooling, reading American idealist writers Thoreau and Whitman. She became a vegetarian, discarded her oppressive corsets, took to wearing sandals and adopted what became her

VOTES FOR WOMEN.

2 Charlotte Despard, WSPU, 1906–7.

distinctive hallmark headdress, a black mantilla. Yet Charlotte went further: she bought a house in the heart of Nine Elms: 2 Currie Street. Here she opened a surgery for local children, then in 1895 buying premises round the corner in Everett Street for a second Despard Club. She also plunged into local political life, making her first speech (brother John loyally accompanying her), and stood successfully for election as Poor Law Guardian. This was the start of Charlotte's long public career, pursuing unscrupulous slum-landlords and mean-minded workhouse masters. 'The Poor Law', she recalled later, 'was my apprenticeship'.[3]

Witnessing the brutalizing effects of unemployment so close to hand, it was but a small step to her conversion to socialism. This became Charlotte's new religion: the Despard Club was renamed Socialist Hall. But some socialists' suspicion of 'women', plus sectarian squabbling in the Marxist Social Democratic Federation (SDF), left her disillusioned. She shifted her allegiance towards Keir Hardie's new Independent Labour Party (ILP), with its idealistic yet practical socialism. She became friends with trade union organizer Margaret Bondfield, who recalled staying at Charlotte's Oxshott cottage; it was an 'open house for tired people' and, seeing her idiosyncratic hostess 'on her knees, weeding her garden at sunrise, she seemed to me like saint at prayer'.[4]

Through such labour networks, Charlotte became an adult suffragist – wanting the vote for *all* adults, rather than just for those women who satisfied the property qualification. Indeed, after the Liberals' landslide victory at the January 1906 General Election, Charlotte joined a suffragist deputation in May to the new Prime Minister, Campbell-Bannerman. She went as an adultist; and was, one suffrage pioneer wrote later, 'unspeakably rough and rude to me – on the sole ground that I supported what she pleased to call the "limited" bill instead of working for

3 John Burns MP, addressing an open-air meeting, 1897.

"adult suffrage" … She then regarded us of the WSPU as narrow-minded foolish people'.[5]

However Charlotte, never one to entertain half-hearted doubt when an idealistic certainty could be grasped, soon radically shifted her stance. Within months, she had transferred her allegiance to Emmeline Pankhurst's recently formed WSPU: 'I had found comradeship of some sort with men … [but] I had not found what I met on the threshold of this young, vigorous union of hearts'.[6] What helped change her mind? Probably Keir Hardie's own women's suffrage commitment and, through her local Guardian experience, what she saw of John Burns and his Tammany Hall electoral domination of Battersea – from which women were excluded.

John Burns was born in 1858 in Vauxhall, south London, into just such over-crowded slum housing that Charlotte had selected as her mission to redeem. The sixteenth of eighteen children only nine of whom survived infancy, John was aged about nine when the family moved into a basement dwelling in nearby Battersea. His mother worked exhaustingly taking in laundry; his father, never a steady provider, was unable to afford the weekly penny to keep John at school, so he had to leave when he was ten or eleven. In 1870, he began working in a Battersea candle factory, later training as a riveter, then obtaining an engineering apprenticeship on the north bank of the Thames. Eating his lunchtime 'piece' here, he could have an eye along the river to Westminster.[7]

Energetic and ambitious, Burns soon left his family behind. He became a voracious reader – Tom Paine, Owen, Ruskin; and was inspired by an exiled French communard from whom he learnt '*Le pouvoir politique est indispensable ... It faut voter.*' Convinced of the absolute necessity of the ballot box, and now in the engineers' union, Burns joined the SDF. Here his powerful oratory won many converts. His voice was likened to a giant gramophone, his earthy epigrams springing straight from his own London streets. Burns was twice arrested over free speech, but just about found time to get married.[8]

The sectarian SDF straitjacket could not however restrain Burns long. To advance urgently needed reforms for the people of Battersea, he was elected in 1889 onto the newly formed London County Council (LCC). Here he distinguished himself with his keenly practical engineer's craft skills – bridge-building, efficient drainage systems; he even attended LCC debates armed with chunks of mortar, all to further the interests of working-class families. After the great London dock strike, Burns became *the* towering labour figure. Everyone wanted his golden voice on *their* side. Even the Battersea Liberals eyed him as a potential candidate. Indeed, in 1892 he was elected as local MP, his salary provided by the Battersea Labour League; and the family moved up to a healthier neighbourhood, Lavender Hill.[9]

Burns trod a fine line between his original labour convictions and growing Liberal loyalty. A metropolitan secularist, he found all the ILP 'religion of socialism' irksome. Indeed, after MPs like Keir Hardie joined with trade unionists in 1900 to form the Labour Party, Burns found himself increasingly out-of-step. A tub-thumper, he still maintained a good line in vilifying opponents as 'the riff-raff of the Stock Exchange and the parliamentary dead-beats'. However, his impeccable proletarian credentials and powerful oratory made him an increasingly desirable ally for the radical wing of the ascendant Liberal Party.

So when Campbell-Bannerman formed his Liberal government in late 1905, confirmed at the January 1906 Election, it was no surprise that Burns was appointed to the Cabinet, its first working-class member. Appointed President of the Local Government Board (LGB), Burns might be vilified as a class traitor by middle-class Fabian reformers like Beatrice Webb; he might be over-shadowed by the instinctively brilliant David Lloyd George, now President of the Board of Trade; he might even be joshed for walking down Lavender Hill resplendent in court dress with gold lace. Yet he remained wildly popular in his own Battersea patch. At his first local appearance as minister, Burns, accompanied by his wife and son, was received with tremendous cheers, and then spoke for nearly two hours. Burns knew that real power lay within grasp: by working hard, he could now *do* things, make real improvements to real people's lives.[10]

So what were his political priorities? He continued to support adult suffrage, including it in his election address. Indeed, for Saturday 19 May 1906 Burns wrote in his diary of the deputation Charlotte Despard had joined:

> Up at 5. Surveyors' gathering at [Battersea] Town Hall, reception and speech. LGB
> in time to see Suffrage Deputation emerge from Foreign Office. Went off well but
> disappointed with C[ampbell-]B[annerman]'s refusal to pledge Government.[11]

It seems Burns shared something of the women's disappointment. He may ironically then have been more sympathetic to women's suffrage than was Charlotte
Despard, still an adultist. And since he must have known her, he would *surely*
have recognized her eccentric profile?

Soon Burns had an opportunity to promote policy close to his heart. He
presided over the first National Conference on Infant Mortality. His speech
makes two points absolutely clear. First that, drawing on personal experience,
Burns spoke with passion. A hundred thousand infants died annually and,
although prosperity had increased, 'the weakest, the smallest, and the dearest
bore unduly the burden of death'. Second, and perhaps surprisingly given his
own bitter family experience, Burns knew where he firmly placed individual
moral responsibility:

> First concentrate on the mother. What the mother is the children are. The stream is
> no purer than the source. Let us glorify, dignify, purify motherhood by every means
> in our power … That is at the bottom of happy, healthy children.[12]

Some local Medical Officers of Health stressed poor wages and irregular employment, appalling overcrowding and insanitary tenement housing. But Burns
pointed his finger at irresponsible married women, with 'delinquent' mothers
going out to work 'another fruitful cause of infant mortality'. The healthy home,
with breast-fed babies, had the mother present all day rather than in the factory.
Additionally, if he had pulled himself out of the slums by dint of hard work and
sobriety, might not others do the same? As part of his crusade, Burns instructed
his LGB officials to collect statistics, so that legislation might be introduced. And
he soon authorized a national survey of infant mortality, the first time a British
government had taken this seriously. In trying to legislate for reform he was
however frustrated by his lacklustre LGB civil servants: Burns was an assiduous
if rather hapless 'yes, minister' in a Cinderella department.[13] At the Board of
Trade, meanwhile, Lloyd George was already honing his free-ranging ministerial
style, exploring daring ways the state could intervene to improve people's lives

Despite Edwardian prosperity and progress, the contrasts in over-crowding
and health inequalities remained dramatic. John Burns, his wife Charlotte and
schoolboy son Edgar lived at 37 Lavender Gardens. These pleasantly suburban
twelve-roomed houses up Lavender Hill, with small gardens front and back,
attracted white-collar professionals seeking a healthy residential neighbourhood.
Next door lived a schoolmaster, three brothers and their widowed mother; on
the other side, a widowed teacher, two adult children, four civil-servant boarders
and a domestic servant. The number of rooms per person was generous, as was

4 'The Colossus of Battersea', the Rt Hon John Burns astride the streets of 'his native borough', *Punch*, 15 Dec 1909.

the ratio of the economically active to their dependants, with noticeably few children.[14]

Lavender Gardens was only two miles uphill from Nine Elms down near where Burns had grown up, but the contrast remained stark. Charlotte Despard's chosen home at 2 Currie Street obviously had an untypical household structure. But those of her neighbours among these edgeland terraces had a pattern. Houses were subdivided, three rooms on either floor, with lodgers upstairs. At No. 8 lived a bricklayer's labourer and his wife, of whose ten children two had died; two sons were in the army, four children at school, plus a one-year-old, with a fourteen-year-old daughter helping her hard-pressed mother. Further along Currie Street lodged a coal carrier and his wife, of whose twelve children ten still lived; two sons also worked as coal carriers, probably at the Nine Elms shunting yard nearby; with five other children living there too, nine people were squashed into just the three rooms. Front doors opened straight on to the street, pairs of households sharing a small back yard.[15]

The political geography of Battersea was shot with similar contrasts. For hard-working John Burns, his daily journey to work down Lavender Hill snaked past Nine Elms and his boyhood home, before crossing the Thames. His political ascendancy had earlier taken him to the doors of Westminster and right into the House of Commons; now he proceeded on to his imposing LGB building

in Whitehall. Here, once the piles of paper were dealt with on Saturday morn-
ings, Burns noted in his diary how he would stand on the Embankment 'to see
work people streaming southward over [Westminster] bridge to their homes …
Although people [are] more sober than of yore still there is a greyness and a
sadness not pleasing to see'. He had witnessed so much during his fifteen years
in Parliament. Then, with his chosen weekend companion, Edgar, Burns would
cycle off through London's green open spaces so dear to his heart, taking in the
'new park to see works for the workless'.[16]

The contrast with Charlotte Despard's journey towards Westminster could
not be more dramatic. This citadel of citizenship remained barred to all women
whatever their social class. Now a WSPU convert, she had risen rapidly through
the suffragette ranks; indeed she had become joint WSPU secretary with scientist
Edith How-Martyn, who had given up a University of London mathematics
lectureship to devote herself to suffrage.[17]

Events were however moving fast, and the WSPU was changing radically.
Prosperous barrister Frederick Pethick Lawrence and his wife Emmeline joined,
putting the small organization on a more financially sound professional basis,
and later started the WSPU newspaper, *Votes for Women*. Christabel Pankhurst,
arriving in London, took control of WSPU policy.

The focus was now on Westminster. In October 1906, at a WSPU demonstration in the House of Commons Lobby, suffragettes were arrested; to her frustration, Charlotte Despard was not among them. Then the following February
a determined Despard, flourishing aloft her umbrella, led the surging crowd
of women marching to Parliament. This time, having taken the precaution of
disguising her distinctive appearance under a thick motoring veil, Despard was
arrested amid the pandemonium and charged. 'I am heartily glad to have done
it at last' she informed reporters later. And like other suffragettes refusing to pay
her fine, she was sentenced to twenty-one days in Holloway, a sharp learning
curve for a woman already in her sixties. She had at last achieved the palm of
imprisonment, but Despard now saw gaol for the degrading experience it was.[18]

In the flurry of WSPU developments, the two co-secretaries became discreetly side-lined. So, when disquiet grew among members about the autocratic
manner with which Christabel especially was now steering the WSPU, Charlotte
Despard, Edith How-Martyn and articulate suffragette Teresa Billington-Grieg
led a protest. The issue of WSPU internal democracy came to a disputatious head
in autumn 1907: Emmeline Pankhurst, scenting disobedience and interpreting
it as treachery, cancelled the planned WSPU conference, vesting power in her
appointees. The 'disloyal' suffragette rebels decided to hold their own meeting
anyway, on 12 October; they claimed (with some logic) that *they* were the WSPU
mainstream, betrayed by an undemocratic leadership. From this dissident gathering sprang the break-away organization led by Charlotte Despard and Teresa
Billington-Grieg. In November it renamed itself the Women's Freedom League.

Despard became WFL president, underwriting its initial expenses and the rent of its London office: 18 Buckingham Street. Between the Strand and Embankment, it stood tantalizingly almost within sight of Westminster.[19]

The WFL's first winter, 1907–8, was hectic. In November, 'sandwich-ladies' began parading the London streets, bearing on their shoulders posters announcing 'Votes for Women', the sandwich-boards prudently made of light cardboard. Local WFL branches, naturally including Battersea, ran meetings addressed by Despard, Billington-Grieg and Victor Duval. Once an active south London Young Liberal, Duval had resigned after seeing a woman thrown out of a John Burns meeting.[20]

Other prominent WFL members included writer Irene Miller, also earlier imprisoned; and Marion Holmes from Croydon in Surrey, wife of a self-employed chemist, and mother of two daughters. She too had been imprisoned after a deputation to the Commons and it was perhaps then that she fell under Despard's spell. Certainly, Marion Holmes brought the whole Croydon WSPU branch across to join the WFL, and later recalled those early hectic days:

> We began almost to live in Buckingham Street. What jolly 'scratch' teas we had on the bare office tables, and what startling plots and plans we hatched up round them! Everyone took a willing hand in the cleaning and washing up, and it was no unusual thing to see Mrs Billington-Grieg or Miss Irene Miller, or some other favourite orator suddenly down her broom or tea-cloth and rush off with a belated memory of an expectant audience.[21]

As with the NUWSS and WSPU, most leading WFL members were middle-class women, able to rely on a reasonably comfortable income. But, as with both the other organizations, there were important exceptions. Emma Sproson of Wolverhampton stands out. Aged forty, Emma described herself as 'a child from the lower depths' who 'worked as a half-timer at nine years of age'. She was married to Frank Sproson, a postman, and they had three children. Frank was secretary of the Wolverhampton ILP branch and naturally Emma was also a member. She too had joined the WSPU and suffered imprisonment; but, concerned about 'a dictatorship of the Pankhursts', Emma switched to Despard's WFL.[22]

For Charlotte Despard, cast in the role of roving firebrand, life had now become, as her biographer phrased it:

> a succession of telegrams, railway journeys and speeches. Seemingly tireless, she shuttled across the nation, weaving the cloth of the Freedom League a little more tightly with each traverse.

She could also be an exasperating chair, refusing to exert her authority until confusion reigned. Confusing some debating detail for a point of principle, she hurled herself into needless quarrels, and then would enquire in endearing bewilderment, 'Now what *is* the will of the committee?'[23]

5 Emma Sproson of Wolverhampton (*second left*), carrying a WFL sandwich board, date unknown.

The WFL had bid for democracy and gained independence. Like the WSPU, it chose militancy but was alienated by autocratic rule. Like the NUWSS, it opted for internal democracy but had little patience with constitutional suffragists' often stodgy cautiousness.[24] Now going it alone, the WFL bravely cast its bread on the choppy waters of Edwardian campaigning, building its own distinctive style of civil disobedience. Like other groups, it focused on those Cabinet ministers who denied women their rightful citizenship. Naturally, among these was John Burns – especially as he had reportedly urged that 'the labour of married women must be enormously curtailed', without suggesting *how* women (and their children) whose husbands did not earn a living wage were to avoid starvation.[25]

Key to WFL demands was the ancient right of a subject to petition. Their immediate focus was the King's Speech at the Opening of Parliament on Wednesday 29 January 1908. When this omitted women's suffrage, the WFL decided to try to present their petition to the King himself. Immediately after this ambitious plan failed, early next morning WFL members diverted their deputation – visiting six ministerial homes, including Burns's at Lavender Hill. *The Times* reported:

> They asked to see [ministers] personally in order to present petitions for signature. Crowds assembled and watched the proceedings of the women, who in some cases caused considerable annoyance by ringing the bells and knocking at the doors of

the houses. The suffragists were disappointed at their reception, and proceeded to make speeches. The police interfered, and requested the women to leave. A number of them, however, refused to do so, and were taken into custody.[26]

Suffragettes visiting Lavender Hill were frustrated, as Burns had just left home. However, nine women were arrested and taken to court, mainly around Westminster, and seven imprisoned. Indeed, during 1908, Lavender Hill Police Court became a regular suffragette location; on one occasion:

the protesters, the prisoners, several policemen, the magistrate and the public all held forth at the same time, which rather spoiled the orations though adding to the excitement.[27]

However, just two months later, an implacable opponent of women's votes moved centre-stage. With Lloyd George his new Chancellor, Asquith shortly became the most powerful and intransigent enemy of women's suffrage.

2

Muriel Matters goes vanning it with Asquith: campaigning cross country

Asquith became Prime Minister in April 1908. Till then, he had been Chancellor of the Exchequer and an adroit deputy leader of the House of Commons. His predecessor Campbell-Bannerman's solution to any problem was 'send for the sledge-hammer'.[1] Yet Campbell-Bannerman's badly declining health meant that Asquith's status as heir apparent was assured. So that spring, when women needed to target their suffrage deputations effectively, they naturally directed them to the Treasury. Then they analysed Asquith's words with sinking hearts.

What made Asquith so distinctively hostile to giving women the vote? Partly it was the clubby masculine world (Balliol, barristers' chambers, politics) he occupied, a world of ambition and achievement. 'Women played very little part in my life', he wrote – though he enjoyed charming female company at country house parties. Partly it was his lifelong party loyalty to Liberalism: nothing must be allowed to ruffle the progress a Liberal government alone could offer, nothing must benefit the Conservatives electorally. Certainly, hostility to women's suffrage was in his blood-stream early: he spoke against an 1892 bill, arguing that most women were uninterested, merely 'watching with languid and imperturbable indifference the struggle for their own emancipation'. He returned to this theme repeatedly, later writing of the notion of women voters as: 'a dim, impenetrable ... element ... They are for the most part hopelessly ignorant of politics, credulous to the last degree, and flickering with gusts of sentiment like a candle in the wind'.[2]

Asquith continued to bring a lawyer's intellectual fastidiousness to all his pronouncements on enfranchising women. In December 1907 while still Chancellor, he offered to lift his opposition 'the moment that I am satisfied of two things, but not before, namely, first, that the majority of women desire to have a Parliamentary vote, and next, that the conferring of a vote upon them would be advantageous to their sex and the community at large'.[3] Asquith then reiterated his patrician aloofness when meeting a NUWSS deputation to the

Treasury on 30 January 1908. *The Times*'s pompous editorial reveals Asquith's urbane deflection of the women's demand:

> He told the deputation that the first thing they have to do is persuade the great mass of women that they ought to have votes, and the second thing is to convince the great mass of men that this country ought to plunge into an experiment for which there is no precedent … Men have never obtained things that they wanted until they had gone through the work of converting the majority to their views and getting it to announce its conversion at the polls. The Government has more than enough work on hand, and would be justly condemned as trifling with the country were it to put that work aside as the ladies demand … The[y] must try to imitate the patience exercised in similar cases by mere man.[4]

So women faced no fewer than four mountains to climb: to convince the majority of women, to convince the majority of men, for an election to be fought on the issue, and finally to exercise patience. A tall order. However, a short-cut through these obstacles soon appeared. In February, a women's suffrage bill was introduced; its provisions were fairly broad, as it would enfranchise both single and married women. With broad support from most Liberal and Labour MPs, it won a majority of 179.[5] When the women waiting outside heard of this victory, and talk of the bill being carried during the current government's term of office, they cheered. They unanimously demanded that the government should give facilities for the Bill 'to become law during the present session of parliament' (i.e. within two to three years).

This was spring 1908: there was still considerable optimism for the new Liberal government, in power for barely two years. Campaigners kept up the pressure; opponents were however alerted. Soon the suffrage weekly newssheet *Women's Franchise* ran 'Save the Bill' alarms. Indeed, the bill was referred to the Committee of the Whole House, and so effectively killed off.[6] Optimism had peaked, prefiguring what was to come. Asquithianism already prevailed.

*

On 1 April, Campbell-Bannerman resigned. Edward VII, holidaying in Biarritz, summoned Asquith: he travelled incognito across France and kissed hands in the king's hotel room on 8 April. By the end of the month, Asquith was confirmed as leader of the Liberal Party – and set about rearranging his Cabinet. John Burns retained the LGB. But David Lloyd George was promoted meteor-like to Chancellor of the Exchequer, Winston Churchill replacing him at the Board of Trade. Asquith thus strengthened the radical reforming side of Liberalism.

This cabinet reshuffle triggered a raft of ministerial by-elections; notably Churchill stood in marginal North-West Manchester. Suffragettes sped north to 'Keep the Liberal Out', and a harried Churchill was defeated. In the other contests, the Liberals retained the seat.[7] Among suffragettes rushing into this by-election fray was Muriel Matters, recently arrived from South Australia and with a flair for flamboyant propaganda.

Muriel Matters blew in on the Edwardian political scene with all the bracing gusto of a fresh young-country breeze. After all, in states like South Australia women already *had* the vote. Her family fortunes had fluctuated, and after studying music at the University of Adelaide, she had to earn her living. Muriel was inspired by Ibsen's *A Doll's House* which played on the consequences of women's financial dependence upon men. She also read Walt Whitman's poetry, determining to work as an elocutionist. She began giving literary recitals in both Adelaide and Sydney – until approached by a firm of theatre managers. Muriel then became an actress, touring Australia and New Zealand, on the road and living in theatrical lodgings. But, alerted to sexual double standards, she recalled: 'I found the condition of stage life for women so repugnant to me that I returned to my old work of teaching elocution'.[8] Until she decided to make an even bolder journey. In late 1905 Muriel boarded the passenger ship *Persic* – and set sail for London.

Twenty-eight-year-old Muriel disembarked on 6 October 1906. It was a timely arrival. Just a week later, Christabel Pankhurst and Annie Kenney stood up in Manchester's Free Trade Hall and demanded: when will the Liberal government give votes for women? Newspaper headlines followed. 'Within six weeks of my landing', she recalled, 'I was attending meetings in Caxton Hall, drinking in all your rebellious sentiments'. Moreover, she brought with her an introduction to the 'anarchist prince' Kropotkin, who encouraged Muriel to use her gifts to make the world a better place. Life in the metropolis was thrilling; though with theatrical jobs highly competitive, she had to take work as a journalist. Muriel plunged right into Britain's new militancy. Among the WSPU suffragettes, she was particularly inspired by the radicalism of Charlotte Despard – Battersea's own Kroptokin. And in late 1907 she joined her in the break-away to form the WFL.

In spring 1908, Asquith's ascendancy meant by-elections, notably Manchester. Naturally, Muriel was speedily talent-spotted by the WFL. Marion Holmes noted how:

> It was in the very earliest days of the Women's Freedom League that Muriel Matters cast in her lot with us. She made her first speech at one of the 'At Homes' held in the offices in Buckingham Street, and I remember how eagerly we discussed her afterwards. Who was she? She had told us in her speech that she was an Australian, but for the rest we knew nothing. Then, in the usual cold-blooded fashion of N[ational] E[xecutive] C[ommittee] members we debated how we could best use her gifts – her enthusiasm, her eloquence, her wonderful magical voice – for the cause.[9]

Asquith had requested that the majority of women be convinced. Where was this 'majority' to be found? Four and a half million people lived in London. But

6 Muriel Matters, Australian actress, WFL. This portrait was made into a 'Votes for Women' postcard for the WFL.

where did the rest live? Well, Surrey, Sussex and Kent had a population totalling over two and a half million, many living in market towns, small villages and seaside resorts. Yet such communities had scarcely been touched by the suffrage message.[10] What better way to reach this 'majority' than to set off in a horse-drawn caravan, meandering down the country lanes to remote communities? If this is what Asquith demanded, then the WFL would deliver – and Muriel Matters would help.

The great processions of June 1908 are now well-known, their beautifully embroidered banners fluttering in the London breeze. Far less familiar are the intrepid caravan tours starting in May. Yet they represent a similarly significant initiative of political persuasion, hitherto largely neglected by suffrage historians. While banners remain well-preserved, wooden vans are far more vulnerable to decay. Moreover, they visited more isolated locations and were photographed less frequently, often just the vanners' own informal snap-shots.

Caravans offered Edwardian bohemians a promise of freedom, and political caravans had their own precedents. For women, vanning certainly became a symbol of liberty; but in taking their controversial message out into the countryside, suffragettes showed considerable daring: it had not been tried before and they had to make it up as they journeyed. They needed a route that would recruit *new* members, but also had to rely on known sympathizers to get meetings going.

So where to start? Well, sandy wooded Oxshott Heath had long been an enticing mecca for horse-drawn vans, both gypsies and children's 'Band of Hope' temperance outings. Caravans were a familiar sight from Charlotte Despard's cottage; and both she and Muriel Matters found inspiration in Whitman – whose 'Song of the Open Road' begins:

> Afoot and light-hearted I take to the open road,
> Healthy, free, the world before me,
> The long brown path before me leading wherever I choose.[11]

Despard obtained a caravan locally, giving it a smart suffrage make-over and providing furniture. Others donated a camp bedstead, lunch basket, kettle and maps. So, on Saturday 16 May 1908, at Despard's invitation, a small crowd of WFL well-wishers gathered at her cottage:

> to witness the departure of the first Women's Suffrage Van on its journey … Before starting, everyone was allowed to explore the inside of the Van, which is most conveniently fitted up for the comfort of the pioneers.[12]

Despard and Matters, Teresa Billington-Grieg and Van Organizing Secretary, Lilian Hicks, another founding WFL member, all made short speeches 'full of hope and courage'. Then it was time to depart.

> Some amusement was caused by the persistent refusal of the Van to go through the gateway of Mrs Despard's garden. This was attributed to the fact of one of the horses being nick-named 'Asquith'. So, naturally, he would feel a reluctance to advance the cause of Women's Suffrage. However the gate was lifted off its hinges, the Van got through, amidst enthusiastic cheers, and made its first official appearance on the King's highway.[13]

The cart-horse plodded its way over gently rolling wooded hills down into Leatherhead. The town offered suffragettes a rough reception at open-air meetings. The 'Liberal elite of the district' rang bells and blew whistles. Indoor meetings were easier, hecklers not being admitted: Edith How-Martyn and Muriel Matters were 'enthusiastically received'. Then, Lilian Hicks reported laconically, 'we were escorted to the railway station by what seemed to be the entire male population of the town – with their musical toys'.

At Guildford, small boys threw orange peel and apple cores. When things grew ugly, Matters told the crowd: 'We are free and independent women … I have been in the midst of a seething mob before, and I am ready to give my life.' At Godalming, even she was drowned out and had to give up speaking. Such propaganda work proved strenuous, despite hospitable WFL friends entertaining the vanners. Reports nevertheless remained upbeat:

> We hope that this van is but the forerunner of others, the pioneer of the movement for awakening in country districts an interest in votes for women, and spreading the knowledge of *what* women want, and why they want it.[14]

7 Muriel Matters in WFL van, probably near Guildford, May 1908.

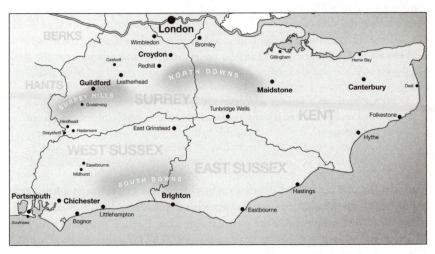

Map 2 South-east England: Surrey, Sussex, Kent and Hampshire.

Poor old 'Asquith' plodded up the Surrey hills, then hurtled down. As the land-scape grew more rural, the vanners grew cannier, alerting the police in advance for protection. On 23 May, they arrived at sleepy Haslemere: Muriel reported that the first open-air meeting was held 'under perfect police supervision'; however, with bells and whistles still making a din, women in the audience were invited to listen in peace to speeches made from the caravan. At nearby Grayshott, 'the hall was packed to the doors', the audience mesmerized at hearing an Australian actress speak in their village, and the vanners departed 'feeling that they had not only left many friends behind, but had secured fresh converts to the cause'.[15] Asquith, beware!

Once the van crossed into Sussex and reached Midhurst, their reception was yet more enthusiastic; indeed, so much so that Matters reported it as 'one of the brightest spots for seed to take root', urging that an organizer be sent down immediately. A Mrs Cummin, wife of the local vicar (undoubtedly accompanied by daughters Vinvela, Christobel, Elsie and Mary) was so impressed by the caravan that a West Sussex WFL branch sprang up.[16] Elsewhere, their reception remained mixed. The Chichester crowd included so many 'hostile roughs' that the meeting ended stormily, with police helping women to their caravan. Afterwards it became nigh impossible to book halls.[17]

From coastal resorts Bognor and Littlehampton, their route then curved inland, skirting Brighton. Matters was impressed how keenly country women, 'who hitherto have known nothing of the movement', listened. Crossing into rural Kent, she noted ruefully how easy it was to lose sight of Asquith – premier, not horse: 'it is difficult to feel strenuous-minded or militant in the midst of cornfields scarlet with poppies, and hedges of dewy honeysuckle, and sweetbriar surrounding the caravan'.[18] Yet they soldiered on, arriving in Tunbridge Wells on 29 June. Here, Muriel found that 'a-gipsying' held new unexpected delights – and her own life changed when she met a particularly warm welcome, as she later recalled:

> As the Caravan made its way slowly up the hill …, Violet Tillard came forward and greeted us. We became friends from that moment … She joined the WFL and worked continuously. It is … not possible to convey what she really was to those of us who were honoured by her friendship …. Courage – sympathy – generosity … shy, elusive qualities accompanying the grim[m]est kind of determination and will.

Tall, slender and delicate, Tillard, daughter of an ancient country house, now threw herself into the campaign – and life with the charismatic Australian actress. Theirs was one of the intense life-partnerships which sprang from the Votes for Women campaign.[19]

Then in August, Charlotte Despard rejoined the van, visiting seaside towns like Hastings. 'I am more and more convinced', she wrote, 'that this is one of the best and least expensive ways of propagandum, and I hope we shall have several such caravans as this moving about the country'.[20] In mid-September, Margaret Wynne Nevinson joined the end of the tour in Kent shortly before it halted for the autumn. She was the wife of war correspondent Henry Nevinson; they had idealistically joined Toynbee Hall in the East End, before moving to Hampstead. Now with her husband frequently away, Margaret had to cope with bringing up their two children; yet she still found time to be an active Poor Law Guardian and a WFL founder-member. Later she recalled those dangerous vanning days:

Perhaps, those of us who went out with the caravan to preach our gospel in remote villages, had the worst experiences … At Canterbury we drew a vast audience to the cattle-market … The audience was very noisy and ill-behaved, and some youths trundled our open lorry up and down, making it hard for us to keep our balance … At Herne Bay, we had a very hostile reception, and finally our lorry was pushed along the parade with loud cries of 'Chuck' em in the sea.' A bodyguard of fisher-man came to our help and escorted us to … where our caravan was parked. They stood as sentinels by the gate, whilst outside the mob howled like wild beasts till a late hour.[21]

This very first tour had taken Asquith at his word: WFL branches sprang up in Eastbourne and Brighton, thanks in part to seeds sown by these intrepid van-ners.[22] The importance of caravans was also symbolic: it inspired women to take campaigns fanning right out cross country, to have the freedom to outface their opponents.

By now, the broader suffrage campaign had expanded beyond recognition – largely due to the giant London rallies of June 1908. The WSPU's carefully planned monster demonstration in Hyde Park on Sunday 21 June, with excur-sion trains bringing in suffragettes from distant towns, possibly reached a crowd of quarter of a million. And the previous Saturday, the NUWSS's giant proces-sion proved a remarkable public spectacle, each contingent bearing its beautifully embroidered banners. The WFL, the only militant society invited to join, was led by Charlotte Despard, her lips pursed in grim determination; this contingent, marching six abreast in Block 7 (including Muriel Matters, who sped up to London to attend) was greatly cheered by an enthusiastic crowd. Behind was Block 8, also six abreast, comprising the London Society for Women's Suffrage (LSWS), arranged alphabetically by constituencies.[23] Such methodical ordering could hardly be the work of anyone other than Philippa Strachey, already a doyenne of London suffrage marches. If any family epitomized the NUWSS, it was the Strachey clan. Some were born into it: Philippa and her literary Bloomsburyite brother Lytton; others married into it – including Ray Costelloe, also now bitten by vanning enthusiasm.

With her Anglo-Indian ideals of noble imperial service, Lady Strachey was the conservative *grande dame* of women's suffrage. While some on the wilder shores of the campaign might wish to link enfranchising women with Indian independ-ence, she did not. Mother of ten children and now widowed, Lady Strachey's family and their five servants lived in an eighteen-room house in Belsize Park. Here daughter Pippa, in her mid-thirties, acted as family pivot. University edu-cation had not been considered for her as it was for her younger sisters. Lytton, Cambridge graduate, deeply attached to Pippa, considered her 'a singularly reactionary woman' owing to 'not having gone to Cambridge'.[24]

Indeed, Pippa, arrived back from India and looking around for the expected

8 Ray Costelloe, Ellie Rendel with two helpers in the NUWSS van, 1908.

liveried rickshawmen, demanded privileges and expected to command. Emily Davies, pioneer founder of Girton in the 1860s, was a neighbour; through her, Pippa was recruited to work for the LSWS in 1906; she became full-time secretary, though undoubtedly unsalaried, in 1907. Her first task was to organize the NUWSS's 'Mud March' (it was ill-advisedly held in February). In this family affair, Lady Strachey walked at its head, followed by daughters and granddaughters; they included Ellie Rendel, with her school-friend Ray Costelloe, who were now at university together. The success of this procession was, Lytton reported, 'entirely owing to Pippa's astounding management'.

From then on, Pippa and Ray never looked back. From a family of American feminists, Ray, was also well-connected: her aunt Alys had married Bertrand Russell, rising young philosopher and an NUWSS by-election candidate the previous year. Ray was studying mathematics at Newnham College, Cambridge, which already had its own suffrage society; here Ellie Rendel took Ray off to her first suffrage meeting. After the triumph of the 1908 NUWSS procession, the two friends sailed together to Amsterdam for an international suffrage congress. Ray fell in love with the Strachey family – most especially Pippa – and soon married brother Oliver, so as, it was said, to able to work more easily with Pippa.

Christabel Pankhurst was not a natural vanner, and the WSPU never became terribly enthusiastic. But the NUWSS, given the success of the WFL tour and of its own London procession, now decided to run its own caravan. So small surprise that the Strachey–Newnham constellation, Ellie and Ray, was the driving force behind the tour.[25]

The NUWSS already boasted a goodly spread of branches across the country and could be more ambitious in its itinerary than the fledgling WFL, deciding to travel right down from Scotland to Oxford. Their van was well equipped with 'three berths, one of which was also a linen chest, its art nouveau curtains ... a china cupboard, a minute bookcase'.[26] Luckily, Ray not only brought a typewriter with her but also apparently a camera, so providing both exuberant letters and snap-shots.

They set off on 2 July. Ray's letters thrilled to the 'glorious fun' of vanning. 'We have a very charming man, a huge and rapid horse and the most heavenly caravan imaginable', Ray typed. They soon reached the Lake District – and Keswick, an NUWSS stronghold. Here, thanks to the Marshall family, 'swarms of suffragists came rushing up to meet us', a crowd of over six hundred listened eagerly in the market, with the Marshalls 'putting us up most luxuriously'. Meandering south down the Pennines, they reached Oxford by late July; here they held a successful meeting of two to three hundred, Ellie and Ray speaking, joined by Ray's Aunt Alys, the Hon Mrs Bertrand Russell.[27] Buoyed by this, the NUWSS chanced a second van tour in August. From the isolated fishing port of Whitby, it journeyed through the North Yorkshire Wolds. They now had a somewhat smarter caravan, 'on which we have now chalked the name of our Society and president in large letters ... In fact we have had inquiries if Mrs Henry Fawcett was inside'.[28]

So why did the NUWSS vanners have so much of an easier time of it than the WFL? It was partly because well-established NUWSS networks could rely upon more local sympathizers. And also partly because constitutional suffragists provoked less antagonism than suffragettes. For, from summer 1908, the militant campaign had taken a decided turn for the confrontational.

After the WSPU's monster 'Women's Sunday' rally, Christabel Pankhurst immediately sent Asquith the Hyde Park resolution, calling on the Liberal government to enfranchise women without delay. Surely Asquith's earlier demand to see that so many women *wanted* a Parliamentary vote had now been met – by *two* impressively large parades? Yet the Prime Minister's cool response remained evasive. Asquith still hedged, with vague patrician reference to some 'remote and speculative future'. Indeed, the more women marched, the more he remained deaf to their entreaties. Frustrated, two suffragettes went to Downing Street with a bag of stones – which they threw at Asquith's windows. Though not agreed WSPU strategy, this individual direct action initiative represented a brand new tactic aimed at government property, a development that would have wider repercussions.

In autumn 1908, militancy developed further. The WSPU invited Londoners to support its 'rush the House of Commons' on 13 October. During scuffles, there were three dozen arrests. In court afterwards, law graduate Christabel Pankhurst's celebrated examination of both Lloyd George and Home Secretary Herbert Gladstone bestowed tremendous publicity on women's claims. Her brilliant rhetoric challenged Liberalism's hypocrisy which still refused to recognize women as citizens: she accused the government of having 'practically torn up' the Magna Carta, 'the title-deeds of British liberty'. This was suffragette militancy as theatre, Bow Street Police Court providing the perfect dramatic backdrop for Christabel's performing women's arbitrary exclusion from the constitution.

More such imaginative audacity soon followed. On the evening of 28 October, WFL members Muriel Matters and Violet Tillard with a third suffragette, Helen Fox, entered the Ladies' Gallery of the Commons. Here the 'vile grille', separating voteless women from MPs, also kept women largely invisible to the parliamentarians below. Under their cloaks, Muriel and Helen hid chains wrapped in wool to prevent clattering. They padlocked themselves to the gallery ironwork and slipped the keys down the backs of their dresses. Muriel's strong voice interrupted parliamentary proceedings, crying out 'Votes for Women'. Meanwhile, Violet, plus supporters in the men-only Strangers' Gallery, showered suffrage leaflets down on the Commons below.[29]

Consternation. Commons' officials found Muriel and Helen could be removed only if they dismantled the grille. When the women were dislodged, the ornate metal was still attached. Once their chains were filed off, they were released. But they were arrested shortly afterwards with other suffragettes and sentenced to a month in Holloway. This WFL drama took everyone by surprise, including press photographers. However, one employed a 'special artist' to conjure up the scene, catching a suffragette (undoubtedly Muriel) still dramatically chained. Like Christabel in court, this political spectacle vividly symbolized the demeaning political purdah in which women were still kept.[30] The NUWSS however did not warm to such WFL 'disturbances': Pippa Strachey and Mrs Fawcett would not raise a smile.

By the end of 1908, the WFL had developed its own distinctive style of symbolic direct action: the constitutional right to petition, highlighting women's exclusion from male parliamentary power. Its propaganda tours were personally exacting too, as Margaret Nevinson later recorded: 'Suffragists lived through strenuous days ... upheld by hope and the nervous energy of enthusiasm ... Speakers, especially, had no rest; I spoke on an average about four or five times a week', long suburban journeys entailing missing meals and sleep.[31]

And during the summer season, vanning remained a favoured tactic for reaching Asquith's elusive 'majority'. During 1909 the suffrage societies reprised the previous summer's imaginative tours. A NUWSS caravan took in Leicestershire and Northamptonshire, plus Yorkshire again; and even the WSPU went vanning, visiting the Midlands countryside around Birmingham. The WFL acquired a new van: Muriel Matters and Violet Tillard journeyed through East Anglia, while a second caravan left Hampton Court, heading up the Thames towards Salisbury. And again, in summer 1910, a WFL van trundled out to Bedford, Buckinghamshire and eventually east to the seaside resort of Felixstowe.[32]

THE SIMPLE LIFE.—Caravanning : A halt by the wayside.

9 'The Simple Life – Caravanning: a halt by the wayside', comic postcard, Ernest Ibbetson. A suffragette in sandals waves a copy of 'Vote for Women' (in WSPU colours) at her wayward horse.

Charlotte Despard could well feel proud of her suffrage vanners and all they withstood. Caravans had entered the public imagination, not only as propaganda vehicles, but also becoming inspiring emblems of women's freedoms and the possibilities of a political vanishing act, should the need arise.

It would however take more than country caravans and multiple meetings to sway Asquith. His government had other more urgent reform priorities. At the Treasury, Lloyd George had developed Old Age Pensions, and now travelled to Germany to investigate its system of social insurance provision. By 1909, his increasingly ambitious welfare plans were turning the Treasury into a real powerhouse. So Votes for Women campaigners would need to be yet more inventive, more creative, more persuasive. A renewed propaganda culture needed to spring from London's bohemian neighbourhoods to win round politicians and public.

3

Propaganda culture:
Clemence and Laurence Housman

The new propaganda culture necessarily centred predominantly on London and its premier bohemian boroughs: Kensington, Chelsea and Hampstead. Here were created rich displays of suffrage publicity by painters, groups of designers, networks of writers and journalists. And here, no site could match the impressive wealth of creativity that flowed from a single household: 1 Pembroke Cottages just off Kensington High Street, home of the inseparable siblings Clemence and Laurence Housman.

They were not however the first. The Artists' Suffrage League (ASL) was formed in 1907, when women artists designed for Pippa Strachey's NUWSS 'Mud March'. Its headquarters were at Brittany studios, 259 King's Road, Chelsea. Here lived legendary banner-maker Mary Lowndes, ASL founder and chair, along with her lifelong companion and ASL secretary, Barbara Forbes. Their studios were a hive of creativity particularly when a suffrage procession loomed, as it was common practice for embroiderers to work on different sections of large banners at the same time.[1]

The Women Writers' Suffrage League followed in 1908. Co-founded by author Cicely Hamilton living nearby, its members employed their pens for the Cause. Margaret Nevinson, who wrote on her experiences of workhouse visiting and of the inequity for women of the marriage laws, became treasurer; Mary Lowndes designed its first banner. The Actresses' Franchise League was formed in December 1908, and these two groups worked together to stage suffrage plays, pageants and large-scale entertainments. Finally, the Men's League for Women's Suffrage founded in 1907 drew on a wide range of influential male supporters, often accomplished journalists: prominent were Margaret's husband Henry Nevinson and Henry Brailsford, both living in Hampstead.[2] So by early 1909, from these four Edwardian leagues sprang a buzzing creativity. In producing this propaganda culture nowhere was more dynamically creative than Kensington and Chelsea: see Map 3.

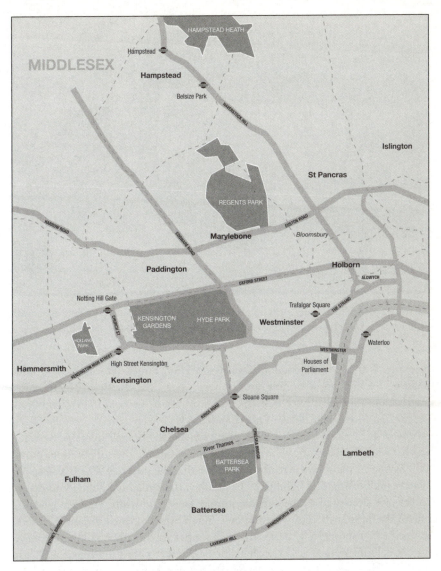

Map 3 West London boroughs: Hampstead via Kensington to Battersea.

From Notting Hill in north Kensington down to the Chelsea Embankment by the Thames, dense networks of artists and writers flourished. It was almost impossible not to bump into suffrage propagandists at every turn. Some lived in substantial and elegant houses: near Holland Park stood the spacious home of artists Georgina and Marie Brackenbury (see Figure 11b).[3] With the WSPU particularly strong in Kensington, their house provided a hospitable venue for

10 Kensington WSPU shop, 1910, its generous-sized plate-glass windows amply decorated with banners. Evelyn Sharp, wearing her WSPU sash, standing outside – also, May Sinclair.

meetings. Further south around Kensington High Street, its tube station now boasting an enticing shopping arcade, were many flat-dwellers. Notable was novelist and journalist Evelyn Sharp, author of *Rebel Women* (1910), who lived nearby in a convenient block of mansion flats.

Evelyn became secretary of the Kensington WSPU branch in 1910. So what was her local campaigning? She collected money outside the tube station, probably having to stand in the road to rattle her tin. She sold the WSPU's *Votes for Women* on Kensington High Street; her satchel, conveniently holding four dozen copies, was decorated in the colours: purple, green and white. And Evelyn supported the WSPU shop on Kensington Church Street; opened in January 1909, it was the first shop run by a branch. Such shops sold literature and merchandise 'in the colours' and proved excellent for day-to-day political advertising.[4] Just off the High Street stood Edwardes Square Studios. Here in a modest apartment (studio, bedroom, kitchen) lived May Sinclair, modernist novelist and suffrage sympathizer.[5]

Over the boundary into Chelsea, more artists' studios flourished. Its riverside location had long been favoured by painters: J. M. W. Turner, John Singer Sargent, William Rothenstein. Here the price of studios was reasonable, yet it was close to the West End's picture-buying public. So Chelsea became the natural home of suffrage painters and designers, particularly clustered around King's Road, with Mary Lowndes's Brittany Studios as ASL headquarters.

Round the corner, Cicely Hamilton, Chelsea WFL branch secretary, wrote *A Pageant of Great Women*; it featured over fifty great women including Elizabeth I and Joan of Arc, and was performed across the country. Just a few doors along stood the picturesque 'cottage' of painter Emily Ford, ASL vice-chairman; her home and studio became 'a meeting ground for artists, suffragists, people who *did* things'. Nearby was imposing Cheyne Walk, home to other ASL artists; with spectacular view over the Thames, its eighteen-room houses required a full complement of domestic servants.[6]

These suffragists and suffragettes might differ on tactics, but all agreed on their aim and all gave their time and talents generously. Amid this buzz of colourful propaganda culture, however, it is siblings Laurence and Clemence Housman who emerge pre-eminent in designing the protest against the coming census.

Clemence and Laurence grew up in a family of seven children near Bromsgrove, Worcestershire. It was not an untroubled childhood; their mother died early, and their father, prone to embroiling family finances in disasters, remarried. Their eldest brother Alfred escaped to Oxford University, where he formed a passionate attachment to another male student. He later became a distinguished classicist and was appointed professor of Latin at University College London. But it is as a poet that A. E. Housman will always remain best remembered:

Into my heart an air that kills
　From yon far country blows:
What are those blue remembered hills,
　What spires, what farms are those?

That is the land of lost content,
　I see it shining plain,
The happy highways where I went
　And cannot come again.

A. E. Housman, 'A Shropshire Lad', XL, 1896

Alfred's memorably poignant poetry gradually found huge popular recognition among the Edwardian book-buying public. Bromsgrove lay just south-east of Shropshire and, Alfred recalled, 'its hills were our western horizon'.[7] So what did 'the land of lost content' mean for Clemence and Laurence? It was not much. After their mother died, Clemence, dutiful daughter-at-home, cared for younger brother Laurence. Always self-effacing, she left scant record of her girlhood.[8] Laurence's own autobiography, however, portrays a boyhood circumscribed by Victorian pruderies and taboos, making even visits to the lavatory torturous. At school, Laurence, susceptible to bullying and caning, early on developed a hatred for cruelty by the powerful to the powerless.[9]

Meanwhile, the family's fortunes drifted downwards: Clemence's financial skills were enlisted to help sort out their father's shady dealings and tax affairs.

Then in 1883 the two siblings fled their stepmother-managed Bromsgrove home to follow their dreams in *fin de siècle* London. Clemence had been enjoined by their mother shortly before she died 'to look after little Laurence', and so was 'allowed' to go to London to help her younger brother. But, with their eldest brother scarcely acknowledging their arrival in the capital, they moved into humble lodgings in Lambeth. Meagre freelancing years followed, always overshadowed by assured academic and poet Alfred.[10] However, both siblings managed to obtain art school training in south London and showed considerable talent. Clemence turned to wood-engraving illustration; in this she was considered by some the most talented of her day. Laurence, always versatile, undertook book illustrations, often of fairy tales, including Christina Rossetti's poem *Goblin Market*.

Then in 1896 on holiday in Shropshire, Laurence met wealthy fellow artist and member of a younger fast set, Herbert Alexander: he became 'Sandro' to Laurence's 'Odrick'. Before long, in the Alexanders' large garden Laurence was 'introduced to tent-sleeping and sun-bathing', naturism and fun holidays. These had 'a touch of the pagan when we varied our diversions by dressing or undressing for dinner … in rather scanty Greek costume … It was all really quite decent, but it was not Victorian.' Clemence who was visiting was less convinced: 'But you are not *dressed*!' she proclaimed as she encountered Sandro as 'a scantily clad Cupid'.[11] Back in London, ebullient Laurence enjoyed sociable evenings at the Café Royal with friends Max Beerbohm and William Rothenstein. Having befriended Oscar Wilde, Sandro and he now visited Wilde in his Paris exile, to deliver money collected by the Café Royal set. In the wake of the Wilde trials however, Laurence, like Alfred, required privacy concerning his own homosexuality; and even years later in his autobiography, Laurence remained understandably reticent about his own male relationships. For solace and escape, he now looked to writing.

Clemence herself remained a wholly private person, quietly producing three novels. Laurence's own writing talents were spotted by C. P. Scott, redoubtable editor of the *Manchester Guardian*; Laurence was taken on as art critic, speeding his reviews north by wire. Such work did generate income, and the siblings, now with a housekeeper, moved about 1900 into a high mansion flat overlooking Battersea Park.

Alfred's reknown as poet was growing: he could not forgo sardonic criticism of his young brother. Indeed, life remained hard for Laurence, the struggling writer – until his first novel *An Englishwoman's Love Letters* was published in 1900. It was mysteriously and sensationally 'anonymous', provoking feverish speculation about its author.[12] Sales were sufficient for brother and sister to move into William Rothenstein's pretty house, 1 Pembroke Cottages, just round the corner from Edwardes Square off Kensington High Street. Their main ground floor room, extended through double-doors from front to back, gave an

11 Suffrage homes, Kensington: (*a*) Clemence and Laurence Housman, 1 Pembroke Cottages; (*b*) Brackenbury family, 2 Campden Hill Square.

unexpected air of spaciousness. At the far end of the garden was a small cottage converted into a studio. Laurence wrote, 'here for the first time, we had a home in London really to our liking, with which we could feel intimate'. Their new life would now start.[13]

The inveterately sociable Laurence enjoyed close female friendships with Evelyn Sharp nearby; with Quakers Sarah and husband Roger Clark in Street, Somerset; and with Janet Ashbee of the 'Arts and Crafts' Ashbees. By contrast, Clemence retained her natural reserve. Overall, we still know far less about her than about Laurence, and both are still less remembered than Alfred. But for Laurence, his sister would always remain one of the 'wonderful ones': steadfast creative women 'who come to know quite early in life that no men will ever wish to make wives of them: for them, then, love in friendship is all that remains'.[14]

Some writers have suggested their relationship to be incestuous. Was it? It seems unlikely. True, they lived together in the closest domestic harmony for over seventy years. True, to their nieces and nephews, Laurence's high voice and Clemence's contralto made them 'Aunt Laurence' and 'Uncle Clem'. True, Laurence wrote to Sarah Clark: '*Clem* is the right man for *me* in the much the same way as Roger is for you: for I think she is as masculine as you and I am as feminine as Roger.'[15] But Laurence retained high-minded views about the body and the need to control sexual desires, whether for men or for women. He wrote to Edward Carpenter, author of *Homegenic Love* (1897), that: 'I have found for my own part that the higher and more passionate has been my attachment for a person the less has it affected the lower parts of my body, while intensifying the desire of embrace in the lips and breast, and above all evoking a passionate wish to be of service'.[16] Rather than an incestuous relationship, the two siblings

12 Laurence and Clemence Housman (*right*), standing in front of Hampden tax resistance
banner, 29 Sept 1911.

offered each other 'love in friendship'. Luckily, we can draw on their intimate
correspondence to illuminate this; at one point, wanting to affirm his devotion,
Lawrence wrote:

> Dearest Own
> … Of all people in the world I find words to you most difficult: try not to need
> them. Believe that I love you endlessly. For our life together my thanks and blessing.
> Be youful, my dear …
> Your ownest
> Lawrence.[17]

Through Laurence's letters we can recreate the tone and texture of life at 1
Pembroke Cottages, with its intersection of the domestic and private with the
public and political. For, from 1908, the pull of the heady Votes for Women

campaign grew irresistible. Both placed at its service their considerable skills as artists and writers, with Laurence also as speaker in heavy demand. As the Housmans hurtled pell-mell into the fray, their friends, who had earlier delighted in Laurence's high spirits and fun, soon grew weary of single-focus suffrage. Certainly, Alfred did not share their enthusiasm, growing irked when people confused him with his prolific younger brother.

Laurence maintained it was Clemence who had influenced his own conversion to the Cause. But if Clem's was a slow-burning commitment, Laurence's conversion was rapid. He had heard Mrs Fawcett speak in the 1880s, and much later Emmeline Pankhurst at a meeting in Chelsea. His bitterness against the Liberals, however, really dated from the killing-off of the suffrage bill shortly before Asquith became Prime Minister, and what he saw as the chicanery of Asquith and his ministers. Laurence recalled later how he:

> found myself to possess that most uncomfortable thing[:] a social conscience ... [which] got badly in the way of my book-work ... [During] those agitating years ... the most devastating blow dealt me by the Suffrage Movement was the discovery it forced upon me that I could speak.[18]

Indeed, he quickly emerged as star speaker, soon criss-crossing the country for meetings with the frequency of an Emmeline Pankhurst or a Charlotte Despard; thus he encountered all manner of surprising people – like suffragettes up in Ilkley, Yorkshire:

> Dearest Own
> ... It's rather amusing to find that not one nor three but five Misses Thompsons are on the premises ... Miss Elizabeth Th our hostess the school headmistress I like very much. Another has been to prison, and is very earnest & eager on the subject.
> They are great fun to talk to ... These amiable & cosy old dears are real 'militants' all of them ... They are only old in a way – ages from 45 to 60, and very unshockable ...
> Love from your ownest
> Lawrence.[19]

Much suffrage journalism and writing had hitherto been rather formulaic, even pedestrian. Importantly, Laurence raised literary standards, reaching new inspiring popularity. He became to Votes for Women what Rudyard Kipling was to patriotism: a rollicking balladeer. His gift was to take the known, and give it a feminist twist. Laurence's rhythmic 'Woman This, and Woman That' opened with acknowledgements to Kipling:

> We went up to St Stephen's with petitions year by year;
> 'Get out!' the politicians cried, 'we want no women here!'
> While bold policemen knocked us down, because we would not run,
> MP's behind the railings stood and laughed to see the fun.
> *Chorus*: For it's woman this, and woman that, and 'Woman go away!' ...[20]

13 Laurence Housman's banner, 'From Prison to Citizenship', here carried in procession, June 1911.

The Housmans supported the WSPU, so strong in Kensington; Clem became 'chief banner-maker to the Suffrage' movement, her needle constantly busy.[21] Indeed, Laurence's first great banner design was his monumental 'From Prison to Citizenship' for the WSPU's 'Women's Sunday' on 21 June 1908; it was worked in the colours, a white figure on purple background with trailing green leaves. The previous Sunday he had written to Janet Ashbee describing the needlewomen stitching silk materials in the studio behind their house:

> My banner for Kensington W.S.P.U. is now practically finished. Everybody says that it is the most beautiful that has been done. It is very simple – just a figure standing against a grille holding broken chains with the motto 'From Prison to Citizenship' but it has taken a lot of time.

A few days earlier, it was displayed at an unveiling ceremony in the Queen's Hall, Langham Place, presided over by Emmeline Pethick-Lawrence. Then the following Sunday, the Kensington contingent lined up along the High Street, stretching for almost a quarter-mile, from the tube station back towards Edwardes Square. Three days after the triumphant procession to Hyde Park, Laurence wrote again to Janet:

> My banner had the honour of being the only one that was kept unfurled throughout the whole demonstration: it travelled on a wagon being too big to be borne by hand, and it really did arouse enthusiasm. Perhaps I am destined to end as a poster-artist!

Thereafter, it became *the* banner in regular demand, used by the WSPU to illustrate its 1908 Christmas card, and regularly borne in subsequent processions.[22]

The Suffrage Atelier was founded in Hampstead in February 1909. It aimed for arts and crafts training in 'effective picture propaganda for the Suffrage ... by supplying Advertisements, Banners and Decorations'.[23] Laurence and Clemence were away in Hereford at the time, so seem not to take part in its founding. However, it is no surprise that soon afterwards Pembroke Cottage became the key site of suffragette cultural production, comparable to Mary Lowndes's ASL studio – though with slightly different inflection. At Caxton Hall in June, Laurence chaired the Atelier's first public meeting and gave the key speech – on 'Art and National Movements'. A month later, when a notice appealed in WSPU's *Votes for Women* for a centrally located room 'to be used for banner making etc at low or no rent', the Housmans offered their own studio. Thereafter, their home became the Atelier's office and workshop. Quietly and unostentatiously Clemence now gave banner-making her all. Certainly Laurence saw his sister wearing herself out with banner work, noting how, with leg trouble, she sat 'on a floor cushion most of the day doing needlework'.[24]

Laurence was the Atelier's outer public face. By now he had also become a key figure in the Men's League for Women's Suffrage; and from May 1909 he regularly spoke for the League on Sunday afternoons in Hyde Park.[25] Increasingly a star speaker, Laurence never looked back.

However, as WSPU stone-throwing and window-breaking increased from 1908, both Housmans began to entertain doubts about this form of militancy.[26] What better suited their style was civil disobedience of women refusing to pay tax. With her financial acumen, Clemence kept an eye on this significant development – which now runs straight as a die through the centre of this story.

> For it's woman this, and woman that, and 'Woman go away!'
> But it's 'Share and share alike, ma'am!' when taxes are to pay;
> When the taxes are to pay, my friends, the taxes are to pay,
> Oh, it's 'Please to pay up promptly!' when taxes are to pay!

Tax resistance had a long and honourable pedigree, stretching back to ancient roots in English constitutional history. Sometimes this was overtly political, as John Hampden's earlier refusal to pay ship money. More recently, quiet resistance to the state sprang from religious roots – as in 1870, when in Bristol Quaker suffragists Anna and Mary Priestman refused to pay their taxes and had their dining chairs distrained (i.e. seized). Later, nonconformists opposing the Conservatives' 1902 Education Act on religious grounds withheld their education rates. The law pursued these 'passive resisters', their goods were distrained and they stoically appeared in court year after year, with their property sold at auction. A recent dramatic example was suffragette Dora Montefiore who, arguing that government must rest upon the consent of the governed, refused to pay her taxes. Indeed, in 1906 she defiantly barricaded her Hammersmith villa against the bailiffs in the 'Siege of Montefiore'.[27]

The WFL now championed 'No Vote – No Tax' civil disobedience, arguing forcibly that 'Taxation without representation is Tyranny'. As Charlotte Despard put it it: 'Women Pay the Piper, Men Call the Tune'.[28]

It was naturally financially independent women who were most liable for tax. Soon the list grew of women passive resisters and sales of their goods at auction. One influential professional group was doctors, notably those well-established women practising in London. One was Dr Elizabeth Knight, a Quaker who had trained at the London School of Medicine for Women; independently wealthy (she inherited a sizeable fortune from her father, a cement manufacturer), Dr Knight had already been to prison after calling at 10 Downing Street to demand of Asquith why he had reneged on his promises to women. With the prosecution of such tax resisters, the WFL could take advantage of the ensuing auctions to stage political theatre. On one occasion, Charlotte Despard 'addressed the people in the sale-room and explained that this was a protest against the unjust taxation of unrepresented women' – until the police forced them to adjourn to Hyde Park, for further suffrage speeches.[29]

Indeed, women's tax resistance met a number of significant propaganda aims. It dramatized the constitutional anomaly of voteless women. It brought suffrage politics right into yet another traditional public space – the auction house; and it was civil disobedience which attracted publicity. And – as if at Asquith's behest for convincing 'the majority' – it reached out to parts of the country previously little-touched by Votes for Women. Like Ipswich near the Suffolk coast.

Ipswich had long had a local NUWSS suffragist branch 'hard at work educating public opinion in the town'. Now WFL member Mrs Hortense Lane of nearby Whitton had refused to pay her 'inhabited house duty'; so when she 'applied the match, the already loaded gun went off in first-rate style'. The tax collector pursued her fruitlessly, followed by a bailiff. The auction on Friday 28 May 1909 was widely advertised by Dr Elizabeth Knight. Soon all the town knew that the 'Suffragettes were on strike'. For the protest meetings, Marion Holmes came up to address crowded audiences. Despite some rowdiness, it was enthusiastically decided to form a WFL branch at once and to get up the WFL caravan.[30]

Ipswich's most notable new recruit was self-employed music teacher Constance Andrews. She was a vegetarian, involved idealistically in the local Social Settlement Hall, and active in the ILP and trades council; she had already stood for election as Poor Law Guardian – like Charlotte Despard and Margaret Nevinson, though in Constance's case unsuccessfully. Local NUWSS branch secretary, Constance now found suffragist tactics too timid and switched her considerable energies to growing the Ipswich WFL branch. And indeed, as we know, that summer Violet Tillard's WFL caravan tour did indeed venture out to distant East Anglia.[31]

But probably the trophy for propaganda *chutzpah* goes to Muriel Matters. In February 1909, the WFL chartered an airship. Muriel, suspended below in a woven cane basket, was lifted aloft from its moorings at Hendon airfield. Across the air-balloon in enormous letters were proclaimed 'Votes for Women' and 'Women's Freedom League'. Muriel sailed over London, addressing those below by megaphone and distributing thousands of WFL handbills.[32] Thus the actress from Adelaide combined daring propaganda with airborne modernity – and so was noticed.

By mid-1909, then, the creativity of Clemence and Lawrence Housman, combined with the political bravado of Christabel Pankhurst and Muriel Matters had taken Votes for Women propaganda culture to unprecedented heights. Yet had their theatrical use of political spaces to stage women's demands for citizenship really managed to persuade Asquith and his elusive 'majority'? Or were the Liberal government's sights still firmly fixed on one reform priority above all others: Lloyd George's welfare agenda?

4

Parallel politics:
Lloyd George plus Midlands suffragettes

During summer 1909, the confrontation sharpened between the government's determination to progress Lloyd George's National Insurance scheme, and the suffragettes' demand for women's citizenship as *the* crucial political priority. It is tempting for historians to treat these two political narratives, Votes for Women and Lloyd George's Finance Bill, as separate. But the two strands would intertwine. Indeed, during autumn, both narratives became locked into bitter, even violent, combat.[1]

Asquith's Cabinet was bent on defeating the peers to push the Finance Bill through Parliament. Constitutional confrontation built up. If his 'People's Budget' fell in the Lords, such a momentous defeat would trigger a general election. The country would have to be won over. So in the autumn, Cabinet ministers packed their bags and headed out of London, to woo the great cities with rousing Budget speeches. And suffragettes followed them: conflict grew particularly turbulent in the Midlands.

Lloyd George left school at fifteen and was steeped in Welsh nonconformist radicalism. Like Burns, he was an outsider in Asquith's Cabinet, and made the most of it. Brutally ambitious, he was also a compelling orator. In Parliament, he championed land reform and nonconformists' resistance to the Conservatives' 1902 Education Act, rising meteorically with the Liberals' ascendancy. Other ministers, Winston Churchill at the Board of Trade and John Burns at the LGB, were outclassed by the unprecedented ambitions fizzing out of the Treasury. His inspired free-wheeling style meant he never got bogged down in the administrative detail as Burns did. Chancellor from April 1908, Lloyd George built upon Asquith's achievements. From January 1909, those aged over seventy with low annual incomes could collect an old age pension from their post office. Nearly half-a-million benefited, mainly women.[2]

But he wanted to go further in ameliorating the harshest effects of poverty and ill-health. During his summer 1908 visit to Germany, he had studied the Bismarckian legacy of social insurance. By autumn, his civil servants were working on plans to introduce unemployment and sickness insurance into Britain. His scheme provoked increasing alarm from the House of Lords, and opposition from doctors, many of whom earned comfortable incomes from well-to-do patients. Other vested interests also grew perturbed: Lloyd George began conferring with insurance companies and friendly societies which collected weekly contributions from lower middle-class and skilled working-class families, as protection against misfortune.

Although it would be a contributory scheme with small weekly payments by those workers who were covered, Lloyd George's proposal would still carry costs. His momentous 'People's Budget' of April 1909 thrust taxation right into the very centre of British politics. The nation would be divided in two: the wealthy who would pay and those in need who would receive. He planned to introduce new direct taxes on higher incomes and, controversially, through taxation of land. Lloyd George's budget speech left few in any doubt that he meant to 'wage implacable warfare against poverty and squalidness'.[3] How would the 'People's Budget' manage to be passed without the Lords killing it off? As it ground its way through Westminster, Lloyd George determined to raise the stakes in his battle with the obstinate peers. On 30 July, he spoke in Limehouse before an East End audience of four thousand. His prentice years of Welsh nonconformist rhetorical onslaught on landlordism now stood him in good stead. Speaking as *un homme du peuple*, he contrasted coalminers' toil with the Duke of Westminster's notorious greediness. Taxation was not robbery of the few, it was the social justice for the many, denying he planned confiscation of a duke's wealth. Rather,

> We are placing burdens on the broadest shoulders. Why should I put burdens on the people? I am one of the children of the people. I was brought up amongst them. I know their trials: and God forbid that I should add one grain of trouble to the anxieties which they bear with such patience and fortitude.[4]

Asquith's Cabinet was bent on defeating the obstinate peers to push though the Finance Bill. A confrontation grew inevitable. The country had to be persuaded. So ministers headed north to deliver their rousing Budget speeches to the heavily populated cities. And suffragettes tracked their steps.

Suffrage campaigners watched Lloyd George – in growing anger. They identified two anomalies. First, the insurance scheme made little provision for the wives and children of those workers it covered. Yet surely, argued feminist reformers, these were among the most needy in the population. Second, despite taxation looming ever larger, women tax-payers remained voteless. Teresa Billington-Grieg demanded to know why women should take any interest in a bill in which they had absolutely no voice: 'Mr Lloyd George is one of the cleverest of our politicians. His Budget establishes the fact ... [Yet] the incapacity of voteless women to escape or alter it, makes even this provocative Budget' unjust.[5]

Soon, the WSPU was pursuing Cabinet Ministers in person. John Burns was accosted by a suffragette who asked him why he taxed women and then refused to give them votes. Undoubtedly the most audacious protest was against Augustine Birrell, chief secretary for Ireland and MP for North Bristol. The city was already a hub for vigorous campaigning: Annie Kenney, WSPU West of England organizer, was based there. When Birrell chaired a Land Taxation meeting in Bristol, suffragettes hid among the organ pipes; just as he began to speak, a voice shouted out 'Votes for Women!' to loud applause. Stewards dashing wildly around eventually ejected the hecklers. The Bristol press headlines ran: 'Suffragettes and Mr Birrell – A Voice from the Organ'. He was also interrupted in London at a public meeting on the forthcoming Budget; when he stated that money did not drop down from Heaven, '"No", called a woman in the audience, "much of it is provided by the women of the country, who pay rates and taxes".' She was immediately removed, despite cries of 'Good old Suffragettes!'[6]

So by summer 1909, the clash between the two concepts of citizenship escalated. On the one hand, Lloyd George voiced urgent health and welfare reform: democracy *for* the people. On the other, increasingly truculent suffragettes demanded a say in policy that affected them, notably taxation: democracy *by* the people. Lloyd George confronted the recalcitrant peers, suffragettes continued heckling. Tempers shortened.

From summer 1909, imprisonment and the clanking of the cell door loomed as an increasingly dark and forbidding backdrop. And, as the suffragette movement spread, the brutal experience of prison reached far beyond London and big cities. So how did Votes for Women play out in the industrial Midlands? The story is introduced here through the waves that imprisonment sent into one WSPU branch, Nottingham, and on one suffragette there, Helen Watts. From there the narrative spreads out to Leicester and then of course the regional capital, Birmingham (see Map 1). It was here, in Winson Green prison, that the confrontation between suffragettes and the Home Office escalated most savagely.

Nottinghamshire's population was nearly two-thirds of a million, of whom almost half lived in the city itself; jobs available to women were largely limited to textile manufacture (notably lace and hosiery), dressmaking and domestic service. Coal was a key male occupation, with miners normally voting solidly Liberal. Such Edwardian cities supported an urban intelligentsia: the Nottingham Art Gallery curator and his family, Nottingham University College lecturers and school teachers, families of lace manufacturers living in the grander houses with views across to the city's imposing Castle. Here Nottingham's suffrage movement had long been a fiefdom of the Dowson clan: Alice Dowson and her daughter-in-law Helena, married to a lace manufacturer. It was an active society, affiliated to the NUWSS.

14 (*a*) Helen Watts, 1911; (*b*) Rev. Watts's church, Lenton, Nottingham. The vicarage stood next to the church, separated only by the graveyard.

Helen Watts, living further out in Lenton vicarage, remained just a suffrage observer with 'a holy horror of the "shrieking sisterhood"'. Then the Pankhursts burst in on Nottingham. Helen heard Christabel speak, and was as 'much impressed, perhaps, by the strong and winning personality of the speaker as by her arguments'. She joined 'the Union'.[7] A WSPU Nottingham branch was formed early in 1908. It was worth the WSPU sending up its star speakers, but the city gave them a rough reception. Emmeline Pankhurst addressing a mass demonstration at Nottingham Forest was almost drowned out by various 'screeching instruments'. Police formed a cordon of protection, and speakers escaped 'in a large brake, with "Votes for Women" posted all over it'.[8] The core membership not untypical of urban suffragette profiles. One founding member was Leonora Shaw, wife of a Nottingham University College science lecturer, living in the suburbs. Another was graduate and teacher May Burgis; she lived near the city centre with her widowed mother, her sister a teacher, and brother a clerk. Certainly, May and Helen fast became friends.[9]

Helen Watts had been brought up with stories of standing up for cherished beliefs in the face of public hostility. Her father, the Reverend Alan Watts, had earlier ministered in Birmingham; here, Helen remembered, he had faced:

> all kinds of prejudice and misunderstanding ... At the first service he conducted ...,
> there were scenes of unparalleled riot and disorder ... But he stuck to his guns and

to his principles … It is a tremendous inspiration to his children to remember that time … [and] our fathers who fought and died for our English liberties.[10]

So Helen was already familiar with the religious language of dedication and sacrifice, of conquering personal fears. She later recalled:

> It was shortly before our Forest Demonstration that I was impelled to offer for active service when the opportunity should arise … One is reminded of Bunyan's little allegory of the lions in the way – how Christian saw them in the distance and approached them fearfully, but passed safely between them because they were chained and could not touch him.[11]

Helen did not have long to wait for an 'active service' opportunity. A WSPU organizer had been appointed for the Midlands: Gladice Keevil. She set up a new regional office in Birmingham and now came to Nottingham. Here Gladice told a large meeting how militant tactics would win the day, amusing her audience by describing pursuing Cabinet minister. Her condemnation of suffragette imprisonment was so eloquent that apparently thirty enthusiastic new members joined.

Helen laid her plans discreetly, confiding only in May Burgis. On 24 February 1909 Helen attended the WSPU's Women's Parliament in Caxton Hall chaired by Emmeline Pankhurst, and she volunteered to join the deputation carrying the resolution to 'Runaway Asquith' highlighting the burdens laid upon women taxpayers. Later that evening Helen scribbled a note to her unsuspecting parents:

> I shall never forget marching on to the platform just as the audience was singing with all their might,
>> 'For what they loved,
>> The martyrs died:
>> Are we of meaner soul?'
> From the 'Women's Marseillaise'.[12]

The notion of martyrdom, providing serenity in adversity, was key to understanding suffragettes like Helen. She was arrested and charged with wilfully obstructing police in Parliament Square; in court the following day she was sentenced to one month imprisonment. She wrote home to 'My darling Mother & all', urging 'you're not to worry about me one moment'. But of course this is exactly what Mrs Watts did. It is worth quoting her letter as it vividly illuminated the dramatic impact imprisonment had on the most respectable families:

> Lenton Vicarage, Nottingham.
> Feb 25th [1909]
> My darling Child
>   I cannot say that your letter was altogether a surprise to me! For it *had* crossed my mind once or twice before that you might think it your duty to do as you have done.
>   … Of course Father & I are proud of your being so brave for what you thought was right.

Only, my child, my heart has ached for you over & over again today …

And what are you going through now, I wonder! Is your room – I cannot say cell – very very cold? …

If I may be allowed to see you, I will try & go town for a day to have a peep at you … Everyone thinks you are very brave! …

I know you did it out of love to [for?] Christ …

Much fond love from Father, Mother, Alice, Ronald and Christopher – and kisses from all.

I hope you will be able to sleep tonight, my darling.

God bless you,

Your fond mother,

Ethelinda W Watts.[13]

With a report in the Notingham paper, congratulations flowed in. The warmest letter came from May Burgis, who wrote shortly before Helen's release:

Dearest Helen –

Three Cheers for you & for the Great Cause for which you have suffered so bravely. Nottingham is indeed proud & if you knew how much worth while it has been you would rejoice – but you will know before long & we shall have you back … The Union [is] looking forward happily to entertaining you … just a happy supper among your friends & admirers – nothing formidable …

Goodbye dear

With my love

Yours May Burgis.[14]

And she added: 'You have made history in Nottingham'. Thus a single imprisonment rachetted up sisterly solidarity in this Midlands city. And at the WSPU's 'welcome home' supper, reticent Helen somehow instinctively grasped what she needed to say:

Dear Friends,

I don't know how I can begin to thank you for all the kindness you have shown me … while in was in prison …

I feel that my experiences and impressions of the past month belong to the Nottingham Union more, almost, than to myself personally; otherwise, I might have hesitated. The last two years have been for most of us a time of new impressions and wider ideals …

Friends, I cannot tell you what a help your loyalty and enthusiasm were to me during those six months of waiting. Your splendid faith in our leaders and in the militant tactics and … the longing that many of you had to be able to join the fighting line yourselves – were all sources of inspiration and strength.[15]

After her public debut, Helen spoke in Nottingham on the right to petition; and in May in Birmingham on how her father's steadfastness in that city had so inspired his children. Then we lose sight of Helen Watts for a while – as suffragette imprisonment on the wider political stage took a darker turn.

On 5 July, imprisoned suffragette Marion Wallace-Dunlop began to refuse food. She became the first suffragette hunger striker. The story of hunger strikers is best remembered through the celebrated case of Lady Constance Lytton, sister of an influential peer. However, rather than tracking the drama through high-profile prisoners, attention switches back to the Midland cities.

These now became key political battlegrounds. In addition to well-established NUWSS branches, the WFL was also active, notably Emma Sproson, postman's wife in Wolverhampton. But it was the WSPU, with Gladice Keevil as Midlands organizer, that remained crucial. In Leicester, Alice Hawkins was WSPU branch secretary. With her husband Alfred, she had been drawn to Keir Hardie's ILP. However by 1909–10, the increasingly polarized politics meant that idealistic socialists like the Hawkinses felt caught uncomfortably between narrow female enfranchisement and full adult suffrage. Alice had left the ILP over this. The companionate couple stuck courageously to their Votes for Women credo, and Alice and Alfred Hawkins now move centre-stage.

Helen was also still firmly committed to WSPU militancy, as she watched the campaign to interrupt Cabinet Ministers stumping the country with their Budget speeches. In late July, Cabinet Minister Herbert Samuel arrived in Nottingham to address a crowded Budget meeting. When women were barred from entering, Helen and other suffragettes protested. She was detained, as was the newly appointed WSPU organizer for Nottingham, Nellie Crocker, a Somerset doctor's daughter and Emmeline Pethick-Lawrence's cousin. When the WSPU opened its new offices in the city centre, speakers included Nellie and Helen.[16] Within days, however, they were both in prison.

Leicester WSPU had been in touch with Nottingham suffragettes to help Alice Hawkins interrupt Winston Churchill's Budget meeting scheduled for 4 September. Helen and Nellie travelled 25 miles down to Leicester. Crowds gathered as the suffragettes mounted their lorry, to denounce Churchill and the government's taxation plans. Helen was clear what political principles were stake:

> 'Taxation without Representation is legalized robbery', and we are not going to stand by and let a member of the Government which is responsible for such legalized robbery of women, discuss the question of their taxation without at least an attempt to let him – and all Leicester – know our view on the matter.[17]

Outside the hall, Helen, Nellie and Alice were among those barred from entering Churchill's meeting. As they walked through the crowd to try and get in, police pushed Helen back into the crowd. 'I offered them no resistance', she recalled, 'but simply held my ground'. Yet police gripped her arms, marched her up the road and Helen was arrested, along with other suffragettes.

Liberal officials felt confident that, with women excluded, Churchill could speak without interruption. However, Alfred Hawkins had stationed himself inside. He waited for Churchill's call to support the Liberal government, and cried: 'Why don't they secure the support of women of the country? How dare you stand on a democratic platform?' He was frog-marched out and arrested. It was a momentous political protest. (However, Alfred, breadwinner on whom his family depended, decided he would have to pay his fine.)[18] By contrast, Helen and the others were sentenced to five days. They quickly said goodbye to friends and were driven off to Leicester Gaol.

Marion Wallace-Dunlop's hunger strike had spread to other gaols. The six Leicester prisoners agreed amongst themselves to 'carry out the same policy of protest as our recently imprisoned comrades'. In Helen's eyes, they were 'representatives of an army fighting for a tremendous principle … Just as a soldier on the battlefield feels that … for honour of our Cause … we MUST protest.' The prison governor grew furious when he learnt they refused food. He told her harshly that if she 'continued to refuse food, force would have to be used'. Helen retorted that it was impossible to compel people to eat against their will. He grew even angrier: 'That's pure nonsense. We can and will do it. We have often forced men in this gaol to eat, and we can force you' – as in lunatic asylums. She dreaded a sudden violent attempt to compel them to eat. That evening, Helen 'heard the most awful choked screams from a cell nearby. "Which of the others is being forced to eat now?" I wondered, and … I pictured myself handcuffed and strapped on to my plank bed, and milk being poured down my throat.'[19]

One morning, Helen even smashed two panes of glass in her cell to let in some fresh air. The visiting magistrate roared at her: 'Of course you are a common criminal'. Her punishment was a day's close confinement in an even gloomier cell; here Helen was cheered to spot some half-obliterated chalk marks 'Votes for Women!' left by previous occupant Nellie Crocker. Helen herself was on hunger strike for ninety hours. It grew painful to lie down; the last day seemed the longest. Food was left in the cells: Helen felt almost tempted to have a sip of the hot steaming tea on her table. Weakened, she repeated the 'Women's Marseillaise' to herself. When morning came, they were hurried away in cabs to recuperate in private lodgings where a sympathetic doctor 'took the invalids in hand'.[20]

The letters congratulating Helen included one from the WSPU in London:

Dear Comrade
    Last night at St James Hall, those prisoners on the platform alluded to you as a fellow hunger-striker & the brave stand you have been making … I can't tell you what I think of you & other women who are behaving so grandly …. I can only from the bottom of my heart say 'thank you'.[21]

Helen was also booked to appear in Nottingham at Morley's Café. She carefully typed seven pages of speaking notes. We cannot hear her voice; but the typescript offers a compelling account of her experiences in Leicester Gaol. Again, Helen spoke in Bunyanesque tones of 'a poor pilgrim tramping patiently along':

Friends

It is difficult to express one's feelings of joy at being among friends again ... Prison is a school in which we learn to understand what friendship and comradeship mean ... We come to see that Liberty is the greatest thing in the world ...

We of the [Women's] Social and Political Union have come to recognise that we ask for an elementary human right in the struggle for which ...we must come down from the various little pedestals on which we have been mounted by birth and education ...

'Votes for Women' will not be won by drawing-room chatter. It has got to be fought for in the market-places, and if we don't fight for it, no one else will ...

It is quite evident that the desperate but deliberate policy of hunger-striking is forcing the authorities upon the horns of a dilemma from which they will only extricate themselves by granting votes to women ... If we hunger-strike now and by doing so bring the day of women's enfranchisement appreciably nearer, it means that a large amount of suffering will be saved in the long run ...

In our movement ... if one faces [fears], one finds that they have no real power to hurt us. The one thing that will matter is –
HAVE WE KEPT STRAIGHT ON?[22]

It is easy to grasp why Helen Watts represented such an inspiring local heroine. She spoke for the growing band of suffragette prisoners whose bodily sacrifices were the price they were willing to pay for the vote. By coincidence, exactly the same day Helen was speaking in Morley's café, 17 September, just fifty miles south-west in Birmingham the conflict between the WSPU and the government erupted savagely.

Suffragettes had harried Herbert Samuel and Winston Churchill. These attacks now escalated when the Prime Minister himself visited the premier Midlands city. With its population now about 750,000, Birmingham included elegant residential suburbs, notably Edgbaston.[23] Its suffrage heritage made Birmingham the natural hub for regional campaigns. The WSPU based its Midlands organizer Gladice Keevil here, and opened a city-centre office. And by autumn 1909, Birmingham WSPU had all the campaigning resources of a major city: *Votes for Women* sellers, a caravan visiting country villages, cycling scouts and, reflecting the city's metal work skills, even jewellery 'in the colours'.

Asquith was to speak on 17 September in Birmingham's Bingley Hall. The police left little to chance. As if in a city under siege, nine-foot barricades lined the streets along which the Prime Minister would travel, with women once again barred from the meeting.[24] However, two determined suffragettes managed to clamber on to a neighbouring roof, then used axes to loosen some slates. When Asquith arrived, these were hurled down, hitting his car. Shouting 'No surrender', they were eventually led away and sentenced to three months' hard labour; other suffragettes received sentences for window-breaking.[25]

Birmingham's Winson Green gaol was a forbidding castellated building. It stood near suburban Edgbaston, yet belonged to a different world. Here the new arrivals also went on hunger strike. Mary Leigh, already an experienced hunger striker, certainly knew how to refuse food to gain early release from a long prison sentence. Such suffragettes presented the Home Office with an impossible dilemma: the guilt-laden prospect of a woman starving herself to death in gaol merely for demanding the right to vote. So the Home Secretary, Herbert Gladstone, son of Liberalism's legendary Prime Minister, ordered the prison medical officers to compel hunger strikers to take food. Thus a Liberal government adopted a chilling new tactic: forcible feeding of suffragettes.

Winson Green's Visiting Committee comprised well-intentioned people, mostly from Edgbaston. They were used to dealing with male prisoners' violence against prison officers, for whom twelve strokes of the cat would induce obedience. An occasional woman prisoner scratched an officer's face. It was all fairly routine. There were no complaints. Until Bingley Hall.

Then on 24 September a letter was delivered by hand to Gladstone from a firm of London solicitors. They had been instructed by suffragette prisoners over 'the legality of the treatment ... of food being supplied compulsorily'. They had also telegraphed the governor to state they wished to visit Winson Green the following morning to take statements from the prisoners. Whitehall reacted fast. The following day, the solicitors received a letter from the Home Office refusing this request: complaints should be directed to the Visiting Committee.[26] They held a special meeting on Tuesday 28. The medical officer duly noted that if:

> the women showed any signs of long collapse owing to the starvation methods they had adopted he had a free hand to act – that they were to be fed with force artificially either through the mouth or the nostrils but all necessary pain to be avoided.

The Committee then heard the many complaints: one suffragette protested, 'people had no right to force food. We are protesting against our treatment'. Another complained: 'we took legal advice ... and the [stomach] pump could not be used unless the prisoner was certified insane'. Yet, when all protests had been heard, the committee still agreed 'that the Doctors had acted in a most humane manner and the prisoners had been shown every consideration and that the Doctors should be commended'.[27]

Such complacency appears extraordinary in retrospect: male professionals, deaf to women's citizenship claims, timelessly commending each other's care and skill, with overtones of the lunatic asylum. Here was revealed Liberalism's great blind spot. Democracy might be working – but not for everyone.

The repercussions of Bingley Hall marked a sharp turning point in the militant campaign. It coincided with the assassination of a government official in London by an Indian protestor. Unwilling to take chances, the Home Office stepped up its surveillance of WSPU activists. At the same time, Birmingham

WSPU organized parades outside Winson Green, singing to give courage to the prisoners inside. The WSPU brought a case against the Home Office and prison governor over feeding Mary Leigh by nasal tube, and her right to refuse forcible 'treatment'. She was eventually released and taken to a nursing home.

Accusations of barbarity were hurled at Asquith's government. Within days, this sense of outrage against the torture of women blazed into nationwide publicity. Two influential radical journalists, Henry Nevinson and Noel Brailsford, took decisive action. Their letter of fierce protest to *The Times* thundered: 'We cannot denounce torture in Russia and support it in England, nor can we advocate democratic principles in the name of a party which confines them to a single sex'. Both journalists announced their resignations from the *Daily News* over that paper's refusal to condemn forcible feeding.[28] Similarly, Keir Hardie MP demanded to know the number of women being forcibly fed. With a gaping hole visible at the heart of Liberalism and the Home Office increasingly on the defensive, suffragettes had won a decisive propaganda coup.

In the equally noisy constitutional drama, Asquith's ministers remained bent on defeating the Lords. Just days after *The Times* 'torture' letter, Lloyd George headed north to Newcastle. Here on 9 October he delivered of one of his most devastating onslaughts on the hereditary House of Lords. The question most people asked, he proclaimed, was whether 'five hundred men, ordinary men chosen at random from among the unemployed, should override the judgement … of millions of people' who worked to produce the country's wealth? No, Lloyd George rounded, 'they have no qualification … They only require a certificate of birth, just to prove they are the first of the litter. You would not choose a spaniel on these principles.'[29]

In direct contrast, he proclaimed, the Liberal government would provide a welfare safety net for those workmen who, by age or misfortune, found themselves brought low by poverty. It was a *tour de force* by Lloyd George and greatly alarmed all those for whom he was a highwayman, robbing the innocent rich; *Punch* depicted the Chancellor as a latter-day John Knox, denouncing 'motorists, golfers and all those miserable sinners who happen to own anything'. Like his earlier Limehouse speech, Lloyd George's Newcastle rhetoric sounded a sea-change in politics: a promise to end the old deferential order at Westminster and usher in new egalitarian welfare reforms. There was no going back.

These two political narratives now grew yet more intertwined. Brailsford's wife Jane plus other WSPU suffragettes had tracked the Chancellor up to Newcastle. Like her husband, Jane wanted to take a public stand against forcible feeding. At Lloyd George's meeting, she concealed a hatchet in a bouquet of flowers, attacked a barrier and was arrested. Also arrested in Newcastle was Lady Constance Lytton: her father had been viceroy of India, her mother a lady-in-waiting to Queen Victoria, her brother was a leading Conservative peer. Yet both

Jane and Constance received a month's imprisonment and both went on hunger strike. There was public outcry that two women so closely connected to journalism and the peerage could be forcibly fed. Indeed, both were released after just three days. So Asquith's ministers were not merely torturers, but also hypocrites. Aghast, some members of local Women's Liberal Associations resigned. For the WSPU, it was another propaganda gift.

In the midst of all this controversy, some suffragettes like Helen Watts with a modest public profile pondered and grew quieter. It seems that after her hunger strike, Helen never fully recovered her health or her hearing, and this seemingly affected her self-confidence as a public speaker. Back at Lenton Vicarage, her mother's anxieties over the prospect of her delicate daughter being forcibly fed, plus her father's growing reservations about militancy, probably dissuaded Helen from risking prison again. Certainly, the Watts family now moved towards the educational Church League for Women's Suffrage, and, as suffragette militancy intensified, towards the NUWSS.[30] Indeed, Helen apparently decided to take time away from Nottingham, and to join her favourite brother Nevile, a schoolmaster near Bath. But if, with forcible feeding, the WSPU branch lost Helen Watts, it certainly retained May Burgis, Nellie Crocker and Leonora Shaw.

By mid-October, then, the government was prepared to go into the coming General Election to defeat the obstructive power of the Lords. Alongside, the WSPU's heckling of ministers and prisoners' hunger strikes had greatly heightened popular awareness of Votes for Women. Yet had suffrage campaigners won over public opinion yet? It is hard to measure.[31] And had they met Asquith's original challenge: persuading him that the majority of women really wanted the vote? The Prime Minister remained obstinately unconvinced.

All these violent confrontations, in public meetings and on the streets, provide the ructious political backdrop to the census story. By contrast, the planning and plotting during the coming eighteen months for the night in April 1911 when the government would count all the people took place quietly and calmly.

PART II

Narrative:
October 1909 to April 1911

5

Plotting across central London:
census and tax resistance

The gaze now swerves southwards from the Midlands and back to the capital, to the homes and offices in central London. Here, two groups of professionals now gathered, each with steely determination to pursue an agreed aim. One was a quartet of senior civil servants. These elite men (and they were of course entirely male) began calmly and efficiently to plan the new census. It would be the most ambitious by far, to be conducted in eighteen months' time. The second group, meeting just two days later, comprised financially independent women, many of them professionals, often doctors, all unenfranchised. They plotted to organize women's resistance to paying their taxes, increasingly timely given Lloyd George's plans.

Both groups had clearly defined beliefs about the state, government and citizenship. When mapped against each other, it was surely inevitable that their political ideologies they would clash before long. However, in autumn 1909 neither group knew of the other's intentions. Though separated by only a short distance across central London, each continued to plot in ignorance of the other. Certainly, suffrage campaigners did not know that the designers of the census planned to elicit highly personal details, especially of married women.

In contrast to Lloyd George, John Burns never mastered the knack of skimming over tedious legislative minutae. His Local Government Board (LGB) remained the Cinderella department of Whitehall. Without skilful civil servants to brief him, Burns became bogged down and left feeling exhausted. Yet in autumn 1909 he faced a crucial political task: his Housing and Town Planning Bill. This ambitious legislation would extend the vital principle of municipally owned housing, widening local authorities' powers to plan health and welfare amenities. Yet Burns's diary makes clear that he felt swamped.[1] His Bill got through the Commons without too many enfeebling amendments; then it reached the Lords – where Burns and his officers endured tortuous negotiations with obstinate peers, who naturally baulked at this creeping state socialism. Burns however cared deeply about the quality of people's housing. His claim to be *un homme du peuple* was infinitely stronger than Lloyd George's. He knew only too bitterly from his own childhood what living in a congested insanitary environment like Battersea meant. So he remained resolute on key points. The more reactionary Lords, viewing his Bill as small beer compared to Lloyd George's revolutionary budget, gave way – and by the end of November the Housing and Town Planning Act became law. It was a major achievement: one sympathetic peer even claimed that in this one act Burns had done 'more to benefit the people than any other Minister before him'.[2] Certainly, in industrial cities like Nottingham, the Housing Act would be a godsend for families living in overcrowded slums, often victims of racketeering landlords.

The LGB civil servants still lacked the skills that Burns really needed to progress his welfare reforms, notably statistical expertise. Indeed, LGB clerks were generally perceived as being inferior to other Whitehall departments, with bills woefully badly drafted. Standards were low, Oxbridge graduates only recently recruited and procedural red tape pervaded. To his frustration, Burns's reform agenda got clogged in swampy detail. However, this now began to improve. A new generation of impressively well qualified and experienced professionals arrived to run the crucial General Register Office, responsible for planning and administering the census.

Bernard Mallet sprang from the gentlemanly world of polished civil servants. At the Audit Office, his grandfather had been a friend of economist David Ricardo, while his father, Permanent Under-Secretary of State for India, was knighted. Mallet himself read Modern History at Oxford, whence followed a string of civil service appointments and promotions: Foreign Office, Treasury, Inland Revenue. In 1909 he was appointed Registrar General, becoming census supremo and joining the clubby world of elite administrators. They could communicate informally across Whitehall, decisions efficiently cascaded down to toiling clerks below. Mallet lived with wife and children in one of Chelsea's more elegant addresses; and to contemporary readers, his 'Sir Humphrey' image suggests a 'Yes, Minister' smooth operator.[3]

Thomas Stevenson beautifully complemented Mallet's social urbanity. Also appointed in 1909 to the General Register Office (GRO), self-effacing Stevenson was fired by towering intellectual goals. After studying at University College, London, he set up in medical practice, gaining qualifications in State Medicine and in Public Health. Unsurprisingly, Stevenson's abilities impressed his examiner, the medical statistician Sir Arthur Newsholme, then Medical Officer of Health for Brighton. Stevenson became his assistant and theirs grew into a powerful partnership. Stevenson's promotions were rapid – including appointment to the new medical service for schools run by the London County Council (LCC). So in 1909, who better to become the GRO's chief medical statistician than Stevenson? That same year, Newsholme himself was appointed as LGB's chief medical officer. This impressively triumvirate – Mallet as Registrar General, Stevenson commanding statistics, Newsholme responsible for health – gave the dynamic leadership essential for the smooth census planning.[4]

Perhaps because he was preoccupied with his Housing and Town Planning legislation, Burns seemed to leave designing the census to these impressive civil servants. So, from October 1909, with professional precision Mallet and Stevenson began detailed planning. A prefabricated Census Office was opened in Millbank to house the staff to be recruited.[5] The first Census Committee meeting was held in Mallet's room on Wednesday 20 October 1909. Four key officials attended: Mallet and Stevenson were joined by by Alfred Waters, chief GRO Clerk; and by Census Office Secretary Archer Bellingham who had already begun census planning. They all knew each other well, so there was no need for preamble, and the Committee promptly got down to business. Given the Liberal government's far-reaching public health concerns, 1911 was always going to be a far more ambitious census than its predecessors, and the quartet plunged immediately into the detail that would be required. This included how the number of rooms would be counted (e.g. including kitchens but not sculleries); and how ages should be grouped (e.g. under ten years). There was no time to waste. A second meeting held two days later, and soon Sunday 2 April 1911 was identified for taking the census.[6]

By the third meeting, the committee homed into the most controversial aspect of the coming census. A key concern was the size of Britain's families, falling birthrate and high levels of child mortality: who was having children, who was not, and whose children were least likely to survive. Burns himself, child in a family of eighteen only nine of whom survived infancy, had sharp personal reasons for wishing to reduce infant mortality. Other Cabinet ministers also had experience of child deaths: Lloyd George had just lost his favourite daughter, Mair, aged seventeen. Welfare and health reforms required accurate data; so into the census schedule it was:

> decided to add after 'condition as to Marriage' – 'duration of existing Marriage'; and 'number of children born to existing Marriage, living and dead'. (In this connection the Registrar General promised to forward to the Local Government Board a copy of Dr Stevenson's Memorandum on the utility of these statistics.)[7]

Thus was quietly slipped in, not only child mortality but also the question of marital fertility and family size. There was a mix of concerns, both environmental factors as the public health movement believed; and that high birthrates in poorer families meant a decline in racial stock, as eugenicists claimed. This was not merely an intellectual debate about the out-breeding of the middle class's small family size. It had personal meaning. Both Arthur Newsome and Archer Bellingham were married with no children. Stevenson's wife had had three children, of whom only one survived. Stevenson began to identify the key factors, notably social class and the age of husband and of wife on marriage. Mallet supported Stevenson's ambitious investigation into the 'fertility of marriage'.[8]

So, the fundamentals of the 1911 census were already emerging clearly. With the best of welfare reform intentions, it would require intrusive inquiries of each marriage: how many children had been born and how many had died. For women, all unenfranchised, this would surely seem the inquisition of an insensitive government still denying them full citizenship. However, beyond the male elite, none of this was known yet by outsiders.

Just two days after of the Census Committee first met, the Women's Tax Resistance League held *its* inaugural meeting. The two gatherings had much in common. Both attracted professionals at the top of their game; and both were built upon earlier precedents. Mallet elaborated upon earlier censuses, while the League drew upon the historical roots: Hampden's refusal to pay ship money; Quaker radical traditions; and nonconformist 'Passive Resisters' refusal to pay their educational rate after the 1902 Education Act, with Liberal support. More recently, Dora Montefiore and Quaker Alice Clark had refused to pay their taxes. Witnessing resisters' local auctions of their seized goods had converted Constance Andrews of Ipswich. This form of quietly dignified, often religious, civil disobedience had been recently inspired by the visit of Mohandas Gandhi, whom Charlotte Despard met in London; then a young Indian lawyer living in South Africa, he had developed his distinctive philosophy of non-violent civil disobedience, *satyagraha* or spiritual resistance to unjust laws.[9]

But to date this calm, considered defiance of the tax-collecting state had comprised individual acts rather than a co-ordinated campaign. Now, with Lloyd George pushing taxation right up the political agenda, the need for organized resistance grew increasingly urgent. And where better to meet than in an eminent women surgeon's spacious Harley Street premises?

The first meeting, held on Friday 22 October at 114 Harley Street, was by invitation of Dr Louisa Garrett Anderson. Daughter of legendary Elizabeth Garrett Anderson and niece of Mrs Fawcett, she was hard-wired into the centre of pioneer feminist achievement. Louisa had studied at the London School of Medicine for Women and qualified as a surgeon in 1897. High profile yet ecumenical, she somehow managed to support both the WSPU and the NUWSS; she protested however at aunt Fawcett's 'manifesto against militancy' after Muriel Matters's grille-chaining in the Commons, and seems to have left the NUWSS then.[10] So, for the fledgling League, Louisa Garrett Anderson carried considerable clout.

The League's neat handwritten minutes record its first meeting. The twenty other women present were certainly impressive. Many belonged to the WFL, now with a growing number of local branches and even its own weekly paper, *The Vote*. The presence of Edith How-Martyn, WFL honorary secretary, indicates the League's close WFL links. Margaret Nevinson, WFL vanner and speaker, brought considerable local government experience. Given that her journalist husband Henry was frequently absent, in one of Margaret's rare references to him she casually mentioned in her autobiography: 'Being a passive resister to illegal taxation, I did not think it my duty to mention my earnings when Mr Nevinson returned our income'. On married women's financial hardships, Margaret added pointedly: 'men and women living out of wedlock are taxed separately and save considerably'.[11]

Other women present included writers like Cicely Hamilton of WFL's Chelsea branch, and artist Mary Sargant Florence who had designed WFL banner 'Dare to Be Free' (though she too remained ecumenical in her suffrage loyalties). Widow of an American musician, Mary was a fairly typical member: she had a Chelsea studio plus a country house set in the beautiful wooded Thames valley near Marlow, which provided weekend rest for exhausted suffragettes. Mary was already a tax resister: WFL had supported her 'Passive Resistance' meeting at Marlow and 'sale in market square'.[12] Another active member was Margaret Kineton Parkes, recently moved to London and previously little known within the suffrage movement. Like Margaret Nevinson, she had two children and a disappointing marriage, seemingly separated from her husband; for such women divorce was not an option. Employed by the WFL, Margaret Kineton Parkes now took up the cause of tax resistance with tenacious zeal.[13]

The key contributors were those combining a quest for justice with their own specialist skills. Of particularly significance was Clemence Housman herself. She unassumingly combined both design talent and networks (Suffrage Atelier meetings at Pembroke Cottage) with patient taxation expertise, honed by years of sorting out her father's dubious muddles. It was an impressive, if untypical, gathering: whether through professional achievement or marriage, they were largely wealthier than the average middle-class Edwardian woman.

Like the Census Committee, momentum had to be maintained. The following Friday, the League discussed various forms of tax resistance, and whether it should be separate from WFL. Opinion was split. However, when Mary Sargant Florence offered to donate £50 if they became completely independent of the WFL (with two doctors similarly each promising £25), independence became a foregone conclusion. Indeed, the WFL even agreed to the request that Margaret Kineton Parkes could work for the Women's Tax Resistance League for three months. So the League now had independence plus one paid official.[14]

By November, the League had set up a working party, chaired by one of the women doctors. It naturally included Mary Sargant Florence, Clemence Housman and Margaret Kineton Parkes. Also present was a Mrs Ayres Purdie, also virtually unknown to suffrage campaigners, but offering invaluable ammunition to challenge Lloyd George. Her advertisement in *The Vote* pulled no punches:

Women Versus the Budget.
Why Not Reclaim Your Income Tax From the Government
And give it to the Women's Freedom League?
If your Income has been taxed before you get it, and does not exceed £700 yearly,
you are entitled to recover a portion of the tax.
NB – Infants, Married Women and Lunatics are not so entitled.
Consult Mrs E AYRES PURDIE ALAA, Certified Accountant and Income Tax
Specialist, Craven House, Kingsway, [London] W.C.[15]

The League got down to business. Preferring to proceed judiciously, it chided precipitate members who wanted test cases to go to court. Kineton Parkes's enthusiasm was reined in: she was to prioritize 'spade work [of] writing letters and arranging interviews with the one object in view of increasing the list of names of women willing to become Passive Resisters'. Two points become clear. First, the League sought prestiguous *names* of women willing to withhold paying their taxes.[16] Second, its choice of the phrase 'passive resisters' must have been made deliberately. Earlier Liberal support of this civil disobedience represented one more stick to embarrass Asquith's government, as it intruded further into women's lives with taxation demands.

Surrounded by this glittering array of feminist talent and achievement, Clemence Housman sat quietly through these meetings. She was conscious of her anomalous position in this new League: she might have some taxation experience, but could not match Ayres Purdie's qualifications. Unlike women doctors or wealthy widows, sharing the house with brother Laurence, she could not be a resister – unless she became liable to pay tax. So Clem determined to do something about this. If the League proclaimed 'No Vote No Tax', then she too would put this defiant principle into practice. At some point during autumn, Clem took a daring step. She decided to rent a modest house of her own. She would make herself liable for at least *one* form of taxation: Inhabited House Duty.

Clem naturally confided her plans to Laurence. His 'Right of Way' article had just been published in *The Vote*, declaring 'Man is an adventuring animal', and certainly seemed to have Clem's tax adventure firmly in mind:

> You cannot claim for one half of humanity the open road and the 'illimitable veldt', while you are driving the other down a cul-de-sac into a compound that is not of her own choosing. Woman must be given, like man, a deciding voice as to her own career; she must be free to make her own risks, her own adventures, her own experiments and discoveries.[17]

For her 'open road' Clem selected somewhere remote from Kensington which she could enjoy visiting unobtrusively. Clem knew Swanage, a seaside resort on the Dorset coast, as this was the where her sister holidayed with her family. Near Studland head, it was a fashionable choice for artists – such as Vanessa Bell and her sister Virginia Stephen. Clem and Laurence did not waste time, apparently visiting Swanage in December.

Clem selected a pleasantly unremarkable residential street, Linden Road, not far from the town centre; here she rented a house called Greycott. She filled it with borrowed furniture, and on 18 December duly paid her *local* rates on this new house to Swanage Urban District Council. However for *national* taxation, Clem refused to pay her Inhabited House Duty. She then had to wait patiently for the Inland Revenue to catch up with her and start legal proceedings.[18] It was to be a long wait. Clem had however now joined the small band of women tax resisters.

For historians, one of the advantages of Clem's periodic visits to Swanage was that her daily conversations with Laurence were now supplemented by intimate letters back home to her brother. Clem, meticulous in all she did, was nevertheless oddly slap-dash in these letters to Laurence. They seem hurriedly scribbled and irksomely undated. Yet, as if continuing a conversation at home, they provide an invaluable record of the loving siblings' daily chat. One example illuminates this vividly, confirming Clem as 'chief banner-maker' to the Suffrage Atelier; it is written to Laurence who was away, undoubtedly speaking for suffrage meeting:

Greycott
Sunday
My Dearest
    … Get a few things for me when you go to Kensington. Cane hoop & iron clamp for embroidery. A bit of pale blue cloth for a pattern … There are only a few inch scraps of this … Also of the gold gauze.

Laurence knew his way round Clem's sewing materials, so essential to her banner-making.[19] What is clear is that for the League Clem now combined three compelling qualities: taxation experience, banner-making and her resistance to paying tax in Swanage. This obscure location made her now extremely well-positioned for 'vanishing for the vote', should that ever be required in future.

To take on Asquith's government, suffrage organizations needed persuasive *chutzpah*. The Women's Tax Resistance League, notably Margaret Kineton Parkes, certainly was persistent. But did it possess the inspirational qualities of, say, Emmeline Pankhurst or Charlotte Despard? Possibly not. Despite trying to persuade other suffrage societies, the number of women willing to add their names the list of resisters never reached near the target of five hundred names.[20] Although was certainly energetic, the League remained small. Rather, its significance was primarily symbolic. It staged resistance 'spectacles' around London and the Home Counties, turning local auction rooms into political theatre. Who knew where these troublesome women would unexpectedly pop up next? One exotic example was Princess Sophia Duleep Singh, a maharajah's daughter who lived in a grace-and-favour house at Hampton Court by the Thames. Her diamond ring was seized for tax non-payment, sold at auction, bought by a League member and duly returned to the Princess. Indeed, all the silver teaspoons and antique candlesticks, passed down in families and polished by parlour maids, allow a glimpse inside upper-middle-class homes, evoking an elegiac picture of Edwardian domestic life.[21]

Along with staging protests at auctions, the League offered a vital model for how women could resist an undemocratic state with acts of civil disobedience, without loss of dignity. To win over members of the public, a great banner was planned and so Clem moved centre-stage at the League:

> The subject of the banner was discussed and … Mrs Sargant Florence offered to send a design and Miss Housman was deputed to order the banner from the Suffrage Atelier. Decided that a drawing of it be made … from the statue of John Hampden & that the colours of the League should be Black White & Grey …
>
> Miss Housman very kindly brought with her the sketch of the banner prepared by the Suffrage Atelier from a design by Mrs Sargant Florence …

After the banner (see Figure 12, p. 42) had been carried in procession, it was minuted that:

> The Tax Resisters' Banner was greatly admired … A very strong vote of thanks was passed to Mr & Miss Housman for their great kindness in putting so much of their individual work into the banner.[22]

All this time, neither the Women's Tax Resistance League nor Mallet's Census Committee knew that the other was hatching plots – just a few miles away from each other. Both continued their work, both operating in their own self-enclosed world, both sure of its own interpretation of the state and of democracy. However, the two visions were so contradictory that before long a clash became inevitable.

Both were, of course, rooted within the wider political realities then pulsating across the country: Lloyd George's budget, his government's head-on collision with the Lords, and the dark shadow of continued forcible feeding of suffragettes in prison. As a result of this rising political crescendo, by the end of 1909 both the Census Committee and the Tax Resistance League halted their meetings. The General Election was set for January 1910; it would be fought constituency by constituency, absorbing everyone's energy. Right across the length and breadth of the country, franchised men and unenfranchised women sharpened their weapons for the vigorous life-or-death political fight ahead.

6

The battle for John Burns's Battersea revisited

Even before the General Election was announced, suffragettes maintained fierce pressure on the Liberal government. The WSPU made excellent propaganda from the violence inflicted on hunger strikers by prison doctors. Meanwhile on 5 July, the WFL, whose request to see Asquith had been snubbed, had begun its patient picket of the Commons. Over 250 women took part in this fifteen-week vigil. Even H. G. Wells found their unbroken 'siege of the legislature extraordinarily impressive', while Margaret Nevinson described how 'our great watch' was maintained:

> Women stuck to their posts ... All through ... the long days and nights of a wet summer and autumn, the supply of watchers never failed. Women, of all ages and all classes, stood patient in suffering and reckless of health ... hoping to gain audience of our elusive Prime Minister.[1]

Meanwhile, a by-election was called in Bermondsey for 28 October. Lying on the south bank of Thames like Battersea, it comprised a largely working-class electorate, often dockworkers. At the 1906 General Election it had been won by the Liberals, who now needed to hold it. The WSPU therefore whirred into action in Bermondsey, distributing a poster which pulled no punches: 'Torturing Women in Prison. Vote Against the Government'. At one crowded meeting Lady Constance Lytton explained that her family 'was founded on chivalry without social distinction', but that 'since the Newcastle incident I have a new picture of justice'.[2]

The local WFL also got busy, dispatching an organizer, opening committee rooms, holding street meetings and running a shop. However, frustration with Asquith's obduracy bred impatience. Their vigil outside the Commons ended on 27 October in sheer frustration. The WFL now informed Asquith that, after thoughtful consideration, it had:

decided that the time had come to make a more direct protest against the injustice of electing members of Parliament without the consent of women.

Members of the League have therefore begun today a new militant policy at Bermondsey, and have invalidated the bye-election by destroying the recorded votes of electors.[3]

So, a new political style erupted. Two suffragettes entered the polling booths and spilled a chemical solution into the ballot boxes to burn the papers placed there by voters. Unfortunately, liquid splashed into the eye of an election official who was temporarily blinded. Despite receiving protest letters, the WFL defended this action publicly: the *Vote* headline was 'The Heroines of the Ballot Box'. But, as with WSPU attacks on Cabinet ministers, some suffrage campaigners looked askance at this new militant tactic which they felt risked personal injury to bystanders and undermined what suffragettes sought: a vote.[4]

More broadly, to the government's dismay, Bermondsey converted a Liberal seat into a surprising Conservative gain. A few days later, Lloyd George's Finance Bill passed its third reading in the Commons. On 30 November however, the unbudging Lords refused to support it, carrying a provocative motion that it would not give its consent to this controversial bill 'until it has been submitted to the judgement of the people'. On 2 December, the Commons duly passed a motion that the Lords' behaviour was a 'breach of the constitution and a usurpation of the rights' of elected MPs. Here was impasse. Parliament was prorogued and polling ordered for late January 1910.

Asquith opened the Liberals' General Election campaign. John Burns felt he had fought Battersea sufficient times already. Now aged fifty-two and among the older Cabinet ministers, Burns was growing tired.[5] He had expended considerable time and energy propelling his crucial Housing and Planning Bill through Westminster, negotiating for final approval with tiresome peers. This strengthened his long-held fundamental democratic faith: 'I have always been a single chamber man but this confirms me absolutely', he wrote in his diary. In the coming Election, Burns stood whole-heartedly in the fight for democracy against inherited privilege. He relished the opportunity to re-ignite his early socialist-cum-temperance rhetoric and recorded in his diary: 'Will present snobbery, past jobbery, ancient robbery unite with dogma and drink to fetter our hands and chloroform our minds again?'[6]

Burns had meanwhile also progressed other welfare reforms dear to his heart; he had authorized a national survey of infant mortality, the first time a government had really taken the matter seriously. Yet while Lloyd George's reforms empowered many crushed by poverty, into those of Burns now sometimes crept an authoritarian moralism. His growing conservatism was particularly apparent in his views on married women's work. Part of his public image was how, in his own upbringing, his over-burdened mother had had to take in washing to support her many children. As a boy, helping his mother carry a basket of washing, he had apparently vowed to her, 'If I've health and strength, no other mother shall have to work as you have to, and no child do what I have to do'. Recently Burns's support of 'greater comfort for mothers, better conditions of life' for healthy children, included 'the prevention of married women's labour in factories and workshops'.[7] While this might make sense in his own Lavender Hill household, it made less sense down in Nine Elms, where hard-pressed women took whatever jobs they could. To many suffrage campaigners it certainly smacked of pure impertinence.

Some local Liberals, while acknowledging Burns's achievements, began to ask questions. There were mutterings in Battersea that the minister had pursued his reform agenda at the expense of his own backyard. Local Conservatives took advantage of his absences to stir up opposition and promote their candidate, Benn. Meanwhile, from Burns's left rose disillusioned accusations of a sell-out. Even his own local Liberal-Radical electoral powerbase began to look shaky. Traditionally astute when it came to election publicity, Burns still had his work cut out to hold Battersea. Socialists ran such a vocal heckling campaign that he made his meetings ticket-only occasions.

Burns's misfortune was to be the only minister defending a central London seat.[8] He represented an easy target. Just over the Thames lay the suffrage strong-holds of Chelsea and Kensington. Both the WSPU and WFL homed in on his Battersea fiefdom. The WSPU organizer advertised a women-only meeting in Battersea Town Hall, just round the corner from Burns's own home. Another WSPU organizer, Annie Kenney's sister Jessie, even managed to corner him on a tramcar, apparently sitting down next to him and asking him to use his influence with the Home Secretary over forcible feeding. Burns crossed to another seat, but she followed him. He reputedly said he would get her locked up, and she jumped off the moving tramcar.[9]

Relations with suffragettes deteriorated further. Both sides believed the other to be hypocrites. Burns certainly saw the militancy of privileged women as both counter-productive to their winning the vote and not in the interests of most of his constituents. By mid-December, he struggled to enter his election meetings at Battersea Town Hall unscathed, and shortly after, women were excluded from them. Christabel Pankhurst retaliated: she told a local meeting that Burns should be rejected as he excluded women from his meetings.[10]

Battersea was of course Charlotte Despard's own backyard, and nearby suffrage families like the Duvals were also very active. So the WFL was quick off the mark. It was soon decided that the General Election priority was first 'asking certain definite questions' of all parliamentary candidates, second 'that campaigns in the constituencies of Mr Burns and other Cabinet ministers should be opened as soon as possible', and all organizers to be under Teresa Billington-Grieg's direction for the Election.[11]

The WFL's Battersea campaign opened both a Committee Room and a shop. *The Vote* helpfully informed readers that, from Charing Cross, the former could be reached by Lavender Hill tramcar and the shop by the Clapham Junction tram. It also kept readers up-to-date with Burns's exclusion of women from his supposedly 'unanimous' Battersea meetings; admission was by ticket, carefully limited to 'those pledged to support "Honest John" through thick and thin'. *The Vote* then added:

> In discussing the problem of unemployment, Mr Burns once more trotted out his … only, remedy. 'The State', he said, 'should prohibit married women from working'. But … it only means to prohibit them working in comparatively well-paid industries, like the cotton factories of Lancashire. There will be no desire on the part of the State to challenge preponderance in the sweated trades or to forbid them to work for a shilling a day at shirt and blouse-making, charring, scrubbing, and washing.[12]

And the WFL produced a special anti-Burns leaflet for Battersea electors. It lammed into Liberal hypocrisies over forcible feeding, excluding women from meetings and the controversy over women's work.

Turn Mr. Burns out!
Why do members of the Women's Freedom League hiss Mr Burns?

Because he has called the women who are fighting for political equality with men 'female hooligans'; and at Mr Burns's dictation women were flung out of his Town Hall meeting and brutally treated by Liberal stewards …

Because he supports, and will, if returned, continue to support, a Government which is Russianising England, and is resorting to the torture of its political opponents by forcible feeding *when those opponents are women.*

Because … [he] refused to sanction … a Women's Workshop in Battersea for the employment of widows with children to support, giving as his reasons that there were plenty of domestic servants [jobs] advertised …

Battersea Electors, stand by your women and prevent this reactionary from returning to power![13]

Prohibiting married women's labour was indeed a particularly weak plank in Burns's political platform: it was not only unworkable but also premised upon a conveniently particular reading of his family memory. At New Year 1910, Charlotte Despard addressed a meeting in Battersea Library. Poking scorn at 'his silvery tongue' and 'his overwhelming vanity', she accused Burns of being 'a traitor to his class'. All this raised the Battersea election frenzy ever higher. One popular paper even ran a cartoon, depicting 'Mrs Despard at The Free Library'.[14]

Particularly memorable was a 'Startling Incident at Battersea'. According to press reports, it kicked off when some women entered one of Burns's election committee rooms and 'offered' clerical assistance'. They duly spent ten minutes

15 'Burns or Benn for Battersea?' Suffragettes (*top right*) and Charlotte Despard (*bottom right*). *Daily Graphic,* 8 Jan 1910.

folding leaflets, then suddenly sped off. Later, one of the women 'supposed to be connected with the suffragette movement' reappeared, on a bicycle. She entered the room, darted to a table and attempted 'to throw some mysterious liquid over papers and canvassing cards'. When the clerk in charge tried to stop her, she ran into his office to splatter more liquid over marked canvassing cards. In the ensuing scuffle, liquid spilt on the clerk's left hand and squirted above his right eye. As a result, he suffered burns. The woman then slammed three doors, jumped on her bicycle and peddled off fast down the road.[15] Like the earlier Bermondsey 'outrage', this spontaneous election militancy raised many hackles, though suffragettes still repudiated 'the stupid deed about which Battersea Liberals profess to be inflamed'.[16]

Elsewhere, electioneering proceeded more conventionally. Among those who probably had more sympathy for Burns than for the suffragettes was Virginia Stephen (soon to become Virginia Woolf). She supported adult suffrage, and during the election she addressed envelopes for the new People's Suffrage Federation at its Bloomsbury office.[17] Her own activity may have been rather desultory, but adult suffragists included for instance the Women's Cooperative

Guild; it represented working-class married women, and the Guild and was busy lobbying the Chancellor to include maternity benefit in his scheme.

Back in Battersea, on polling day, 17 January, Burns noted that in the Town Hall 'women in gallery hissed me before and after the Count'. As the result was announced, he added, 'a triumphant cheer went up from the people' and outside the 'crowd seized us', chairing him shoulder high through the streets. Burns was indeed returned, though with a reduced majority. He however remained uncomfortably aware of his many detractors: 'brewers, distillers, ... Socialists, and the ladies'.[18]

Lloyd George was also re-elected. By end of January, the results of this historic Election became clear. Some Liberal voters had been alarmed by Lloyd George's uncompromising language about the House of Lords and his new land taxes. Their huge 1906 majority was swept away: it was less a question of the Liberals winning the election than their remaining in office. Asquith's government now had to rely on the support of Labour and Irish Nationalist MPs.

There was some reshuffling: at the Home Office hapless Herbert Gladstone was replaced by Winston Churchill, who now was responsible for forcible feeding of hunger strikers. Overall, the government's dependence upon other parties left ministers feeling uncomfortable. By mid-February, a miserable Asquith was visibly floundering. Burns wrote in his diary, 'PM feels keenly the situation. I am deeply sorry for him. Little or any blame is his.'[19]

With the Election results now clear, suffragettes rejoiced optimistically. Charlotte Despard, so often given to rhetorical flights of biblical hyperbole, celebrated the Liberals' downfall. She proclaimed to a Trafalgar Square crowd: 'Never perhaps in all history has there been so dramatic an illustration of the Nemesis which falls upon the perpetrators of injustice when the cup of their iniquity is full'.[20] And when the WFL held its annual conference on 29 January, it could reflect back on a successful year. In her presidential address, Despard declared: 'Before the present Parliament has run its course, we shall have the vote'. Edith How-Martyn's survey of WFL highlights included Muriel Matters's flight over London in an airship, two caravan tours, the sixteen-week vigil, plus 'passive resister' protests and sales of their seized goods. The Bermondsey and Battersea incidents were skimmed over (despite disquiet among branches) and the WFL's militant policy was unanimously endorsed.[21]

So what were the political prospects in spring 1910? Despite its wobbles, the Liberal government still determined to pursue the constitutional war with the Lords, and to win approval of Lloyd George's budget. On suffrage, there was cautious optimism. The two militant organizations were willing to offer a truce to Asquith's government, to give it an opportunity to state its intentions.[22] Brailsford and Nevinson began consulting with Mrs Fawcett's NUWSS over what might now be possible. The aim was to find a compromise women's suffrage measure. It had to be sufficiently narrow a property-based franchise to retain Conservatives' support, yet broad enough to appease Liberal and Labour.[23] A cross-party Conciliation Committee of MPs was formed; it was chaired by Lord Lytton, a Conservative peer and Constance Lytton's brother; with Henry Brailsford as its secretary, it had direct links to the WSPU.

After considerable behind-the-scenes lobbying between suffrage campaigners and politicians, a Conciliation Bill eventually emerged. They had ended up with a narrow bill that would at least establish the principle of equal voting rights for men and women. But it was so limited that it would enfranchise only one million women who satisfied a strict property qualification: women householders, usually well-to-do widows and unmarried women. There was unease among radical Liberal and Labour circles, who felt their adult suffrage beliefs were being badly compromised. The suffrage societies however placed their faith in this Conciliation Bill as their best practicable option during the coming year.[24]

7

The Census Bill and the boycott plan

By February 1910, Asquith's government was living hand to mouth: Irish MPs demanded Home Rule, while ministers wanted to get Lloyd George's Finance Bill passed. Other legislation seemed far less contentious by comparison. John Burns's LGB needed to get its bill through Parliament in time to plan the April 1911 census. After a lengthy hiatus while the General Election results became clear, the Census Committee could at last resume its deliberations.

The four key civil servants got into their stride again: Mallet as Registrar General, Stevenson as GRO Superintendent of Statistics, plus Alfred Waters, Chief GRO Clerk, and Archer Bellingham, Census Office Secretary. Taking advantage of London's rail and tube links, the four men all commuted into the city from the healthily salubrious suburbs: Mallet from Chelsea, Stevenson from Finchley in Middlesex, Waters from Limpsfield in rural Surrey, and Bellingham from Wimbledon. Dedicated professionals, they immediately got down to business, despite the political eddies still billowing around Westminster.

In February, they routinely discussed how best to present the 'Social Statistics' showing individual ages and 'Condition as to Marriage' in various urban and rural districts. Bellingham's model census schedule page was accepted.[1] Then it was time to get down to seemingly innocuous detail. How precisely would census questions be framed? Social reformers required information on certain controversial questions. Was the population reproducing itself at a healthy rate? If not, what were the main obstacles to maintaining a healthy birthrate? Were people marrying at too early or late an age, and how did this vary across different social classes and occupational groups?

Stevenson had been busy, with a Memorandum on how the census could record the duration of each marriage and number of children born to each of these marriages. It would exclude any previous marriages of husband or wife, it having already been established by 'statistical investigation that the advent of sterility is hastened by early marriage'. Stevenson outlined 'his scheme of presenting fertility statistics', inviting criticism of it; he suggested how a table would show 'the prospects of fertility for any given union of husband and wife of specified ages'. Such tables could be prepared for different occupations or for 'upper middle and lower class', and in this way:

> precise information could be obtained as to the extent to which prudential consid-
> erations and other factors influence the size of the family in each rank of society
> and for each combination of father and mother ... [These] are at present our only
> source of information as to the reproduction of the population. It seems likely that
> the information obtained would be of great interest and utility.[2]

Stevenson suggested that these refinements on the data available from previous censuses would for the first time enable 'an accurate comparison of the fecundity of females of different ages ... [by] comparing wives of one age with those of another'. And by looking at 'expectation of birth' figures, the tables 'would indicate the most appropriate age of spouse for a man or woman of any given age'. Stevenson then warmed to his theme of comparisons across social class:

> such Tables would throw much light upon the tendencies for one social stratum
> to replace another, especially if, as in New South Wales, the children could be
> returned separately in the Schedule as living and dead. The fate of the children so
> recorded might have an interesting bearing upon the problem of infantile and child
> mortality, and might afford valuable information as to the best ages for marriage
> from this point of view.

The tables would also show 'at what ages the economic shoe pinches in the different classes of society, in different occupations and different parts of the country'. All this, he added persuasively, would be of keen interest 'both to the vital statistician and to the social economist', as well as 'a wider class of readers' among the Edwardian public.

Despite the somewhat chilling wording, Stevenson's good intentions do still shine through. He *wanted* to identify the best way for producing and raising healthy children, and knew that politicians and other welfare reformers were relying on this census data, and how it was presented. So Stevenson's aim was 'to present fertility statistics by three dimensions – age of husband, age of wife and duration of marriage', but reasonably succinctly. Yet how could they meet criticism of those 'indisposed' to accept the figures, unless *complete* data were presented? Stevenson proposed applying two tests for social status: (*a*) number of rooms occupied; and (*b*) occupation – though 'he feared the numbers in the higher occupations might be too few to admit deductions being drawn from them'. And at this point Stevenson (in census meetings normally the public health intellectual) now reveals himself also as husband and as father of three children only one of whom still survived. Probably heart-felt, he admitted he was, the minutes record:

rather anxious if possible to get fertility co-efficients for three grades of society. The Upper and Middle Classes were constantly being accused of not reproducing themselves and he thought it desirable that statistics should verify or deny this accusation.[3]

Both professionally and personally, Waters and Bellingham may well have agreed with Stevenson about the need for this detail. Mallet however wanted just broad brush occupations (e.g. mining, textiles) and discussion moved on to other refinements – like the grouping into broad five-year bands of age difference between husband and wife, which could mask either a few days or ten years. Stevenson thoughtfully took all comments on board and went away to fine-tune his scheme. Meanwhile, the others met to discuss the mechanics of enumerators' duties and use of new machines to speed up tabulation, rather than relying on copying by enumerator as previously. The new tabulating machine speeds, and the employment of temporary female staff to operate them, were welcomed.[4]

By this point, however, the Australia model of the efficiently detailed census conducted in New South Wales had won the civil servants' admiration. And statisticians' need to access detailed data had the influential backing of the Royal Statistical Society, the Society of Medical Officers, the Institute of Actuaries and the Royal Society of Medicine – as well as that of John Burns. The Census Committee was aware that inquiries into the duration of a marriage and the number of children born to it, both now living and dead (as included in the Australian census), might be regarded as too inquisitorial, but that was a price that reformers keen to tackle health inequalities were willing to pay.[5] Would the British people swallow it?

With these broad census principles established, the four men now needed to consult with the local officials whose responsibility it would be to implement this ambitious enumeration. On 4 March, they were joined by five central London Superintendent Registrars, whose fears needed to be soothed. One expressed anxiety about enumerating common lodging houses, as lodgers might fear their information might be passed to the police. Another warned that 'many Occupiers concealed the number of their Children for fear of being turned out from their dwelling'. Mallet offered urbane reassurance about the confidentiality of the information provided, plus the professionalism of registrars and enu-merators. But still further assurances were required. The National Federation of Registrars had got wind of the unprecedently elaborate enumeration plans they would be required to put into practice and was preparing a deputation. What to tell them? That registrars would be encouraged to recruit local government officers as enumerators; school teachers would instruct children in filling up the family schedule; the timetable for Registrars to send in their enumeration books would be relaxed slightly, to minimize the risk of inaccuracy; and police alerted to rounding up local vagrants for enumerating.[6]

It was all progressing smoothly. The census would be taken on the night of Sunday 2 April 1911. Wrinkles were ironed out and anxieties assuaged. The Census Bill was ready for its first reading in the Commons. Even at this stage, however, Burns seemed content to retain a low profile, just keeping in touch via Mallet; and the Bill was introduced by his LGB Parliamentary Secretary.[7]

Then Archer Bellingham suggested consulting a former Australian government statistician about his own experience of the detailed census taken in New South Wales. Mallet agreed to invite him to 'call' and Bellingham then reminded them that, with the four new columns added to the schedule, 'it was most important that the patience of the Occupier should not be strained by his being asked to furnish too much information'.[8]

Helped by the Australian statistician's experience and with a copy of the census schedule back from printers, the Bill proceeded through Parliament during the early summer. It duly included questions for 'any person ... being married, the duration of marriage, and the number of children born of the marriage, [and] the number of such children living', and those who had died.[9] When Mallet and Stevenson, Waters and Bellingham met again in late June, however, they all agreed that some final polishing of the precise wording on the schedule page was required. For these most contentious questions, headings for the four key columns were now amended to read:

Column 6 – 9. 'Married Couple' altered to 'Married Woman' ...
Column 7. 'Total born alive' altered to 'Total children born alive'.
Column 8. 'Still living' altered to 'Children still living'.
Column 9. 'Now dead' altered to 'Children who have died'.[10]

So, the final wording under the 'Particulars as to Marriage' columns, to be filled in by 'the Head of Family' now read: 'State for each Married Woman entered on this Schedule', the number of children born alive to the present marriage, the number still living and the number who have died.

This committee-room census-speak needs to be disentangled to glimpse how it might have been perceived by the suffrage world. 'The Head of Family', normally the husband (or brother, father) and invariably enfranchised, would complete the census schedule. This now included his answering questions 'for each married woman' enumerated on the schedule, how many live births she had had and how many of those children had died. Women, till now merely deprived of a vote, were apparently also to be deprived of a voice: their own experiences of childbirth and child deaths were now to be recorded *for* them *by* their 'Head of Family'. Women not only could not vote: they could not even hold the household pen. Thus in one fell swoop was insult added to injury.

Once the decision had been taken to ask their intrusive questions in this manner, it apparently never occurred to these civil servants that some women, notably married women (whose husbands were required to provide information

about them), might object. It appears that, in their clubbily male professional
world, such problems were simply not envisaged. Yet it is possible they *did* have
a hunch that suffragettes might object. After all, the Mallets lived in Chelsea,
and it seems nigh impossible that Mrs Mallet could have missed the presence of
Votes for Women campaigners on her local shopping streets, and likewise Mrs
Bellingham in Wimbledon. It is however highly likely that the four men had
absorbed the Asquithian creed: that until the majority of women manifested
their desire for the vote, government officials need not overly concern themselves. Nor was it their responsibility to oversee the Conciliation Bill's progress.
Suffrage could be seen as a minority irritant, compared to the urgent imperative
of improving public health.

Certainly this revealingly illuminates the workings of both Whitehall administrators and ministers. It was a Liberalism premised on the smooth working of the
state apparatus, but which remained – even by 1910 – myopic about those adults
excluded from political citizenship. Complacent about the brilliance of British
parliamentary democracy, it could turn a blind eye to Votes for Women.[11]

Yet the Census Committee plans for very detailed data collection had additional fears for feminists. The government's reform concerns included the degree
to which women's employment affected female fertility.[12] Occupational data
was required if certain types of women's labour were to be curtailed by law.
Suffragists might welcome the other welfare uses to which the information on
fertility and infant mortality would be put, for instance to demonstrate the ill-
effects of family overcrowding. But they strongly feared that future laws would
limit women's economic freedoms, especially the freedom to earn a living – and
this gave them an additional strong motive to oppose the census.[13]

However, during the 1910 run-up to the census neither side, though both
working a short distance apart in central London, was really aware of what the
other was planning. Suffragettes remained a problem for ministries other than
the LGB, notably the Home Office, with its police and prison service – not for
the census planners. And at this stage suffrage campaigners remained unaware
that the designers of the census were to elicit such personal details, especially
of married women.[14] After all, the Census Act itself had merely referred to 'any
person' who was married, the number of children born and the number still
living. Surely little to object to in that?

With the 1910 Census Act now out in the public domain, though of course
its devilish detail not yet grasped, the government's plans for April 1911 soon
caught the beady eye of suffragettes, notably the WFL. The WFL, and particularly Charlotte Despard, wished to avoid the impetuous militancy of suffragettes
rushing on bicycles into elections with phials of acid. The truce, observed by both
the WFL and WSPU while the Conciliation Bill progressed through Parliament,
provided a positive context. The WFL however still supported women's tax

resistance. Despard was being pursued by the Inland Revenue over unpaid tax: with their leader threatened with arrest and imprisonment, WFL activists volunteered to be ready for 'danger duty'.[15]

This was also a summer of great processions through London, confirming the suffrage movement as impressively well-supported and creative: the Housmans' 'From Prison to Citizenship' banner carried aloft and displayed resplendently: see Figure 13. Additionally, Despard's meetings in London with Mohandas Gandhi had inspired her with his theory of *satyagraha*, spiritual resistance to unjust laws. Indeed, the idea for a census boycott sprang from the WFL's developing philosophy of non-violent 'passive resistance'.

The WFL was certainly quick off the mark.[16] It brought together fears about Asquith's real intentions on the Conciliation Bill, with suspicion about his government's census planning. At its National Executive Committee in June 1910 the WFL therefore proposed a boycott. The idea grew from a suggestion by Edith How-Martyn, with her experience as a mathematics lecturer and now as head of WFL's Political and Militant Department. She held that violent militancy hindered the chance for a suffrage bill, whilst peaceful resistance to unjust laws would greatly impress both Parliament and the public. How-Martyn now proposed that 'if the Conciliation Bill be killed', the WFL should adopt a policy of passive resistance to all government business, and 'that the form for immediate interference shall be to boycott the Census'.[17] Of course, neither then nor during other discussion of the census boycott in 1910 was there any suggestion that they were aware of the new questions to be asked about married women. Rather, the predominant suspicion was of Asquith's government betraying women once again by ditching the Conciliation Bill.

So, by late July 1910, the WFL was poised ready for the census protest. A letter was circulated, probably by Edith How-Martyn, to eighteen suffrage organizations; these of course included the NUWSS and WSPU, plus smaller professional pressure groups like the Artists' Suffrage League. This letter is worth quoting fully, for it carefully sets the framework for the coming eight months:

STRICTLY PRIVATE AND CONFIDENTIAL
July 30 [1910]
Dear Madam,

The Women's Freedom League has had under consideration a plan of protest for Suffragists in connection with the Census, to be applied if the Conciliation Bill does not pass into law during the autumn session. We believed that this plan of campaign offers remarkable opportunities for both militant and constitutional action such as will impress the Government and the country at large with the widespread nature of women's discontent.

The National Executive Committee at its meeting on July 25th decided that a general concentration of all suffragist forces upon the Census was desirable, and resolved that invitations should be issued to all suffrage societies ... I therefore ask if your society would be willing to send delegates to a private conference to be called by the Women's Freedom League in September or October when the possibilities of our suggested plan of campaign can be discussed and a system of co-operation, official and unofficial, may be devised.

Will you please place this matter before your Committee and let me have as early a reply as is possible. I do not need to call your attention to the fact that while the fate of the Conciliation Bill hangs in the balance any leakage of this suggestion to the public or to the Press would be most ill-advised … We have taken the precaution to disarm Press curiosity by issuing a brief statement … about co-operative action among suffragists …

Sincerely hoping that your society will send delegates,

I am,

Yours faithfully.[18]

The WFL nuanced language is clear. It was keen to work with constitutional suffrage societies, notably of course Fawcett's NUWSS and Pippa Strachey's London Societies (LSWS). Its language is moderate with danger words like 'resistance', 'unlawful' or 'prison' edited out. Rather, attention is drawn to the Conciliation Bill, so dear to the Stracheys and other influential suffragists.

Replies to this Census Conference invitation gradually trickled in. Responses from the two major organizations were equivocal. The WSPU replied that it 'would confer informally only' (and, recalling the WFL rebels, undoubtedly let the matter lapse, at least for the moment). More helpfully, the NUWSS said it would send delegates. Of the smaller suffrage leagues, the Actresses, Writers and Artists all agreed to send one or two delegates, as did the Conservative and Unionist Women's Franchise Association, a New Constitutional Society and others; and four organizations apparently did not reply.[19] So far, reasonably good. It vividly illustratee the width and cultural range of the women's suffrage movement in mid-1910, with hopes united round for the Conciliation Bill.

The WFL's 'Militant Report' for June–July noted that: 'Copies of the Census Bill were obtained and one was sent for comment to Mrs B[illington] G[rieg] and another to Dr Earengey', a sympathetic lawyer and Edith How-Martyn's brother-in-law; but otherwise 'further particulars of the Census' were not yet obtained, the details still unknown outside Whitehall.[20] And there matters might have rested during the summer.

The Conciliation Bill, sufficiently limited in its provisions to be palatable to Conservatives, had passed its second reading with a large majority, even Asquith feeling obliged to provide it with further parliamentary facilities. But, by being constructed so narrowly, it had of course alienated backbench Liberal MPs and many in the labour movement who wanted a far more democratic measure. Lloyd George for one wanted more sweeping and ambitious franchise reform that would give the vote to far more adults. So, despite all the NUWSS's cam-

RE-UNITED.

Prime Minister (*Shelving Woman's Suffrage Bill*). "WELL, GENTLEMEN, NOW THAT YOUR INDIVIDUAL CONSCIENCES HAVE HAD THEIR FLING, LET'S GET TO WORK AGAIN."

16 'Re-united', Asquith shelving the Conciliation Bill, watched by Burns (*far left*), Lloyd George (*fourth left*), and a pudding-like Churchill (*second right*). *Punch*, 20 July 1910.

paigning, organizations like the People's Suffrage Federation, the Women's Co-operative Guild and some Labour MPs grew decidedly lukewarm about the bill, preferring a full adult suffrage measure.[21]

During July, suffrage organizations campaigned vigorously to 'Pass the Bill'. But then, in late July, Asquith informed Lord Lytton that the Conciliation Bill would be granted no further time that session, and in the Commons announced that he would grant it no further facilities. Henry Nevinson noted sadly in his diary: 'So another hope is killed'.[22] The same day, the WFL issued an angry press statement:

> We secured the second reading in the face of Mr Asquith's ultimatum and we will secure the third. Every suffragist must rally to the fight and prove to Mr Asquith that we are as powerful as the Nonconformist conscience.

This was undoubtedly a reference to Liberal support for Passive Resisters over the 1902 Education Act. And the WFL added a strongly worded threat: 'There will be no rest for the Government and no peace in the country until we secure justice'.[23] With the Census Act now on the statute books and Lloyd George polishing his plans for new taxes, it was going to be another hotly contested autumn.

8

Lloyd George goes a-wooing
versus Burns's 'vixens in velvet'

Against the backdrop of the parliamentary crisis, Lloyd George pressed forward with his 'People's Budget' and his insurance scheme, proposing that the state should make a contribution to health insurance. In this ambition, he had won wide support among the progressive Liberal intelligentsia and idealistic social policy experts; as one MP put it, 'we encouraged each other to dream dreams but to base them on existing reality'.[1]

First however Lloyd George had to woo certain crucial interest groups. One was the medical profession: doctors remained wary of any health scheme that might encroach upon their own incomes. The second was the powerful insurance industry itself, which feared Lloyd George's proposal would upset their lucrative apple-cart, while friendly societies worried about their well-established place in working-class life being destabilized. Considerably lower down on Lloyd George's list of groups which needed to be wooed and won were women – all still unenfranchised. Women's groups began to ask: would women workers be covered by the new insurance scheme? Would the wife of an insured worker be covered if *she* fell ill or suffered a dangerous pregnancy? The Women's Co-operative Guild, voice of working-class married women, urged that maternity provision be included.[2]

Lloyd George, thrusting taxation ever further up the political agenda, proposed new taxes. In September, a storm blew up over a new land valuation census requiring landowners to provide Whitehall with basic information: they berated it as 'an inquisition unknown since the Middle Ages'. Financially independent women wanted to know if they too were once again required to pay for the scheme through these new forms of taxation – over which they had absolutely no say or constitutional influence. Particularly for those wealthy women who already entertained a deep political distrust of this jumped-up rabble-rousing Welshman, this additional intrusive social levelling seemed a step too far.

Month by month, the differences between these two concepts of citizenship grew sharper. The notion of a welfare democracy *for* those who would benefit from National Insurance was pitted against a participative democracy *by* all adults, especially those directly affected by the scheme or contributing to it. As the outlines of Lloyd George's National Insurance scheme grew clearer, it would certainly be a conflict-ridden autumn.

The great insurance industry was based upon an army of agents going door-to-door each week to collect a few pence premium from working-class homes. They visited families on modest wages where prudent wives kept their insurance money in a sugar bowl on the parlour mantelpiece, put by against dreaded misfortune: an accident befalling the main bread-winner, unforeseen funeral costs. The major industrial insurance companies (notably the Prudential) plus large friendly societies commanded the bulk of this business. For an ambitious working-class man, an insurance round offered desirable career prospects and an enviable weekly income. There were about seventy thousand insurance collector-salesmen, even boasting a National Union of Assurance Agents. With their entrée into millions of working-class homes, such men wielded undeniable political clout. Insurance was big business based upon millions of small financial anxieties: they could not be ignored and would need appeasing.

The influence of these agents had already become chillingly clear. When Lloyd George interviewed their delegation, they stated uncompromisingly that they would oppose any government plan to pay, on the death of a worker, widow's benefit or other benefits aiming to soften the bereaved family's financial difficulties. Upon just such fears were their profits based. And not even Lloyd George's reform momentum could afford to oppose such a formidable lobby. So widows and orphans would have to go.[3]

In all this continued political turmoil, voteless women were therefore becoming doubly disadvantaged. Impoverished widows and their orphan children would be excluded from the government's grand new insurance scheme; meanwhile women tax-payers – also voteless – had to contribute to it. How aware were suffrage organizations of these impending small-print threats to groups of women?

Naturally, the Women's Tax Resistance League tracked Lloyd George's every move with an eagle eye. It could not however wield the clout of large numbers. Its aim of reaching five hundred names of women willing to refuse paying their taxes (or at least sympathetic to League aims) was clearly over-ambitious. Neither Mrs Fawcett's NUWSS nor Pippa Strachey's LSWS was encouraging about receiving a League deputation.[4] More positively, local meetings to win potential resisters held in seaside resorts like Eastbourne and Hastings were productive, while persistent Margaret Kineton Parkes visited residential towns like Bath. The League's banner that Clemence Housman had organized was greatly admired when carried in procession; and naturally Laurence was among those happy to speak on the League's summertime platform in Hyde Park.[5] Though small, it had already emerged as an extremely effective pressure group, offering specialist taxation expertise. And taxation had moved steadily to the top of the political agenda.[6]

So the League was strategically positioned for the autumn's brewing storms. One key founder member was Winifred Patch, a doctor in north London. Her medical practice kept her too busy for much campaigning; but during the summer holidays, she would advertise in *The Vote* for local WFL 'friends' to assist her suffrage campaigning at her seaside resort.[7] So when Dr Patch received an Inland Revenue form requesting information about land tax, with a penalty of up to £50, her anger erupted. She immediately wrote to *The Vote* with a robustly uncompromising retort. It is worth quoting fully, as Dr Patch spoke for many other confident professional Edwardian women:

> As I am denied the rights of citizenship I absolutely decline to facilitate in any way the carrying out of the provisions of Mr Lloyd George's Finance Bill, and am returning my paper with this written across it. I am hoping … to obtain expert information which will make it impossible for the Government to exact the £50 penalty, and will leave them with no alternative but to imprison me in default. Will other women join me in making this protest. I feel that there must be many like myself who would gladly risk imprisonment for the cause, but who, for various reasons, find it very difficult … to take part in the more active protests which have hitherto brought women into conflict with the law. I cannot help hoping that we have here another vantage ground from which to attack a Government which refuses us justice.[8]

The League met a week later, in the Kingsway office of its income tax special-ist Mrs Ayres Purdie. She took the chair, others present including Dr Patch, Clemence Housman and Margaret Kineton Parkes. The most urgent business was of course the legal implications for women refusing to complete their land tax forms, and naturally this was linked to the fate of the Conciliation Bill. So Kineton Parkes was instructed to:

> approach different Suffrage Societies with a view to placing before their members at an early date the desirability of every woman suffragist who is a tax payer declaring now, that should the Conciliation Bill fail to become law this session, she will refuse to pay next year's taxes …
>
> That Mrs Fawcett be seen if possible and asked to declare her attitude with regard to Tax Resistance as it is affected at the present moment by the Conciliation Bill

and to see Henry Brailsford who had kindly offered to help. Drawing room meetings in London would be organized, and Clemence would consult a sympa-thetic magistrate for legal advice.[9]

Meanwhile, Ayres Purdie wrote to *The Vote* protesting against 'the extraordinary system of "bluff" which is constantly practised by the Inland Revenue on women'. For instance, married women could not legally be charged with income tax, so legally 'neither her money, her goods, nor her body may be seized'. Yet 'abominable cases' brought to her notice already included that of two elderly ladies, in 'penurious circumstances' receiving a threatening letter from Somerset House demanding immediate payment. Ayres Purdie wished 'to earnestly warn all women to be on their guard where the Inland Revenue is concerned'; for, when complaints were made about delay in repayment of income tax, the official excuse given by Somerset House was:

> 'delay caused by the unusual difficulties in connection with the last Budget'. Now I should like to know what women had to do with these 'unusual difficulties'. They did not cause them, or want them. They were not consulted by anyone in regard to the Budget … yet they are penalized by having to wait for months for their money.[10]

Given these mounting grievances, the League was now poised for a publicity attack. A November conference was planned to ascertain 'under what conditions each [tax] resistance is promised'; Dr Patch outlined a circular for women doctors, with everyone delighted that both Garrett Andersons had agreed for their prestigious names to head the list. The League, now renting its own office near Trafalgar Square, prepared more new leaflets for printing; and December's General Election was discussed. Events were moving fast.[11]

The WFL also remained as alert. It now needed eyes not only for the Conciliation Bill, Lloyd George's new taxes, but also for the Election. By dint of its propaganda campaigns, WFL confidence had grown. Its active branches now included Portsmouth and Cheltenham, Manchester and Sheffield; in smaller communities, there was even a new branch formed in rural Hadleigh, near Ipswich where Constance Andrews remained busy. Additionally, cordial relationships continued with the Suffrage Atelier: a Market Fete was held at the Housmans' Pembroke Cottages, with a stall selling sweets and WFL merchandise.[12]

The WFL too was incensed that income tax was being extracted from married women, and the legal muddle over whether, if she refused to pay, the woman's husband was liable for prosecution.[13] A well-publicized letter was sent to Lloyd George, asking about income tax levied on married women and new taxes on women land-owners. However weeks passed, with Teresa Billington-Grieg impatiently asking: 'Has Lloyd George answered yet?' and urging that he should be reminded. Her forthright article in *The Vote* on 'Women and Taxation' proclaimed 'No Vote, No Tax' and even incited hitherto loyal Liberal women to 'rise to the occasion', because 'definite impeding of the Government business is the only policy that will carry weight now'. Eventually, Charlotte Despard did receive a reply from a Treasury civil servant; couched in impeccable bureaucratese, it stated that before considering receiving a WFL deputation, Lloyd George required in writing 'the precise points which the League desires to raise through the medium of the proposed deputation'.[14] In other words, the Chancellor prevaricated.

Meanwhile, the census in six months' time was not forgotten by the visionary few. Laurence Housman recalled later:

> before the Census began, I drew up a scheme for organized resistance, and offered it first to the WSPU, which rejected it, then to the Women's Freedom League, who had already, I found, started a similar scheme of their own. So with them I worked.[15]

Indeed, the WFL was quietly plotting a historic conference in Caxton Hall for 27 October. Teresa Billington-Grieg's briefing paper made its serious intent absolutely clear. The WFL provided the framework for next six months:

> *Suffragist Resistance to the Census.*
>
> *Passive Resistance.*
>   1. *Women Housholders* – 1,000,000 will receive Enumeration Forms as heads of households. It is recommended that all suffrage societies combine to persuade Women Householders to refuse to fill [them] up ... to be endorsed with the phrase
>   No Votes for Women; no information from Women.
>   2. *Women Residents not Heads of Households* ... It is recommended that:
>   (a)   women residents should refuse this information ...
>   (b)   ... should absent themselves from home for the night ...
>   3. *A combination of 1 & 2* ...
>   (a)   A Woman Householder ... can throw open her house for the night of the
> Census to as many fellow suffragists as possible ...
>   (b)   ... run all-night entertainments and socials.
>   (c)   walking parties could be organised for the hardy ...
>
> *Active Resistance*
> *Destruction of Forms.* This seems to be the only active course possible...
> *Penalties* ... to a maximum fine of £5.
>
> *Co-operation*
> ... It is recommended that each society should work up the scheme among its own members and that local co-operation between branches should be advocated and encouraged.[16]

The range of suffrage groups sending delegates to this conference was impressive. Despite inflammatory reference to 'destruction of forms' (reminiscent of the Bermondsey and Battersea incidents), organizations included Fawcett's NUWSS, carrying considerable clout right across the country. Significantly, also represented was the Women's Co-operative Guild; with 27,000 members, it was already expert at lobbying Lloyd George on behalf of married working-class women. Of the professional suffrage leagues, the Actresses, Artists and Writers were all present, as was the Conservative and Unionist Women's Franchise Association. Others organizations included the Men's League for Women's Suffrage and the New Constitutional Society. Conspicuous by its absence however remained the Pankhursts' WSPU.[17]

In all a dozen suffrage societies assembled at Caxton Hall. Charlotte Despard, delighted at the prospect of united action, welcomed delegates. Then Teresa Billington-Grieg outlined the WFL scheme, explaining that 'the time had come for Suffragists of all Societies to unite in impeding big national undertakings' like the census. Then the meeting was thrown open for discussion.

Anxieties about legal risks and penalities were understandably at the forefront of many delegates' minds. Lawyer Herbert Jacobs founder of the Men's League suggested that census resisters might be liable for a common law misdemeanour; but Billington-Grieg quickly batted this away by suggesting that this would apply only to signatories on any public statement. Mary Lowndes of the Artists' Suffrage League asked whether a special penalties bill might be rushed through Parliament, but the general feeling was that this would be a government own goal; and Herbert Jacobs suggested that the maximum penalty for refusing to pay a fine would be three months. For the NUWSS, Edith Palliser, by coincidence the Housmans' close neighbour, voiced the fear that the proposed scheme 'might not be sufficiently effective'; however Billington-Grieg pointed out curtly that effectiveness would depend on delegates present persuading their organizations.

Discussion moved on to imaginative census night tactics; the Women Writers' Suffrage League suggested householders display a notice on their doors saying that 'the residents had gone away to escape the Census'. Then they debated timing: how advisable would it be to announce the census plan before Parliament opened or 'when the [Conciliation] Bill was killed'? However, Edith Palliser's careful resolution was in end carried: to defer decisions about tactics until each delegate had a mandate from their own organization; and it was agreed to reconvene on 9 December for report back from the societies.[18]

A few points are immediately striking. First, the degree of amicable unanimity. All present at this conference were united around fervent hopes for the Conciliation Bill. Even Edith Palliser was cautiously upbeat. Second, concerns focused on two specific areas: anxieties about likely legal penalties, and the likely scale of the boycott and so its public impact. But so far so good. Charlotte Despard, Teresa Billington-Grieg and other WFL leaders could go home with a warm glow in their suffrage hearts.

Yet, to be fully effective, the WFL scheme needed to win over the WSPU, with its high profile leaders and amazing flair for publicity. The WSPU however had other more immediate challenges on its mind.

The WSPU continued its truce during 1910, while keeping up pressure on the government over its Conciliation Bill intentions. It held its own tax resistance meeting, addressed by Christabel Pankhurst: 'No Vote, no Tax! No Conciliation Bill, no Surrender!' The *Votes for Women* headline was 'A Bonfire of Tax Papers!'[19] The WSPU leadership grew suspicions that the Cabinet was prevaricating still further on the Bill. Meanwhile, the government itself could see no way out of its constitutional deadlock for supremacy over the obstinate Lords, and on 10 November Asquith agreed to dissolve Parliament, triggering a second 1910 General Election.

The WFL had also determined to 'take effective militant action' if the government refused to pass the Bill, but did not know exactly what the WSPU planned. Diplomatic spirits like Brailsford grew alarmed at talk of a WSPU deputation to Parliament planned for 18 November, with suffragettes volunteering for 'active service'.[20]

Everything then happened very fast. When Parliament reconvened on Friday 18 November, Asquith informed the Commons that he had asked the King to dissolve Parliament, and this would take place on 28 November; until then, government business would take precedence over all else – like the Conciliation Bill. On hearing this government announcement of dissolving Parliament without progress on the Bill, the WSPU promptly ended its truce. While Asquith spoke, the WSPU met nearby in Caxton Hall and, learning that the Conciliation Bill was not even mentioned, a deputation of over three hundred women set out for the House of Commons in small detachments. The first included such prestigious names as Emmeline Pankhurst and Elizabeth Garrett Anderson, Princess Duleep Singh and scientist Hertha Ayrton.

Battle erupted in Parliament Square as suffragettes sought to interview Asquith. They tried to make a rush past the police, who responded with considerable brutality – kicking, punching noses, twisting arms. After six hours of struggle, 115 women and four men had been arrested. From its notorious violence, it was dubbed 'Black Friday', Brailsford and others collecting evidence of police brutality. The following day, however, charges against most of those arrested were dropped, on order from Winston Churchill at the Home Office. Was Churchill embarrassed by a possible court case, or merely distracted? He was certainly preoccupied, a few days later ordering troops to Tonypandy in south Wales to confront striking miners. Of other ministers, Lloyd George spoke on 21 November to a crowd of five thousand in a Mile End Road music hall in London's East End, with his usual rousing class-warfare oratory. Nor, as the Election neared, was he allowed to forget pledges made to woo the insurance agents.

So the minds of Liberal ministers were elsewhere. The WSPU however had no intention of letting the matter rest. Individual women roughly handled by police would never forget 'Black Friday'. Asquith merely offered a statement. But it was mealy-mouthed: if the Liberals won the Election, they would

17 John Burns , 'Taxation and Representation', Suffrage Atelier poster. MoL.

introduce a franchise bill open to amendment to include women; yet even this would be eventually, rather than soon. So the Prime Minister remained grudgingly unhelpful. The furious WSPU now dispatched two hundred women to Downing Street; here stones were thrown at government windows – and a total of 206 women were arrested (although only 75 were charged).

Other suffrage campaigners looked on apprehensively. NUWSS pessimism grew that WSPU militancy would spoil all their careful consensus-building. Mrs Fawcett was in absolutely no doubt: Asquith's statement had given hope for post-election suffrage, but 'then those idiots go out smashing windows and bashing ministers' hats over their eyes', adding 'I deeply deplore the futile silliness'.[21]

It is easy to lose sight of John Burns in this mêlée. On Friday 18 November, sitting in the crowded Commons, he had been so impressed with Asquith's 'marvellously clever and compact speech' that he scarcely noticed the 'Black Friday' battle raging outside. Indeed, it was not till four days later that Burns, walking between a Cabinet meeting and his ministry in Whitehall, noted:

> Tuesday 22nd … Streets filled with the Vixens in Velvet till 6 when they broke LGB windows, and at the same time were re-planting [a blow, i.e. damaging] Pattie's front parlour [window] at Lavender Gardens – of such is the dynasty of Pankhurst …
>
> Police Officers called at 37 L[avender] G[ardens] – they agreed with my suggestion [increase domestic security?] Pattie quite cool and plucky but has almost had enough worry with public affairs.[22]

Suffragette anger had invaded the privacy of ministers' homes: stones were also thrown at Churchill's houses. Within days it had grown very nasty. And into this 'Vixens in Velvet' window-breaking scrimmage arrived the December General Election. For a sixth time, Burns got busy with the rough and tumble of Battersea electioneering. He remained a suffragette target:

> Saturday 3rd ... Park at 3 for final Demonstration. A large patient and kindly crowd of 4 or 500. Suffragettes encircled by 40 men and quietly rolled out of crowd to the amusement of all even themselves ...
>   Election work till late – hoarse and tired but quite certain of 1000 [majority?] at least.[23]

By Tuesday, after visiting Battersea polling stations, Burns was rewarded once more with victory – and was again chaired by supporters through the streets. Reflecting back on his five years in Cabinet however, he confided to his diary his growing tired and 'not enough daring, but oh so much useful work slavishly carried out for the benefit of all'.[24]

More broadly, the December Election left the balance in the House of Commons little changed, and so disappointed the government. Lloyd George's star was nevertheless in the ascendant, as he banked on the popularity of his Insurance Bill. He set off on holiday to the south of France; on the Riviera he was joined by expert civil servants from both the Treasury and Inland Revenue. Rather incongruously, detailed briefings on administering health insurance began on the pier at Nice, accompanied by brass-band music.[25]

So where did the Election leave suffrage organizations? Women's suffrage had not generally been a deciding issue in constituencies up and down the country. The NUWSS had sponsored three suffrage candidates, though without much success. By late 1910, the main NUWSS achievement lay in the impressive expansion of both its membership and its local branches, both grown by about 50 per cent in just one year. Otherwise, with hope dimmed for the Conciliation Bill, the NUWSS grew pessimistic about trusting the Liberals; and, after Black Friday, its enthusiasm dwindled for even non-violent civil disobedience – like the census protest.[26]

So when the WFL reconvened its meeting on 10 December to discuss census resistance, it all had a very different feel from the conference six weeks earlier. No longer in Caxton Hall, it was now held in a room of a club near the Strand. Noticeably absent were certain crucial delegates: from the NUWSS, the Women's Co-operative Guild and from the Conservative women. The big guns were staying away. And there was no WSPU – as yet. Even the Men's League and Actresses' Franchise League now said they 'would do their utmost as individuals' but could not take part as societies. So what exactly had caused this *diminuendo*? It is difficult to gauge how much arose from distaste for 'Black

Friday' and 'bashing ministers' hats', and how much from a belief that, with the Liberal government returned to power, future welfare reforms must rely on accurate statistical data.

The WFL was still strongly represented of course, and five small societies did send delegates – including of course the Women's Tax Resistance League. From the chair, Charlotte Despard invited delegates to report back. The New Constitutional Society delegate said it would wait to hear the NUWSS decision and, till then, census resistance would be made only unofficially by individual members; other societies reported that they too were unable to take part officially.

Those present must have felt somewhat beleaguered. There were however sufficient people present absolutely determined to boycott the census, rather than comply with the dictats of an undemocratic government. The Women's Tax Resistance League naturally remained keen. Margaret Nevinson, no stranger to braving a hostile public, said the Women Writers would also adopt the census protest. As an imaginative idea for maximizing publicity for the boycott, she suggested meetings held on census night in Hyde Park. There was also widespread enthusiasm for boycotters' opening their houses to friends and sharing the £5 fine among those assembled. One supporter proposed exchanging houses to evade responsibility, as the Census Act applied only to the householders themselves. Another suggested that the great strength of the boycott would be discrediting the data collected by enumerators, as it would be impossible to estimate how many or how few had evaded the census or refused giving information. Such ideas were soon to bear rich fruit.

Charlotte Despard spoke about timing, and it was agreed to announce the protest immediately after the text of the King's Speech was known. As the WFL now soberly recognized that some suffrage organizations had grown nervous, it was agreed to draft a special leaflet for use by societies willing 'to circulate the suggestion'.[27] Now they just had to wait a few weeks for the King's Speech.

So at New Year 1911 what were the political prospects for reform? There was cautious optimism. The power of the reactionary House of Lords would be curbed, to allow Lloyd George's budget through. The suffrage movement meanwhile remained suspicious of government intentions towards women, especially married women. Campaigners were absolutely determined – and cautiously optimistic – as they waited for the King's Speech, due on 6 February. And hence an announcement of the census boycott.

After New Year the census battle went public. The WFL national executive ratified the decision that if the King's Speech included no mention of women's enfranchisement, the plan to boycott the census would be announced that day, plus 'protests at Public Offices'. Meanwhile meetings addressed by WFL leaders were arranged for local branches.[28] And the WFL's annual conference in Caxton Hall at the end of January confirmed the health of these local groups. Delegates arrived from three dozen branches across England, stretching from Brighton and Portsmouth, Cheltenham and Ipswich, up to Wolverhampton and Manchester, Middlesbrough on Teesside and South Shields on Tyneside.[29]

Two days later, the Women's Tax Resistance League held *its* first AGM and, after routine discussion of married women's test cases, it was agreed that the League would 'strongly advocate that all Tax Resisters refuse to give Census information'. For the League, a refusal to pay tax segued logically into a census boycott of an undemocratic government. Indeed, the League identified the census boycott as of such urgent importance that it became a special initiative.[30]

By then, the exact wording of the new census schedule had become known – and immediately raised suffrage hackles. In January, an article in *The Vote* alerted readers to the new census questions to be asked of married women: how long the present marriage has lasted, how many children were born alive, still living, and how many have died? This, the article added, 'is a direct attempt to ascertain whether, as is so frequently stated, the family [size] decreases with the ascent in the social scale'. Suffrage campaigners by contrast looked for the causes of too few healthy children in malnutrition of the mother, her unpaid home drudgery and families struggling in poverty. Women winning the vote was key, for 'race improvement cannot be affected without the direct co-operation in legislation of mothers'. The new census questions were impertinently intrusive: voteless mothers, and indeed all women, remained without any direct say in legislation.[31]

The 1911 census would of course be conducted countrywide. It allotted as much space to families living in an industrial city as it did to those of suffrage doyennes in Hampstead or Kensington. The battle for the census would be fought out where women really lived, in the major industrial and commercial cities, plus distant market towns, seaside resorts, country villages. Political theatre in Britain might be enacted most dramatically in Westminster and Whitehall. But to observe the census plans unfold, attention swerves northwards again – up to Manchester, that great suffrage city.

9

The King's Speech: Jessie Stephenson parachutes into Manchester

By New Year 1911, census night was just three months away. Suffrage ears were trained on the King's Speech to the House of Commons, due on 6 February. Meanwhile, with dark shadow of 'Black Friday' still looming, the WSPU was busy collecting evidence of police brutality. So far, it kept its distance from

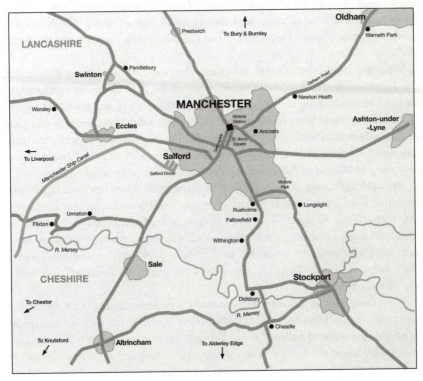

Map 4 Manchester and its suburbs.

the WFL's census boycott plot. From its headquarters at Clements Inn by the Strand, the WSPU dispatched a band of organizers fanning out across the country, to stir up cities and their regions.

Among the regions, pre-eminent remained Manchester, the world's first industrial city. This massive conurbation included neighbouring Salford, plus Stockport and the north Cheshire suburbs. The city also served the Lancashire cotton towns of Oldham and Rochdale, and further north Burnley, Blackburn and Preston. From their mills, money flowed into Manchester. The commercial vibrancy of the city centre was visible in the grandeur of its bank architecture, with imposing financial and insurance offices clustered around Deansgate. Its cultural richness included not only theatre and art galleries but also the University of Manchester; here new disciplines like Sociology carried growing intellectual influence.

Many businessmen had by now moved out of the city for the southern suburbs. One woman recalling her Edwardian childhood wrote how every morning 'the business men caught the 8.25 or the 8.50 or the 9.18 trains into Manchester. The times are graven on my memory ... After the 9.18 train had pulled out of the station [Alderley] Edge became exclusively female.'[1] Suburban ladies could catch a later train into the city. For them and for women working in the city centre offices, Manchester's money could now be spent in style: elegant shopping arcades linked Deansgate to fashionable St Ann's Square and the Royal Exchange.

Since the 1860s, the city also comprised the cradle of the suffrage movement; and it remained – half a century later – one of the richest sites of campaigning for the vote, embracing suffragists and suffragettes of every stripe and shade. The NUWSS was strongly represented across the region: the Manchester Society had its headquarters in Deansgate Arcade itself. The WFL was also well organised too, especially out in residential suburbs like Sale and Eccles. Notably Mary Manning, living out in Sale, filed regular branch reports in to *The Vote*.[2]

The suffrage name most vividly associated with Manchester undoubtedly remained the Pankhursts. It was of course in their own home that Emmeline had formed the WSPU. They had all now left Manchester for London, of course (though Emmeline's youngest – and least well known – daughter Adela had returned north to Sheffield, as WSPU's Yorkshire organizer). Despite the exodus down to London, the WSPU nevertheless retained a powerful Manchester base.

All of these suffrage organizations needed the influential ear of C. P. Scott. For towering over it all was the mighty *Manchester Guardian*, the regional newspaper he edited that wielded national clout. Brought up as a Unitarian, C. P. Scott was now a member of the Liberal political elite. After studying at Corpus Christi, he had joined the *Manchester Guardian* which liked to recruit its staff from Oxford; he was now not just the paper's editor but also its proprietor. With four grown children and recently widowed, Scott lived in the nearby suburb of Fallowfield. The Firs, virtually an urban palace, had ample garden and noble trees; and from here Scott regularly bicycled into his newspaper office. He would also cycle at weekends down to Knutsford to visit his suffragist friend Helena Swanwick and her husband, a mathematics lecturer at Manchester University. Helena, editor of NUWSS's weekly *Common Cause*, held an extremely high opinion of Scott: 'I never knew a man of strong feeling so incapable of personal animosity ... He was a great encourager'; indeed, he had emboldened Helena herself to write for his *Manchester Guardian*. On their bicycle runs and walks out around Knutsford, Scott would fill her in on the latest high-level suffrage negotiations.[3] For Scott was not only a major NUWSS donor, he was also closely involved in Conciliation Committee negotiations.

Scott was *the* voice of progressive Liberal intelligentsia in the north. He supported both women's suffrage *and* the government's reform agenda. Constantly on the train shuttling between Manchester and London, he acted as an influential go-between, having the ear of both suffragist leaders like Swanwick and key Cabinet members. As *Manchester Guardian* editor, he was regularly consulted by leading politicians, all of whom wished to secure the good opinion both of the editor himself and of his influential paper. Indeed Scott's correspondents read like a list of the great and the good.[4] Thus Lloyd George enquired in mid-January, 'If you could turn in for breakfast Friday morning 9.15, I shall be glad to see you. In fact I am anxious to have a talk with you on the whole situation' (probably about his National Insurance Bill, shortly to go to Cabinet).[5]

Scott's support was also regularly sought by Brailsford as he tried ingeniously and patiently to weave together effective parliamentary support for the Conciliation Bill. In mid-January he warmly thanked Scott 'for sending me news of [Lord] Grey's attitude. It sounds very hopeless. I suppose he has quite forgotten that he ever said "next (i.e. this) session"' of Parliament.[6] Likewise, both Christabel Pankhurst and her mother, who knew Scott from their Manchester days, were also regular correspondents. Emmeline had written to him earlier, imploring him to use his influence on ministers; he had responded advocating patience, and now in early January, Emmeline, emotionally battered by family sadness, wrote again:

> Dear Mr Scott
>
> Were it not for the faith I have in the courage and loyalty of women your letter would make me despair ... You tell me that nothing can be done until the so-called constitutional crisis is settled. I know quite well that if we wait there will always be something that must be settled first. Our turn will never come until women & the friends of women *make it come*.
>
> Have we not done & suffered enough? How many more women must die before you say 'The time is now' ...
>
> The opening of Parliament is near at hand. Will you not do something to make

it certain our Bill shall have its chance in the coming Session if not for the sake of justice & women at least for the honour & Credit of your Party.

Our duty as women is clear. We must go on no matter what the danger or the cost …

Do, I beg you, help us to retain our belief in hu[man] justice & recover our faith & respect for men by pr[ompt] action.

Faithfully yours.

E Pankhurst.[7]

Such were the high political emotions swirling in early 1911, with Scott near the eye of the storms. It was at this point that the WSPU parachuted Jessie Stephenson into Manchester.

Jessie Stephenson had a comfortable Edwardian family background. Now in her late thirties, with a clerical job in a barrister's office, she already had three to four years' experience of campaigning with the WSPU. Dressing well was paramount for Jessie: the night before the 1908 Hyde Park rally for which she was a marshal, she had prayed that her 'white lacy muslin dress … and … a white shady hat trimmed with white' would cut a dash, for 'my milliner and dressmaker took endless pains with my attire'.[8] Then in November 1910, in protest at 'Black Friday' police brutality, Jessie was among the window-breakers sentenced to a month's imprisonment in Holloway.

Jessie's typescript autobiography records how the Pankhursts had cast their magic spell. At night as she lay on her pillow in her dismal little Holloway cell, her last words were: 'Thank God for Mrs Pankhurst'. Then at the Christmas lunch for the released prisoners, Jessie sat next to Christabel – whom she also revered. Rising apprehensively, she made a speech, saying: 'before I went to Holloway I had the greatest admiration for the Suffragettes who faced imprisonment, but that is all changed now'. Still a nervous speaker, she paused. Mrs Pankhurst glanced at her, a look that Jessie carried with for years. '"Yes", I continued gravely, "[it] changed into reverence". There was a gasp of relief.'[9]

Afterwards, dazed Jessie found herself overwhelmed even by ordinary family conversation. Indeed, it took several weeks for her 'recurring queerness' to subside. The price she had paid for her militancy was to lose both her job and, worse, her family support, being ostracized by her sister 'and doffed of my parental dress allowance … rather a bitter pill'.[10] So how would Jessie now meet her living expenses? Feeling unwanted, her dark cloud of despair and loneliness continued.

She was however just the kind of spirited woman, inspired by the Pankhurst charisma, whom Christabel looked to recruit. Such women must be snapped up as itinerant organizers, and despatched off to places often unfamiliar to them. The WSPU's democratic branch structure had generally weakened in big cities; and so it was upon its organizers that the WSPU's country-wide fortunes now heavily depended.[11] So it was the Pankhursts who came to Jessie's rescue:

> When Christabel's wire came asking me to town [Clements Inn?] to 'fix things up for Manchester', I was mightily troubled … whether my ability was adequate for the many and often unusual calls to be put on it, for which … I had no training or experience whatsoever.

Manchester had recently had to resort to stop-gap arrangements, but now the WSPU could not afford to do without a regional organizer in the city for long. Jessie was to take over.[12] Summoned to appear, Jessie continued that she:

> did not breathe a word of it [my anxieties] to Christabel and only hoped for the best when I found myself installed as Political Organiser in Manchester with a delightful office, three intelligent and – can I not say? – devoted secretaries and five hundred or so members; innumerable and violent 'antis', but some splendid stalwart friends.

Jessie arrived in Manchester with her luggage, and found herself some dingy rooms. She worked in the WSPU's strategically situated premises in elegant St Ann's Square just off Deansgate. The office even boasted telephones, which was just as well, for 'a Political Organiser's work consists very largely in getting up meetings … and above all getting people to come to them … Many celebrities came to Manchester to speak for and help us.'[13]

Jessie's memoirs offer vivid centre-stage testimony of spring 1911 in 'suffrage city'. Her 'many celebrities' included Laurence Housman – now one of the stellar speakers rushing around the circuit like Emmeline Pankhurst and Charlotte Despard. Laurence probably knew Manchester fairly well; and Jessie recorded a rare behind-the-scenes insight into what he was like – the moment *before* he stepped into the limelight of the meeting platform. On this occasion, the WSPU's normal hospitality arrangements had fallen through; Jessie had to book a room at the Midland Hotel, but when she met him Laurence protested:

> 'Oh, no, no, no,' he said, 'no costly room at the Midland running up your bills for me. I'll rake up some friend who'll put me up for the sake of the Cause.'
>
> 'But where will you sit now and prepare your notes and lunch and so forth?'
>
> 'Can't you give me a little nook at your office anywhere, and can't you secretly cook me an egg?'
>
> He wouldn't have it otherwise, so we arranged a corner with a desk and chair and a screen round it, and my secretary got him a little lunch, and the business of things went buzzing on around – telephones, typewriting, callers and what not. He then wrote notes for his speeches and every now and then looked round smilingly at me at my desk and said, 'very happy here; much more after my heart's desire than Hotel grandeur' …
>
> There was a small meeting first at our offices. I was in the chair of course. I loved the way he spoke. Surely even a granite block would have been converted. Towards the end he said he could always speak better to a small audience – it was more intimate.

> When I got up to close the meeting I said –
> 'Mr Housman says he speaks best to a small gathering. I should rather like to test the truth of that statement. Let us have an enormous crowd to-night.'
> And so we did ... and ... an overflow meeting. He spoke splendidly.[14]

Not all of Jessie's tasks as WSPU organizer for Manchester were quite so pleasurable. Her autobiography records how, 'in her final exhortations to me Christabel had said, "call immediately on [C. P.] Scott and enlist him as your friend"'.[15] This was of course easier said than done, for Jessie was not yet familiar with the world of northern suffragists like Scott and Helena Swanwick, a strong critic of WSPU militancy.

From February 1911, Scott would record his political conversations in London during his return rail journeys. For instance, he knew Augustine Birrell, Chief Secretary for Ireland. Like Scott, Birrell also sprang from Liberal nonconformist tradition, and, like widowed Scott, Birrell was cast low by his wife's brain tumour. With so much in common, the two men grew friendly. Scott now wanted to enlist Birrell's support in Cabinet 'for the solution of the Women's Suffrage question'. Birrell however had of course already been noisily heckled by suffragettes. On the train home, Scott recorded Birrell's story of his suffragette 'attack'. As with Mrs Fawcett's distaste for 'bashing ministers' hats over their eyes', Scott's sympathy for Birrell was far-reaching:

> He was walking alone from the House to his club ... when a body of about 20 suffragettes ... came right on to him.
> 'Some one cried "Here's Mr Birrell" ... and the whole body immediately swarmed round me. I was not kicked, but they pulled me about and ... knocked off my hat and kicked it about and ... harangued me with "Oh! You wicked man ..." I struggled to get free ... and slipped the knee-cap ... It was excessively painful and I was in terror ... that they would knock off my spectacles in which case I should have been absolutely blind.'

A passing civil servant came to the rescue. Birrell was:

> deeply exasperated against the women who had attacked and injured him – perhaps permanently, and evidently quite prepared to see the suffrage question shelved in this Parliament and indefinitely postponed ...
> He said I could have little idea of the great and increasing exasperation caused by the methods of the militants ... Evidently no active support can be looked for from him ... [Yet] he is in favour of the sort of solution proposed in the Conciliation Bill and dead against adult suffrage.

Birrell 'kept wringing his hands in a way I have never seem a man do before'.[16] This was one Cabinet supporter now lost to women's suffrage, and any sympathy Scott had with militancy was also ebbing away.

So this was the political context in which Jessie Stephenson sought her interview with Scott. She noted that 'the *Manchester Guardian* had to be curt-seyed to by all not least by [suffrage] propagandists'; and, Jessie was told that such newspaper editors could only be 'seen at their offices round about midnight' shortly before tomorrow's papers went to print. Hoping for publicity for a coming WSPU meeting, and accompanied by a friend, Jessie:

> sallied forth ... to keep a nocturnal appointment with the mighty Scott. He kept me waiting an interminable time, insultingly interminable, for was I not representing the WSPU? And somehow we were made to know that it was meant to be insulting ...
>
> At last we were admitted and saw a slim, distinguished-looking white-haired gentleman. He shook hands hastily but offered us no chairs.
>
> 'I'm in a hurry,' he explained. (Everyone was when suffragettes arrived.)
>
> I showed him the ... notice [of the WSPU meeting].
>
> No, no, he couldn't have anything to do with it ... Then he suddenly burst into really an uncontrollable rage. I stood perfectly quietly, never attempting to interrupt him while he drenched fire and brimstone over me. Terrible invective. A suffragette, he told me, had just knocked off Mr Augustine Birrell's hat and nearly injured him ...
>
> He didn't mind this and didn't mind that, that the suffragettes had done, but this new step – no – it was intolerable ...
>
> I remained perfectly silent.
>
> 'Now what have you got to say to it?' he asked blazingly after this long and fiery tirade.
>
> Very quietly I answered, 'What a tiny trifle Mr Augustine Birrell's crushed hat is compared to the injury done to women by keeping them from their just due these many years'.
>
> I looked him gravely in the face – a red-hot face it was – and he returned my look for quite a long time ...
>
> Suppressing [my] rage was really an act of heroism on my part.
>
> 'Well,' he continued, 'do you think for one instance you are going to get the vote like this?' ...
>
> 'Tell me, Mr Scott, do you think if we all sit quietly in our drawing-rooms, knitting, we shall get it?' I asked ...
>
> With a quick and angry goodbye we were dismissed.

Despondently, Jessie felt she had let Christabel was down. Next morning at the office, however, just as she was about to go out canvassing:

> back came my secretary with a note ...
>
> I ... sank wearily into a chair to open it. Signed 'P. Scott' – all in his own hand-writing – gracious!!
>
> ... It ran somewhat as follows ...
>
> 'I was very heated last night. I said things I very much ought not to have said and you were so quiet and so unmoved. I am ashamed. I apologize. Send what you will to my paper and I will do what I can for you.'
>
> Hip, hip, hip![17]

In fact, it was never going to be simple – especially in a sophisticated suffrage city like Manchester, where Liberalism and Liberal MPs were so well rooted.

At one level, these flared tempers was little more than one newspaper editor losing patience with one suffragette, then hastily regretting it. Just a northern storm in a teacup? Maybe. But at another level, it prefigured the political battle for the census shortly to erupt. For it revealed the complexity of suffrage aims, tactics and allegiances by 1911. At one end, were the massed ranks of 'Antis' and foot-draggers, led by the prevaricating Prime Minister. Not far away, were the adult suffragists, unhappy at the Conciliation Bill's narrowness. Elsewhere stood one-time sympathizers like Birrell, now disenchanted with militants. Not far away were ranged suffragists such as Helena Swanwick and sympathizers like C. P. Scott, bending ears to progress the Bill. Nearby stood other valued intermediaries like Brailsford, keen for a public enquiry into 'Black Friday', and whose wife Jane remained active in WSPU. Meanwhile, speakers and writers such as Laurence Housman (while sympathetic to the WSPU) inclined towards the WFL's growing Ghandhi-ist civil disobedience. Finally, and not too far away, was the WSPU with its busy organizers like Jessie Stephens, poised to do Christabel's bidding.

All these points-of-view would soon erupt very noisily over the census boycott plans, to be sparked by the King's Speech. Everyone waited to see whether it included reference to a women's suffrage bill in this Parliament.

The omission of women's suffrage when the King's Speech was read to the new House of Commons on 6 February was of course the immediate trigger. When Asquith's government, through the King, remained silent on the matter, the WFL wasted not one minute enacting its plans. Within three days, at a WFL 'At Home' in Caxton Hall, Charlotte Despard announced she would tear up *her* census form and hoped every other woman householder would do the same; meanwhile Margaret Nevinson suggested 'taking walking parties down Fleet Street and round the newspaper offices' on census night.[18] The next *Vote* had a dramatic front-page 'Boycott the Census' headline. Inside, Edith How-Martyn's 'Boycott the Census' editorial sounded a strong battle-cry to members:

> The King's Speech has been read … But because this Government does not need to rely upon women's votes for its support, therefore, anything and everything is more important and more urgent than women's right to political freedom.
>
> It is time that men and women realise what party policy and trickery are disgracing our Government today … Mr Asquith contemptuously sweeps aside all those whose urgent grievances have become inconvenient to him …
>
> It is clearly evident that Suffragists must change their grievance from an inconvenience to a menace. Any Government which refuses to recognize women must be met by women's refusal to recognize the Government …

Tax resistance has already been used, and used successfully to point the injustice of taxation without representation, but an even greater injustice, which can be summed up as 'legislation without representation is tyranny', is daily affecting the lives of all British women. To this tyranny we must not become consenting parties ...

Woman Suffrage is not in the King's Speech, ... an omission which is deliberate and dishonourable. What is the reply of the Women's Freedom League to the callous indifference and heartless dishonesty ...? Is it to be expected that we shall without protest or hindrance fill in Census papers and thus assist and make easy the task of governing women while denying them the elementary rights of citizenship? ...

The Women's Freedom League ... now openly calls upon women all over the kingdom to boycott the Census, to refuse all information about themselves and their households ... We intend to do our best to make it unreliable and inaccurate.

This census was no abstract political grievance: as How-Martyn added, John Burns's LGB had already attempted to restrict women's labour; and the WFL now considered it likely that the detailed census questions about marriage, children and women's occupations would together be used to develop legislation along these lines. And she ended defiantly:

[Such] legislation is to be hindered, hampered and obstructed – Suffragists will cease to be merely persons with a grievance; they will become a menace to that good feeling [i.e. consent?] upon which even the most powerful Government must ultimately rely. To boycott the Census is an important step in this campaign of obstruction.[19]

So, no room for hesitation or doubts there. All WFL the organizers and branch secretaries – Mary Manning in Manchester, Constance Andrews in Ipswich – were now exactly aware of their organizational strategy. Speakers like Laurence Housman became even more in demand, his feet scarcely touching the ground during the next seven weeks. No one wrote more persuasively on the census than Laurence. He immediately began his imaginative series of boycott articles in *The Vote*. The first, adapting Kipling's popular verse 'If – !', proposed 'a Census strike'; Liberals would be hypocritical to condemn the 'strike' since they had earlier condoned nonconformists' passive resistance, and Housman ended with a clarion call: 'it will be difficult for a Government ... to argue with any show of consistency that a Census strike of women ... is anything else than a protest public-spirited in character, constitutional in aim, and in substance right'.[20]

On a smaller scale but no less determined, the WTRL met just four days after the King's Speech. A resolution to support the census boycott was discussed and 'members spoke for & against'. Was it one of the women doctors, mindful of the need for accurate census data for future health reforms, who voiced reservations? When the vote went in favour, however, the League decided to set up a working group, to recruit an organizer and produce a leaflet. Indeed, the working party meeting agreed to Mary Sargant Florence's design for a postcard, to be printed by the Suffrage Atelier.[21]

Soon after the WFL's boycott proposal went public, the WSPU announced that it too would join the protest. Having hovered in the census wings for so long, overnight it lent the census boycott real clout. For the WSPU brought all its well-known names, notably Emmeline Pankhurst and the Pethick-Lawrences, plus its considerable panache for publicity and fun.[22] With the WSPU on board, the boycott suddenly moved centre-stage. In her *Votes for Women* editorial, Emmeline Pethick-Lawrence incited women to participate in this:

> act of passive resistance to a great and intolerable wrong … Let women and men join in their thousands … It is only by making government without consent impossible that voteless women can force the Government to accord them the rights that should coincide with the duties of citizenship.[23]

From now on, WSPU organizers and local activists became central to the census story – Jessie Stephenson in Manchester of course, Adela Pankhurst in Sheffield, Annie Kenney in Bristol among many others. So within a fortnight of the King's Speech, all the main militant organizations – WFL, WTRL, now strengthened by WSPU – were absolutely determined to resist. They were raring to go, and that meant publicity.

In all the boycott propaganda, it was undoubtedly the WFL's uncompromising Manifesto 'No Votes for Women – No Census' that had most dramatic impact. Circulated under the names of Edith How-Martyn and Charlotte Despard, it alerted the boycott's opponents to what was being planned, providing them with ample ammunition for rebuttal. In particular, the Manifesto quickly caught the unsympathetic eye of *The Times*, which immediately quoted from it extensively. *The Times* dilated upon WFL plans to refuse 'to give intimate personal details' to the enumerator, and under the heading 'Obstruct Government Business', it noted that the WFL even incited members to:

> oppose, hamper, destroy if possible, the power of an unrepresentative Government to govern women, refuse to be taxed, boycott the Census, refuse all official information until women have won that which their absolute right – the right of a voice and vote.[24]

Hackles were raised from within Liberalism's scholarly intelligentsia, and indeed on C. P. Scott's very own doorstep: Manchester University, seedbed for emerging evidence-based social science research. The immediate shot was fired by eminent educational reformer Professor Michael Sadler, a colleague of Helena Swanwick's husband; C. P. Scott, whose business it was to know everyone, certainly knew Sadler. After all, Scott's daily cycle ride to his newspaper office passed the University, and the two men, both loving walking, occupied the same *Weltanschauung*.[25]

Educated at Oxford like Scott, Sadler had progressed into schools reform. Like Lloyd George with his social insurance scheme, Sadler had found visits to Germany particularly helpful in examining comparative educational provision across Europe. Winning considerable distinction, he had moved into running Oxford University's extra-mural extension lectures, then been appointed to the post of Professor of the History and Administration of Education at Manchester University. So Sadler remained firmly committed to enshrining independent authoritative research at the heart of policy-making. For which ends, of course, reliable and accurate data were absolutely essential.[26]

The very next day after the Manifesto was publicized, *The Times* published Professor Sadler's short yet extremely pointed letter rebutting the Manifesto argument. Sadler warned the WFL that 'to boycott the Census would be a crime against science' because 'upon the completeness of the Census returns' depended future legislation to better the conditions for all people. 'To sulk against the Census', Sadler concluded fiercely, 'would not be a stroke of statesmanship, but a nursery fit of bad temper'.[27] This Manchester academic spoke from the very heart of intellectual Liberalism. Had he been a lone voice, Sadler would have carried less weight. But he articulated a deep distaste, increasingly held by the progressive Liberal intelligentsia, for the planned suffragette boycott. It found a ready echo with C. P. Scott: his *Manchester Guardian* even reprinted Sadler's letter to its rival paper as a news item.[28]

Sadler's jibe of a 'crime against science' reverberated – and stung. Immediately, Edith How-Martyn (herself a scientist and now signing herself ARCS, BSc) immediately retorted in *The Times* that for women to comply with the census 'when governed without their consent is a crime against the fundamental principles of liberty'. Indeed, she stated, 'the Census is designed, not by a scientist for scientists, … but for politicians with the knack of juggling with statistics' to make the figures support their own theories, including curbing women's right to work.[29]

So, within a fortnight of the King's Speech, an extraordinarily fierce political debate had flared up among academics and writers, newspaper editors and suffrage leaders – about the very nature of democracy and so what constituted a political 'crime'. It pitted scientific statistical accuracy against women's rightful citizenship claims, it raged for and against the census boycott. Battle was joined, up and down the country. The battleground for democracy. Science or citizenship? It would be a hard call.

10

Battleground for democracy:
census versus women's citizenship

By early March, the main battalions were ranged upon the battleground for democracy. On one side stood the Pankhursts' WSPU, Charlotte Despard's WFL, alongside Laurence Housman and pressure groups like the WTRL. On the other, Sadler and Scott lined up behind John Burns's Census Act. Both sides of this 'census versus citizenship' fight would hone their arguments during March, with other groups and individuals, occupations and regions each forming their own views.

By now, the Census Committee was so well organized it had little left to do but to polish a few final details. Indeed, so well-oiled was this state machinery, it had already co-opted schools, the labour movement and the press to help persuade the population of the vital importance of accurate census data. Together, these crucial social institutions were all now poised to maximize compliance among pupils, workers and newspaper readers. Indeed, census administration increasingly developed into a matter of civic pride, with local Registrars vying with each other to produce the smoothest enumeration on census night.[1]

Meanwhile, Lloyd George finessed the small-print of his National Insurance legislation, ready to go before Parliament. He remained adept at squaring opponents. Faced by continued lobbying by the big industrial insurance firms, he had not only dropped widows' and orphans' pensions, but had also allowed these companies to help administer his new scheme. He now prepared an outline of his insurance proposals for Cabinet: a weekly contribution from wages (4d for men, 3d for women), topped up by 3d from the employer and 2d from the state, making 9d benefit for men and 8d for women. An insurance 'stamp' bought from a local post office would entitle contributors to care by an approved doctor, plus the weekly sickness benefit. Although the 'stamp' was mocked by opponents, Lloyd George's popular slogan was 'ninepence for fourpence'.[2]

At the beginning of the new 1911 parliamentary session, the WSPU resumed its truce. With the Liberal government re-elected, suffragettes and suffragists

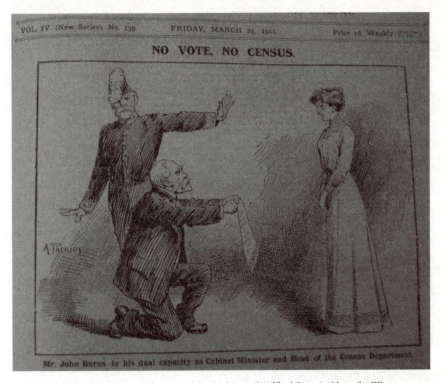

VOL. IV. (New Series), No. 159.   FRIDAY, MARCH 24, 1911.   Price 1d. Weekly

NO VOTE, NO CENSUS.

Mr. John Burns in his dual capacity as Cabinet Minister and Head of the Census Department.

18 'No Vote, No Census', cartoon by 'A Patriot' (Alfred Pease), *Votes for Women*, 24 Mar 1911.

alike now placed their hopes in a *new* Conciliation Bill. It would be brought forward by Sir George Kemp, Liberal MP for North West Manchester and yet another friend of Scott's. Urged on by the NUWSS and its Manchester Society, Kemp agreed to introduce it as a private member's bill. It passed its first reading on 9 February, with its crucial second reading scheduled for 5 May. However, the bill, still promising to privilege propertied women, was even narrower than before; so there remained disquiet among some Liberals that it was essentially undemocratic compared to full adult suffrage. In the weeks leading up to the census, nevertheless, all women's suffrage societies were united in pursuing a non-militant campaign in support of Kemp's Bill.[3]

This then was the context for publicizing the census boycott. Imaginative propaganda now included postcards, posters and the written word. *Votes for Women* published weekly 'Census Resistance' articles, plus a memorable front-page cartoon mocking Liberal Government hypocrisy.

The WSPU certainly ran an impressive operation: its spacious headquarters alone occupied thirty-seven rooms. The energies of its 110 salaried organizers and assistants now focused on the census. One photograph depicted a dozen women, bent over their tasks along a table piled with paper, quoting a Scottish newspaper's caption:

> The women warriors are in deadly earnest over their Census boycott. Any number of zealous young ladies are working at high pressure at the WSPU's headquarters in Clements Inn, sending out hundreds of Census-resisting forms to the people of Britain.[4]

Votes for Women meanwhile promised that 'a midnight promenade in Trafalgar Square' would be followed by a concert at the Aldwych with prominent actresses; chaired by Emmeline Pankhurst, it would include singing 'The March of the Women' conducted by its composer, Dr Ethel Smyth. Here the novel 'Rinkeries' would be open for early morning roller-skating, then highly fashionable: 'all those who are wanting a little exercise will have a chance of practising skating', accompanied by a special band. Tickets for the Aldwych Skating Rink would be 6d each, hire of roller skates a shilling a pair, with roller skating lessons for younger members. From midnight, the sympathetic Gardenia Restaurant nearby would offer meals for a shilling a head, with WSPU members as waitresses serving breakfasts; attached to the restaurant were rooms for whist parties. 'Everything has been thought of to conduce the welfare, comfort, and pleasure of all who are willing to take part in this memorable protest.'[5] Indeed, the WSPU promised daring plus fun, appealing both to the roller-skating young and the whist-playing experienced campaigner.

Now, at WSPU meetings, the audience was urged to fill in 'promises cards'. These had four separate sections: for women occupiers; for lodgers, boarders or hotel residents; for male occupiers; plus other women. Those signing promised to resist the census and 'to write across the form the reason for my refusal'.[6] Soon *Votes for Women* could report the vigour with which census resistance plans were being adopted:

> Private houses are being thrown open, and dances, whist drives, and other festivities are being arranged ... Many members have written to us offering to put up 60, 80, and 120 people in one house. All these arrangements will be carried out privately ... Secrecy will be observed with a view to keeping the authorities in the dark with regard to numbers ... In London, every hour of Census night has been planned out with a view to giving protesters a merry time.

Secrecy was of the essence – to out-wit the government and local Registrars. WSPU members in the London area – from Hampstead to Redhill, Kew to Crouch Hill – planned to open their houses; and readers who contacted the Census Secretary at Clements Inn would 'be put in touch with hostesses' locally.[7] The front page of the final *Votes for Women* showed a resister's model schedule, with 'No Vote No Census' written right a cross it. Upbeat, it reported that 'an army of women very much larger than was originally supposed, running into many thousands, will resist or evade enumeration'.[8] So how would these 'many thousands' respond on census night?

Ecumenical Laurence Housman wrote for both WSPU and WFL. At census journalism he remained unmatched. In *The Vote*, his whimsical 'News from No-Man's Land' series reported from that country – where the census had fortuitously been taken a month earlier i.e. early March. Housman promised news of how 'things actually fared with your sisters "over the way"'. With 'No Man's Land' a month ahead, he offered this reassuring 'precedent' to the undecided in Britain, stressing the low legal risk for evaders:

> In choosing Census-resistance as a suitable means for demonstrating their fundamental principle that 'Government depends on the consent of the governed', the No-Man's Land Suffragists have taken good account of the fact that a Census … without accuracy is valueless …
>
> Another good reason for this choice of [boycotting] the Census lies in the fact that the militant feeling among Women Suffragists is far more widespread than their ability to take militant action … A great many women … cannot afford to face imprisonment or fine. In Census-resistance, however, it will be seen that all who are militant-hearted can join, without incurring risks which, for the sake of others [family], they must avoid. They can swell the numbers of those who boycott the Census without being themselves in the fighting line … They can be in a house where Census-resistance is intended; they can be there just for one night in any numbers you like to name – in what precise number it will require a whole army of detectives to discover.

Housman warmed to his multiplication theme, ending on:

> The humours of the situation are developing … But under all the humour there is a grim determination that the blow shall be a really damaging one against a form of government which has long been an anachronism, and is now becoming a crime.[9]

'News from No-Man's Land' ran practical tips about house-swaps and census-night walking tours. In another instalment, Laurence rebutted Sadler's 'crime against science' jibe, stating:

> Science … depends for its steady workings on the consent of the governed, and if the scientists cannot secure from the Government which employs them a fundamental act of justice to one half of the community, then, quite scientifically, they must expect to have their elbows jogged and their scientific calculations disturbed.

Laurence even took a tilt at the hypocrisy of Liberal leaders who had earlier supported passive resisters to the Education Rate. So popular was his 'News from No-Man's Land' political fable that the WFL reissued it as a penny pamphlet (10d a dozen for branches), including helpful tips on how 'To Evade the Census'.[10] Invited by Adela Pankhurst up to Sheffield, Laurence was also happy to speak as provocatively as he could:

19 'Census Meeting April 1st Trafalgar Square 3pm', cartoon, *The Vote*, 25 Mar 1911, and
WFL postcard, A [E] Winterne.

I have invited one of the women's suffrage societies to send as many of its members
to my house on the Sunday evening as my house can comfortably hold. Of course,
in nearly every case the ladies will be strangers to me. I shall put questions to them;
but on my census form will be the words: '[Census] return defective owing to the
lack of information from the occupants of my house'. (Laughter and applause)
The attitude of women is this: 'We women are treated as though we don't count,
therefore we say we won't be counted'. (Applause).[11]

Another boycott inciter whose feet now scarcely touched the ground was
Charlotte Despard. At Caxton Hall, she inspired her audience by reporting she
had 'everywhere met with success in persuading women to boycott'. She herself
would 'have a large house-party' on census night and encouraged her audience

'to get as much fun as possible out of this protest', trusting none of women listening would so 'lose her self-respect as to give information asked for on the Census forms'. Indeed, soon Edith How-Martyn reported almost all branches had arranged local census meetings.[12] Members were urged that 'every effort is now directed towards filling Trafalgar-square for the Census mass meeting' on the Saturday afternoon at 3pm, immediately prior to Sunday's census night. WFL postcards selling at 1d each (or 24 for 1/-) even depicted a petulant Asquith and Burns, drowning in a flutter of census 'No Votes for Women, No Census' handbills.[13]

During the final fortnight, daily poster parades spilled out from WFL Adelphi headquarters, at Knightsbridge tube station and High Street Kensington. Charlotte Despard's caravan would be brought in to publicize a 'Hackney Town Hall Census meeting'. This all added to WFL's appeals for all members to help put the ambitious plans into practice.[14] Yet how many members and sympathizers, perhaps with health reforms or legal penalties on their mind, were willing to run the risk?

For its part, the Tax Resistance League's meetings now grew increasingly urgent, a special Census Organizer appointed and census postcards printed. It sought legal opinion on the likely penalties for, say, exchanging flats or houses on the night. Would it be a choice of a fine *or* imprisonment (like suffragette militancy), or would it be a fine *or* distraint (like tax resistance)? Meanwhile, the League also now spread its tentacles out to new territory with a northern tour: Kineton Parkes spoke in Birmingham and Leicester, Nottingham and Sheffield, making some converts. Invaluably, Elizabeth Garrett Anderson 'was now in favour of the Boycott', with her daughter Louisa requesting census details. A few League supporters did oppose the boycott for tactical reasons: its timing was just weeks before Kemp's Bill came before Parliament. By the end of March, however, every energetic League member was fully stretched persuading others.[15]

Suffragette organizations were determined that boycott propaganda be fanned out right across the country: there was no point in the WFL, Women's Tax Resistance League or even WSPU persuading merely their own supporters. So who best to lobby? Why not start with the large women's organizations that had sent delegates to the WFL's original census conference in Caxton Hall?

The Women's Co-operative Guild's 27,000 members were predominantly married working-class women with children. Persuading them immediately proved tricky. At its annual conference, the Guild had debated the Conciliation Bill, but had voted unanimously for full adult suffrage: to 'give the vote, and one vote only, to all citizens, male and female, on a short residential qualification'.[16] The *Co-operative News* now ran a vigorous exchange of letters between an adult suffragist and a woman suffragist. The paper exhorted Guildswomen to recognize their 'large, clear, and vital public duty' in ensuring the census was completed accurately to assist welfare reforms, rather than bowing to 'any individual or sectional' interests.[17] They were left in little doubt about how their husbands should fill up the family schedule on census night.

Perhaps the large constitutional suffrage societies, notably Fawcett's NUWSS, would be more amenable to persuasion? Its membership was now about thirty thousand, with three to four hundred local societies. The NUWSS however had long taken a view of citizenship and the state that was different from suffragette organizations. Mrs Fawcett, approached earlier about tax resistance, had replied she *was* interested, but significantly she dissented from the Women's Tax Resistance League's creed 'that women have no duties to State' until they are enfranchised.[18] The NUWSS also retained its own opinions on tactics most effective in wooing politicians. While suffragists and suffragettes alike agreed on the aim of supporting Kemp's Bill, they diverged on militancy – however non-violent the civil disobedience proposed. Indeed at New Year, despite persistent lobbying, the NUWSS executive decided *against* recommending census resistance to its local suffrage societies. So during spring, the NUWSS remained absent from boycott planning. A few members did express alarm at the intrusive questions to be asked of married women, suspicious they could be used as a pretext 'to turn out the married women from the labour market'.[19] But the likelihood of many NUWSS suffragists boycotting the census was growing distinctly small.

The third major group who had attended the Caxton Hall conference last October was the Conservative Women's Franchise Association. Edith How-Martyn wrote to Lady Strachey, a vice-president, to invite support for the boycott; but Lady Strachey replied that she certainly did *not* agree with the WFL:

> I am strongly of the opinion that nothing but harm can result to our Cause from any action that would frustrate the efforts of the State to arrive at the truth concerning the numbers, status and occupations of the women in it … The Census is not work of any particular Government or party; it is a scientific attempt to arrive at an accurate knowledge … without which no effort for social amelioration can be other than empirical, and for women to refuse their co-operation would be … to throw doubt upon their capacity for understanding the problems with which progress has to deal.[20]

Neither Fawcett nor Strachey left much room for negotiation. Both the WFL and Women's Tax Resistance League nevertheless persistently lobbied NUWSS societies, dispatching literature and requests to speak at their meetings. The League widely circulated its 'Women and the Census' leaflet, which argued that:

> The WTRL urges you to make up your mind at once to adopt an attitude of passive resistance to the Census of this year. Such an attitude is dignified, logical, and effective; it will render the Census unreliable, and will greatly inconvenience the Government without embarrassing yourself.

> This year Special Intimate Questions relating to Women as Mothers have been added. Refuse to assist a Government which denies you Citizenship – withhold the information which helps to make laws which govern you without your consent …
> Census Day is April 2nd, 1911. Be Ready for it …
>
> Write at once to the Hon Sec, WTRL, 10 Talbot House, St Martin's Lane, W.C.

When this reached Pippa Strachey's large London Society for Women's Suffrage (LSWS), it was already well-practised at polite yet bureaucratic stone-walling of lobbying by impetuous militant organizations. At the LSWS, it was duly filed – and ignored; indeed the LSWS refused to place the boycott proposal on the agenda of its next meeting.[21] When lobbied by the WFL, it also refused to display a poster on the grounds that 'our Society has not adopted the policy of resistance to the Census'. The LSWS's correspondence with its many London branches invited members to judge for themselves – but offered absolutely no encouragement to boycott. Its voluminous files make it crystal clear that Pippa Strachey's LSWS would have no truck whatsoever with the census boycott.[22]

Almost as weightily influential as the LSWS was the Manchester Society for Women's Suffrage. It comprised well-supported branches in suburban strongholds like Fallowfield, Withington and Didsbury, and also now ranged widely across the region: Ashton in the east, Knutsford to the south, and Bolton in the north (see Map 4). Its long list of vice-presidents and donors included Scott himself, and sympathetic MPs Sir George Kemp for Liberals plus Philip Snowden for Labour. *Common Cause* editor Helen Swanwick was its honorary secretary, and its chair was municipal philanthropist Margaret Ashton of Withington. Now with its own elegant city-centre offices at 85 Deansgate Arcade, it too employed an organizing secretary.[23]

At its AGM in January, the Manchester Society discussed Kemp's Bill, cheerful that most regional MPs were sympathetic. Prospects looked promising. During the spring however Manchester apparently grew alarmed at plans for the census boycott locally. Suffragists needed to demonstrate that suffragettes were not the only show in town. They believed their own constitutional tactics to maximize support for Kemp's second reading would be more effective than any irresponsible midnight promenading. Certainly, at least two meetings seemed to have been timed for the few days before the boycott; for instance, on 31 March, Margaret Ashton spoke in Eccles Town Hall, along with visiting speaker Ethel Snowden, wife of the MP.[24]

For the boycott really to work, suffragettes required thousands (ideally tens of thousands) of other women to join. Yet the likelihood of many suffragists or Guildswomen boycotting the census was growing remote.

Rather than just in Kensington, Hampstead or even Withington, the effectiveness of the census campaigning would be played out in the houses and streets of communities right across the country. During March, the arguments, no longer confined

to suffrage leadership and Liberal intellectuals, fanned out to newspaper correspondence columns and public meeting halls the length and breadth of England.

In these public arenas, this pell-mell battle to win hearts and minds, for and
against the census boycott, was depicted in public discourse not only as a political
conflict, but also as a moral choice. It became a choice between the moral wrong
wrought by a government that persistently denied women a political voice, and
the moral imperative of health legislation to meet the needs of future generations
of women and children, currently burdened with poverty and victims of over-
crowded slums. Two examples from Yorkshire conjure up this battleground for
democracy, starting with the WSPU's iconic figurehead.

On Thursday 30 March in the West Riding textile town of Halifax, Emmeline
Pankhurst spoke in the Mechanics' Hall. This WSPU meeting was chaired
by impressive local suffragette, Dr Helena Jones. Before a crowded audience,
Mrs Pankhurst urged the government to grant facilities for Kemp's Bill. Women
had too long been patient, while the government gave pledges to all sorts of other
people – the Irish, Welsh, Labour Party; and she added provocatively,

> it is a farce to talk about representative government, about the free institutions of
> the country, and the campaign against the House of Lords – until the House of
> Commons is, first of all, made representative. Women have no votes whereby we can
> enforce a pledge from the Government to grant facilities for the Conciliation Bill.
> We have to look around, therefore, to ask what lever we can use, because … until
> people make themselves politically inconvenient, they never get what they want.
> One of the most effective ways we have found this year is our census protest … The
> protest is being entered upon by us with a full sense of our responsibility … all the
> more because of the uses to which the census statistics will be put …
>
> Until women rank as people, in the full sense of the word, we refuse to be
> numbered among the people, and we advise other women to join us in this protest.

Emmeline's inspiring speech won enthusiastic support; but it also prompted
a local Unitarian minister to challenge her ethical argument for undermining
census accuracy and so future welfare legislation. 'In view of the tremendous
moral and social significance of a correct census', he asked, was it 'quite a moral
argument … to withhold information that later might do good for legislation?'
Mrs Pankhurst rebutted him robustly:

> the greatest moral wrong I know in modern civilization is the tyranny exercised
> over women. (hear, hear) The greatest danger I know is the legislation, very
> well intentioned, but passed without [the] necessary experience, knowledge and
> information … Women are prepared to hinder and defer legislation by every means
> in their power until we get the power to control that legislation, and see that it is of
> the right kind. (hear, hear) If our friend does not like the census interfered with, don't
> let him remonstrate with women who have made up their minds. Let him go to the
> Prime Minister. One word from the Prime Minister will ensure the census being got.

Despite Emmeline's magnificent oratory, the minister persisted, asking if she 'admitted there is a certain immorality implied in withholding information', for 'does not the history of morals and religion all the world through prove that good cannot come out of evil?' She refused to admit for a single moment any immorality, any more than there had been in Hampden's protest. 'The immorality is practised by the people who, while they have certain principles, and who admit the injustice done to women, resolutely refuse to do them justice'. He persisted, flinging at her the accusation that the suffragettes were 'attempting something which to me is grossly immoral'. Mrs Pankhurst secured the last word, asserting how she had been 'working for public morality for many years longer than my young friend'.[25] She had won the battle but had she won the war?

The second example of a local battleground comes from Sheffield, coal, steel and cutlery city. It was south Yorkshire's major suffrage centre, with all three main organizations well represented, plus strong local opposition to suffragette tactics. The WFL branch had organized a census boycott meeting in the city's Cutlers' Hall; at the end, about twenty women volunteered to fill their houses with friends on census night and to refuse the enumerator any information. The *Sheffield Daily Telegraph*, however, editorialized disparagingly that the census boycott would be merely as 'annoying as feminine ingenuity can make it'.[26]

It was Emmeline's youngest daughter Adela who pushed the boycott argument forward most passionately here. Working as WSPU's Yorkshire organizer, she shared a large house in one of Sheffield's residential suburbs with suffragette Helen Archdale and her family. When a *Telegraph* editorial decried women tax resisters and the proposed boycott, Adela Pankhurst retorted: 'until I exist as a voter I am not going to exist as a taxpayer, or ... fulfil duties very properly expected of citizens, who have the rights of citizenship'. Indeed, a Tax Resistance League speaker was invited up, who urged 'taxation without representation is tyranny', and promised such trouble when women's goods were distrained that 'we will make auctioneers so [nervous] that they won't trouble to sell our things'.[27] Then Laurence Housman came up to speak at Adela's meeting: women had been told that 'this evasion is a crime against science' but, he countered, 'they are fighting against a much greater crime' – the crime of unrepresentative government.[28]

Sheffield was also the fiefdom of elite suffragist Helen Wilson. Dr Wilson, daughter of a nearby Liberal MP, was president of Sheffield's NUWSS branch. Like many pioneer doctors she had trained at the London School of Medicine for Women; she shared her father's Liberalism and now worked for social purity reform. Adela and Helen Wilson had long clashed over militant tactics. Dr Wilson now made her opinions on the boycott robustly clear in the NUWSS's *Common Cause*; and, because her argument came from a reform-minded woman doctor writing powerfully from the heart of respectable Liberalism, it is worth quoting:

Statistics are not compiled for the amusement of the Government of the day. Their main usefulness is to serve as a storehouse where statesmen and social reformers of every shade of thought may find the material from which to forge the weapons for fighting battles. The census of 1911 ... is of value chiefly for comparison with former and future enumerations, and as a basis for all kinds of human statistics ...

The strength of the suffrage movement makes it certain that if the proposed form of protest is widely adopted, the returns will be seriously vitiated [impaired], and the census of 1911 will in the statistical tables of the future have to be marked with an asterisk, and a note, 'unreliable as regards the female population.' That will be an enduring monument to the women of 1911 – but it will be a monument placed where it will hinder the march of future progress ... Some of those who are now urging this step may have cause to rue it five years, or fifteen years hence, when they are seeking to promote some great reform by the aid of the women's vote, and they find that a closely wrought statistical argument breaks in their hands, owing to the 'unreliable census returns of 1911'.[29]

Before long, Adela Pankhurst was battling it out with Dr Wilson in the *Sheffield Daily Telegraph*. Helen Wilson condemned those 'who enter light-heartedly' on the boycott as having little grasp of the vital purpose of census accuracy. From her WSPU city-centre office, Adela retaliated: Dr Wilson had failed to understand that 'the nation which ignores women must be ignored by its womanhood until the lesson is learned. It is the Government that is today preparing to commit a crime against science, and the blame should be put upon the shoulders of those responsible', Asquith and his Liberal cronies.

Dr Wilson immediately retorted: 'neither votes nor statistics are an end in themselves'. Readers then joined the argument. One WSPU sympathizer supported the boycott: 'the Cabinet need only promise facilities for the Conciliation Bill, and all forms of protest will cease'; one suffragette demanded of Dr Wilson 'why does not she, and all Liberal women who think the same, protest against that [i.e. government] attitude [to women] in every way possible to them?' including forsaking 'the present so-called Liberal Party'.[30] Overall readers nevertheless largely sided with Dr Wilson's health reform argument rather than with Adela's civil disobedience tactics. Would many Sheffield women support the boycott on census night?

Meanwhile, in the *Manchester Guardian* two suffragettes argued that 'women will have cleared their own consciences by refusing to give facilities for being governed against their consent'. Scott retorted angrily that their boycott would not merely harm current legislation, but also compromise women and children's future welfare. Rather pompously, he accused them: 'so far from clearing their consciences, evaders, we fear, only show how their turbid the[ir] conscience may be rendered'.[31]

The arguments for the census boycott have been well aired; but what were the main arguments *against*? Some entailed abstract debate on citizenship: that though unenfranchised, women still did have duties to the state, as Mrs Fawcett argued. Along similar lines were practical considerations, for those supporting both women's suffrage and adult suffrage aims. Guildswomen were urged to recognize their 'large, clear, and vital public duty', to ensuring census accuracy. Likewise, Professor Sadler's ringing denunciation that the boycott was 'a crime against science', as it would reduce its usefulness for future social policy reforms. Dr Wilson's argument was similar: census data provides 'the material from which to forge the weapons for fighting battles'. To compromise accuracy would, as Scott put it, scarcely help evaders 'clearing their consciences'.

In addition to these moral and practical arguments, strategic political considerations were also evoked. Suffragists shared suffragette franchise aims, but believed militancy such as a boycott to be irresponsible and so counterproductive; Pippa Strachey was wearied with being constantly badgered by militants. Then there were the immediate political consequences of a boycott. Timing was crucial, dignified patience essential. Kemp's second reading was only five weeks after census night. So boycott opponents argued that midnight militancy would merely reveal women as peevishly 'sulking against the census', in 'a nursery fit of bad temper'. In Lady Strachey's words, for women to refuse to co-operate would 'throw doubt upon their capacity for understanding the problems with which progress has to deal'.

Would these moral, practical and tactical arguments win in the nation's households on census night? For suffragettes determined on boycotting, the time for abstract arguments had long run out. They now put all their energies into finalizing census schemes. Some planned small-scale individual evasions. Clemence Housman carefully finessed preparations by visiting her secluded Dorset hidey-hole again; meanwhile, Laurence himself continued to race to and fro.[32]

Jessie Stephenson illustrates preparations for an ambitious mass evasion. When she arrived in Manchester, one of the most 'stalwart friends' she first met was 'that Giantess of Good Sense and Kindness and Generosity, Mrs Rose Hyland', one of the wealthy widows upon whose largesse the suffrage movement so depended. She lived in a spacious house in residential Victoria Park, not far from Scott, and had long been a supporter of local radical causes, subscribing £25 to the 'Dr Pankhurst Fund', and she certainly was friends with Emmeline in Manchester.[33] Mrs Hyland had also resisted paying her taxes, with bailiffs sent round to her home. Like Laurence Housman, she ecumenically supported the WSPU and WFL and was a Manchester Society vice-president.[34] Such suffrage benefactors now played a crucial role. Jessie's autobiography recorded how:

> our splendid friend Mrs Hyland sent for me one Sunday afternoon from my couch of snows [unheated lodgings] … All the Town was talky-talky as to what was going to be done [for census night].
> After a delightful tea – it was the surroundings I enjoyed after my dismal digs …

Mrs Hyland switched on to 'The Census'. I explained all [our WSPU plans] to her and she was in full accord with the refrainment [abstention, evasion]. She said she had empty [i.e. unoccupied] a large unfurnished house and garden in the neighbourhood, and I could make any use of it I chose. This was too scrumptious, and … my face, I expect, beamed forth my delight.

She got a key and we went round to it to see the possibilities. It would house four or five hundred – packed in of course, I mean – and a good point was that it had several entrances from its various frontages [and] park-like surroundings, so arrivals in numbers could split [up] and not attract attention.[35]

Elsewhere suffragettes gave their plans a final polish too. If near London, they could attend the WFL meeting in Trafalgar Square on Saturday afternoon. On Saturday evening at Queen's Hall, Dr Ethel Smyth would give a special concert of her 'March of the Women'. Later, the energetic could reach for a pair of roller skates for WSPU's Sunday night at the rink. The notion of the census boycott had entered public consciousness and so popular culture – which meant a comic postcard. Significantly, it does not pointedly caricature suffragettes, but suggests airy and imaginative fun.

Meanwhile, Bernard Mallet's census machinery was ready to roll. This was the most ambitious enumeration ever conducted. Newspapers depicted scenes at the Census Office: bundles of schedules piled high, primed for delivery by a hired army of 35,000 local enumerators. Sitting poised for the return of completed schedules were rows of temporary female clerks, ready to work with their 'ingenious' Hollerith counting-machines, hole-punching and card-reading. According to his diary, John Burns himself remained fairly pragmatic about plotting by the 'vixens in velvet':

Tuesday 28th – LGB 9.30 [a.m.] … Orders. Letter to Churchill about Census, Suffragettes, and their fatuous tactics on Census night. Mallet R[egistrar] General called and I cheered him up and discounted Christabel's minions.[36]

The press had also urged householder responsibility; schoolteachers, particularly in working-class and immigrant (e.g. Yiddish-speaking) communities, had primed pupils to help parents who were struggling. It all now depended on local efficiency. By Thursday 30 March, one paper reporting 'Enumerators at Work' interviewed a 'tired and harassed-looking individual hurrying from house to house in one of Sheffield's meanest streets'.[37] By Friday 31 March, Mallett made a final appeal for compliance.[38] All his civil servants' months of carefully thoughtful planning would now be tested.

Midnight on 2 April Sunday was the witching hour. Householders the length and breadth of the land, supposedly sleeping, might be mentally totting up exactly who was present under their roof, eliciting their personal particulars, especially sensitive for married women.

On Sunday evening, suffragettes raced into action. They trusted all their

20 'Beyond the Reach of the Census', 'Reliable' comic postcard, no date, but undoubtedly March–April 1911.

eloquence and plotting would bear rich fruit across the country. The battle-ground for democracy, census accuracy versus women's citizenship, grew quiet as darkness fell.

PART III

Census night: places and spaces

11

Emily Wilding Davison's Westminster – and beyond

The Borough of Westminster sprawled from the Houses of Parliament, across to Kensington and north up to Oxford Street (see Map 3). Even within central London, Westminster, with its official government offices and peers' town houses, was untypical. At weekends it could feel deserted, uninhabited Whitehall buildings clustered around Parliament's majestic yet empty architecture.

By 1911, for suffragists and suffragettes alike, the Palace of Westminster's great doors had acquired compelling symbolism. They acted as a metaphor for women's debarment from parliament. A *Votes for Women* cartoon had recently depicted how:

> the Womanhood of the Country stands outside the Closed Door of the Free Human Commonwealth; behind it sits secure the Manhood of the Race … The spirit of Womanhood knocks once again for admission, crying … 'I have paid the price for Freedom'.[1]

Any census evader who successfully penetrated these massive iconic barricades would therefore, a Houdini-like escapologist in reverse, achieve a tremendous propaganda coup.

The name Emily Wilding Davison, now so memorable, remains forever linked to her suffragette martyr's death two years later. In 1911 however, she was little known beyond WSPU circles. Her family had experienced financial problems, but Emily had determined on higher education – and received a first-class degree in English from St Hugh's, Oxford. Then she had to earn her living, and, like so many other women, found her options severely limited. Emily sought work as a governess and as a teacher in a private school – until 'the call' came.[2]

By time of the census, Emily had over five years' experience in the WSPU. In March 1909, after a deputation to Asquith, she was sentenced to one month in prison. She wrote revealingly of how, 'through my humble work in this noblest of all causes I have come into a fullness of joy … never before experienced'. She was among the suffragettes interrupting Lloyd George at Limehouse, in full flow against dukes; Emily, one of the first to go on hunger strike in prison, was released within days. Then later, she threw iron balls through a window during a meeting addressed by Birrell. Sentenced to two months' imprisonment and hunger striking again, Emily was, to her surprise, released again fairly sharpish.

With these spells in gaol, Emily by now must have left her teaching job: indeed, she was described by the WSPU as 'one of the most devoted voluntary workers in the Union'.[3] Arrested once again, she was sentenced to lengthy hard labour, and again went on hunger strike. This time however Emily was forcibly fed, being one of the early victims of this brutal treatment. After just one feeding session, Emily barricaded her cell door. A hose-pipe was turned on her, eventually her cell door was broken down, Emily was again forcibly fed, and, after just eight days, she was released from prison.

By spring 1910, Emily had become a paid WSPU organizer. Her personal focus increasingly became the Palace of Westminster. She was already uncannily familiar with the building, having managed to evade its security officers and remain hidden in a ventilation shaft. Sustained by bananas, Emily passed the time surreally reading a guide to the Houses of Parliament; once discovered, she was formally banned from the building. Then immediately after November's 'Black Friday', Emily once again managed to get inside the House of Commons; she threw a hammer at a window, to which was attached notes addressed to Asquith, requesting he desist from obstructing the Conciliation Bill. Prison, hunger striking and forcible feeding once again followed, with her release after just eight days.[4]

So, by spring 1911, three points are crystal clear about Emily Wilding Davison. She was prepared to go to extraordinary lengths to achieve her propaganda goal, whatever the personal cost. Second, she was now far better acquainted than any other suffragette with Westminster's interior architecture, its maze of pipes and hidey-holes.[5] Finally, she remained independent and unpredictable, her freelance militancy nor always winning WSPU approval.[6] Emily remained not only something of an outsider, but she also continued living in straitened circumstances, eking out an existence in a single room of a boarding house in Bloomsbury.

Probably on Saturday 1 April, Emily somehow wriggled an entrance into Westminster. Feeling her way through the daunting maze of corridors, perhaps reassured by landmarks familiar from earlier escapades, she descended the imposing stone stairway to the ornately Victorian Crypt Chapel, its stained glass windows with decorative gold leaf. And, right by the chapel entrance, Emily found an inconspicuous broom cupboard. Here on, her story entered the public domain, with all its glare of press and publicity. Among those who took up her tale, *Votes for Women* elaborated upon the iconographical significance of her cupboard of rebellion:

Armed with some provisions, Miss Davison took up her position in a cupboard of about 5ft by 6ft. What at first sight appeared to be a mere lumber room was, in reality, a spot of great historic interest, for on the wall were written the words, 'Guy Fawkes was killed here'. In this small dark place, taking only occasional walks in the crypt, Miss Davison remained until Monday morning.[7]

While it was Emily who immediately captured the public imagination, the census also recorded other Westminster residents that weekend. Cabinet ministers had houses a convenient distance away. John Burns remained in Battersea just across the Thames. For him, helping Lloyd George with his Insurance Scheme ('Oh, these elusive and winning Celts') was still the political priority. On Saturday morning Burns was hard at work in Whitehall. Bogged down with paper-work at his desk, he also quickly completed his census schedule:

Sat 1 – 9am. LGB. Filled up Census Paper. Orders. Decisions ...
    A long conference ... on Maternity Insurance Scheme of L[loyd] G[eorge] ....
2pm. Home early, [working] on Insurance Scheme till late.

On his schedule, Burns duly recorded himself as fifty-two-year-old 'Head of Family', giving his occupation – perhaps with justifiable pride – as 'Privy Councillor'. He and Pattie had been married for thirty years: Burns added schoolboy Edgar aged fifteen, but there was apparently no domestic servant living at 37 Lavender Gardens. With his unpretentious lifestyle, Burns did not relax until Sunday afternoon, when his ministerial duties were finally interrupted 'by a "high tea" with Pattie and 6 of Edgar's boy and girl friends who had a pleasant time'.[8]

Another Cabinet Minister with an unusually modest household was forty-eight-year-old Lloyd George. His wife Maggie, usually secluded away in Criccieth, was with him on census night, and he recorded her as married for twenty-three years; of her five children, four still lived. (To his immense sadness, as we know, his favourite daughter Mair had died from appendicitis aged seventeen.) On census night, Lloyd George's private secretary was also present, plus just three servants.[9] Other ministers lived more palatially. Asquith's household listed over a dozen domestic servants, ranging from governess and butler to a bevy of maids and a 'hallboy'. Similarly thirty-six-year-old Winston Churchill, newly married to Clementine, living in an elegant Belgravia square, had eight servants. Slightly further away, in fashionable Chelsea, Bernard Mallet recorded himself as married, looked after by four servants.[10]

Yet even in these elite families, their schedules confirm how many children died young. Asquith's wife had four children 'born alive to the present marriage', of whom two had died in infancy.[11] Out in Middlesex, forty-year-old Thomas Stevenson, completing census details for his wife, wrote soberingly that she had been married for ten years, with three children born alive, two of whom had

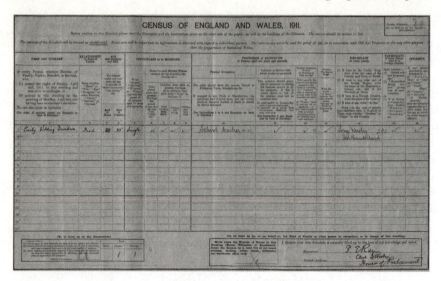

21 Census schedule, Emily Wilding Davison, Houses of Parliament, Westminster.

died, and just one, a seven-year-old son, still living. In Edwardian England, behind closed doors, death still scythed down infants. Yet these families could afford expensive doctors. Of course, the highest infant mortality rates and lowest life expectancy were still found in working-class households among the congested streets of Nine Elms, north Kensington or northern cities. Not, however, exclusively. And these common mortality experiences provide the sobering family backdrop to other more exciting tales of census night which now follow. The 1911 schedules recorded it all.

Immediately after census night, rather than these ministers or civil servants, it was of course Emily Wilding Davison who attracted most public attention around Westminster. *Votes for Women*-recounted her tale of Monday morning when:

> finding all the doors locked, she decided to remain in the cupboard until some visitor, coming to view the crypt, should cause one of the doors to be unfastened. About an hour after midday footsteps and voices were audible, and there appeared on the scene a Member of Parliament, accompanied by a lady and gentleman, to whom he was showing the glories of the crypt. 'And this is where Guy Fawkes was killed', said the MP, and, throwing open the door, he displayed the writing on the wall. Having gazed with due interest at the place where the great conspirator met his death, the visitors passed on, blissfully unconscious of the unwonted presence of a Suffragette crouching behind the boxes!
>
> About an hour later a cleaner arrived, who discovered her presence. She was taken to Cannon Row Police Station, and after being detained in the matron's room there for a few hours was released.[12]

This was early Monday afternoon. And it was apparently here that Emily's census schedule was completed for her, and signed by the Clerk of Works for the Houses of Parliament.[13]

Emily was in fact one of a handful of suffragettes who, despite all their ingenuity on census night, was counted twice. In her Bloomsbury boarding house, the landlady, perhaps wishfully hoping her troublesome boarder was indeed asleep upstairs, had also recorded Emily as – more accurately – a thirty-eight-year-old 'Political Secretary', and had signed it. *Votes for Women* reported that Emily had written on her schedule: 'As I am a woman, and women do not count in the State, I refuse to be counted. Rebellion against tyrants is obedience to God!' Yet, if Emily *did* somehow scribble that statement, the documentary evidence has not survived. Possibly she did write those defiant words, then when the enumerator came round her landlady was persuaded to complete and sign a fresh schedule. Or is it more likely that Emily's outspoken statement reflected her wished-for intention, that frustratingly, as just a humble boarder, she had no opportunity to add to her landlady's schedule?[14] This remains one of the census night puzzles.

Certainly, Emily was *not* in her room on census night, for there are plentiful press reports of her being found in her cupboard the next morning. *Votes for Women* continued:

> In the House of Commons on the same day [Monday] Dr Esmonde [Irish MP] asked the Treasurer of the Household whether it was true that a lady had been found in the crypt, and, if so, when she got there, and what he proposed doing?
> Mr Dudley Ward: I have just been informed that a lady was found in the crypt this morning. I have not yet had time to make myself fully acquainted with the circumstances. Presumably the lady went there in order to avoid the Census. The only step I propose to take at present is to inform the President of the Local Government Board so that she may be enumerated with the rest of the population.[15]

Emily Wilding Davison's Westminster night alone remains the most daring and celebrated of census evaders. She was not however the only suffragette to be caught by an enumerator against the best of intentions. *Votes for Women* reported that Emmeline Pankhurst too had refused to fill in her schedule and also scrawled a defiant statement across it: 'On the schedule left for her at her hotel, Mrs Pankhurst wrote "No Vote, No Census", and explained to the hotel proprietor that she took full responsibility for her action'. In fact, Emmeline *was* caught by the enumerator that night, wrongly transcribed as 'Mrs G. Pankhurst', one of over a hundred guests listed at the Inns of Court Hotel, Holborn. Recorded with her were a WSPU friend, Ada Wright, and a solicitor.[16]

The autobiography written two decades later by esteemed musician Ethel Smyth offers a different account. Apparently Emmeline and she were in the hotel together. Towards the end of census night, according to Ethel, they stood in their dressing gowns watching the dawn rise beyond the Thames:

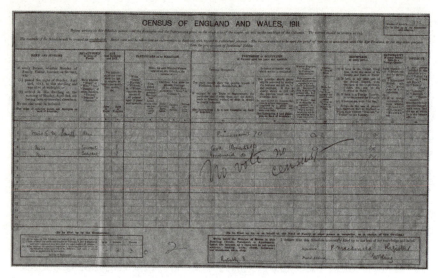

22 Census schedule, Ethel Smyth, Woking, Surrey.

Our foreheads pressed against the window pane staring silently into the dawn, gradually we realised that her love for down-trodden women … her hope of better things for them … my music … our friendship … that all this was part of the mystery that was holding our eyes. And suddenly it came to us that all was well; for a second we were standing on the spot in a madly spinning world where nothing stirs, where there is eternal stillness … Not a word passed between us, but we looked at each other, wondering why we had been so troubled … Neither of us ever forgot that dawn.[17]

This rather mystical portrayal may be misleading. Earlier that weekend Ethel Smyth had apparently been out of London, down in Woking, Surrey, where she had her own home. And as householder here, she received her own schedule, and so could refuse the enumerator information. Ethel, a resister, just scribbled 'No vote no census' right across it, as the WSPU had instructed. After this, she apparently left her schedule with the two servants and set off for Queen's Hall to conduct her Saturday evening 'March of the Women' concert, probably staying on after in a hotel, though seemingly not the same one as Emmeline.[18]

Emily, Emmeline, Ethel: these three vivid examples from Westminster and neighbouring Holborn immediately make striking points. First, for committed suffragettes the census boycott signified a highly charged personal moment, with every sinew strained to confound the enumerator, solitary Emily most particularly. Second, with the schedules now available, discrepancies appear between the various sources of written evidence. Both Emily and Emmeline asserted they wrote defiant statements on their schedules – which, if so, have since disappeared. And the schedules now challenge Ethel Smyth's autobiography, a romantic account of evading with Emmeline in the same hotel. Was her memory playing tricks, or was she wishing retrospectively to position herself alongside Emmeline, her original suffrage inspiration? All this made hard work for enumerators and their registrars in 1911, and subsequently makes challenging detective work for suffrage historians, deciding which evidence is the stronger.

Luckily, however, such high-profile boycotters, attracting reporters and biographers, are not typical. Hereon in, it becomes easier to rely upon the documentary evidence. So from Westminster's forbidding doors, 'Places and spaces' now turns to Trafalgar Square and Aldwych, and then out to London's bohemian suburbs. The first visit is up to convivial Hampstead to discover how boycotters' hopes for such suffrage heartlands were realized on census night.

12

The Nevinsons' Hampstead – and central London entertainments

Twenty-nine-year-old Virginia Stephen, soon to marry Leonard Woolf, lived in Bloomsbury. As Virginia Woolf, her *Night and Day* brilliantly evokes the excitement of central London's busy street-life, its anonymous passers-by often unaware of each other. Her heroine Katherine Hilbery, living in the family's spacious Chelsea home, had sufficient time on her hands:

> to walk all the way from Bond Street to the Temple if she wished it. The flow of faces streaming on either side of her had hypnotized her ... She ... looked at the faces passing, and thought how much alike they were, and how distant, nobody feeling anything ... 'Oh, dear', she thought ... 'I don't care for any of them.' ... She ... wondered – should she walk on by the Strand or by the Embankment?[1]

Katherine's friend Mary Datchett lived in rooms just off the Strand, here hosting literary gatherings. There was buzz of male conversation on the 'Insurance Bill', and Mary speculated about this political talk: 'I suppose, if we had votes, we should too'. In fact, Virginia (probably drawing upon her desultory People's Suffrage Federation experience) depicts her working hard in a suffrage office: 'From ten to six every day I'm at it'. Yet Mary found the laborious tasks there, constantly trying to catch Asquith's eye, vexatious. Indeed at the point when 'the question of the new census will have to be gone into carefully', she put on her hat, left the office and caught the tube back home.[2] Virginia Woolf's heroines might feel cynical about such questions. Yet London offered a cityscape well suited to female census evasion: women could live independently, host gatherings 'in their rooms', disappear into tube stations and could amble the Edwardian streets unchaperoned – all without forfeiting respectability.

Whether Katherine sauntered 'by the Strand or by the Embankment', she would pass near no fewer than three women's suffrage headquarters. Sandwiched between these two busy thoroughfares, at 1 Robert Street in elegant Adelphi (and almost within neck-craning sight of Parliament), stood the current WFL offices.

The WTRL was based nearby, just beyond Trafalgar Square; while the WSPU headquarters stood just at the far end of Aldwych. The imposing architecture of these offices spoke of the centrality of women's suffrage organizations within Edwardian politics.[3]

During census weekend, Trafalgar Square and Aldwych would be the destination for many. Yet for sending a powerful message to Asquith's government, the effectiveness of the census boycott in London would not lie here. It would be found where most people actually lived, predominantly in suburban boroughs like Hampstead. This lay on the city's northern slopes, past Marylebone with its women doctors' Harley Street consulting rooms, past Belsize Park, up Haverstock Hill – to Hampstead Heath itself (see Map 3).

Hampstead might not boast all of Chelsea's artists' studios or Kensington's enticing department stores; yet it housed an impressive number of intellectuals, often journalists, writers or lawyers. Despite its tube station, it remained something of a village, a bohemian village, particularly clustered just below Hampstead Heath; and like Kensington and Chelsea, it supported a goodly share of suffrage organizations.

So what were local plans for census night? Of the two WFL branches, West Hampstead invited sympathisers willing to evade the census to send in their names urgently. The WSPU ran a shop on Heath Street where Census Resistance cards could be obtained, and urged that paper sellers were badly needed, such as outside Finchley Road tube station. The overall impression of both the WFL and WSPU here is of a vibrant, well-supported suffrage branches. Yet, as census night neared, it all felt rather fraught, committed volunteers pushed near their limits, stressed branch activists straining to meet national leaders' expectations. The branches did however hold together, partly because sufficient well-to-do supporters gave time running the shop and helping financially: Dr Elizabeth Knight, the wealthy WFL tax resister, lived near the Heath. At this demanding time, WFL and WSPU branches sensibly co-operated, planning a joint meeting on 'Women and the Census' in Hampstead Town Hall for 21 March. Even so, the WSPU organizing secretary had to entreat members to volunteer as 'the time for working this up is short, and many workers will be necessary'.[4]

Some of the keenest 'battle for the census' arguments were aired in these neighbourhoods. After all, here lived many of the most active campaigners, all sharing the same aim – votes for women – yet with different tactics to promote that aim. Among the fiercest critics of militancy remained Lady and Pippa Strachey of Belsize Park; their home was a stronghold of opposition to the census boycott, with Pippa's views holding sway for LSWS suffragists across London.

Given Hampstead's village-like proximities, those holding distinct views were likely to live in the same street, use the same pillar box, even encounter each other on the stairwells of Hampstead or Belsize Park tube stations – undoubtedly to mutual embarrassment. One telling example: next door but one to the Stracheys lived a prosperous German merchant; here his daughter Daisy Koettgen chaired a WSPU meeting, with a speaker from south London.[5] Conversation undoubtedly focused on the planned boycott, with confidences exchanged about personal plots, and observations on neighbours – Daisy apparently planned to evade.

Luckily, the *Hampstead and Highgate Express* kept readers well informed on all local events. Suffrage was good for business and it happily advertised competing meetings: LSWS branches' performance of Ibsen's *The Pillars of Society*, the WFL–WSPU joint 'Women and the Census' meeting, and the delights of 'Rinking in Harem Skirts', daring dress indeed for WSPU roller skaters.

Alongside this, progressive Hampstead saw support for broader adult suffrage legislation: sympathizers included the Women's Labour League. So rather than a two-sided debate, here there was a three-way argument. Both the WSPU and WFL supported the census boycott; both the NUWSS and labour opposed it (united on census night compliance though of course disagreeing vehemently on suffrage aims). Thus the People's Suffrage Federation publicized its adult suffrage meeting on 27 March, also in Hampstead Town Hall. Significantly, speakers included Women's Co-operative Guild leader, the influential and persuasive Margaret Llewelyn Davies (who, Virginia Woolf later stated, 'could compel a steamroller to waltz'), and Marian Ward for the Women's Labour League; both naturally stressed the crucial importance of accurate census data on which to base future welfare reform.[6]

It is at this point, during the last ten days before census night, that our gaze can luckily be swerved from Hampstead's general suffrage picture, to focus on two crucial suffrage households: Henry and Margaret Nevinson plus Noel and Jane Brailsford. Their four stories are already threaded through this book, from Margaret's initial WFL vanning and Commons picket, Jane Brailsford's WSPU hunger strike, plus their two journalist husbands' public resignation from the *Daily News* over forcible feeding.[7] Till now, the narrative has largely focused on their role as political campaigners operating in public places. Now, thanks largely to Henry Nevinson's daily journal, we can open wide the two front doors and walk inside their private domestic spaces. The two homes stood just a convenient walk apart up Haverstock Hill; and this diary offers an hour-by-hour, blow-by-blow play-script, as the four actors prepared for census night.

By 1911, Margaret had been married to Henry for nearly thirty years, and they had a son and daughter. Their artist son recalled an uncomfortable childhood of the progressive Hampstead intelligentsia, his mother with her shingled hair, championing of modern art and social justice. Henry Nevinson certainly cast himself as a 'new man', embracing modernity, a journalist happily promoting radical causes – like Votes for Women. Given his frequent trips abroad and inveterate socializing, the couple increasingly led emotionally separate lives, while formally still sharing the same domestic space. Certainly, Margaret, for whom the first betrayal was always the bitterest, remained deeply wounded by Henry's affairs with other women.[8] She had decided to live her life as independently as she could, with regular Guardian meetings and a punishing schedule of suffrage speaking. Yet it was scarcely a companionate marriage, and Margaret often felt lonely.

When back in London, Henry effortlessly strode the city and glided up and down Haverstock Hill. Amongst those he most regularly socialized with were of course the Brailsfords up by Hampstead Heath. Here Jane represented all that luckless Margaret lacked: flower-like beauty, sweet femininity. His remained more an infatuation than a love affair however, not least because Henry had considerable respect for Jane's husband, with whom he shared so much. It was also partly because Henry's premier affair was then with Evelyn Sharp of Kensington WSPU – also now criss-crossing the country speaking at census meetings.[9] Thus references to Evelyn, shortened to 'ES', regularly occur in his diary.

Like Margaret, Henry had thrown himself into suffrage. Yet, as his biographer perceptively remarks, he 'trod a thin, equivocal line' between public politics and private morality. For Henry, the domestic now meant the mundane, the restrictive and the commonplace, unbefitting his 'new man' image. He had earlier made barbed references in his journal to the 'usual abuse & contempt at home from the woman who lives here'.[10]

Margaret's story, that of an unloved Edwardian spouse, was shared by so many other neglected or deserted wives, for whom, should they wish to cling to their remaining self-respect, divorce was scarcely an option. Margaret however had a pen and so a voice, often writing in *The Vote* on the legal and financial inequities endured by married women.[11] Indeed, one of Margaret's most pointed stories concerned a husband leaving money to his mistress, rather than to his widow and her children – yet the law protected him. Her sketch, 'Detained by Marital Authority', highlighted 'the abominable slavery of wives and the advantages of vice under the law', and the workhouse 'where the victims of men's lust can hide, when the price has to be paid by the woman'.[12]

What is starkly striking is how seldom either husband or wife mentions the other in their writings. For the census period, Henry maintained his refreshingly candid diary plus his vivid journalism; for Margaret we have to rely just on her *Vote* articles and brief references in her later autobiography. Since the boycott was WFL-initiated, Margaret was naturally in the thick of it, but just curtly recalled later how 'all-night entertainments were organized', and how 'speakers had a hard time … speaking up and down the country, inciting to passive resistance against a Government in which women were unrepresented'.[13] She had every reason to be unrevealing about her household's activities. Yet the census, with its new intrusive questions, throws up – a century later – personal information otherwise hidden.

In the preparations for census weekend, Henry Nevinson's diary opens on Tuesday 21 March. Along with Noel Brailsford he attended a press lunch, followed in the afternoon by the joint WFL–WSPU boycott meeting in Hampstead Town Hall conveniently situated on Haverstock Hill. Margaret, a local Guardian, presided, while the main speakers included Jane Brailsford. Jane stated that many men also planned to resist, and that her own husband would 'have his house full of suffragettes on the night of April 2'. In the light of the platform line-up, Henry Nevinson's diary entry is revealing laconic:

> Came away early [from *Nation* lunch] for Town Hall meeting on women on census.
> J.E.M. [Jane] spoke most beautifully: I gave her tea in a shop & went to her house
> … She was most sweet & gracious.[14]

While Jane's initial 'M' referred to her maiden name, Malloch, Margaret, unacknowledged and un-entertained to tea, presumably returned home alone.

The following day, Wednesday, after some desultory writing, Henry left home smartly and travelled down to meet Evelyn Sharp. She was returning from Cheltenham, where she had spoken at two meetings in its Town Hall:

> Met E S on [her] return fr[om] Cheltenham and lunched very unhappily …
> Went home & changed. Then to Lady Brassey's meeting of aristocrats in their Egyptian room. Sir George Kemp [MP], Ellis Griffiths [Under Secretary of State at Home Office] & ES spoke. She was not at her best, her brain tired, forming words, & not quite catching people.
> Went back thro Park, depressed & unsatisfied. Dined at Square Club.

Home was where one changed one's shirt, ready for next political soirée. On Thursday, Henry popped up the road to his favourite household, before proceeding to a major WSPU event:

> Went to 32 [Well Walk] & found H. N. B[railsford] had been working the whole night. We discussed Men's League … She [Jane] was very sweet & gracious & merry …
> Dined in restaurant … Then to great Albert Hall meeting, sat in front arena. Mrs Pankhurst, Mrs [Pethick] Lawrence, Christabel admirable. Christabel up to her old level except that once she ranted … Vida Goldstein calm, fluent, pleasing, but rather uninteresting, like Australia. Back with … the Brailsfords.[15]

Busy Henry then treated himself to a long weekend in the country. On Friday 24 March he travelled out to Great Missenden in the Buckinghamshire Chilterns. He was, after all, an energetic journalist belonging to a Saturday Walking Club, and these group outings provided a discreet means of spending time in public with Evelyn Sharp, also a member. This was also Hampden country and John Hampden was *the* inspiration of tax resistance, and it is revealing that Henry strolled over the Chilterns in Hampden's footsteps, while Margaret remained at home. After trying to sort out an irksome Men's League splat, he set off for

Great Missenden and, despite snow, walked the 'wide country … under varied sky, hidden sun & long beams'. The next day:

> Saturday 25 … Walking to Missenden, arriving like a snow man. Bought cake and tea. Met the [Walking] Club at 1.15 train – [including] E.S … Had lunch in snow at a porch of empty house, and reached cottage at 2.30 … The view not so exquisite as yesterday. But all were pleased. Long tea and discussion, chiefly theatrical. Walked to Missenden again, & they went by 7 [pm] train, happy & pleased.[16]

On Sunday, Nevinson was on his own again, and on Monday, with sleet blotting out the views, he 'drove to the station at 3 and was home by 4.30', back to muted marriage, the Men's League and WSPU soirées in Kensington:

> Tuesday 28 … Went to Actresses' Franchise [League] performance at the Löwes' [Lowys'] in Holland Park. E.S spoke admirably, and there was a finely acted little scene of beautiful suffragette courted by a magistrate the evening before he was to sentence her. Miss [Louisa] Garrett Anderson was … really 'femininely' sweet.
>
> Went to Men's League Committee … The whole League is not worth the labour I put into it.[17]

In these last few days, the crescendo built towards census night. No speaker was spared. On Friday, Evelyn Sharp travelled down to Bournemouth and spoke at 3 pm, then caught the train back to London. 'Met E.S. from Bournemouth at Waterloo & dined. She was worn out & querulous with overwork & others' stupidity.' The following day, she was back on a long train journey, this time to Bath, speaking at the Assembly Rooms at 3.30 pm: 'Went to Paddington & saw D [ES] on [her] way to Bath'.[18] A punishing schedule.

Nevinson himself remained in central London for the big census-night set-piece rallies – starting at 3 pm with the WFL's 'No Vote, No Census' mass meeting. Here is his diary entry for what would be a packed day:

> Saturday 1 April … Afternoon in Trafalgar Sq[uare] for Freedom League meeting. Mrs Despard, Mrs Cobden-Sanderson, Mrs How-Martyn … I had to speak to fill up time at end. [I was] not good; no passion or wit. Things don't come to me at the moment, as to an orator …
>
> Waited long in vain at Rendez-Vous restaurant. Then H N B[railsford] came, but she [Jane] was too ill. So we walked down Oxford St and he went home.
>
> I got a shilling dinner & went to Queen's Hall for Dr Ethel Smyth's concert. A superb occasion. She conducted throughout. Parts of The *Wreckers*, mass in D & French songs – all her own work. Suffrage things at end – a piece of comedy with catch-words, a very beautiful lament of waiting, & the marching song [March of Women]. All went with intense enthusiasm … Met Christabel with Ellis Griffith coming out: she turned to greet me & held my hand long. I got her a taxi in the rain; again she took my hand to lead her through the crowd – that little hand, so eloquent, so vital. So they drove off, Ellis Griffith with them. I came back alone in the rain.[19]

23 Census schedule, Nevinson household, Hampstead.

Nevinson, long with a weakness for small female hands, had a shine for Christabel.

Sunday would of course end with census night. And, as he planned to attend the all-night boycott entertainment at the Aldwych, Nevinson may have completed his census schedule before setting out. If so, he neglects to mention it – but Figure 23 shows what it recorded.

Henry provided all the required data for himself (journalist, fifty-four, working at home), for his son (Christopher, twenty-one, art student) and for two domestic servants, Louisa and Emily. Of his wife there is no mention, and the official note reads:

> Other women were staying in the house but they refused consent to the Census on the ground that Women have no representation in this Country's Government.
> Copy: 'Original handed to Mr Bridges [Registrar] 4.4.11, A.P.' [enumerator].
> Signed by H.W.N.[20]

This then is a resister's schedule offering considerably more information than say Ethel Smyth's hastier form. First, it is a political document. The 'other women' staying overnight in the house, undoubtedly his wife and probably daughter, has 'refused consent to the Census' on citizenship grounds. Second, it seems highly likely that Margaret had offered her home as an overnight hideout. So how many evaders sheltered in the Nevinsons' eleven rooms? Were they all the WFL members, or, given the joint Town Hall meeting, other suffragettes too?[21] We will never know. With disappointing reticence, her autobiography remains impersonal: 'up and down the country, thousands of quiet, innocent-looking houses were crammed from attic to cellar with passive resisters. We all expected a penalty of £5 or a month or two in gaol.' Third, this schedule is untypically a copy made by a census official, possibly because Henry had scrawled all over it his illegible eloquence.[22] Finally, this schedule bears only scant relation to the life-as-it-was-lived in that house then. It records a husband who is present, with his son; unrecorded is his wife and daughter. There is scant consistency. Here we see a disjucture between the LGB's intended documentation and the realities of daily life in one bohemian intellectual home. Certainly, it proved such a headache for the local enumerator, the schedule was not handed in until Tuesday.

Through his diary and journalism, Henry remains the most compelling eye-witness guide to census night in London. On Sunday 2 he left home fairly early, and as usual 'called at 32 [Well Walk] & found her [Jane] better, busy with census' – perhaps putting finishing touches on her boycott plans? Henry then set off for the city centre: his diary for Sunday night now segues effortlessly and without break to Monday morning. This is also reflected in the census night report he wrote for *Votes for Women*; it draws upon his diary and confirms him as a compelling journalist:

It was between eleven and twelve … Trafalgar Square gleamed with wet pavements … Police stood formed in squares round all the statues … The crowd kept pouring in along the Strand … chiefly men …

By midnight the square was crowded … But nothing [no trouble] happened, though many hundreds of Suffragettes had come there, simply for the beginning of their all night's protest. The people walked or stood about, listening in closely-packed groups to the improvised debates … At 12.20 they [police] began to request us to 'pass away', as though we were but shadows of a shade. So we passed away up the Strand. But before we went I had noticed three gypsy caravans passing in the opposite direction. They were driven by women, who whispered me the names of woodland regions not very far off in Surrey … They vanished silently down the road …

To the rest of us it seemed a long time waiting, crowded together in a dense mass before the Aldwych Skating Rink. When at last the doors opened, something after one o'clock, there came a struggle, as in the good old days of theatrical first-nights, when everyone fought desperately for the front row of the pit.[23]

Henry's own diary painted a similar picture, though naturally more personal:

Sunday 2 … At 10.30 to Trafalgar Sq met E.S … & many others; but mainly a quiet crowd in Square.

Then to Gardenia [restaurant in Covent Garden] (no that was before the crowd in Square). The others went home & I to the Aldwych rink … Immense crush at entrance. Fine sort of concert & speeches. Mrs Pankhurst in chair & Miss Decima Moore … and a lot more. Christabel spoke at the end, & Mrs [Pethick] Lawrence told some admirable stories … [24]

Nevinson's *Votes for Women* article also noted the entertainment included an

24 Census-night refreshment stall, probably in London, possibly near Covent Garden.

25 Aldwych Skating Rink, the audience enjoying a sketch by Decima Moore, 3.30 am on
3 April 1911.

Actresses' Franchise League performance, Ethel Smyth's 'Marching Song', plus
'admirable speeches on "Woman This and Woman That", … "The Woman's
Cause" (with an eloquence partly due to Mr Housman again)'.[25]

The photograph in Figure 25, with its notice prohibiting 'Fast Skating', captures nearly a hundred of the people present.[26] Nevinson's article quoted two guesses, one of 70 and one of 2,500, and he added impishly: 'poor statisticians! Will they add the estimates together and divide by two?' He added that standing outside the Aldwych Rink at 3 am were 'four policemen and a sergeant, evidently attempting to make a rough count'.[27] In fact, the police seemed unfazed by this unorthodox task: the schedule 'At the Skating Rink Aldwych. Report from Census Office' records in cursive script '500 women, 70 men', giving a total of 570 'persons'.[28] This rather surreal schedule, providing no names and no details, was signed by the local Registrar. Here were 570 evaders very publicly defying the census and cocking their snook at the law; and alongside operated the state's administrative machinery, the Registrar and police, who took it all in their stride, their procedures running as smoothly as clockwork. Surreal? Yes. Yet this document of London's largest mass evasion is also surely invaluably revealing about a tolerant pragmatism within Edwardian Liberalism.

Nevinson's diary continued:

> Monday 3. About 3.30 am I went to the Gardenia with [ES] … Stayed long talking there – Mrs [Pethick] Lawrence & Christabel & others. Then back to Rink and I put on skates again after all these years – at 6 am, I was skating with Decima Moore, a thing I never dreamt of.[29]

Census-night skating certainly lodged in the memory. Over sixty years later Marie Lawson still vividly recalled it as terrific fun. As a member of the Tax Resistance League, she said 'we formed immediately a census resistance group' which determined:

> We … would not be counted, would stay out somehow – out of a house or [on] roof during the period when you had to be recorded. Our group, we took the Aldwych skating rink for the night – we hired it. Nobody was supposed to be sleeping there. [*Laughs.*] We had roller skates and we spent the night on roller skates and there was no-one to declare us, and when we went away in the morning we were very weary, very tired, with our roller skating, but we felt we had done the government out of so many names on the census resistance … We used to grab at every little thing, you know, that we could make a protest about. It was advertising, really.[30]

Nevinson's *Votes for Women* report continued, describing early morning:

> The lamps were going out as we returned to the Aldwych Rink. Then we began skating with the comfortable sense of being exemplary early risers … So the coming day found us enjoying old English sports on skates [like] potato races … whirling backwards in unwonted curves … Never in the wildest dreams of youth did I picture myself skating with a celebrated actress in the Strand at five o'clock on an April morning.

On this celebratory note, Nevinson's article ended – though his own diary continued:

> Came away soon after seven by the awakening Strand. At 5 we had been in Covent Garden, & I got some roses for J.E M's birthday.
>
> Hours with the model & breakfast with various skating figures after the night.
>
> Went up to 32 [Well Walk] with Covent Garden roses for her [Jane's] birthday which were very sweetly welcomed … Her rage because he [Brailsford] had written 'Head' of family on Census papers. She scratched it out & wrote 'Nonsense'.[31]

Jane had presumably also spent census night elsewhere, and on the Brailsfords' schedule is noticeably absent. Only one single name, her husband's, is listed; the word 'Head' is indeed deleted; and the one word on the line below (presumably handwritten 'Nonsense!') has clearly been erased. All that remains visible of Jane's defiance is a solitary exclamation mark after the erasure. Brailsford had however signed the schedule, vouching for its accuracy 'save as regards the women in the house', with not even servants recorded. At the foot of the schedule in another hand, is added 'All Other Information Refused', and it is initialled by the Registrar. (Indeed, the enumerator's summary page for Well Walk merely noted: 'Mr Brailsford refused to fill up Form.')

Nevinson's diary then rounds off his glittering census night later on Monday. At the end of a Queen's Hall meeting, Christabel and Decima Moore asked him to write up his experience for *Votes for Women*. By now everyone was exhausted: 'Called on D [ES] who was very sweet & repentant [for tiredness] if querulous [with] weariness'. On Tuesday 4 April, Nevinson on a rare visit back home sat down and wrote his 'long account of Census night for *Votes* & took it to WSPU', which printed his memorable article under the bold headline: 'Complete Success of Census Protest'.

So here we have four defiant people and two census-boycotting Hampstead households (albeit one more complex than the other, as it was really five individuals, since the story included Evelyn Sharp too). So how typical were the Nevinsons and Brailsfords, even for Hampstead? Whom else did local enumerators have to contend with, and what was the broader neighbourhood census scene that night?

Edith How-Martyn, who lived in Hampstead Garden Suburb, wrote a report for *The Vote*, 'Paying Calls' around London; with a fellow WFL suffragette, she travelled southwards:

> We went to Hampstead, where we not only paid calls but greeted many evaders who were beginning their all-night vigil with a walk. At one house we were pressed to stay to a Census supper timed to begin at 11.30 pm, and which promised to be very lively. Reluctantly we departed.[32]

26 Census schedule, Lady, Pippa and Lytton Strachey, 67 Belsize Park Gardens, Hampstead.

Who were these midnight walkers? And was it Margaret Nevinson who rustled up the hospitable 'Census supper'? Elusive figures slipping along darkened streets of the night proved daunting to pin down for enumerators then – and for suffrage historians now. However, it seems clear that across Hampstead, with its resilient WSPU and WFL branches, its tax resisters and Men's League journalists, few of those suffragettes who might be expected to boycott decided to comply. It is now possible to identify with some certainty the schedules of about forty boycotters across the borough (see Gazetteer, pp. 251–6). Two neighbourhood suffrage clusters offer a closer picture.

Near the Nevinsons in Belsize Park lived Amy and Lilian Hicks, Lilian a founding WFL member and vanner. For them, the enumerator's summary page could record only 'information refused'. Nearby, on the Koettgens' schedule at 63 Belsize Park Gardens, Daisy's father, sister and three servants are duly returned – but of Daisy, undoubtedly evading, there is no sign. Two doors along, the Stracheys all complied; it is only unorthodox in that Pippa signed, rather than elderly Lady Strachey, who perhaps found the schedule's inquisitorial questions impertinent. Pippa's compliance, was, of course, entirely due to the NUWSS opposition to the boycott. Nearby, eighty-year-old feminist pioneer Emily Davies likewise complied. These were just two householders across the borough of the many thousands completing their schedules just as the law required.

Up near the Heath, round the corner from the Brailsfords, tax resister Dr Elizabeth Knight had likewise refused to complete her schedule, to the despair of the enumerator who wrote: 'No information. Mrs Knight refused to fill up Form.' One indication that this corner of Hampstead sheltered a nest of suffragettes is that, in the enumerator's summary book, these two boycotting households appear on adjoining pages. Finally, downhill nearer the city centre can be found one of the resisters' strongest statements. Dorothy Bowker, WSPU organizer for Hastings, was then living in Marylebone. Refusing information, she defiantly inscribed right across her schedule: 'No Vote – No Census. I am Dumb politically Blind to the Census Deaf to Enumerators. Being classed with criminals lunatics & paupers I prefer to give no further particulars', and she signed her statement 'Dorothy A Bowker, Member of WSPU'.[33]

So questions remain for historians. First, how typical was intellectual Hampstead, with its determined WSPU and WFL branches, its writers, adult suffragists and its tube links straight down to central London? With so many boycotters, how does Hampstead compare with other London boroughs and with other parts of England? Second, more broadly, how worried should Burns and Mallet have been about the overall accuracy of their census data?

13

Laurence Housman's Kensington, with Clemence in Dorset

Kensington and Chelsea were exactly where suffragette organizations entertained high hopes for an enthusiastic boycott response. In addition to the bohemian clusters of artists' studios and writers' small apartments, these pleasant suburbs attracted affluent residents seeking desirable homes near the green spaces of Kensington Gardens and Holland Park. Its attractive old houses or newer mansion flats were home to women doctors, wives of retired army officers and well-provided widows of businessmen. Along with women working in meagrely paid white-collar jobs, the New Women determined to make their independent way in the world, and all had convenient easy access to central London via Earls Court or Kensington High Street tube stations (see Map 3).

Yet there were two Kensingtons. The borough stretched through four miles of urban housing. To the north, casual employment and overcrowding were rife, with significant pockets of grinding poverty – notably Notting Dale with some of 'the most notorious slums in London'. Families losing a male bread-winner made do as best they could. One such household was that of Mrs Nightingale, a sixty-eight-year-old widow who worked in her greengrocer's shop, living above it with her son and his wife. Of this daughter-in-law's seven children, no fewer than six had died. To make ends meet, the Nightingales took in four boarders: thus eight people squashed into six rooms. Other households nearby told similar stories – of over-crowding, widows going out charring, girls working as domestic servants.[1]

Unsurprisingly, Kensington's pattern of health inequalities remained brutal. Across the southern wards, infant mortality rates were 69–92 per thousand, yet in the northern wards these doubled to 122–56. While such stark statistics were echoed in boroughs like Battersea, Kensington had no John Burns to champion working-class families. Borough politics remained dominated by councillors keen to protect their rate-payers and loath to fund health improvements. Poor living conditions surely arose from individual fecklessness: if there was a problem, it could be solved by voluntary philanthropy.[2]

Some local women active in the labour movement refused to accept this; notable was Dr Ethel Bentham, one of the early generation of women doctors trained at the London School of Medicine for Women. She had practised in Newcastle, here becoming a leading member of both the NUWSS and Women's Labour League. Then in 1909, Dr Bentham moved down to London. Her sizeable north Kensington home now served as a centre for a group of like-minded women. Closely linked to the Fabians, the labour think-tank, they were involved in feminist campaigns towards a democratic welfare state.[3] It would however take time to win election on to Kensington borough council to put this ideal into practice; so in the shorter term, they sought locally based health initiatives, notably baby clinics. Meanwhile, Ethel Bentham had shifted her sympathies towards adult suffrage. So, her household would hardly look kindly on suffragette plots to render crucial statistics unreliable.

They favoured census compliance – like the constitutional suffrage movement. There were two branches of the LSWS in Kensington, plus another in Chelsea; here Mary Lowndes's Artists' Suffrage League continued designing for suffragist campaigns. Of the militants, the WFL was not well-represented locally – though, of course the WTRL was keenly supported by resisters like Clemence. Rather, it was the WSPU that remained particularly strong, with writers and actresses like Evelyn Sharp and Decima Moore. Not only did the Kensington branch run its own suffrage shop, so did Chelsea – at 308 King's Road. Indeed, Chelsea WSPU branch took newspaper stands in Sloane Square, with poster parades 'sent out into the neighbourhood' to advertise weekly meetings in the Square.[4]

So as census night neared, across Kensington and Chelsea boycott plans were laid, sympathetic neighbours consulted and plots exchanged. After all, neighbourhood networks became increasingly vital when contemplating night-time law-breaking. Now private homes, long converted into suffrage platforms from which to address the wider world on women's citizenship, grew yet more sharply politicized. Between these domestic interior spaces, pavement pathways solidified the sense of neighbourly connectedness for those within comfortable walking distance.[5]

Few neighbourhoods better reflected this social glue of suffrage than Edwardes Square, its writers including May Sinclair, with painter Louise Jopling Rowe, Suffrage Atelier supporter, round the corner. Nearby, and with a slightly different suffrage inflection, lived Edith Palliser, now taking over as NUWSS parliamentary secretary. And five doors down at Pembroke Cottages, tucked round from Edwardes Square, the Housmans were making their final census plans.[6]

While it was Laurence who had been inspiring begetter of the census boycott, it was tax-resisting Clemence who had quietly determined on audacious long-distance evasion. As the crisp summary in his autobiography suggests, Laurence remained buoyantly optimistic: he worked with the WFL planning census resistance, and 'in a very short time the idea "caught on"; even among the "Constitutionals" it found a certain amount of favour, especially perhaps when the size of the demonstration made legal penalties become less likely'.[7]

During March, Laurence combined writing and addressing London rallies with a punishing travel schedule. In the space of just three weeks, he spoke in Manchester (undoubtedly for Jessie Stephenson); in York, then travelled down (probably staying overnight in Ilkley with the five 'very unshockable' Misses Thompsons) to Sheffield for Adela Pankhurst's meeting where he talked up house-swap fun. After more speeches in Scotland, he raced back south via Birmingham and Bristol, to talk in Harrow, Chelsea, Ipswich and Bury St Edmunds, before his final Trafalgar Square speech.[8] Yet somehow in all this, Laurence seemingly never lost his affability or grew, in Nevinson's phrase, 'querulous'. What magic kept him so good-humoured? Partly he was sustained by his talent for female friendships, partly by his loving sister, one of the 'wonderful ones'.

By now Clemence had packed her bags and set off for Swanage, having sent her luggage, including a portmanteau and a crate, on in advance. The main railway ran down to Bournemouth, then once she reached Dorset she changed on to a branch line for Swanage. Among the town's holiday visitors, inconspicuous Clemence attracted scant attention as she made her way to Linden Road and her house, Greycott. How long she was in residence before census night is unknown. What is certain is that thoughtful Clemence had left clear household instructions for Laurence as to what he had to do. This included scurrying around the house searching for sewing materials or her missing book: 'perhaps that book is in the window seat with the Suffrage literature and cookery books. You need not root, for it is near the top if there.'[9]

It was a rather surreal time at Greycott for Clemence. Her original purpose had been to wait for the wheels of tax officials to catch up with her. Now she was waiting with an additional purpose: to evade the enumerator. Would the long arm of the Census Office track her down? Meanwhile, Clemence's almost daily letters kept Laurence entertained with domestic news of her friendships. For Clemence it seems planned to share census night with a few other evaders, including a friend, Miss Gertrude Wilson. A second visitor, she informed Laurence,

> came in and out very comfortably – she had your room, and loved the blue curtains ... This afternoon Jane [maid] & I took her round the Lulworth Lanes. It was beautiful and bright ... Miss Wilson is most willing and kind and capable. She and Jane do all the laying [of table] and washing up.[10]

Equally hospitably, Laurence, just returned from speaking in Trafalgar Square, opened his home to evaders wishing to vanish. Luckily, his autobiography is far more forthcoming about census night than Margaret Nevinson's memoirs:

Those who were behind the scenes of that midnight orgy of resistance did not trouble to wonder how he [enumerator] managed to count them; they knew that he did not. To this day I do not know whether my own house contained ten, twenty, or thirty resisters [evaders]; for though I slept in the studio adjoining [my home], I found my door barred to me in the morning when I presented myself with the forms [schedule] which the law required me to fill [in]; and when I finally obtained entry the house was empty.

A few hours later I informed an official collector [enumerator] that my house had been full of women of uncertain ages and numbers who had refused me all information (though through the keyhole I begged for it), and had then decamped, leaving me by way of recompense a nicely-prepared breakfast. He took it all lying down, as one already inured to the tale; and the paper [schedule] he carried away had nothing on it but my own name and particulars, with the additional note: 'A quantity of females, names, numbers, and ages unknown' – or words to that effect.[11]

Likewise in Swanage, during census night Clemence lay low. On her schedule she had modestly written just: 'No Vote No Census Clemence Housman'. Luckily, a pencil note hastily scribbled to Laurence the following evening, Monday 3 April, allows us to recreate the tensions of this household's census drama, with its anxious aftermath. Laurence knew the house well and those it was now sheltering: servant Jane, Miss Wilson, perhaps two other suffrage visitors. So, when his sister updated him on her daring plot, he could envisage this remote evader's domestic scene:

Greycott
My Dearest
    The enumerator young man comes late this afternoon when I was out, and Miss Wilson interviewed him kindly & discreetly. He asked if anyone had slept at the house, but she said she could not answer. She posed as a caller keeping house while I was away. So he will call again.
    Oh joy, there is another [evader] in Swanage. Gertrude & Jane recognized an old fellow [art-school?] student, now a widow with two children. She has brought them down and her mother & a governess, and has taken rooms for the purpose – and has claimed a paper [schedule] and seems to be well prepared. She leaves tomorrow. She is the sweet-firm type – admirable … She seemed placid, but was nervous underneath, & very glad to come here and talk to another …
    We all want so much to hear how you got on.[12]

Clem's letter appears to end abruptly, without the usual 'love from your ownest'. In her anxious haste to keep her whereabouts secret from the prying Post Office, she did not even sign this note. But the romantic language in the word 'another' is audible, almost like the yearning for a beloved partner. Does it suggest female networks that must remain vigilant and alert? If so, Laurence would readily empathize with his sister. He probably did not have time to write back before her next note arrived, for almost the next day, probably Wednesday 5 April, a second scribbled note from Clem confirmed her return:

27 Enumerator's summary page, Linden Road, Swanage. Miss Housman, Greycott (*second line down*) is listed as inhabited, but with the population columns left blank.

Greycott

My Dearest

... [My] portmanteau and crate have gone [from Swanage] and should be delivered [home] tomorrow. So put out the label [sign for delivery?] when you are out. I have a latch key.

After the enumerator came the registrar. He came yesterday [Tuesday?] morning, but was not at all troublesome and did not try to question beyond the necessary or to persuade. He said he had to carry out his duty, and I said ditto ditto.

He would probably be going on to Mrs Smith [the other evader] and would find her flown for I think she was off about 9 – and it was then after 10.

It is evident that [boycott] results cannot be known to the Press, for [news of] Swanage [census] deficiency would not reach headquarters till today at the earliest. It is amusing that the dunderheads say of course we shall be counted in willy nilly – reckoning [up] the householders and unaware of the in-wardness of [intimacy between] the evaders.

I went to say farewell to [friends who] asked after the Census and guessed I should not fill it in. I ventured out in a bright interval but when I got down to the sea there was a black, black sky travelling fast up ...

An early train tomorrow is not likely.

Love from your ownest

Clemence.[13]

This is amazingly polite dialogue – given that her schedule was bare, apart from her four-word resister's statement, and it was unsigned. The officials merely added a note: 'Information refused'. Indeed, the civilized Registrar permitted 'Miss Housman' of Greycott to be returned on the eumerator's summary

28 Census schedule, Laurence Housman, 1 Pembroke Cottages, Kensington.

page for Linden Road with merely her name recorded. Even though Clemence had refused to comply, hers is listed as an inhabited house, but with the key 'Population' columns significantly left blank.[14]

Whether or not Laurence had time to reply to these breathlessly hasty notes, they vividly evoke census evasion as a mysterious adventure into the unknown. Unlike tax resistance where case law had built up gradually, census night was completely uncharted territory. For as unflamboyant an Edwardian woman as Clemence, she could feel reasonably pleased with her quiet achievement: outwitting the enumerator and even out-facing the registrar. She returned home, probably on Thursday 6 April, to Pembroke Cottages and back to day-to-day suffrage life. Her daring is less celebrated than Emily Wilding Davison's crypt-cupboard adventure, but was no less courageous. It was one thing for WSPU bravadoes to vanish overnight, quite another for forty-nine-year-old Clemence, respectable family mainstay, to challenge the might of the law with all its unknown consequences.

In Laurence Housman's schedule the historian can at last to find corroboration of a resister's own memoirs written decades later. His recollection proved admirably accurate. Except on one point: rather than his imagined 'ten, twenty, or thirty' evaders, there were recorded just four. Would Laurence have been desperately disappointed had he known? And what would he have thought of the census boycott more generally across Kensington and Chelsea? Did it justify Laurence's heart-felt optimism?

Well, he would not have had to look far to find out. Five doors along, Edith

Palliser, cautiously upbeat at the WFL's initial census conference, six months later unsurprisingly complied. Her schedule records her aged fifty-one, engaged in 'literary work', as joint occupier with Dr Mabel Paine, 'medical practitioner', plus a cook and housemaid – not an untypical Edwardian female professional household. Round the corner and more surprisingly, painter Louise Jopling Rowe apparently also complied. Surely as a Suffrage Atelier supporter organizing afternoon teas and giving speeches, she would have heeded Laurence's call? Her husband completing the schedule recorded his wife as an artist, married seven years, no children. Had she had reservations about breaking the law?[15]

And in her Edwardes Square Studios, May Sinclair also surprisingly complied. Her schedule records her modest three-roomed flat (studio, kitchen, bedroom) with herself as the 'sole occupier', aged forty-seven, self-employed, working from home. May supported the WFL and WSPU, so might be expected to boycott. So why did she not? Was she preoccupied with earning her living and making a name for herself as a woman writer, rather than creeping around inconveniently in the dark?[16]

Finally, the other side of Kensington High Street lived Ernestine Mills, WSPU enamellist, and her husband, Dr Herbert Mills. Both of them were Fabians, and Herbert cared deeply about health reform; he bravely championed Lloyd George's health insurance legislation, despite organized opposition from doctors. Like other professional families, the Millses were away on holiday for census night, in Studland, by coincidence not far from from Clemence. Perhaps surprisingly, Ernestine complied, her schedule recording herself ('artist in silver and enamel'), Herbert plus their daughter and her governess.[17] What had persuaded Ernestine? Was it the 'crime against science' jibe about jeopardizing future health reforms?

Elsewhere across Kensington and Chelsea, census schedules were completed more as might be expected. Compliers included NUWSS, LSWS and ASL members: Mary Lowndes at Brittany Studios and Emily Ford nearby; Ellie Rendel, one-time vanner, now aged twenty-six and seemingly still 'daughter-at-home'.[18] In north Kensington, Dr Ethel Bentham's schedule records herself, with Marion Phillips 'Author, lecturer, trade union organizer' and likewise 'Political Organizations' secretary, Mary Longman.[19] They all complied, though for slightly different reasons. Further north, in the overcrowded tip of the borough, few boycotters are apparent.

Elsewhere across both boroughs, the Housmans would be more cheered by the significant number expected to boycott who now did so. Hardly surprisingly, the enumerator had a job to pin down Evelyn Sharp – who wrote a strong statement on her schedule. Further up Kensington Church Street, the Brackenburys' spacious home hospitably sheltered one man and twenty-five females; nearby, there was a mass-evasion of a further one man and thirty-five women, making Campden Hill a veritable nest of evaders.

Nearby, a few boycotters, like the Lowy family mentioned in Nevinson's diary, refused to provide the enumerator with any information. Other resisters were more flamboyant. Not far away Catherine Pine (WSPU) ran a 'medical and surgical nursing home' providing shelter for recuperating suffragettes. She recorded the details of three patients and a nurse; but instead of providing details for herself, she wrote defiantly across her schedule: 'Above names at request – for the rest, No Vote, No Information', underlining these words emphatically in both red and black ink.

Across both boroughs many of the suffragettes in the Actresses' Franchise League were predictably absent. Certainly we know Decima Moore was entertaining crowds at the Aldwych and roller skating with Nevinson. For some other households, the enumerator encountered surprises. Near King's Road, he hesitantly pencilled in 'Miss Wolfe', a suffragette, 'particulars not known', who popped up from nowhere. She was probably Lilian Wolfe, socialist and anarchist, unwilling to assist the overweening state.[20]

But probably the most dramatic discovery here cropped up in Edith Road on the Kensington – Fulham border. Thirty-eight-year-old Eleanora Maund was the wife of a considerably older African explorer and mining magnate, now turned prosperous businessman. Eleanora's name is crossed through on Edward Maund's schedule, and added below (probably by the enumerator) is 'Wife away'. But then her husband must have intercepted it, and in red pen had tetchily added:

> My wife unfortunately being a *Suffragette* put her pen through her name, but it must stand as correct. It being an equivocation to say she is away. She being always resident here and has only attempted by a silly subterfuge to defeat the object of the census to which as 'Head' of the family I object.
> E. A. Maund.[21]

Edward Maund has thus left us a rare insight into one discordant marital conversation on census night. Here is a husband controlling the census pen, in the face of his wife's intentions. What motivated Eleanora, apparently not previously active in suffrage campaigns, to defy her blustering sixty-year-old husband? If she had talked to a suffragette while out shopping, we will never know who. Certainly there was at least one other evader in the suffragette enclave of Edith Road that night, and it seems probable that hasty conversations between neighbours may have taken place.[22]

Laurence Housman may not have known of this particular evading attempt, but he must have had a good inkling about such women. For in his autobiography he later summed up:

> The main reason why Census-resistance succeeded so well …was that it was an act thoroughly representative of the feelings of the rank-and-file, and of the [moderate]

amount of risk they were prepared to take to express those feelings in a concrete form … Census-resistance was well suited to the mentality of the non-heroic many; thus it ensured numbers [and] it was also good principle.[23]

How typical were these London boroughs of England as whole? How many other mass evasions were hosted in suburban homes, how many other resisters popped up from apparently nowhere? Some of the schedules here have thrown up puzzles: women who might have been expected to boycott, who instead complied. Were there many other census returns elsewhere surprising in their compliance? And for such women, how widely shared were the personal motivations suggested here: disenchantment with the narrow Conciliation Bill, reservations about militancy, prioritizing health reform over the census rebellion?

Hampstead, Kensington and Chelsea boycotters could all easily reach central London, to congregate in Trafalgar Square and roller skate at the Aldwych. And all shared a high proportion of bohemian literati and journalists, artists and actresses. Perhaps a sounder test of the boycott's reach lay far from such suburbs – in the streets of distant towns and cities. First, travelling out west, to where Annie Kenney was regional WSPU organizer, and where Laurence Housman and Evelyn Sharp had recently spoken on their whistle-stop tours.

14

Annie Kenney's Bristol and
Mary Blathwayt's Bath

To help peer into boycotters' domestic spaces behind their formal census schedules, Henry Nevinson's diary, Clemence Housman's letters and Laurence's own autobiography provide revealing personal testimony. For the large west of England region, the autobiography of chief WSPU organizer Annie Kenney, *Memories of a Militant* (1924), can be consulted. However, Annie, while the central actor-observer of Bristol's census boycott, wrote her *faux naïf* recollections selectively, telling us more about travelling to London for WSPU spectaculars than about local suffragettes on the ground. Luckily, not far away there was a family of eye-witnesses. There are no fewer than three concurrent Blathwayt diaries: those of our key figure Mary, her mother Emily and father Colonel Linley Blathwayt, all living at Eagle House just outside Bath.

Bristol had long been *the* regional suffrage city. As early as 1870 the Quaker Priestman sisters had, after all, refused to pay their taxes in protest against women's exclusion from the franchise.[1] More recently, the WSPU had ensured a high-profile regional organizer was put there. By now, Annie Kenney had been working from her Bristol base as WSPU organizer for almost four years. So, when charged with planning the census boycott, what were the challenges she faced across the south-west? What was distinctive about her area?

Bristol faced the Atlantic. With a commanding position on the River Avon flowing into the Severn estuary, the city had long been a trading port. Atlantic traffic made it a major transport centre, importing and processing sugar and tobacco; it was also the focal point for distributing goods produced in its rural hinterland, for to the east lay Cotswold country with its ancient honey-coloured cloth towns like Trowbridge. Now with a population over 350,000, Bristol had grown into the key commercial city for the west of England.[2] From the Avonmouth docks, the river wound its way up to the city's wharves and coal yards, charcoal mills and brick works. All were inter-cut by the Great Western Railway sidings and

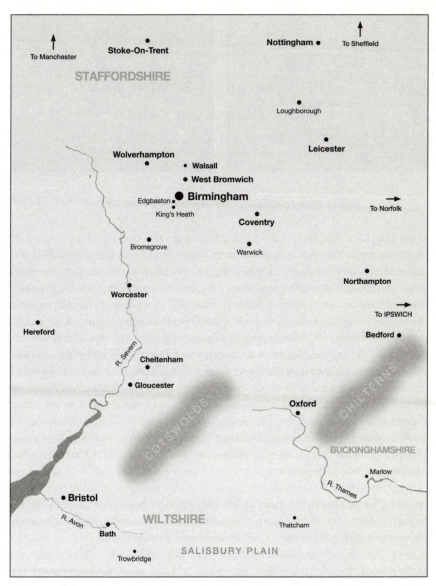

Map 5 The Midlands and south-west: Nottingham down to Bristol.

goods depots. As a result, the predominant male occupations in Edwardian Bristol were dockers or railway workers, with women working as domestic servants or in factories producing consumer goods.

Bristol therefore appeared a different world from the suburban sophistication of Hampstead, Kensington or Chelsea, scarcely a city where the suffragette

29 Suffrage homes, Bath area: (*a*) Blathwayt family, Eagle House, Batheaston;
(*b*) 12 Lansdown Crescent, with its panoramic view over Bath.

census boycott was likely to flourish. However, the continued popularity of
local spas across the region attracted both visitors and residents, often education
professionals, retired clergy or army officers. Notable was Bath, just ten miles
away, the small if mightily elegant spa city, its beautiful crescents rising uphill,
immortalized by Jane Austen. Clemence Housman, for instance, regularly visited
the family of her sister Kate, wife of a headmaster of a prestigious Bath public
school.[3] Similarly, 35 miles north, residential Cheltenham was also home for
the well-to-do. Indeed, Bristol had its own spa: Clifton, high up by the majestic
suspension bridge spanning the Avon gorge. Clifton's elegant crescents, dignified
hotels, zoological garden (with its own museum and even skating rink) were all
served by trams into the city, up and down Queen's Road past the university
college. Clifton had provided the local focus for Victorian women pioneering an
active role in public life. Annie had lived in a series of digs around Bristol until,
tiring of constant moves, she herself moved up to Clifton in 1910, into a flat
looked after by a housekeeper.

Bristol itself was strongly Liberal, and unsurprisingly boasted a Liberal Cabinet
Minister: Augustine Birrell, target for suffragettes. Across the region, however,
there was a balance between Conservative and Liberal MPs.[4] On the face of
it then, Bristol with its Clifton suburb plus Bath and Cheltenham might not
seem exactly the right location for the WSPU to despatch ex-mill-worker
Annie Kenney to. Indeed, it did look like a mismatch: Rebecca West mischie-
vously wrote, 'I think that it [WSPU] wasted a wonderful opportunity when
it encouraged its working-class members with a genius for revolt to leave their
mills and go to south coast watering-places to convert retired Anglo-Indian
colonels'.[5] However, in this instance the WSPU's deployment worked like a
dream. This was partly perhaps because, as Teresa Billington-Grieg observed,
although the WSPU promoted Annie as 'the suffragette mill girl' in clogs and
shawl, in fact her 'factory work was a very temporary affair', for 'the Kenney

30 Adela Pankhurst (*left*) and Annie Kenney (*right*), in the arboretum at Eagle House, c.1910. Behind them is visible the latticed Suffragettes' Rest.

family came from a home where there was a basis of culture and the ideals of a cultivated life'.[6]

And Annie was extremely effective as WSPU regional organizer largely because she was charismatic and could indeed charm 'retired Anglo-Indian colonels'. Of these, most significant was of course Linley Blathwayt, retired lieutenant colonel who had indeed served in Bengal, now moved to the pretty Cotswold village of Batheaston just outside Bath. Here he lived with his wife Emily and daughter Mary at imposing Eagle House, offering welcome country hospitality to recuperating suffragettes: thus the Blathwayts had become very well-networked within the WSPU.

There were other similarly well-connected organizers in the region too. In Bath itself, Mildred Mansel, local WSPU organizer, was wife of Colonel Mansel. Another key figure was daring widow Lillian Dove-Willcox who had hostessed WSPU 'At Homes' in Bristol and been an early hunger striker. Her country cottage also offered suffragettes a chance to recuperate; one described Lilian's flower garden as 'more full of enchantment than I had imagined'.[7] The WFL was well-represented in Cheltenham: here branch secretary was Edith How-Martyn's sister, Florence Earengey, whose sympathetic lawyer husband later became a judge. This then was the suffragette world across the Bristol region: understandably, it had little trouble getting glittering London speakers down to grace its

31 (*a*) Mary Blathwayt, portrait, 1911; (*b*) Lillian Dove-Willcox, portrait, 1911.

local platforms. The dominant figure remained Annie Kenney, whose charisma inspired and shaped WSPU campaigning here. Yet, as Annie's autobiography left local questions unanswered, the diaries of Mary Blathwayt and family at Eagle House become even more invaluable.

With her brother William away working, Mary Blathwayt remained very much the 'daughter at home'; she was able to live on dividends from investments plus an allowance from her parents, giving her at least some financial independence. Mary was a member of the Bath Ladies' Microscopical Society: here she found an outlet for her liking for lists, apparent in her diarist's cataloguing of many mundane 'facts'. Her mother Emily had a more relaxed approach to life, her diaries often more reflective that her daughter's. Meanwhile, talented Colonel Linley not only ran a car (thus enhancing Eagle House's hospitality attractions) but was also a semi-professional photographer whose images retain their power to impress. Many of these depict the Blathwayts' arboretum, with visiting suffragettes caught informally at their tree-planting ceremony. Annie Kenney regularly returned there to recuperate, learning to play tennis, swim, ride and even drive.[8]

Suffrage – and Annie Kenney – had changed Mary's life. In 1908 she became treasurer of Bath WSPU. Soon afterwards, persuaded by charming Annie, she made her WSPU commitment full-time – though still unpaid. Indeed, for eighteen months Mary lived in Bristol, sharing lodgings (and probably a large double bed) with Annie, organizing propaganda around the west country. Shy, protected Mary's confidence grew. She became active and busy, if occasionally harassed; travelling to Torquay and other seaside resorts with Annie, she felt fulfilled and 'intensely happy'.[9]

However, Mary refused to take part in militancy that might lead to imprisonment. In fact, her mother now resigned from the WSPU; and in October 1909 Mary had to discontinue her WSPU organizing owing to poor health: exhaustion and eye problems. Additionally for Mary, flat-living had implications of immorality, and she returned from Bristol back to live with her parents at Eagle House.[10] Thereafter, Mary's world shrank back to its earlier dimensions: mainly helping run Bath's WSPU shop, working alongside Mildred Mansel on local propaganda. Mary looked back poignantly to the earlier time when she was caught up in suffrage excitement, before she became painfully supplanted by other women for a favoured place in Annie's affections. She still however kept in contact, as her diary for March 1911 records:

> 8 Wednesday … I left Bath [by] G[reat] W[estern] R[ailway] at 11.40 & arrived Bristol at 12. Went to Annie Kenney's flat at 9 Whatley Road, Clifton, and had lunch with her at 12.30. Mrs Hatfield [housekeeper] lives with her & does the cooking & everything for her. I took over some primroses etc. After lunch rested on Mrs Hatfield's bed. Then took 5 pairs of stockings for Annie to Miss Porteous, 40 Hampton Park East, to be darned … Had tea with Annie … I left Bristol at 6 o'clock. A postcard from Aethel & Grace Tollemache this evening.[11]

Now aged thirty-two, here then is the texture of Mary Blathwayt's life now: domestic errands, suffrage friends – like the Tollemaches, near neighbours. Living back in parental Batheaston, hapless Mary was run ragged by WSPU demands – notably for keeping accounts which the WSPU required to be submitted. Conscientious Mary did extra shifts, further wearing out her eyesight: she was, her mother perceptively noted, grown 'powerfully weak'.[12] Yet she just about coped, improvising a suffrage talk when the key speaker could not come. Meanwhile, the Blathwayts' regular stream of visitors kept them up-to-date. For instance, on Saturday 18 March, Jane Brailsford and Helen Watts arrived and planted their trees. Helen, apparently grown somewhat deaf, now lived with her schoolmaster brother Nevile, 12 miles south of Bath, spending time together with Mary.[13] The two had much in common: both had been invalided out of full-pelt suffrage campaigning, Helen after hunger striking, Mary for broader health reasons. Both families drew away from earlier sympathies with militancy.

Living out in country villages as they did the post was crucial for keeping in touch. Both Mary and Emily noted in their diaries for March that WSPU census resistance information arrived, urging sympathizers to boycott. Emily wrote:

> Tuesday 14 … Census resistance circulars came from WSPU. Numbers of women will stay away from home all night & public halls are hired; a £5 fine will exempt [deter?] a number of people. The Government Census will be unreliable & only Asquith to blame.

(Mary, who slept badly the previous night and had a temperature, merely tersely noted: 'I have received a Census Resistance form from the WSPU 4 Clements

Inn today'.)[14] *Votes for Women* also brought weekly news of how organizers and supporters were now gearing up for the census boycott in four local centres: Cheltenham and Bath, rural Wiltshire and of course Bristol.

Cheltenham excelled itself. A new WSPU organizer had arrived. Ada Flatman, keen to book star speakers, did of course secure Evelyn Sharp, and also Emmeline Pankhurst. Emmeline's meeting in Cheltenham's Town Hall attracted record crowds, while a 'large and fashionable' audience gathered to listen to Lady Constance Lytton. A Cheltenham woman had even written a new play, a one-act comedy, *How Cranford became Militant and Boycotted the Census*, performed by local members. Meanwhile, those wishing to lend their houses for the boycott were urged to send in their names post haste.[15] On census night, Ada Flatman suggested that 'a midnight supper party shall be held, each one bringing her own provisions'. For Cheltenham's WFL branch, Florence Earengey not only persuaded key speakers down, but publicly also took on the mayor in scorching correspondence in the local paper. *He* was anxious that the census boycott would be bad for the town; *she* hit back, demanding to know 'what has Cheltenham done to gain exemption?' and stressing the national importance of local women 'joining hands with our sisters all over the kingdom'.[16]

Mildred Mansel had Bath similarly well organized, reporting: 'Census resistance is what everybody is thinking about, and friends must come and hear how they can take a share in it'. Activity naturally focused on the WSPU shop: 'a "Census Fund" is open to meet resisters' expenses ... Recruits are warmly invited to share in the protest ... The all-night meeting will be made as delightful as possible.' Indeed, a large empty house, 12 Lansdowne Crescent, had been rented; here 'there will be short speeches and some singing. Evaders are asked to bring food, a rug, and pillow'.[17] Soon Mansel was exhorting: 'Women, make up your minds now ... Shake off doubts'.

Basing herself out in Trowbridge, Lillian Dove-Willcox whizzed dynamically round rural Wiltshire; she drummed up support, speaking to a local Sewing Guild to whom 'the subject ... was quite fresh'. Lillian even reported how 'a letter dealing with the Census protest has been sent to all the municipal women [voters] in Trowbridge, and has been followed up ... with a house-to-house canvas'. Evasion arrangements had been made, but she added realistically, 'owing to the smallness of the town it has been thought wiser to keep these a secret'.[18]

And in Bristol? Annie Kenney was away for some of the time, but energetic propaganda was still kept up: suffragettes 'going out with a costermonger's cart, selling cakes, sweets, and fruit' on the Clifton and nearby Durdham Downs. The city naturally attracted its share of star visitors: when Jane Brailsford spoke on census resistance, it was reported that half those present promised to boycott. And of course Laurence Housman included Bristol in his whistle-stop tour, with a reading of his new play *Pains and Penalties* about Queen Caroline; it depicted how a defenceless woman was victimized by a heartless government, a theme sufficiently near the bone to alert the nervous censor. The local paper, echoing *Votes for Women*, ran headlines: 'The Census: Suffragists' Efforts to Evade Enumerators: Weekend Programme' – including a whist drive and refreshments.[19] But national speakers are one thing; local activists are quite another. And it remained unclear how many of the 'promises' came from Clifton and salubrious northern suburbs rather than from the great urban stretches further east across the city.

By the end of March, then, suffragettes, especially in Bath and Cheltenham, were poised for the census night boycott, some understandably keeping their locations secret, others more debonair about publicizing their plans in the press.

And there historians might have had to leave it, relying heavily upon the census schedules themselves, amplified by suffrage and local press reports. (Annie Kenney's autobiography merely notes with characteristic vagueness that 'we held another Albert Hall meeting. We all refused to fill in our census papers', but offers no word at all about the Bristol area.)[20] Luckily, however, we can also consult the three Blathwayt diaries; in contrast to Nevinson, they provide a foot-soldiers' view of census weekend around Bath. Each provides a personal running commentary. Linley was too ill with gout, rheumatism and his liver to do much, so sadly there are no photos.[21] Mary, perhaps emboldened by her father's illness, was preparing to join the Bath evasion herself – and so was busy making lists. Luckily her mother Emily, at home in Eagle House, while anxious about ailing husband and evading daughter, provides an observant overview. These daily journals, read alongside the formal schedules, allow us to re-evaluate some of the press claims.

For 23 March, Mary Blathwayt's diary, plaintively poignantly, notes of the WSPU: 'They are having a meeting in the Albert Hall, London tonight. I believe that Annie has gone to London for it.' Mary was now too removed from the action to be certain even of Annie's whereabouts: life was happening *else*where. As census night neared, with all its myriad responsibilities, Mary anxiously jotted memos to herself in her tiny pocket diary. For other suffragettes, census night promised hilarity – even rinking, daring fun and japes; for burdened Mary it was a time for scribbled 'to do' lists, making a stock-list in the WSPU shop, 'wash head, iron blouses', and noting that her skin itched.[22]

On Saturday 1 April, in her pocket diary, Mary's memos-to-self continue, opening with 'sent Petty Cash Book to 4 Clement Inn'. For Emily, her day largely mirrored Mary's: various errands in Bath, including making dentist appointments for them both. Then, as if routinely going shopping, Mary added almost prosaically her housekeeping tasks for tomorrow night's evasion:

> Saturday 1 ... I had lunch in Bath. Bought some [Bath] Oliver biscuits, & ordered bananas & oranges for Mrs Cave [WSPU volunteer?] for tomorrow night ...
> At 3.20 went to a Bath Ladies' Microscopical Society Meeting ... a paper on 'Cotton Fibre' ... I went to a WSPU Meeting at the Assembly Rooms. Mrs Mansel

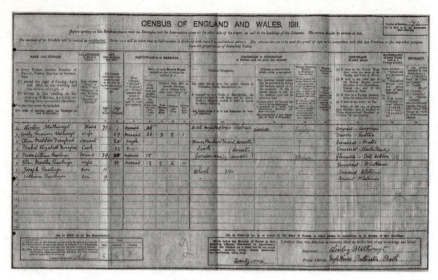

32 Census schedule, the Blathwayt family, Eagle House, Batheaston.

was in the chair & the speaker was Evelyn Sharp. I went to Batheaston Villa [Tollemaches'] with Miss Cave who fetched a number of green branches for [decorating] the house in Lansdown Crescent tomorrow night. Grace Tollemache has been ill.

And so ends Mary's diary entry: mundanely imperturbable. For the following day, Sunday 2 April, she wrote just five brief lines – understandable, as she was so busy; but these five enigmatic lines seemingly draining excitement from Bath's census evasion:

> Sunday 2. Batheaston. I did some gardening this morning. This evening I am going into Bath to spend the census night at 12 Lansdown Crescent, the house Mrs Mansel has taken so we can evade the census.

Meanwhile, Mary's tiny pocket diary reminds herself anxiously: 'Census Day … bring banana & oranges'. Luckily, Emily's own journal tells us about what Mary did during the weekend; and it also provides one of the few diary accounts of a woman who, while still offering hospitality to WSPU visitors, does herself comply with the census:

> Sunday 2 … M went after supper to 12 Lansdown Crescent where Mrs Mansel has taken a house for the Census evaders, as women say they will not be counted if they do not count. M expected there would be about 30 in that empty house. They all subscribe towards the £5 fine & all take food for the community. M pays for a bed too. She will stay in Bath till after midday. I do not blame women for taking this action. There is no justice with the rulers, & some methods which they feel must be used or women remain as they are.

Monday 3. L filled up Census paper. This time we have to say how long we have been married, how many children we have had & if they are alive. As Rawlings [gardener] did not get a paper delivered to him, L put the family on ours including Joseph 11 & Willie 9 last birthday. Our two servants are Mabel & Ellen Durnford. L still feeling poisoned & trying living on peptonised milk.[23]

Emily's comments on the schedule are not only totally accurate, but also unusually reflective. In direct contrast to the Maunds in Kensington, theirs is obviously an amicable marriage: she has not only seen the schedule, but also probably discussed it with Linley. So why did they decide to comply? With access to private doctors and dentists, it was hardly the 'crime against science' jibe. More probable is their ambivalence about WSPU militancy: this civil disobedience entailed breaking the law.[24]

Mary's own diary for Monday 3 April does however recount her previous night's evasion experiences:

Mon 3 April. I went into Bath last night by tram and walked to 12 Lansdown Crescent, to spend the night there and so evade the census, as a protest against the Government for not giving us Votes for Women.

I got there before 10 o'clock. A little crowd of people were standing in the next doorway on the east side to watch us go in. I took a nightdress etc with me, and had a room to myself on the 1st floor and a bed. Everyone else slept on mattresses.

Mrs Cave has arranged everything very well, & we had a charming room to hold our meeting, beautifully decorated and very comfortable. There were 29 of us.

Mrs Mansel took the chair and spoke. Mrs Rogers came over from Bristol and recited, but left us again at midnight.

Grace Tollemache played the violin and Æthel accompanied on a piano. Mrs Forbes Williams gave a lecture on Clairvoyance, but did not stay all night.

We had food in the next room; Mrs Berriman & Miss Pavey worked very hard washing up etc. We sat up until 2am this morning.

Breakfast 8am. I helped wash up afterward. Some of us went out by the back door, as I found the key in a green house.[25]

Mary presents the domestification of law-breaking. She was surely one of Laurence Housman's 'non-heroic many', women who had so far avoided risky militancy, to whose mentality 'census-resistance was well-suited'? Mary had attended local tax resistance sales but, unlike Clemence, had not taken any steps herself. Quietly courageous, after she left Lansdown Crescent, Mary met her mother going to the dentists in Bath and Emily, her diary records, heard how:

The people kept up revelries last night ... and there was good deal of feasting. Detectives were trying to count the women but M explored & found keys hidden (as keys generally are) near back gate of which they partly made use. M could not sleep much because of the noise. She had her bed and paid for everything, (house rent, gas, rates & fine included) £3. When she made her offer others followed with theirs till they nearly paid [all] expenses. Some of the people were poor. Numbers

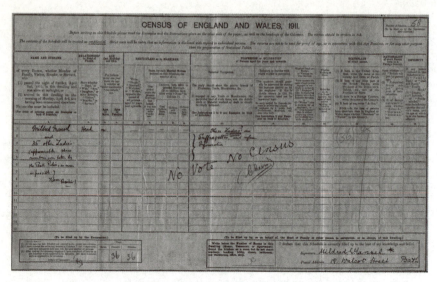

33 Census schedule, Mildred Mansel, 12 Lansdown Crescent, Bath.

of rugs were hired in for [the] occasion & mattrasses [*sic*] … Evening. Both local papers give long & friendly account.

Again, domestic detail prevails. Yet the Lansdown Crescent schedule really was dramatic and vivid. 'No Vote No Census' was written at a defiant angle across it, to which some wag added 'Cheers!' It records as present 'Mildred Mansel and 35 other Ladies', with a note adding of the 35: 'approximately. These numbers were later [provided] by Bath Police, or [as] near as possible'; and it was signed by the Registrar. To this palimpsest schedule, another wag had in green ink queried the word 'Ladies'. And Mrs Mansel had added underneath her own signature, 'with whom are a number of Suffragists who are boycotting the Census as a protest against the disenfranchisement of qualified women'. The poor enumerator may have hoped to keep his summary pages neat; but the registrar had added in red ink the new numbers of evaders obtained from the police, so the female total at the bottom of the page now shot up by an extra thirty-six.[26]

For Cheltenham there is no eye-witness tesimony. However, Monday's *Gloucestershire Echo* ran a lengthy interview with Ada Flatman, headlined 'DETECTIVE'S ALL-NIGHT VIGIL. THEY FIDDLE WHILE HE FREEZES'. Ada was certainly still in high spirits after census night, as she talked up the town's mass evasion to a reporter:

We have had rather an exciting time. Evidently they [police] know that we are a dangerous people, for we were very closely watched.

A good friend lent me her house in her absence for the week-end, asking no questions, and that made me *pro tem* the legal occupier.

I and another friend sallied forth on Sunday evening to take up residence, and we were immediately shadowed by detectives, who sprang from some area [basement] steps where they ... [were] watching for the ringleaders to show them the way to the Suffragist Mecca. This we did not in the least mind doing, knowing that the majority of our party were already awaiting our arrival.

We parried the detectives [for] some time, first walking in one direction and then in another, sometimes holding long conversations at street corners. At last I held them at bay while my friend disappeared down a side street. Then I hid myself behind a corner where a detective immediately passed by, thinking to follow me.

I advanced and asked him why he was following me, and we had a little conversation ... I afterwards went to my [evasion] house, but lost sight of my shadower ... At the house we had a blaze of light ...

It was necessary, though, in some cases, to keep the house in absolute darkness ... many hiding ... From this point of view it exceeded my expectation ... The exact numbers ... is part of our secret.

We were sitting up in the small hours ... hoping of course that the poor detective whiled away his time listening to the violin solos and peals of laughter of the merry Suffragettes ... He was blue with cold ...

I filled in the schedule for the house with the words 'As women do not count politically, I and the guests in my house refuse to be counted for the census', and signed it with my own name[27]

and Ada ended her interview with a challenge to Cheltenham's mayor. This breathless press report does roughly correspond with the census schedule itself; except there are only thirteen occupants, with really only ten evaders, and apparently no statement.[28]

For the Cheltenham WFL, Florence Earengey lived further out, in a village with more than its fair share of retired generals. On his schedule, her husband recorded himself as the sole occupier (thirty-five years old, solicitor) and duly signed it. However his defiant statement reads: 'the other members of this household were away as a protest against women having no parliamenta[ry vote]'. Florence was of course evading, apparently taking her daughter and servant with her – probably joining one of Cheltenham's evasions.

The most daring evader was Lillian Dove-Willcox (see Figure 31b). As we know, Lillian had headed out south-west from Bristol into rural Wiltshire, possibly travelling by caravan. She based herself in the old cloth town of Trowbridge; here she worked as co-secretary of West Wiltshire WSPU with a Miss B. Gramlick, daughter of a wealthy Viennese family, and took lodgings across the town. Lillian was absolutely determined to evade officialdom (and so finding her exact whereabouts has posed a particular challenge to subsequent researchers). Though she was resolute to leave no trace, a schedule *was* however completed for her. It records an 'L Dove Willcox, Head (apparently), 30, widow', and adds 'Suffragette worker who spent the night of the 2nd April 1911 in a Caravan at [obscured]', noting rather surrealistically that it was a two-roomed van. Then, in lieu of Lillian's signature is appended a note probably by the registrar: 'As per letter from Archer Bellingham Esqr to me dated 7th April [1911]', signed by a T. S. Hill (who also initials the enumerator's box) at Trowbridge Town Hall. To the summary page for Lillian's Trowbridge lodgings is added another note: 'Schedule 254 collected. No particulars entered. Information refused', and it is initialled by the fraught enumerator; under this, another line had been added: 'Subsequently filled up by authority of A Bellingham Esq', and signed T. S. Hill.

So, from this search for elusive Lillian, first in April 1911 and second a century later, three points are clear. First, that it was only with considerable difficulty that her caravan had been tracked down in the remote Wiltshire countryside. Second, that Lillian's evasion had risen right up to the top: Archer Bellingham, one of Mallet's elite civil servants, handled only the most vexatious evasions, its obstinacy suggested by the date, 7 April. Lillian had foxed the enumerator, stumped the registrar and got herself referred up to the top of Whitehall. Third, Lilian was among the most daring of suffragette evaders on census night, out in a caravan near Salisbury Plain at midnight. The recent release of the census provides a sudden flash of lightening catching the suffrage movement in full fearless motion, freezing the night-time frame. Civil disobedience, indeed!

One caravan in Wiltshire was all very well, but would scarcely perturb Bernard Mallet. Of more official concern would be the strategic city of Bristol, its population more than three times Bath and Cheltenham combined. How many evaders there?

Bristol remained Annie Kenney's regional base of course. So the first place to look is Annie's four-roomed flat at 9 Whatley Road, Clifton. The information on her schedule is sketchy: just her name, signature, address plus her occupation (seemingly written by Annie) merely as 'Suffragette'. The enumerator added a question mark in the 'age' column, and noted 'Information refused'. However, even his summary page has just one sole female occupant for her flat.[29] Yet when Annie was interviewed by a *Bristol Times & Mirror* reporter on Monday about midday she, like Ada Flatman, happily proclaimed herself 'distinctly pleased' with the boycott. She had put up a poster on her door proclaiming 'No Vote, No Census', and added:

> I have had my house crowded out all night. They are just beginning to leave now, so they cannot reach home before noon. We commenced a bridge party as soon as Monday morning broke, and some played bridge all night. Others ... played other games, or went and got what rest they could.[30]

So the question remains: how many card-players can you squeeze into four rooms? If Annie's account of her home being 'crowded out all night' is accurate, why were the city's police and detectives so dilatory? Or might Annie here, as more generally in her autobiography, be exaggerating Bristol's mass evasion? Were there other census boycotts across the city that night? Annie expanded to the reporter on events in various homes:

> Each hostess organized her own party. The movement has been taken up in Bristol more universally than we ever expected, and more active resisters came forward than we reckoned upon.

The report claimed, on the basis of Annie's testimony, that so many hostesses were prepared to cram their houses with guests that the public 'Rooms' she had booked earlier 'were not needed'.

So who were these other Bristol 'hostesses' prepared to cram in evading guests? Here difficulties with evidence continue. The Misses James, inhabiting a ten-roomed Clifton Down House, did refuse to provide information. The enumerator noted on their schedule: 'Suffragettes. This information obtained from next door neighbour'. Though little seems known about them, they might have gone to Annie's flat. Mary Blathwayt noted that a Mrs Rogers of Clifton had joined the Bath evasion; and further north, in more rural Westbury-on-Trym, one of Bristol WSPU's shadowy figures, Gertrude Fowler, wife of an industrial manager, is missing – and is probably evading. Right across the city in east Bristol, one other undoubted evader was twenty-year-old Lilian Lenton, a recent suffragette convert. Flamboyant Lilian and also her mother are missing from the family schedule, and probably evading together. Otherwise, evidence of specific local women evading remains decidedly hazy.[31] Annie however continued to paint for her press interview a vivid picture of wide-scale and imaginative evasions:

> 'Then there was a caravan, with upon one side [a poster] "A Few Census Resisters", and upon the other "No Vote, No Census". In this ark of refuge from the flood of census questions some members of the local "militants" spent the night, taking a drive in the night air over the [Clifton] Suspension Bridge …
>
> In view of the weather, the tent idea was discarded. Even Suffragettes are in some respect very human. They don't take kindly to bedraggled skirts and wet-rag millinery.'
>
> Miss Kenney … says it would not do to give the number of parties held or the total number of the guests, else she would be supplying her friends at the Census Office with information they would like to get hold of. And that she would be very sorry to do.
>
> 'Upon leaving the parties, some Suffragettes went to business, some went shopping, and some went home – but took care not to get there before noon.'[32]

Census searches have however not so far identified this particular caravan; and it may be that Annie Kenney, like other WSPU organizers, felt under pressure from London to put the best possible gloss on Bristol's boycott. Given the conflicting evidence, it remains difficult to be certain.

Nevertheless, the overall pattern emerging in the south-west is of the boycott flourishing in the spa towns of Bath and Cheltenham, and possibly in Bristol's fashionable Clifton suburb, rather than across the rest of this bustling commercial city. Overall, Bristol appears to have produced broad census compliance. This was partly due to the resilience of NUWSS locally – like the Priestman sisters; and partly to strength of Liberalism across the eastern industrial working-class parts of the city.[33] (Possibly in her heart Annie Kenney, one-time mill worker, knew the daunting financial risks for even lower-middle-class women to defy the law.) Certainly, the large urban area of Bristol has thrown up not only problems of inconsistencies of evidence, but also its limitations: other than the Blathwayt diaries, historians have to rely upon Monday's press interviews for what took place in interior spaces on census night itself.

Mapping patterns across the south-west more generally, it seems residential spa towns, suburbs and coastal resorts like Torquay threw up more boycotters than urban terraced streets. So it is time to head north to Manchester, where such ideas can be tested. For here a dynamic press dispatched not only reporters but also a photographer into the city's 'census lodge'.

15

Jessie Stephenson's Manchester and Hannah Mitchell's Oldham Road

Manchester remained *the* suffrage city. The population of this massive conurbation had reached one and a half million, half living in Manchester, half further out – west to Salford, south towards Cheshire, or north-east up the long Oldham Road. Here stood row upon row of red-brick terraced houses interspersed with Co-op stores; and beyond Oldham rose the Pennine slopes, dotted with large cotton mills, birthplace – and workplace – of Annie Kenney (see Map 4).

Manchester was of course the site where the 'battle for census' was fought out particularly sharply. From Manchester University had sprung Michael Sadler's stinging 'crime against science' jibe; similarly, a strong labour movement, notably the ILP and Women's Co-operative Guild, now largely supported adult suffrage. On the eve of census night, however, all the main women's suffrage organizations – NUWSS, WSPU, WFL and Men's League – remained energetically supported right across the region. The NUWSS, boasting branches in almost every small suburb, was led by suffragists like journalist Helena Swanwick, and local councillor Margaret Ashton.[1] The offices of the NUWSS and WSPU in the city centre were linked by elegant shopping arcades; meanwhile the WFL's strongholds lay in outer suburbs like Sale. Both WSPU and WFL now actively urged boycotting, and with Jessie Stephenson's arrival battle was joined, all suffrage groups appealing to local women as census night drew near.

For Jessie Stephenson, that 'Giantess of Good Sense and Kindness', elderly widow and tax resister Rose Hyland, with her spacious house in Victoria Park, remained the pivotal benefactor. And Jessie invited up to speak a glittering succession of speakers. On 10 March, Laurence Housman addressed a WSPU 'At Home' at 3 pm, chaired by Rose Hyland's sister, then spoke on 'Census Resistance' in a public hall at 8 pm. Enthusiastic audiences at both meetings expressed 'great willingness to resist and evade the Census', with several houses offered to her for Census night, and Jessie appealing for others.[2]

Another of her big meetings was addressed by Adela Pankhurst, whom Jessie liked even though she saw her as 'a blazing socialist'. Adela stayed with Jessie 'at my rooms', while the other speaker, Australian Vida Goldstein, stayed with Rose Hyland. Jessie had worked hard on publicity, and Rose brought with her to the meeting 'a large party and many, I was told, of the professorial profession' from Manchester University, though some men in the audience remained decidedly unsympathetic. Jessie remembered how she was mesmerized by Adela's oratory: 'My eyes were riveted on her. She seemed made of fire ... The whole house, I felt, was gazing enthralled at her ... the martyr in the flames ... I could not believe she was the same rather insignificant mortal who had been sitting by my fire that evening'. Afterwards, however, conversation between Jessie and Adela was prevented by 'too big a rush on' – as so often in the days plotting the boycott.[3]

Up to the last minute, Jessie urged 'all those wishing to evade the Census without incurring any penalty' to contact her, stating in *Votes for Women* that she had:

> rented a large house in Manchester and extends a cordial invitation to every woman who can help in this great protest. Guests will incur no liability whatever. The house will be open from 4 pm on Sunday April 2, to 4 pm on Monday April 3. There will be various entertainments. Sacred music, recitations, speeches, and (after 12 midnight) a whist drive will take place. Rooms will be set aside for those wishing to sleep. Please bring refreshments, rugs and cushions. Musical friends should bring their instruments. Every evader is asked to make it a solemn duty to bring at least ten women with her.

And she followed this up with publicizing a 'Census Sunday' At Home at her 'Census Lodge', the address undisclosed, still remaining mysterious.[4]

Jessie Stephenson's typescript autobiography offers one vivid portrait of WSPU census eve in Manchester, her focus being city centre and Victoria Park. Annie Kenney's memoir offers a romantic picture of growing up in a mill village beyond Oldham and then of WSPU organizing in Bristol. By contrast, Hannah Mitchell's spare and poignant autobiography, *The Hard Way Up*, presents a third and distinct picture of suffrage around Manchester.

Hannah was denied access to education as a child: her second chapter is just headed 'A Fortnight's Schoolin''. She took what jobs she could, and later with her husband Gibbon, as an active socialist, became lectures secretary of her local Labour Church and, supported by the ILP, was elected as Poor Law Guardian in Ashton. Her baby Frank was born 'after twenty-four hours of intense suffering' and Hannah, aghast at the prospect 'of bringing a second child up in poverty', determined 'to bring no more babies into the world'.[5]

Hannah joined the WSPU, speaking in towns around Manchester, even heckling Liberal cabinet ministers and being thrown out of one meeting. She spent only one night in Strangeways, however, as Gibbon arrived and, against her wishes, paid her fine. Hannah wrote memorably: 'no cause can be won between dinner and tea, and most of us who were married had to work with one hand tied behind us … Domestic unhappiness, the price many of us paid for our opinions and activities, was a very bitter thing.' Hannah became paid part-time organizer in Oldham, throwing herself into by-election campaigns.[6] But all this, combined with family responsibilities, took its toll on her health. Her nervous breakdown was, the doctor said, caused by overwork and under-feeding. Charlotte Despard sent money to ensure she got nourishment, and even visited her. For Hannah, this contrasted starkly with the Pankhursts, none of whom bothered even to write a letter of sympathy. She was deeply hurt by this and suffered bouts of depression. With no 'Suffragettes' Rest' nearby, Hannah found solace afterwards walking miles till her suicidal feelings lifted and she eventually recovered. Disillusioned, she left the WSPU.

Gradually, her interest in politics returned. She joined the WFL and indeed became one of its organizers, eventually being employed organizing in Manchester. However militancy, even in the kindlier WFL, still took its toll on her health. 'A nervous breakdown is like breaking a spring', Hannah later wrote:

> which may be mended, but never has the same resilience again … I realized that the strain of suffrage work, and militant work at that, was more than I could continue, although the pay was adequate … I loved the work too, but for me there was always more joy in voluntary service. So I gave up the full-time work, and returned to the domestic life, giving my spare time helping the WFL with such work as I was able to do … [But] my nerves were so shaken, that whenever I was in a meeting, however orderly, I found myself trembling for fear disorder would break out.[7]

Soon the Mitchells – Hannah, Gibbon and fourteen-year-old Frank – moved into a neat red-brick terraced house at Newton Heath, just inside Manchester's boundary with Ashton, half-way up the Oldham Road. Gibbon had obtained a tailoring manager job in one of the area's many Co-operative stores. This better wage was sufficient to allow Frank to remain at school, where he was doing well. Gibbon and Hannah joined Manchester's dynamic Central Branch ILP; at this time, however, it campaigned more for welfare reforms than for local MP George Kemp's upcoming suffrage bill, the ILP being disenchanted with its narrow proposals.[8] However, as her health improved, things grew easier for Hannah and:

> I almost made up my mind to live a quiet domestic life, and let others agitate for the reforms they wanted. However, … I began to attend a local debating society and I was very soon asked to open a debate on the suffrage question, in defence of the militants. This was a task after my own heart, but it led to so many requests from other organizations that I soon became fairly busy again … My chief interest was in the suffrage fight, now being waged with intense vigour.

Hannah retained some misgivings about suffragette tactics, recalling 'my most lawless act was fly-posting'; it 'needed a quick-eyed confederate to watch out for the police … A whole district would wake one morning to find … posters on every church door and PO letter box.'[9]

Her autobiography is casual about dates but gives the impression that by spring 1911 Hannah, with her Co-operative and ILP welfare loyalties, did not entertain full sympathy for Manchester's boycott plots being brewed up both by Jessie's WSPU and by the WFL.

WFL membership, strongest in the less fashionable outer suburbs of north-west and south-west Manchester, represented a range of occupations notably school teachers. Based in Sale just inside Cheshire, Mary Manning, WFL organizer for Lancashire and Cheshire, remained the key mover and shaker. She was a rather shadowy figure, throwing herself into suffrage and then like many others apparently disappearing. More is known of her scholarly father, a Missionary College tutor in Hebrew and Old Testament Studies, who had been a Unitarian minister. Mary grew up in a book-loving, play-acting family; one of three daughters, her youngest sister Ruth led a noticeably more exotic life, full of horse-drawn caravans and travelling circuses. Their father had just died, and Mary, her mother and sisters occupied the sizeable family home.[10] By now Mary could boast a strong Sale WFL branch, led by energetic Lucy Geiler, daughter of a prosperous businessman. Charlotte Despard came up to address a large audience in the local Free Library, urging the importance of the census boycott; at the end 'an eager group of women surrounded Mrs Despard to discuss ways and means of evading the Census'. Next day, Despard also spoke in Eccles and in Pendlebury, both Salford suburbs.[11] This was WFL heartland.

By March, Mary Manning was busy urging 'all men and women anxious to boycott the Census' to write to her at home, adding: 'I have a number of houses promised for Manchester', and enquiring of other branch secretaries about their local census plans. Rooted in their local communities, WFL members knew they must also confront the 'crime against science' jibe that the boycott would hamper health reforms. In Eccles for instance, branch secretary Janet Heyes spoke to a local Socialist Society on women and child-bearing, and the Urmston branch discussed a Midwives' Bill. The WFL also promoted suffrage culture. At Sale, to an overflowing meeting in WFL quarters at the Temperance Rooms, Mary Manning spoke on Shakespeare's female characters, with her sisters Ruth and Bessie reciting scenes from the plays (Ruth's *Romeo and Juliet* potion scene 'was illuminated by the most intense dramatic feeling, and created a vivid impression'); meanwhile Mary's presentation distinguished between Shakespeare's active women 'whose action moulded', and passive characters 'moulded by circumstances' – a difference unlikely to have been lost on her audience.[12]

But the direct focus was now of course the census protest itself, with joint branch meetings, plus whist drives and jumble sale to raise needed funds. In Sale, Mary now held twice-weekly committee meetings, adding 'plans for a Census "At

Home" on a large scale are in hand'. In Urmston, branch secretary Muriel Hudson reported she had 'several houses and offices promised for the night', some of which would house at least a hundred evaders, with support from local Men's League members. Eccles branch's active resisters organized whist drives and dances for the night, and even 'a Census breakfast'. 'Well done, Eccles!' pronounced *The Vote*.[13] Particularly in central Manchester, there was amicable WFL–WSPU co-operation. Rose Hyland invited WFL members to her spacious Holly Bank drawing room in Victoria Park. For the WFL Central Manchester branch, Agnes Horden worked flat out; and by census weekend, all four key WFL branches were poised to boycott, Mary issuing her final last-minute appeal for any other resisters to contact her.[14]

For the WSPU, Jessie Stephenson was similarly immersed in eve-of-census frenzy. She had moved her lodgings to be nearer her St Ann's Square office, and from here she spent her days 'tearing here and there, hardly time to eat, coming back a-hungered only to be faced with a wire [telegram] to hurry off forthwith'. So punishing was this pressure that Jessie was 'knocked up for three days on a bed of anguish, [then] up and out and at it again as soon as the flesh was – not willing, but tolerably able'.[15] Rather than WFL's dispersed local evasions, her plot centred on Rose Hyland's empty rented mansion, Denison House, Denison Road near Victoria Park. Her autobiography offers an hour-by-hour account:

> How well I remember being on the road near it [house] the day before Census [night] when a milk cart stopped, and I ordered, quite blindfold [blindly] thirty gallons of milk to be delivered there on the morrow … [even though] the house was an empty one! Anyhow it all came eventually.
>
> Great preparations, all in secret, were being made. Some were making up parties for the moors [Glossop], and no end of adventurous plans were mooted.
>
> I issued a general invitation to all women who wished to evade. We got hundreds of chairs – the house was empty – and a few tables, arranged a room for dancing – a room for cards – and so on. The day would be Sunday, but at midnight it would be Monday, and revels would begin.[16]

Jessie had already been summoned by the Chief Constable in Manchester Town Hall who outlined the legal penalties facing her. As hostess to a few hundred suffragettes, she would be liable for a £5 fine or imprisonment for each visitor, the prison sentences to be served consecutively. He remained courteous but apparently warned her that 'the sentences, in [the] case of large numbers, might mean the rest of your life in gaol'. Yet Jessie remained resolute, relieved that her invited guests would be immune from prosecution. 'It isn't nice to have a party and feel they may be imprisoned for coming.'[17]

Meanwhile, experienced WSPU organizer 'General' Flora Drummond arrived to lend ballast to Jessie's plans, while Rose Hyland supervised elaborate house preparations. Her late husband, like Linley Blathwayt, had been an army officer in India and, knowing about improvising sleeping comfort, Rose:

got her man to fill with hay endless tick mattresses, which opened down the middle and laced up. She also had glorious fires laid and lit all over [the house], looking very cosy and home-like. The large oak-panelled dining-room was ever so nice. Some of the antique furniture was still left in, one bit was an enormous ceiling-high carved oak piece opposite an immense oak fireplace. I had lovely bowls of flowers put about near the old oak, and blue grapes with muscatels in quaint vine-trimmed baskets on the long dining room [side]board.[18]

Mindful of the Chief Constable's gloomy warnings, Jessie got 'a notice typed and put very conspicuously in the hall, stating that only I was liable to imprisonment or fines and that if the police entered no one but myself could be touched'. But, she added ruefully, 'I fear some of my guests were a trifle sceptical' about this reassurance. Then at last, Jessie's 'eventful Refraining Sunday' arrived. From her lodgings, Jessie sallied 'forth to "my" house to welcome my guests'.

As hers is an hour-by-hour account of Manchester's mass evasion, it is worth pausing on Jessie's words. It was about 4 pm on Sunday when finally:

the women poured in – flocks of them with suit cases – all very pleased with the place. During the evening Mrs Hyland came. I took her round everywhere, every room swarmed [with evaders].

Engaged in some work at the Town Hall, her niece often lent us a hand but she could not do this too openly. She had offered to superintend the kitchen. I had ordered crowds of stuff in, and then appointed stewards sold [the food] at a nominal price to any desiring guests. It was catering blindfold because many brought their own grub.

I took Mrs Hyland into the kitchen. There was her niece, the 'Chef', in a cap and busy apron, very occupied and merry … When we had been all round, Mrs Hyland who was not given to over-praising people, said 'it is splendid. I am proud of you'. That was a great reward and pleased me mightily.

I asked her to say a few words to them all – and gathering them together – such crowds all through the open doors and on the stairs – and she spoke a few words to them and at a sign from me, after thanking her, they broke into a ringing cheer.

I walked back [round corner] to her house with her and had a cup of coffee, using on my return the Password to enter – 'Census Lodge'.[19]

The precise sequence of night-time events is necessarily fairly confused, especially around midnight. At some point newspaper reporters had arrived, accompanied by Robert Banks, Manchester's premier photographer.

In Figure 34, it is difficult to be certain about any of these faces. For instance, who is the monocled man on the stairs, and are the women wearing ties university students? All are dressed in their best for the occasion, including many hats and at least one fur muff.[20]

We can be more certain from what Jessie wrote in her memoirs. About eleven o'clock, her secretary informed her half-a-dozen men had arrived at the door, thought to be plain clothes police. She immediately went and spoke to them

34 (*a & b*) The staircase of 'Census Lodge', Denison House in Manchester, presumably depicting the evaders listening to Rose Hyland's speech. The photo is probably illuminated by limelight, as their expressions look startled.

'through a chained door slit' and ordered coffee to be brought to them outside. This they enjoyed, but said that '*copy* was what they wanted. They were reporters.' Eventually Jessie let in the pressmen, showed them around but gave them no chance to count how many women. They were impressed with the hay mattresses, and Jessie led them into her 'own sanctum' where 'General' Drummond 'was already sampling one.

The newspaper men did Jessie proud: their reports corroborated her later testimony. The *Manchester Courier* described 'Census Lodge' as ivy-covered, richly wainscoted, its staircase wide enough for six abreast; signs on the walls announced 'No vote no census', 'Buffet', 'Concert' and 'To the Whist Drive', while a women's suffrage banner hung conspicuously in the hall. With its garrets and cellars, an underground passage leading into the garden and access out on to the roof, it was indeed perfect evaders' premises.[21]

The outstanding *Guardian*, despite its editor's grave reservations, had of course also dispatched a correspondent to Denison House (irritatingly for C. P. Scott, near his own home). The reporter noted that entry was gained only furtively as the house stood in its own grounds with a carriage drive up to the front door:

> admission, however, was not to be had that way. A notice stated that all visitors must apply to a small side door, which proved to be round a dark corner and up a small flight of steps, which a single candle faintly illuminated. A knock caused a hurrying of feet inside. The 'sentry' on duty apparently gave a warning and someone came … to open the door on a chain. A man was a highly suspicious object, and [even] though he had the credentials of his newspaper an incautious question about the number of inmates revived but half-allayed fears, and the prompt rejoinder was 'then you are an enumerator'.[22]

Jessie had organized for suffragette scouts to guard the mansion's seven exits, with its seventeen rooms laid out with mattresses, evaders tucked away in all its rambling garrets and cellars. Just after midnight, the *Guardian* continued:

> Mrs Rose Hyland led a party from the house, which is her property, to her home [Holly Bank] a short distance away. This party was to spend the night in the rooms she had prepared for their reception. Shortly afterwards sounds of revelry (!) broke out.[23]

The reporters, Jessie recalled, 'thought the whole show extremely good fun and begged in vain to be allowed to remain all night for the revels'. However, a steely Jessie, gathering the men into her sanctum, told them she had allowed them access 'to the whole show, including our splendid kitchen', and so they should allow her to make a serious statement, for 'a nice fat paragraph'. They instantly agreed. Years later Jessie remembered the scene: 'I can see now those men all around me with their note books, the candles flickering, and Mrs Drummond gazing at me from her lowly Indian hay-bed'. Jessie then escorted them all off the premises – except one reporter (probably the *Guardian*), plus a photographer, undoubtedly Robert Banks, who were allowed to stay.

Jessie had a deal table in her den ready for the long-awaited supper. Her secretary rushed in to say it was nearly midnight and forced her to have something to eat. Flora Drummond was snoozing after her long journey, so Jessie 'tucked up the General' and flew off. 'A huge gong was to be sounded for the revels including bridge tournament to begin, shortly *after* midnight, to be sure it was really Monday, and not still the Sabbath'.

At midnight, the *Guardian* continued, the women squashed into the magnificent oak-wainscotted room:

> As many of the 'evaders' as could crowd themselves in and the others standing in the hall pledged themselves to resist the census so long as they are denied the vote. 'No vote, no census' was the cry. Afterwards, to the tune of the 'British Grenadiers', a song was sung …:
>> Then let us fill a bumper
>> And drink despair to those
>> Who call for census papers
>> And wear official clothes.
>> Oh! You want to take the census
>> And count us every man;
>> With a tow-row-row-row-row-row,
>> Then catch us if you can.[24]

With real fears about the ringleaders being arrested, the suspense was acute. If a bell rang or crunching on gravel was heard, a cry of 'the police' added to the tension. Exhausted evaders staggered off to bed in relays, collapsing on straw mattresses, instantly dropping asleep, some still clutching their hats (see Figure 35).[25]

There was not much time for sleeping. Breakfast began at 6.30. Jessie addressed 'the thronging crowds', Flora (now well slept) speaking with verve and humour. Jessie orated: 'We are living in Runnymede times again. The Conciliation Bill is our Magna Charta … Mr Asquith is King John.' Then 'all leant forward to witness' as Jessie filled in her census schedule. She recalled later that she wrote on it: 'This house is crowded with women who refuse to fill in the Census form until women are recognized as persons and have the vote'. Three cheers and singing the National Anthem followed. Immediately afterward, the enumerator called – but would not enter. So Jessie went out and delivered her schedule to him personally, reading it out to him. 'He looked pale and simply galloped off', she added. Then, when all her guests had flown – to jobs or to children – Flora and Jessie strolled round the rather neglected grounds in sunshine, 'feeling wrecks – but happy wrecks'.[26]

Jessie has proved a pretty reliable memoirist. But the schedule as she describes it appears not to have survived; instead, the available copy was in fact completed and signed by the Registrar, and merely records Jessie's name as 'Organizing

35 Manchester 'Census Lodge', sleeping evaders. The best-known of the 'sleeping evaders' photographs, this appeared in *Daily Sketch*, 4 Apr 1911, and was also made into a postcard. One evader, Mabel Capper (who had been among the original Winson Green prisoners to be forcibly fed) sent this card to her friend Nellie Hall. On the back, Mabel wrote: 'Dear Nellie, the p.c. shows one of the sleeping apartments at our Census party. Don't look for me among the sleepers. I would not dream of being photographed in so undignified a position!'[27]

Secretary WSPU'; altogether there were 156 women plus 52 men, giving an impressive total of 208. Additionally, round the corner at Rose Hyland's were a further 88 people, making central Manchester undoubtedly the largest mass evasion outside London.

So who were all the others who evaded there that night? Certainly Mabel Capper of the WSPU, already a hunger striker, probably accompanied by her mother and Men's League brother: it was she who wrote the postcard. Eva Gore-Booth and Esther Roper, suffragists defending women's labour rights, were probably present too: it was certainly very convenient for them, as they lived just round the corner. For the WFL, Manchester Central branch secretary Agnes Hordern of nearby Longsight also undoubtedly evaded at Rose Hyland's; she reported how, thanks to Rose's kindness, other branch members 'joined with great ease in the Census Protest', enjoying the luxury of beds and sleep denied the resisters in the suburbs'.[28] (See Gazetteer, pp. 342–4)

Other evaders spent the night less comfortably. The *Guardian* report continued:

a large party left Manchester for Glossop last [i.e. Sunday] night … [to] spend
the night on the moors … Others devoted the night to making a series of calls on
their friends. They went about in large companies, trusting to evade the policemen
enumerating tramps and loafers in the street, and taking care to stop nowhere long
enough to require inclusion in a census schedule.[29]

Most of these were WFL suffragettes, out and about on census night. From her
home, Mary Manning reported triumphantly how across:

Manchester and the suburbs [in] sixteen houses and offices … lurked large numbers
of resisters. The largest party gathered at Harper-hill, Sale … mothers of families,
with their children, business and professional women, all ready to put up with
temporary inconvenience [so] that they might not be party to the continuance of
unrepresentative government. 'This,' said one of our protesters, 'is the best thing
we have done; this is real revolution.'
    In the early dawn four enthusiasts stole out and [bill]posted Sale's public build-
ings with 'No Vote, No Census.' Even the police-station did not escape.[30]

Naturally Sale was proud to be *the* WFL focus. Indeed, no schedule appears to have
been filled in for Harper Hill. The enumerator's summary page merely lists for Mrs
Manning's house, twenty female occupants – Mary, her two sisters and mother,
plus other branch members (undoubtedly including the Geiler mother and
daughters), plus evaders from Urmston, three miles away. Indeed, Muriel Hudson
reported how 'on Sunday night several members of the Urmston branch walked
over to Sale and took part in the Census protest there', the daring Urmston walkers
undoubtedly including Muriel, her mother and perhaps sister. Up in Eccles, Janet
Heyes, naturally also evading, reported in *The Vote* great success on the night:

A spice of adventure was felt by the cyclists who sped at midnight through Swinton,
Pendlebury … and Eccles, posting the 'No Census' bills, and by those resisters
who, realising the resistance houses were being watched, hired a room in Eccles,
and spent the night there.

To which she added: 'From Eccles comes the story of a lady of seventy-six who
evaded the Census by walking from one daughter's house to another during the
night'.[31]

Among the hundreds of thousands of households across the region complying with
the census were of course the very many NUWSS members. Out in Knutsford,
Helena Swanwick certainly complied, as did Margaret Ashton in Withington. All
this was just as expected: WSPU and WFL members defiantly evading, NUWSS
complying. Yet certain compliant schedules are surprising: it is initially puzzling
to encounter militant suffragettes who fully complied. Two examples. The first is
Hannah Mitchell, living in her five-roomed house half-way up the Oldham Road.

36 Census schedule, Hannah Mitchell, Newton Heath, Manchester.

Hannah seemingly complied with the census requirements. Why? She was certainly very isolated from WSPU–WFL activity five miles distance down in Victoria Park, probably two tram-rides away.[32] Additionally, as an ILP member, Hannah very probably felt limited enthusiasm for such a narrow Conciliation Bill. And as a Co-op employee, Gibbon undoubtedly supported adult – not women's – suffrage

Yet reading the Mitchells' schedule is scarcely straightforward. In his carefully formed, cursive script, Gibbon had filled in his name, his wife's and son's, his occupation, plus their three birthplaces, and then signed it. However, other entries are written in crude capitals: relationship to head of family, ages, fifteen-year marriage plus one fourteen-year-old child. This is surely not the handwriting of proudly self-educated Hannah or of schoolboy Frank or of the enumerator. Had Gibbon rushed off to work before completing his schedule; did he and Hannah agree to omit some personal answers to intrusive questions; did she want to leave some defiant omissions; were the words added by a nosy neighbour? It remains a mystery. But it perhaps suggests some domestic tension, not as bitter as that of the Maunds of West Kensington, nor yet a marriage as companionate as that of the Blathwayts in Batheaston. Rather, Hannah's census schedule captured her, frozen in a moment of time, without a paid occupation, 'one hand tied behind us' – wanting Votes for Women, yet pulled different ways in spring 1911.

Finally and similarly perplexing, in Stockport why did Jennie Baines comply with the census? Jennie, an experienced itinerant WSPU organizer already imprisoned

37 Census schedule, Jennie Baines, Stockport, Cheshire.

several times (indeed one of the first hunger strikers), apparently did not refuse information to the enumerator. Her husband, George Baines, a boot-maker with a wage of about 25s, supported his wife's militancy, despite their young children. Indeed Christabel even acknowledged this, writing to Jennie to send 'best wishes, please, to Mr Baines who is making his sacrifice for the movement in sparing you'.[33] Jennie was one of the few WSPU organizers who had young children; yet Christabel often hounded her to start on the next campaign before the current one had finished: if necessary, Christabel urged, 'take your bicycle' to work up a surrounding area. Unsurprisingly given such pressure, Jennie's health suffered, with regular attacks of chorea, a nervous illness involving jerky spasms (popularly called St Vitus's dance) associated with emotional stress. However, there was no let-up from Christabel, always keen for Jennie's swift recovery so she could continue working up local pestering campaigns. As with Annie Kenney, Jennie's value to the WSPU lay in her labour credentials and ability to rouse working women.[34]

Jennie had already experienced other hardships. Two of her five children had died. By 1911, her surviving children comprised her married daughter Annie (twenty-one, 'assistant housekeeper'), plus two schoolboy sons. Annie's husband was a cotton spinner, then unemployed, and, with their toddler son, a total of seven people lived in the Baines's six-room terraced house. It was congested and money tight, Jennie and Annie having to stretch the one reliable wage seven ways.

Probably owing to recurrent illness, evidence of Jennie's life for 1910–12 is sadly scanty.[35] Questions raised are not readily answered. It seems unlikely that

Jennie's inclusion on the form was against her wish. So *why* was she willing to be counted? Was Jennie's isolation out in Stockport and the absence of neighbourly militant support networks, as with Hannah Mitchell, a factor? Was the £5 fine – four times George's wage – a sobering deterant? Did Jenny comply because, although a suffragette, she had also experienced the deaths of two of her five children? Did she feel Lloyd George's health reforms for working-class families were now a priority even over women's citizenship? Perhaps the Baineses' labour movement sympathies pulled her away from women's suffrage at this point?[36]

So, across the vast Manchester region, rich local clusters of WSPU and WFL boycotters sat amid extensive tracts of census compliance. In that sense, Manchester was not dissimilar to the south-west: here the WSPU was strong in Bath and Cheltenham, both boasting mass evasions – while the key city Bristol appeared more compliant. Across the Manchester area, boycotters sprang from a wide range of occupations, in the south-west's spa towns less so.

So how do these patterns map on to the rest of England? This requires a final journey, down the length of the country – from Teesside in the north-east, to the south coast, and finally to the Thames, back to Charlotte Despard's Battersea and John Burns's Westminster – where it all began.

16

English journey:
sweeping back down from Teesside to Thames

The diaries of Henry Nevinson and the Blathwayts, the Housmans' correspondence, plus Jessie Stephenson's autobiographical typescript and Hannah Mitchell's published memoir – such evidence is as precious as it is rare. For most local communities, there is sadly little personal testimony to supplement the census schedules themselves, and only limited press coverage. Yet we need to look more widely across England than these four case studies, to visit a more representative range of local communities. They will help investigate the boycott for its broader themes: spatial patterning and distance from London; local economic structure and occupations; experience of health inequalities, notably infant mortality. But how to penetrate additional local networks on census night? What other sources have survived; in particular, do any local branch minute books provide names and addresses of members whose schedules could then be tracked? These are sadly rare for spring 1911. In the West Riding, Huddersfield WSPU branch minutes end in February 1909, over two years earlier; and the Manchester Men's League minutes do not begin until mid-1912. Luckily however one set of local minutes for spring 1911 has survived: that of the WFL branch in Middlesbrough on Teesside.[1]

Middlesbrough lay 100 miles north-east of Manchester, beyond the North York Moors, with smaller industrial communities spreading up the Durham coast (see Map 1). The minute book reveals this northerly WFL branch as small but impressively active. Particularly dynamic were the Coates clan: Alice Schofield-Coates and her sister-in-law Marion Coates-Hanson, both married to businessmen grown prosperous on Middlesbrough's rapid industrial expansion, and both living in residential suburbs. Members such as Amy and Lottie Mahony were school teachers; Winifred Jones was a head-teacher; others occupations included a cashier in the local Co-op, and a self-employed insurance agent's wife. The branch was committed to improving health provision; and,

38 Census schedule, the Mahony family, Middlesbrough on Teesside, North Riding.

like the Sale branch, it was culturally creative, with discussion on Ibsen and on 'Rossetti's women'.[2]

So it is no surprise that at New Year, Middlesbrough was quick off the mark with its census campaign: a WFL speaker travelled up from London and a local census agent was appointed. Soon however members' apprehension grew: the minutes record that, 'as this matter [boycott] was new to the majority' of members, it was agreed that the secretary write 'for further particulars as we should like to know what risks we ran'.[3] In a predominantly working-class community, for members on meagre wages or school teachers employed by the local authority, anxieties already loomed. Margaret Nevinson came up to address a meeting in the local Co-operative Hall chaired by Winifred Jones. Margaret pressed her pro-boycott 'battle for the census' arguments, proclaiming that: 'Women have been urged not to take this step in the cause of science. Well, we may all love science, but we all love liberty a great deal better, and science must go.' The boycott was however scathingly derided by the local press as 'the action of a spoiled child'.[4]

Indeed, on census night itself, it is hard to find local WFL members who did boycott, other than the two Coates sisters-in-law: both of their husbands confidently inscribed defiant statements on behalf of 'the female residents in this house'. For others, running the risk of a £5 fine seemed to have been sobering. Even Winifred Jones the head-teacher complied. So did highly active members Amy and Lottie Mahony. As with other surprise compliers, it is hard to identify personal motives – whether it was because they were both teachers in local authority schools and so might well entertainment economic fears about their employer; because three of their siblings had died; because their father, local Co-operative hall-keeper, was probably an adult suffragist; or because the price of living in a tightly knit local community was that both the enumerator and registrar were likely to know their family.[5] As with Jennie Baines, it was probably a mix of all these factors, a question returned to in Chapter 19.

Teesside's census night experience was of New Year's high expectations seemingly dashed upon the rocks of daily realities. So how representative was this pattern in other industrial communities across the north? As might be expected in the Lancashire cotton towns, where radical suffragists like Selina Cooper were active in the NUWSS, compliance was widespread. But elsewhere, on the eastern Pennines flank, across vast Yorkshire, were boycotts well-supported, and if so where?

In Bradford, 60 miles south of Teesside, the WSPU had positioned one of its most experienced organizers, Mary Phillips; she compered an impressive mass evasion in the WSPU's city-centre office. As in Manchester, the local paper had apparently dispatched a pair of keen reporters, who provided a vivid account in Monday's paper. It was headlined 'Suffragists "Night Out" – Revelry at "The Vote" Shop', and sub-headed 'With the Suffragettes – A Night at Headquarters – "Telling Fortunes", Whist & Patience':

> It was the witching hour of a quarter past one when we approached the headquarters of the Bradford branch of the WSPU, situated in Manningham Lane. The Lane itself at that hour was [a] scene of loneliness, long drawn out … There was no one about, not even a policeman. The Votes for Women shop was in darkness – a blind and desolate frontage. The door was securely locked. We stepped back and looked up. There were signs of life at last: a lighted window, inscrutably veiled by a blind …
>
> There, faintly heard, came … sounds of merriment immured and muffled. Naturally, we wanted to get in closer communication than that – for professional, of course, rather than personal reasons. But how to do it? …
>
> Suddenly the dark silence of the shop below was thrilled by a telephone call … At length, steps were heard descending. When it seemed the call was over, we ventured to knock gently. There was a pause, and then 'Who's that?' came a voice, not frightened of course (remember, these were suffragettes) …
>
> 'What do you want?' it further asked. The door blind was pulled aside, revealing the features of Miss Mary Phillips, the local organizer …
>
> 'It's only the Press', said we, 'and we want to know all about it'. The door was unlatched and grudgingly half-opened … Sounds of sociability; feminine voices simultaneously speaking …
>
> 'We're having a fine time,' said Miss Phillips … Some, we were told, were fast asleep … Possibly Mr Asquith haunted their slumbers hideously … The rest amused themselves … with cards, with whist … One pictures them at Bridge, using the Census schedule as scoring sheet …
>
> Miss Phillips told us … some walked to Ilkley, but not … over the moors. They

chose the road way, because it was so dark a night … A number of rebels also walked from Ilkley, whither they had proceeded by train during Sunday.

This [Monday] morning … a Census paper was fixed in window of the 'Votes' shop … 'No Vote, No Census', and a somewhat lengthy prophesy … that posterity would know how to judge the Government for thus falsifying the Census returns.[6]

An enticing night-time challenge for a couple of cub reporters, filing an account that was both evocatively witty yet sympathetic. Mary's own schedule had an uncompromising statement right across it: 'Posterity will know how to judge this Government if it persists in bringing about the falsification of national statistics instead of acting on its own principle & making itself truly representative of the people'. The enumerator guessed at ten females present, and this suggests that the presence of a confident organizer could be crucial. Mary also worked in neighbouring Leeds; although this was a larger city, there were about a dozen boycotters.

Elsewhere in Yorkshire, it also was patchy, with possibly no boycotters at all in the port of Hull. Meanwhile, in the Pennine textile town of Huddersfield, the WSPU minutes, though ending two years earlier, do record names and addresses of members. Given this was a very stable community, it is therefore possible to track down schedules. Of previously active branch members, it is hard to identify a single one who boycotted. Why? Probably most pressing were financial fears, given modest textile wages. Yet even Bertha Lowenthal, an unusually prosperous supporter whose name was given in *Votes for Women* as the local contact, complied with the census.[7] And Edith Key, WSPU branch secretary who remained an active suffragette, complied. Given the number of Huddersfield suffragettes who had earlier risked imprisonment, there is by 1911 a distinct sense of diminuendo, the branch apparently having dwindled away two years earlier.[8]

A further 30 miles south in Sheffield there is however a different picture. WSPU regional organizer Adela Pankhurst still shared the house with Helen Archdale, experienced suffragette who was married with children. Together Helen and Adela master-minded Sheffield's mass evasion in their own home. Adela's census night experiences had much in common with Jessie Stephenson's: a central WSPU evasion plus smaller WFL boycotts around the city. And, as with Jessie's 'Census Lodge' and Mary Phillips's evasion in Bradford, a reporter made his way on census night to 'the House of Conspiracy' to record Helen and Adela's activities. Hugging Sheffield's deepest shadows, he was eventually admitted – to a room 'packed with ladies':

'I thought you were a policeman', said the young lady as she ushered me in. 'We were hoping for a police raid. Never mind, you can join in the chorus. We're wanting someone to take the bass part.'

… 'Political charades,' said someone. 'Excuse me,' said the dark young lady … 'We want to know if you'll take the part of Mr Asquith.'

39 Census schedule, Adela Pankhurst and Helen Archdale, Sheffield.

> … It was the merriest of parties … I tip-toe out to find some coffee. The door of the Day Nursery is open, and the floor is crowded with sleepers, fully dressed … Their faces are white and drawn with weariness.[9]

This English journey then proceeds 30 miles further south, to the industrial Midlands, to revisit Nottingham, Helen Watts's home town. As we know, Helen herself was away, boarding with her schoolmaster brother near Bath – and she complied with the census. Back at Lenton Vicarage, her family also duly completed their schedule, recording the Reverend Alan Watts, his wife Ethelinda, four of their children, plus a cook and housemaid. One of Helen's sister was a school teacher employed by Nottingham council, while another sister's occupation was given as 'Secretary Suffragists Society' – her father making it clear that she, like himself, was a constitutional suffragist, not a militant suffragette. Elsewhere in Nottingham, however, WSPU members – like May Burgis – did indeed boycott. There were possibly at least a dozen evaders, all vanishing for the vote. They had decided 'to make up private parties, arranging that the head of the establishment [household] should give an incomplete return,' but, the local paper suggested, with 'not more than a score of so' evaders.[10] Certainly, the impression gained is that the local WSPU had hunkered down as a small yet strongly committed suffragette group, amid a wide sea of Nottinghamshire compliance.

To the south-west, among the industrial Black Country's furnaces, foundries and iron works, the boycott also found some support. In West Bromwich, local WSPU members warmed up towards census night by performing a sketch entitled *How Cranston was converted to Militant Tactics and Boycotted the Census*.[11] One of the most active households locally was the Brockhouses. Their much scribbled schedule records Henry Brockhouse, a well-to-do iron industry businessman (see Figure 1). His wife, WSPU secretary, is mysteriously missing, possibly taking one of her daughters with her to evade on census night.

In nearby Wolverhampton, Emma Sproson, wife of ILP postman Frank, lived with their three children in a modest semi-detached villa. Emma is hard to track in early 1911: though nominally a national figure, she may have grown slightly distanced from the WFL.[12] What is interesting about Emma is that, other than Margaret Nevinson's briefly impersonal account, she wrote one of the few WFL memoirs of census night and was the only working-class woman ('a child from the lower depths') who subsequently recorded *her* recollections of that night:

> When the census was taken, it was not a true census owing to our policy. We decided that as women did not count in the state, they should not be counted. We packed numbers of women in places w[h]ere they would not be counted … and in my own case after my husband had filled up the paper [schedule] I took it out of the envelope and cut out all the females that slept in our house that night; in due course the collector [enumerator] called for the form. I handed him the paper and he took it out of the envelope, after looking at it he said with amazement 'what does this mean?' 'I have nothing to say on the matter' I said 'except that as women do not count in the state I do not see why they should be counted. Good day', and closed the door … This was a serious breach of the law.[13]

Unfortunately, this later account of census night bears little relationship to Emma's schedule, now accessible. Apart from occupation or birthplace not being recorded for Emma, it is perfectly compliant with no signs whatsoever of any unlawful snipping. Perhaps Emma's memory had played tricks over the intervening years, and she remembered what she would have *liked* to have done on census night: invite other local suffragettes for a sleep-over. But in April 1911, did the Sprosons' ILP preference for adult suffrage strongly shape their behaviour? Yet, unlike Hannah Mitchell's schedule, there is no hint of domestic discord. Across Wolverhampton generally there were indeed very few who were prepared to evade.[14]

This English journey continues southwards, first to visit Ipswich on a south Suffolk estuary. Music teacher Constance Andrews had continued to channel her considerable energies into the local WFL branch, stimulating outlying rural communities like Hadleigh and the seaside resort of Felixstowe. Certainly, come census night, Constance was kept busy. She lived with her sister and brother-in-law George Pratt in a spacious house; and on his schedule George recorded himself (married, teacher of music) and his two sons. He signed it, but it was left to the enumerator to add below: 'there were two female Suffragists in this family who went to some place unknown for the night. The female servant went with them.' Had he waited he could have read that this 'place' was indeed in the town centre, for Constance impishly provided full details to the local press:

> As a protest against the Government's attitude, we thought that a sleepless night would be a small trial, but our vigil turned out to be a real joy on account of the large numbers of talented people who gave their services. The first arrivals at the Old Museum Rooms, the 'storm centre' of the Ipswich movement, were from Felixstowe. They came about six o'clock, and others from Hadleigh and elsewhere, but chiefly Ipswich comrades, kept arriving up till midnight, when we had a good muster.
>
> Our commissariat department was well organized, and, though only for one night's siege, no detail was left out …
>
> After supper we assumed various disguises in case of intruders appearing. Some of the younger members of the party looked very ancient, and some others more youthful than usual. Hiding places were arranged in case of any official appearing. Speeches and songs were now the rule, and we all began to enter with zest into the spirit of the thing …
>
> There was an agreeable diversion in the shape of some ghost stories … Some of the younger members of the party gave a capital exhibition of physical drill, which was much applauded.
>
> People began to leave to catch trains and go to work quite early, and after breakfast there was a gradual dispersal.[15]

Constance's press report is corroborated by the enumerator's summary sheet for Ipswich's Old Museum Rooms, which does indeed record five men and sixteen women, totalling twenty-one 'Suffragettes'. Overall across East Anglia, the nearer a community was to London, the greater was the number of boycotters.

On the Hampshire coast, Portsmouth was dominated by its Royal Dock Yard and barracks, naval occupations predominating. Nearby was the holiday resort of Southsea, with its piers and elegant Esplanade. Portsmouth might appear unpropitious suffrage territory; but all three groups – NUWSS, WSPU and WFL – turned the area into a vibrant suffrage hub. Dynamic organizers inveigled national headline stars down to speak, boosting local membership.

Three stand out particularly vividly. WSPU organizer was Charlotte Marsh, one of the first suffragettes to be forcibly fed. Charlotte arrived in Southsea for a WSPU holiday campaign in September 1910 and remained as popular Portsmouth organizer for eighteen months. She was described laconically in the local paper as 'a quite young lady and of attractive appearance'. Charlotte visited Batheaston in early March 1911, Emily Blathwayt writing in her diary: 'Miss Marsh planted her tree … All her friends call her Charlie … We liked very much what we saw of her. She is very fair with light hair and a pretty face.'[16] In the weeks before the census, Charlie had Emmeline Pankhurst down to speak and

40 Charlotte Marsh, 1911.

organized a poster parade in Southsea, yet still found time for house-to-house canvassing.[17]

Second was dynamic Norah O'Shea, commanding the NUWSS. Living outside Portsmouth on a private income, 'red-haired rebel' Norah and her sister Margaret shared their mis-named 'Cottage' with its fourteen rooms. It was stately Margaret who wrote the words of the rousing suffrage song: 'Forwards, brave & dauntless / Daughters of this earth, Let your dormant talents / Spring to glorious birth'.[18]

For the WFL, sadly far less is known about branch secretary Sarah Whetton. She lived with her civil servant husband and children in lower-middle-class Southsea respectability. Her active members clustered nearby, notably a Mary Mottershall who lodged with a retired army officer by the seafront. Plans were hatched for persuading WFL supporters to boycott, with regular meetings at Mary Mottershall's and 'promises' obtained. To urge more boycotters, Sarah had down Charlotte Despard, who 'spoke in her usual eloquent manner on the Census protest', with evaders recruited for census night.[19]

Soon both the WSPU and WFL publicized their boycott plans in the local paper. Charlie Marsh was emphatic about the WSPU's steps 'to vanquish the enumerator'; Portsmouth might not be able to 'imitate the suffragette Bohemianism of London', but many heads of families would agree to be absent from home on census night, finding their homes 'occupied by strangers who are suffragettes'.[20] Equally optimistic, Sarah Whetton boasted to a reporter that nearly a hundred WFL supporters would evade, sounding debonair about plans 'to completely vanquish the enumerators'.

All this suffragette braggadocio naturally provoked angry correspondence in the press. One anti-suffrage letter stated that assembling like this 'for a kind of orgie [orgy]' merely offered 'up-to-date proof of the folly of giving them a vote'.

Unusually, an adult suffragist wrote in, arguing, not unreasonably, that if women could resist the census, what about unenfranchised men living in low-rent flats or rooms? Norah O'Shea retaliated: 'in spite of many and repeated invitations the Suffragist fly has not yet agreed to walk into the parlour of the adult suffragist spider!'[21] One boycotter pointed out that census resisters merely asserted 'that we are not recognized as citizens, and until we are recognised as such [we] do not intend to fulfil the duties of citizenship'. 'Battle for the census' arguments continued to rage.

To finesse their plots, Charlie Marsh hired not only St James's Hall in Portsmouth town centre, but also an empty shop in the elegant shopping arcade nearby.[22] She announced she was 'arranging a muster of Suffragists [suffragettes]' at the hall, with a reading of Ibsen's play *Ghosts* given by a theatrical company. And Sarah Whetton held a final meeting at Mary Mottershall's for gingering up boycotters: a room had been secured for evaders to spend the night, its location kept mysterious.[23]

Afterwards, a local reporter interviewed the ring-leaders. Charlie Marsh sounded jubilant. 'Possibly we have been counted, for there were two policemen standing at the door, but they have no particulars.' Her WSPU evaders had 'met at an empty shop in the Arcade from nine to ten last night, and proceeded in detachments to St James's Hall'. Here the theatre company read Ibsen's banned *Ghosts*, so that 'we were evading the Censor as well as the Census', Charlie added with a triumphant smile. They then went back to the Arcade: here the reporter noticed a spirit lamp, a copper kettle, portions of a cake, indeed 'signs of an enjoyable, if not sumptuous, repast', with make-shift curtains 'to baffle any keyhole-pryer'. Charlie told how some evaders 'went to sleep on chairs or wrapped in rugs on the floor, but the greater number of the sixty or seventy ladies we had here passed the night laughing and talking'. She remained defiant. (However, police informed the paper that constables stationed outside St James's Hall had 'carefully counted the audience' entering and leaving the hall, and counted them for a third time when they entered the empty Arcade shop.)

Meanwhile, Sarah Whetton also pronounced the local WFL 'well satisfied with what we have done'. She said a member had opened her house 'from 9 o'clock in the evening, and between that hour and midnight, they came in in twos and threes, so that no suspicion was excited'. WFL members had been provided with sleeping accommodation, evaders taking turns resting, while others played cards. Next morning, Sarah added, some evaders (often school teachers) had to hurry back to work, others being careful not to return home before noon. She reported herself 'pleased and surprised at the large number that responded'. So who was her mystery hostess? Sadly, the name of this WFL member remains elusive, a 'known unknown'.[24]

Indeed, a century later, most of Portsmouth's evaders remain just shadowy figures. But we do now know that Charlie Marsh's 'sixty or seventy ladies' turn out to be in fact fifty-two evaders: thirty-nine female, thirteen male. Exactly who boycotted with her remains shrouded in mystery. Not least because many known WSPU members apparently complied, leaving us with dozens of evaders who, vanishing for the vote, also vanished from history.[25]

Sarah Whetton's own schedule, signed by her civil servant husband, records her as absent too. More intriguingly, who were her other evaders? They too remain shrouded in mystery. Sarah had been conspiratorial about the exact location of the evasion, merely offering 'thanks due to the member who kindly opened her house to us. We completely mystified the authorities as to our whereabouts and numbers, although they were on the look-out for us.'[26] The smart money is on Mary Mottershall. She lived in a sizeable house, conveniently away from town-centre spying eyes. Perhaps her seventy-one-year-old landlord was prepared to turn a blind eye to overnight visitors at his house, and to state on his schedule that his nine rooms 'at present are empty'. Would a retired soldier returned from India, perhaps with no liking for the new-fangled Liberal government, collude with suffragettes, as other retired military officers did? Certainly, the WFL boasted that its evaders had completely evaded police vigilance. (See Gazetteer, pp. 313–15)

Rebellious Norah O'Shea and her sister Margaret, despite NUWSS directives, completed their census schedule but then added a most defiant statement: 'We have filled in this paper under protest because Women should vote for Members of Parliament, Margaret O'Shea, Norah O'Shea'. This puts the two sisters in a tiny minority among suffragists.

So Portsmouth remains an intriguing enigma. There were two sizeable evasions, yet few names. Who were these women of mystery? What is certain is the crucial role played by the three charismatic organizers: Charlie Marsh, Sarah Whetton and Norah O'Shea. Theirs were three distinct boycott strategies. Two NUWSS dowagers comply, but remain decidedly defiant. The WFL, undoubtedly in darkened Southsea, kept its secrets, thanks to Sarah Whetton. The WSPU's town-centre mass evasion achieved publicity, but evaders got counted – three times. Elsewhere across Hampshire (e.g. in Southampton), other boycotters are hard to find. Given Portsmouth's suffragettes' isolation, their numbers and creative spirit are the more remarkable.

Finally, this English journey meanders back down the Thames, from its source in the Cotswolds, past Oxford, destination of the first NUWSS caravan and still largely a suffragist stronghold. Below Reading, certain well-to-do suffragettes fleeing congested London had country retreats. Near Marlow, Mary Sargant Florence, designer of the WTRL census postcards, now inscribed across her schedule at a defiant angle 'NO VOTE NO CENSUS'. Downstream, 'Black Friday' veteran and tax resister Princess Duleep Singh had a grace-and-favour house at Hampton Court: her sparse schedule signed by the registrar, tersely

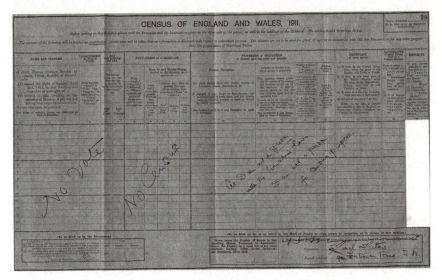

41 Census schedule, Muriel Matters, Lambeth, London.

noted 'Best Information obtainable'. Further downriver stood the gypsy caravans Henry Nevinson had spotted, 'driven by women, who whispered me the names of woodland regions not very far off in Surrey', before vanishing silently down the road. And indeed, the front page of the *Daily Sketch* was devoted to photographs taken on darkened Wimbledon Common near Putney Bridge at 2.30 am; visible are three parked caravans and at least ten chilly evaders (see Figure 42).[27]

At last, the journey returns to central London again. On one side of the Thames lies Chelsea, on the other Battersea. Here Charlotte Despard had provided her name but, of course, otherwise had resisted: her schedule, signed by the registrar, merely notes 'Refused further information – a Suffragette'. Not far away, Muriel Matters, the original Australian WFL vanner and distinctive balloonist, lived in lodgings with Violet Tillard. She inscribed her schedule particularly defiantly.[28]

Across Lambeth Bridge lay Westminster and Whitehall: here John Burns completed *his* schedule at his LGB desk. And Emily Wilding Davison left her Bloomsbury boarding house and hid here in her crypt cupboard behind Westminster's forbidding doors. Till Monday, with its daily newspapers – read by public, by politicians and by civil servants alike, as they made their way back for the start of another working week.

PART IV

The census and beyond

17

After census night:
Clemence's resistance, Asquith's betrayal

On Monday 3 April, enumerators collected in their schedules and reported to their Registrars. So it might seem precipitate for the press to report on the boycott. Yet newspaper readers expected *something* on the census to read at their breakfast tables and on their tube journeys to work. The press obliged, the tabloids reluctant to waste any exciting photo opportunity. Monday's *Daily Mirror* front page was devoted to census night over the headline: 'Numbering the Nation: Suffragettes suffer great discomfort to avoid being included in the population returns'. A photograph depicted a respectable kitchen table, husband in shirtsleeves, pen poised to complete his schedule, surrounded by wife and small children. Below were images of uncomfortable evaders huddled under blankets. Tuesday's *Daily Sketch* ran a similar page: 'Tired, but not beaten – more Suffrage-Census Martyrs', showing slumbering bodies inside Denison House, Manchester. One photo was taken inside Aldwych rink, another interior showed 'resisters' playing bridge; its front page was reserved for the Wimbledon caravans.[1]

While photographs in the tabloids fed public fascination, it was however the broadsheets that carried clout with the political elite. When civil servants like Archer Bellingham commuted in from Wimbledon, their newspaper of choice was *The Times*. Such papers, mindful of fears about inaccurate data, tended to downplay the boycott as insignificant, headlining the smooth running of the census enumeration. Indeed, Tuesday's *Times* editorialized 'The Census: Failure of Suffragist Efforts at Evasion'.[2]

By Wednesday morning, there were still no stories of any suffragette arrests – however ingenious their evasion, however defiant their resistance. Hours ticked past. Would there be no summonses, no court appearances? Given the legal proceedings against women tax resisters, surely the government would never let suffragettes get off scot free with flouting the law? After all, Jessie Stephenson had been summoned and warned by Manchester's Chief Constable. Up and down

42 *Daily Sketch*, Tuesday 4 Apr 1911; Wimbledon Common, 2.30 am, depicting three caravans and at least ten chilly evaders.

the country, suffragettes waited anxiously: if required, would some pay their £5 fine and be done with it; would others, for the sake of principle and publicity, endure imprisonment? At the WSPU and WFL headquarters, with weekly press deadlines looming, they waited for news. It was a tense couple of days, watching to see how the government would respond.

Then at last, on Wednesday afternoon at 2.45 pm, John Burns stood up in the Commons to make his ministerial statement. Asked 'whether the suffragette agitation against the Census is likely to affect prejudicially the accuracy of our statistics', Burns pronounced on behalf of the government. What did he say?

By Wednesday, the government's attention, including that of Burns, had swung right back to its primary concern: welfare reform, notably the Insurance Bill. Burns's diary records that on Monday, he had 'a long conference with Chancellor at Treasury. Criticized [Insurance] Scheme. Suggested improvements with which in the main he agreed.' Tuesday was similar, the census already overshadowed:

Wednesday 5 – 9am Insurance Bill Cabinet. Sat (in) Cabinet L.G[eorge] paid us a great tribute for help suggestions and criticisms … House of Commons. Questions on Census. Housing etc. Amusing reply. Back to Treasury for 2 hrs with L.G.[3]

So what lay behind Burns's 'amusing reply'? Unbeknownst to the suffragettes, Burns had come to a gentlemen's agreement with the Home Secretary. On 28 March, Burns had written to Winston Churchill. This LGB letter, doubtless drafted by a civil servant, is worth quoting as its pragmatism is so revealing:

Dear Churchill

No doubt you have noticed that the militant suffragists are endeavouring to defeat the Census which is to be taken on Sunday evening next. It appears that in London the [Aldwych rink], the Gardenia restaurant and some large private houses are to be occupied for the night by women who wish to be omitted from the count and who would refuse to give the full information required for the purpose of the Census schedule.

The Registrar-General who is responsible for the Census does not propose to force matters unduly and will be satisfied if he can obtain an estimate of the number of persons who congregate in the buildings referred to, but he is very anxious that the enumerators should receive all possible assistance in their task from the Metropolitan Police …

Seeing that the organisers of the movement are engaged in a deliberate attempt to set the law at defiance, I think that you will agree with me that the police in London should render every assistance to the Registrar-General and to his enumerators and I should be obliged if you could arrange that this should be done. A rough enumeration of the persons gathering in the selected building is all that is desired.

I may add that if this plan of countering the movement can be made a success, the necessity of prosecuting any large number of persons in default may be obviated and the main object of the suffragists may thus be defeated.

Yours sincerely

John Burns.[4]

Here then is the LGB's position on the suffragette boycott stated baldly. The primary census aim remained obtaining accurate statistic data, or at least 'a rough enumeration' of people in each building on census night. Police co-operation was clearly crucial. Was this the Edwardian state being astute? Burns professed to care little for suffragette infringements: if reliable data was collected, then there was little need to prosecute 'any large number of persons in default'. So, even beforehand, the LGB seemingly felt confident that suffragettes would not succeed in undermining statistical totals. Subsequently, perhaps on Tuesday, registrars would have contacted the LGB with information on the rough size of local boycotts (plus any other problems), with official relief conveyed to the minister.

And so on Wednesday, responding to the question of 'whether the suffragette agitation against the Census is likely to affect prejudicially the accuracy of our statistics' Burns could indeed offer his unperturbed ministerial reply:

I do not anticipate that the suffragette agitation against the Census will have any appreciable effect upon the accuracy of the statistics of population. (Cheers) According to the information that has reached me up to the present, the number of individuals who have evaded being enumerated is altogether negligible. (Cheers)[5]

He was then pressed by Labour MP J. R. Clynes: 'is it intended to take proceedings against those who deliberately evaded the Census?' Burns's urbane response was both airily patrician and succinct – 'In the hour of success mercy and magnanimity must be shown', which was greeted by MPs with cheers and laughter.

The remainder of the Commons' census questions continued along more conventional lines. Burns stated that he hoped the population totals (including male and female) would be published in June. One MP persisted, enquiring: 'whether any special difficulties have been experienced in taking the Census; whether the population ... have co-operated willingly in filling in the Census schedules; and whether ... the results of the 1911 Census will show increased accuracy and reliability?' Burns still remained unruffled: 'So far as I have learned at present there have been no special difficulties experienced ... and I hope that the results will be certainly not less accurate and reliable than those of preceding Censuses'. This put pay to further MPs' questions – allowing Burns to answer more routine questions on health visitors and motorcar speeds.[6]

When Burns's statement about not prosecuting reached suffragette headquarters, it was received with relief and joy. Surely this ministerial 'magnanimity' spelled a resounding victory over the government? The *Votes for Women* front page reported triumphantly: 'the Census protest has been a great and unqualified success'; it demonstrated 'the impotence of the authorities in the face of determined resistance [by women] to government without their consent'. The exact number of evaders would never be accurately known, but from reports the paper had received 'the number was far larger than anything anticipated by the authorities'. Prosecutions would thus have turned 'every police court in the country into a pulpit, from which a sermon would be preached on the subject of Votes for Women'. Faced by two undesirable alternatives, the government had opted for the lesser of the two evils and climbed down, completely beaten by the suffragettes – however much Burns puffed out his chest.[7] *Votes for Women* hammered home Burns's 'mercy and magnanimity' climb down: 'the moral of it all is that victory lies near at hand': just 'one more deputation' was needed finally to convince the government of the futility of resisting further women's citizenship demands.[8]

The *Vote* reports were similar, if less triumphant: the WFL could 'congratulate itself on having initiated and on being largely responsible for the carrying through of the most effective protest yet made by women against government without consent ... The 1911 census has been made memorable by the organized revolt of women.' 'In the Hour of Success', Charlotte Despard mocked her old Battersea adversary, proclaiming:

> Mr John Burns *dare* not allow the record of those who refused to register themselves in the Census of 1911 to be published. That is his mercy and magnanimity. 'For heavens sake,' I can hear him whisper, 'keep quiet! Assume that all is well and it will be well'.[9]

Suffragette organizations were now confident there would be no prosecutions to prepare for, no fines to pay. As with any campaign, it was crucial to avoid any sense of anti-climax, to bounce back. With schedules whisked away by civil servants, the census had become yesterday's news. Suffragettes moved on to the next significant event. On 5 May, Sir George Kemp introduced the Conciliation Bill in the Commons: here it resoundingly triumphed with 255 votes for and a mere 88 against. (However, many Liberals who voted for it believed it was too narrow to go further without more democratic amendments. And both front benches were virtually empty; yet it was crucial the government grant facilities to the bill. Brailsford urged the NUWSS to cajole Lloyd George in particular, and wrote to Fawcett: 'I think the insurance scheme is the golden opportunity. The moment he thinks he can be the hero of the women of England our Bill will pass.')[10]

Buoyed up by Kemp's success and keen not to lose momentum, suffrage organizations quickly immersed themselves in staging the *next* spectacle: the Women's Coronation procession on Saturday 17 June. The WFL, headed by Charlotte Despard, marched seven abreast; they were followed by WFL's new 'Census Protest Banner'.[11] The WSPU was similarly strongly represented, the NUWSS agreed to participate and even Pippa Strachey's LSWS came round. In all, forty thousand women marched together, constitutionalists and militants alike, joined in a spirit of optimistic and determined co-operation.[12] Rather than the recent 'battle for the census' differences, this surely confirms the combined strength of the suffrage movement in the summer of 1911. The movement could roll forwards optimistically.

For John Burns's civil servants, however, their work had only just begun. On Friday 7 April, letters were sent out to individual census dissidents: Archer Bellingham wrote to Trowbridge, chasing up Lillian Dove-Willcox.[13] By Saturday 8 April, enumerators had to deliver in person to their Registrars all schedules and paperwork. The final meetings of the Census Committee were held on 26 and 27 April. Present were Bernard Mallet, Thomas Stevenson and Archer Bellingham. They discussed population figures, revealing some obvious sensitivity about exactly how to present the 1911 ratio of males to females compared to earlier censuses.[14] These methodical civil servants kept Burns informed – as his diary for May records:

> Tuesday 23 … Back to H of C at 7 to get Census figures …
> Wednesday 24 … Saw to publication of Census Figures.
> Thursday 25 – LGB – many callers about Census … Census Figures well received [–] not the least leakage from anywhere. Somerset House done well. Wrote Mallet and officers.[15]

On 10 June, the *Preliminary Report* giving population totals was signed by Mallet, Stevenson and Waters, with Archer Bellingham as Secretary, and thanked the press, TUC and school teachers for their 'special Census lessons'. It noted an increase of population (11 per cent since 1901), confirming the rapidly growing suburbs outside London, now over seven million people.[16] Moreover, as its first table carefully showed, there was no significant change in the female–male ratio: indeed 'Sex Proportions' since 1901 remained unchanged at 1,068 women per 1,000 males – undoubtedly to the LGB's unspoken relief.[17] In other words, in Burns's phrase, any under-enumeration of women was 'altogether negligible'. Thus, when asked for the 1911 population total of males and females in the United Kingdom, Burns could comfortably reply: 45.2 million, 21.9 million male and 23.3 million female.[18] By the autumn, with the boycott largely forgotten, the daunting task of analysing the mass of information continued routinely: data, no longer laboriously copied, were mechanically sorted by the new card-punching-machines, as Burns's visit confirms:

> [Nov] Friday 10 ... To Census Office ... where men girls and boys were tabulating by machines and other devices the figures of the Census. Secured a Card as illustrative of the process ... B. Mallet Reg General called to report progress.[19]

Meanwhile, at the Treasury negotiations progressed the National Insurance Bill. On 5 April, Lloyd George put his proposals to the Cabinet: weekly contributions from employees would be supplemented by employers and the state – hence the slogan 'ninepence for fourpence' (even if the prospect of licking an insurance 'stamp' was both welcomed and derided). The Bill was introduced into the Commons on 4 May, to widespread praise for the scheme, despite continuing opposition from doctors. Alongside, the constitutional crisis rumbled on: Liberal government reforms stymied by House of Lords obstinacy. In July, Asquith requested the King to threaten the Lords with the creation of new peers. Thus the Parliament Bill was eventually passed in August. Lloyd George was nearer achieving his long-awaited National Insurance Bill.

Suffrage campaigners maintained other priorities that summer. After the resounding success of John Burns's census climb down and no prosecutions, plus Kemp's Bill and the impressive Coronation Procession, the political landscape seemed to look promising. It was an inspiring time for those committed to non-violent civil disobedience. Rather than tracking the story of the larger suffrage organizations, here we follow a less familiar narrative, to the beat of John Hampden's drum.

Individual tax resisters felt distinctly optimistic. Within days of Burns's 'mercy and magnanimity' statement, they began to stage high-profile protests. After all, if the government did not prosecute census evaders, might it now not take a more lenient line on tax resistance? With their growing sense of injustice, many of these otherwise quiet women found imaginative ways to stage their rebellion. In Buckinghamshire, one sale of resisters' goods was held in the ancient inn standing

43 Constance Andrews on her release from prison, accompanied by Charlotte Despard, 27 May 1911.

when Hampden represented Wendover in Parliament. Margaret Kineton Parkes spoke to a very sympathetic audience, proud to remember that Hampden's 'work of resistance was done in their own neighbourhood'. At another sale in a west London auction room, the large Hampden banner fluttered, then a procession marched to Hyde Park for a Protest Meeting. A gold watch seized from Dr Elizabeth Wilks, WTRL treasurer, was auctioned in Hackney, again with the Hampden banner unfurled. So iconic was his precedent that the WTRL even ran a caravan for a fortnight in July 'for a campaign in the John Hampden county'. Muriel Matters, who had shifted her allegiances from WFL to the WTRL, was the organizer and set off accompanied by Violet Tillard. In Buckinghamshire they successfully ran meetings in Great Missenden, Wendover and nearby towns, WTRL congratulating their 'very excellent work for The Cause'.[20]

Two tax resistance cases stand out particularly, both springing from census boycotters: Clemence Housman and Constance Andrews. In Ipswich, Constance had purposely bought a dog, refused to pay the licence and was charged on 20 April at the local county court with keeping it without a licence. Her defence was, of course, no taxation without representation. Constance refused to pay her fine, and smilingly proclaimed 'they have not got me yet'. Indeed, she had made her goods over to her sister so that the officers would have no choice but to imprison her. A warrant was issued for her arrest and eventually, on 20 May in the local Mechanics' Institute library, she felt a hand touch her shoulder: it was a policeman who took her straight off to prison. Constance spent seven days in Ipswich gaol.[21]

Constance was released on 27 May to rapturous welcome celebrating Ipswich's own suffrage martyr. A great crowd assembled outside the prison gates, and Constance was taken in triumph with Charlotte Despard in an open cab. Quite remarkably, one girl, a twenty-year-old tailoress, could remember 'that May morning 74 year ago', and the vivid impression dignified Constance made on her:

> some of the girls … said, 'The mean thing, wouldn't even pay the dog licence' … We all went to see her come out …, and before she came out this girl said 'I'm going to throw stones at her', she said, 'being mean enough'. And she stood beside me when she came out and Miss Andrews just turned round and said 'Good morning, Emily'. And she said 'Good morning, Miss Andrews'. (laughs) I said, 'I thought you were going to throw stones at her' … She was marvellous really.[22]

The procession made its way to the WFL rooms for a ceremonial breakfast, followed in the evening with a celebratory meeting in the Old Museum Rooms where the census evaders had hidden away so very recently.[23]

Other tax resisters during that May included Emma Sproson of Wolverhampton. Emma decided that, denied citizenship, she too would resist paying her dog licence. This was one of the few taxes that a working-class woman, wife of a postman, could be liable for. In her memoir, Emma recalled what happened: after the census boycott, she was imprisoned in Stafford goal and 'I protested by going on hunger strike'; the WFL held nightly meetings while Emma remained in prison.[24] More exotically, Princess Sophia Duleep Singh, the maharajah's daughter, continued her own tax resistance: the League gladly recorded 'her most successful protest' and recommended a lawyer to appear for her in court.[25] But it was quietly determined Clemence Housman who achieved the highest tax resister profile: her case went right up to Asquith. She had three points in her favour: a well-known surname, a London home, and it was a house (not just a dog) protest. So her case is worth looking at more fully.

It took eighteen months before the law finally caught up with Clemence, patiently sitting it out during visits down to Swanage. As Laurence put it, this was the Government's 'vain attempt to extract 4s 2d from a pocket which could not be picked', so ringing up a much larger bill in process. The tax authorities wrote to her on 28 July that unless she paid £2 14s 6d she would be liable for arrest. Clemence, not to be hurried, replied she was on 'a brief holiday' and would not be home for a while; Somerset House wrote back politely that that would not be convenient.[26] Clemence bided her time.

Meanwhile, Laurence was writing his witty satire, *Alice in Ganderland*. Rather like his earlier Gulliver parable, Laurence cleverly adapted Lewis Carroll's story to satirize current party political hypocrisies over women's citizenship. At the Mad Hatter's tea party, the high-sounding posturing of the three main parties was wickedly mocked. The Liberals' poster proclaimed 'Taxation and Representation go together', while Alice in WSPU colours bore a 'Votes for Women' sandwich board which she propped against the Liberal poster.[27]

Then Laurence's work was interrupted. The first intimation came on Wednesday 27 September: Laurence left his desk – and visited the WTRL office, 'to give the news that Miss Housman would be arrested on the following day'. They immediately arranged for a meeting 'to be held at Mr Housman's residence'. Suffrage societies were circulated with the news of Clemence's imminent arrest on Thursday 28 September – and arrived at the Housmans' home. Emmeline Pethick-Lawrence, Laurence and others made speeches – yet, the WTRL minutes record, with uncharacteristic drama, 'Miss Housman was not arrested!!'[28] Indeed, it was not till the next day, Friday 29 September, that officials finally arrived and, with excruciating politeness which for Laurence combined comedy with pain, took Clemence away.

Laurence informed the press that his sister 'has no furniture, and she therefore actually forced the authorities to imprison her', and a photographer was on hand to capture the moment (see Figure 12). Both siblings had dressed carefully for this occasion, Laurence in formal three-piece suit, fob watch neatly positioned. Clemence, confident at her brother's arm, wears a dark jacket and tie; she looks smilingly defiant and is casually hatless.[29] She was escorted by Laurence in a taxi, through the gates of Holloway.

In prison, Clemence immediately petitioned the Home Office, explaining that as a woman lacking representation she had 'personally fulfilled a duty, moral, social and constitutional, by refusing to pay taxes into irresponsible hands'. This petition made its way up the Home Office chain. Clemence could wear her own clothes and have books in her cell. Afterwards, Laurence enquired how she had whiled away her time inside, and she replied: 'I sat and bubbled'; her brother 'realized that triumphant mental satisfaction' meant so much to Clem. Indeed, when asked by the prison governor how long she was in for, Clem's riposte was 'For life'.[30]

The suffrage movement was soon galvanized, with a demonstration held outside Holloway on Sunday 1 October and more protests planned. At the Home Office, resolutions of protest demanding Clemence's immediate release were received from the WSPU, the WTRL and the Men's Political Union. By Monday 2 October, her case had even reached 10 Downing Street; here a note records 'the PM cannot intervene with the ordinary course of law' unless there were 'special circumstances'. The Home Office likewise felt that 'resolutions of this kind should be simply acknowledged'; on Tuesday 3 October, Churchill agreed: Clemence should not be released 'until she has served a substantial term & sufficient to deter others from following her example'.[31] So what would constitute 'substantial'?

Suddenly and unexpectedly, Clemence was released on Friday 6 October.

Why was she treated more leniently than others? Laurence suggested that it was concern about her health, prompted by the medical officer who told her 'You are eating too little'. Then there was the realization that Clemence would never pay up, so perhaps it was a battle best dropped quietly. Certainly press publicity was far greater in London than elsewhere, especially for someone with such influential connections. Clemence was, after all, sister of renowned A. E. Housman, poet of 'the land of lost content'; and, through Laurence, Clem was known to everyone. (Their elder brother however took a decidedly dim view of her action, writing sarcastically to his publisher of 'a lovely picture of my disreputable relatives' in the newspaper.)[32]

Clemence's release certainly won considerable publicity. On Saturday, the planned protest march turned into a triumphal procession from Kingsway up to Holloway, with speeches delivered (despite the rain) outside gaol. Christabel Pankhurst addressed the crowd, huddled under umbrellas. Clem herself made a rare public speech: 'I felt I have done my best, and that I have effectually registered a woman's vote … in the women's polling booth at Holloway. And I hope many other women will follow me and give their vote before long as I have done'. She had, Constance Lytton commented, 'Hampdened the Government to her heart's content'.[33] And *Votes for Women* devoted its front-page cartoon to official embarrassment, under the headline 'Government without the Consent of the Governed is Impossible'. It depicted Lloyd George outside prison protesting, 'You know, we cannot go on paying this week by week for ever'. A uniformed Winston Churchill retorted: "Well, then, you will have to let her out". (And he did)'.[34]

All the press coverage ensured Clem's case became well-known. So in December when the WTRL held its Hampden dinner, both Housmans had every reason for quiet pride. The elaborate menu included 'Vol au Vent à la Hampden' and 'Bombe Tax Resistance', with Charlotte Despard offering a toast to the queen, Earl Russell to Hampden and Frederick Pethick-Lawrence to 'The Cause', while Laurence gave a toast to 'John Hampden's Successors', notably his sister.[35] Laurence did not stop there. Shortly after Clem's release, his play *Alice in Ganderland* was performed by the Actresses' Franchise League at its grand annual matinée at the Lyceum. This was 27 October 1911.

All this suggests good grounds for suffrage optimism: after all, John Burns had magnanimously climbed down, Kemp's Bill had won a resounding majority and Churchill had released Clemence. However within days of the *Alice* matinée, even before the WTRL dinner, all this changed dramatically.

The People's Suffrage Federation remained extremely wary of enfranchising propertied women alone, preferring full adult suffrage, as did so many Labour and Liberal MPs. On 7 November, the Federation presented a memorial to Asquith requesting the introduction of an adult suffrage bill. To the surprise of this Federation delegation, in reply Asquith casually announced a new government-backed Reform Bill for the next parliamentary session. However, this bill would include only a *man*hood suffrage measure, giving the vote just to all adult men. But, the Prime Minister added graciously, it would be so drafted that, if the House wished, a women's suffrage amendment might be added.

Why did Asquith act so provocatively? Certainly he could feel confident of his having trounced the Lords. And certainly he could be sure of wide distaste among Liberals for a narrow female franchise; this was of course coupled with his own innate distaste at the prospect of *any* women voters, so 'hopelessly ignorant of politics, … flickering with gusts of sentiment like a candle in the wind'. What is clear is that Asquith's bombshell announcement threatening manhood suffrage had fierce repercussions right across the entire suffrage movement.[36]

All organizations reacted furiously. The sense of outrage was palpable. Sympathetic labour supporters like the ILP felt betrayed; and the NUWSS, despite its traditional Liberal loyalties, now moved towards a labour–suffrage alliance. Also absolutely incensed, the WSPU responded with an outbreak of window-smashing. By the time of the Hampden dinner in mid-December, WSPU suffragettes were regularly appearing in court at Bow Street.

Clemence Housman continued her active WTRL support; but the space for the Ghandian philosophy of civil disobedience personified by Charlotte Despard now shrank. A few days later, Lloyd George's National Insurance Bill at last proceeded to royal assent and became law. It was a historic achievement by the Liberal government to reduce health inequalities, yet it felt increasingly hard for women's suffrage supporters to celebrate.

It is not the task of this book to track in detail the full Votes for Women narrative of the last two-and-a-half peacetime years, which is told elsewhere. The NUWSS set up its Election Fighting Fund to support Labour candidates at by-elections, and later organized its impressive pilgrimage from all corners of the country down to Hyde Park. The WSPU expelled the Pethick-Lawrences, and in 1913, as prospects for women's suffrage receded, WSPU window-breaking turned to arson. With so many suffragettes hunger striking in prison, the government introduced its controversial 'Cat and Mouse' Act, releasing suffragette 'mice' from goal on temporary licence, then attempting to re-arrest them. Tensions ran high that summer. Particularly dramatically, Emily Wilding Davison ran on to the racetrack at the Derby, and died a few days later: the magnificent funeral procession of this suffragette martyr was staged a week later through London.

For Emmeline Pankhurst the winter of 1913–14 was particularly dramatic. She sailed for New York; here she was detained by immigration officials on notorious Ellis Island, this lending her tour enormous publicity. Eventually she arrived back at Plymouth, where she was re-arrested by inspectors dispatched from Scotland Yard. In gaol, Emmeline embarked on both hunger and thirst strike – and was soon released. In May 1914 she was re-arrested while attempting to petition the King at Buckingham Palace. The photograph of this elegant widow, clasped round the waist and lifted by a burly chief inspector, became one of the iconic images of the suffragette movement.[37]

Less well known, the LGB continued all the while methodically to sort its copious census data with its crafty card-punching machines. The next report, issued in July 1912, gave population totals within smaller geographical districts, revisiting in more detail 'Sex Proportions'. This reduced proportions from 1,068 down to 1,050 females per 1,000 males. (With the suffragette boycott overlain by more recent events and largely forgotten, perhaps the LGB felt more confident to adjust female figures down.)[38] When war broke out, Mallet, Stevenson and their staff were only part-way through their mammoth task. They just noted imperturbably that other urgent tasks had of course become priorities.[39] The 1911 census and the boycott soon became overshadowed by rapid and dramatic warfare on a totally unprecedented scale. It was in this context, of fierce pre-war suffrage antagonisms followed by war, that the historiography of the census began to be written.

18

Telling the story:
suffrage and census historiographies

The relationship between public-political places and private-domestic spaces runs as a central theme through this book. In accounts of political protest, this linkage between public places and private spaces now seems self-evident. Yet histories of the suffrage campaign and of the census remained distinct and separate until very recently. So it is time to pause and consider each in turn. This chapter brings both literatures together, prior to final analysis of 'the battle for the census'.

The 1911 census boycott till recently had been regarded as a fairly minor theme within the wider suffrage narrative.[1] It was easy to miss. Where noted at all, initially the distinct impression was given that this WFL initiative was adopted widely across country, not only among suffragettes but also by NUWSS suffragists.

Within just two years, Margaret Nevinson gave the boycott its first retrospective consideration. In *The Suffrage Annual and Women's Who's Who* (1913), she noted that census resistance was WFL-inspired and that its support was widespread:

> In 1911 the WFL organised resistance to the Census as a protest against government without consent. Later on, other societies joined us officially, as well as individual suffragists of all shades of opinion. All over the country the names of thousands of women are missing from the Census papers, proving the great axiom of the British Constitution – that government must rest on the consent of the governed. Every resisting householder, both male and female, was prepared for fine or imprisonment; but, to the astonishment of offenders, no action was taken. The Government preferring to ignore the whole thing – probably reflecting that the more people summon[s]ed, the more would the inaccuracies and defects of the Census be proclaimed to the public.[2]

Likewise four years later, *Woman's Effort*, also for a committed readership of suffrage enthusiasts, devoted considerable space to the boycott. The author was

Agnes Edith Metcalfe, a London science graduate and secondary schools HMI; she became 'an inconspicuous worker in the ranks' of the suffrage movement, until campaigns were temporarily checked by war. She nevertheless remained WTRL treasurer and, perhaps through this tax resister link, Laurence Housman wrote a very sympathetic Introduction, and undoubtedly inspired Metcalfe's account of 1911:

> On April 2, census night, another demonstration was given of the growing spirit of rebellion among women. The idea originating with the Freedom League that as women were not regarded as person, they should not submit to be enumerated as such, was eagerly taken up by thousands. Many women householders … either tore them [schedules] up or returned them blank, or with some message of defiance written thereon … In a considerably larger number of cases various means were adopted to frustrate the authorities, and to evade the census, while evading at the same time the possibility of prosecution. Some householders, men as well as women, threw open their houses to rebels for the night, and the number of refugees thus sheltered was never revealed. Some women spent the night *al fresco*, or attended the many all-night entertainments … specially organised … in London and elsewhere.[3]

With no summonses issued, Metcalfe continued: 'Nothing happened' – merely John Burns's comment on 'negligible' numbers, followed by his 'mercy and magnanimity' statement. And her account ended on upbeat Housmanite optimism: 'it was estimated by those conversant with the extent of the movement that the number of evaders ran into six figures' – that is, at least a hundred thousand. Yet, she concluded jubilantly, 'this sin against science went absolutely unrebuked and unpunished', boycotters having successfully asserted 'that Government must be by consent'.

So these two quiet accounts reported the boycott both as WFL-inspired, and as an extremely widespread, effective protest. However, both books soon fell from favour, and, in the new century, attract the attention of only the most dedicated suffrage historians.[4]

This was partly because they were eclipsed by far more popular accounts. In late 1913, rushed out soon after her sensational martydom, *The Life of Emily Davison* by novelist Gertrude Colmore naturally included Emily's census night evasion 'in Guy Fawkes' cupboard' at the House of Commons. Colmore recounts that on her schedule Emily wrote: 'As I am a woman and women do not count in the State, I refuse to be counted', followed by her chosen motto; 'Rebellion against tyrants is obedience to God' – so replicating the somewhat unreliable account in *Votes for Women*.[5]

It was of course Emmeline Pankhurst's tremendously popular autobiography that outshone even Emily's *Life*. *My Own Story* (1914) reached a far wider readership – both then and long afterwards. It could not have been composed in more dramatic circumstances. In late 1913 Emmeline had sailed to New

York for her lecture tour; here she was detained, returning once released. On both journeys, Emmeline was accompanied by American journalist Rheta Child Dorr – who put the long days at sea to good use by taking down in shorthand Emmeline's dramatic words, dictated as they steamed across the Atlantic. Vividly ghost-written, Emmeline's successive imprisonments and re-arrests made the publication all the more compelling. *My Own Story: the autobiography of Emmeline Pankhurst* was published in 1914 (and indeed the closing paragraphs were written in late summer as European armies were mobilizing). The life-story of so iconic a figurehead powerfully shaped received wisdom on the boycott for decades, and so it is worth pausing to hear Emmeline's own words. When the census was to be taken:

> we organized a census resistance on the part of women … Our plan was to reduce the value of the census for statistical purposes by refusing to make the required returns … We made the announcement of this plan and instantly there ensued a splendid response from women and a chorus of horrified disapproval from the conservative public [like] The *Times* …
>
> We carried out, and most successfully, our census resistance. Many thousands of women all over the country refused or evaded the returns. I returned my census paper with the words 'No vote no census' written across it … In some places unoccupied houses were rented for the night by resisters, who lay on the bare boards. Some groups of women hired gipsy vans and spent the night on the moors.
>
> In London … many of us walked about Trafalgar Square until midnight and then repaired to Aldwych skating rink, where we amused ourselves until morning … and on the whole the resisters had a very good time.[6]

Emmeline's account also ends on Burns's statement of insignificance. 'But', she declared, 'every one knew that this was the exact reverse of the facts'. Given the tensions of winter 1913–14, Emmeline's account is understandably broad-brush, and has been criticized by some historians. Certainly the first person plural is a slippery pronoun: Emmeline's artless claim, 'we organised … and most successfully, our census resistance', placing the WSPU centre-stage, may have raised a few eyebrows. And by suggesting 'many thousands of women' boycotted, she thus established in the mind of the reading public that other suffrage societies did indeed join in.[7]

Emmeline's death in 1928 saw a statue raised to her at Westminster; she remained, and remains, *the* suffragette leader. It is scarcely surprising then that public memory of the boycott remained shaped by her two suggestions: that it was WSPU-initiated and organized; and that it was a resounding success, with any grumpy cavilling restricted to 'the conservative public'.

Meanwhile and completely separately, the government continued publishing its census reports. However, during the war, with many civil servants called away to fight, other administrative tasks became urgent priorities. Eventually in 1923, the 'Fertility of Marriage' report was published; its Preface admitted that 'the war conditions ... postponed indefinitely the continuance of this programme', despite 'the wealth of material' gathered. In other words, all the data collated from the questions about children born alive who had since died, which some Edwardian women had found so intrusive, would never see the light of day. And of course the war had so changed health and welfare politics that comparisons between 1911 and 1921 were no longer really useful: there was now even some state provision of mother and baby clinics, plus women over thirty could not only vote but even be elected as MPs. Indeed, for the 1921 census, 'it was decided not to repeat the fertility inquiry'.[8]

During the interwar years, then, where it was mentioned at all, the boycott continued to be presented as WSPU-inspired and as successful. Annie Kenney's *Memories of a Militant* (1924) just noted extremely briefly how 'we all refused to fill in our census papers'; but of her role in gingering up boycotters in the Bristol area, there was not a single word.[9] However, Evelyn Sharp's 1926 biography of eminent scientist Hertha Ayrton, who up to then was sympathetic to WSPU and militancy, did note that the protest was organized by WFL, and offers a more nuanced account:

> Mrs Ayrton turned her rooms into dormitories for the night, hiring beds, and giving hospitality to some forty census-resisters, all of [whom] ... could thus with her help escape notification, their hostess having declined to fill in her census paper or give any particulars of the people under her roof.[10]

Sharp stated decidedly that Ayrton had been made a rebel by 'her passionate sense of the injustice to women ...; for, very naturally, as a scientist, she would attach special significance to the accuracy of the census returns', undoubtedly alluding to Sadler's 'sin against science' accusation.

Otherwise, in the two key interwar suffrage histories, both long retaining their popularity, the boycott was ignored. One-time student vanner Ray Costello, married into Pippa's family and now Mrs Oliver Strachey, looked back on the campaign in *The Cause* (1928) through staunchly NUWSS eyes. Strachey did not refer to the boycott (and indeed, the WFL merited only a single sentence), possibly recalling sister-in-law Pippa's irritation with militant lobbying about it.[11]

Three years later and even more influential was middle sister Sylvia Pankhurst's *The Suffragette Movement* (1931). This too ignored the census boycott. Perhaps this is unsurprising. The book is subtitled *An Intimate Account of Persons and Ideals*, and Sylvia was away on a two-month speaking tour in America during the whole census period. So understandably, the boycott rather passed her by.[12] Sylvia's history, acquiring canonical status, set the seal on how the history of Votes for Women would be popularly viewed by future generations.

Broadly then, in interwar memoirs and suffrage histories, the 1911 boycott was presented either briefly as WSPU-inspired, or received no mention.[13] There were only two exceptions, both written by those centrally involved in, or very sympathetic to, the WFL. Margaret Nevinson's autobiography, *Life's Fitful Fever* (1926), conjured up something of what breaking the law felt like at the time:

> In 1911 the WFL initiated the census boycott; speakers had a hard time all those months, speaking up and down the country, inciting [audiences] to passive resistance ... The WSPU ... officially decided to adopt the policy ... Up and down the country, thousands of quiet, innocent-looking houses were crammed from attic to cellar with passive resisters. We all expected a penalty of £5 ... The authorities preferred to regard the effect on statistics as "negligible"; but as those of us conversant with the roll of their own members consider the figures of the 1911 Census were out by some hundreds of thousands, we had sinned heavily ... against the science of political economy – quite unpunished, which is bad for law and order.[14]

So, thirteen years after her earlier account, Margaret now claimed not just 'thousands of women' but 'some hundreds of thousands' of missing women, suggesting at least two hundred thousand. Why was she now talking it up? One possible reason is that Margaret felt increasingly lonely and depressed, her domestic life an empty shell; in her last years, did she wish to lend greater significance to her personal past?[15] Perhaps. Sadly, her autobiography fell out-of-print and is now near-forgotten.

The other crucial interwar memoirist was of course Laurence Housman, key begetter of the boycott. His poignant autobiography, *The Unexpected Years* (1937), has already been cited. Looking back a quarter-century to those prewar days, Laurence wrote tellingly about census night and its significance:

> Before the much darker days that followed, there was one happy and successful interlude, in which I took an active part. This was the Census-resistance of 1911, one of the very few things in the way of militancy which the women Suffragists did on so large a scale that the Government was unable to touch them. It was the only act of defiance to imperfectly constituted authority which that authority – in spite of much threatening beforehand – did not attempt to punish.

While 'well suited to ... the non-heroic many', yet Laurence stated that it:

> could not be despised by the heroic ones who preferred to get their shock of battle in more active form. It proved, indeed, so representative that the WSPU, which had at first been held back by its leaders from organized participation, was forced by the restiveness of its own rank and file to come in, give the protest its official blessing, and as a result make it doubly effective, and safe. Honest John Burns, when informed by his enumerators that he was against resisters to the tune of many tens of thousands, amounting quite possibly to figures in the hundred thousands, climbed down in a night, and announced ... he would be magnanimous and let the offenders off.

Laurence's vivid account remains probably the most evocative, yet also fair and balanced:

> It is not to be pretended that the Census-protest had a devastating effect upon the Government, but it had its uses none the less. It was good argument, and it got – if not a good press – plenty of publicity … With comparatively little wear to themselves, the Women Suffragists were able to undo the accuracy and therefore the efficiency, of a very elaborate and costly piece of government machinery …
>
> In the Suffrage camp it … gave the women a sense of numbers and solidarity which heartened all, and an opportunity for action to many who had previously done nothing; it was also a distinct score in another direction, at that time rather rare – the women had come off victors from the field, without rough-handling or bruises from the mob or the police, or any subsequent imprisonment from the Government; they had a thoroughly enjoyable time seeing friends, keeping late hours, sleeping in strange beds. They had a virtuous 'night out', and were none the worse for it. Taking it all round it remains, I think, one of the happiest memories of the Suffrage Movement …
>
> As a souvenir of my part in the business, the law-breakers gave me a library chair, with a brass plate on it recording the event; and it is in that chair that I am now writing, and have written nearly all my work from that day to this.[16]

Was Housman's estimate of 'figures in the hundred thousands' (at least one hundred thousand) about right? In the 1930s there was still no way of knowing, nor any likely prospect of finding out in his own lifetime. Together till the end, having both moved down to Street in Somerset, Clem died in 1955, Laurence in 1959.

By the Second World War, memory of the suffrage campaign increasingly defined militancy solely in terms of actions which led to imprisonment; civil disobedience like boycotting the census attracted no such penalty, and was of little consequence in establishing personal credibility as a 'suffragette'. Indeed, the very triumph of the boycott – no fines, no imprisonments – turned out to be its Achilles heel: it did not 'count'. Those passive resisters who had merely broken the law with impunity became erased, occupying an odd historiographical twilight world.[17]

However, memories of the census were not completely forgotten. By the 1970s, popular interest in suffrage enjoyed a renaissance. In *The Militant Suffragettes* (1973), Antonia Raeburn not only acknowledged the boycott as Housman-inspired and WFL-organized, but also interviewed a surviving suffragette tax resister, Marian Lawson, about Aldwych roller skating on census night. Indeed Raeburn, having discovered the Batheaston collection, even quoted from Mary Blathwayt's diary for census night. Moreover, she was the first writer to look beyond the suffrage papers for contemporary reports, reading the *Bath Chronicle* report on the local boycott, and quoting its 'Census Ditty'.[18]

The following year, Brian Harrison began recording his suffrage interviews; these magnificent oral histories included not only the interview with Marie Lawson just a year before she died (quoted in Chapter 12), but also that with Cicely Hale who worked for the WSPU:

CH: We all gathered in a house – somewhere in Bloomsbury, I think. Some lay on the floor … Some were preparing a bath, to sleep there. We just spent the night there.
BH: This was a house that the inspectors didn't know about?
CH: Yes, the group that I was in – there were 10 or 12 of us – I think they were doing it all over London. We tried to sleep, we lay down … My parents were very good about that sort of thing. They never made a fuss about my being out.[19]

Sadly, tape-recorded oral testimony is not readily accessible to the general public. In contrast to television drama. During spring 1974, BBC TV broadcast its memorable suffragette drama serial, *Shoulder to Shoulder*. It relied upon Sylvia Pankhurst's *The Suffragette Movement*, so ensuring, more than ever, that this book was seen as *the* history of Votes for Women. Yet ironically, Sylvia was one of the very few who had actually been out of the country during the census.[20] So in the popular mind, the boycott remained a minor theme; where mentioned it was seen as a WSPU achievement, with the WFL, tax resisters and Housmans getting short shift.[21] With lives of participants now passing into the past, the census boycott faded into insignificance – for a further two decades.

By the 1990s, a new confident generation of suffrage historians had emerged. They wanted to look beyond the Sylvia Pankhurst or *Shoulder to Shoulder* versions, and beyond the two main organizations, the NUWSS and the WSPU; they wanted to deploy imaginative techniques to find neglected connections and to revisit familiar suffrage stories. Among the new *Women's History Review* invaluable series of historiographical articles was American historian Laura Mayhall's 'Creating the Suffragette Spirit'. It discussed how 'the very definition of militancy … equates it with the material practices of window-breaking, arson, and hunger striking', and talked of how 'the stranglehold of the WSPU on the historical imagination' privileged actions leading to imprisonment – rather than the census boycott which had successfully avoided prosecution.[22]

Then in 1996, Sandra Holton's *Suffrage Days* offered an innovative focus on lives that had previously slipped from view. In her chapter 'Women's Suffrage Among the Bohemians', she highlighted the importance Laurence Housman attached to the civil disobedience tactics; in contrast to his 'growing unease at the suffering which militancy increasingly brought to the women', he took 'particular glee' in his creative role of organizing census resistance. Holton's research was indeed pioneering, given that Housman's *Unexpected Years* had long fallen from favour.[23] Two years later, in her short study of the WFL, Clare Eustance discussed the census boycott within its programme of passive political resistance, and included the photograph of Manchester evaders sleeping, crammed like sardines on the floor, below the notice proclaiming 'No Vote No Census'.[24]

It was however Elizabeth Crawford's *The Women's Suffrage Movement: a reference guide* (1999) which really drew attention to the research potential of surviving census evidence. As the WFL-instigated boycott produced incomplete or spoiled census returns, she noted, these will hide from history many interesting women, 'which historians will soon regret'. She even quoted that forgotten 1917 source, Agnes Metcalfe, on 'this sin against science'.[25] Crawford thus presciently linked the boycott to future availability of archival evidence – as yet unavailable.

This brings us to the new millennium and two final contributions to historiography. Laura Mayhall's *The Militant Suffrage Movement* (2003) deftly placed the boycott within the radical tradition of the right of the unenfranchised to rebel against the state. Subtitled *Citizenship and Resistance in Britain, 1860–1930*, the book made visible 'the tangle of connections' between political radicalism and women's suffrage, citing tax resistance precedents like the 1906 'Siege of Montefiore'. Mayhall explored how suffragettes' withholding their consent from a tyrannical government flowered into the staging of theatrical constitutional spectacles – such as WFL Muriel Matters's 1908 grille chaining, and of course 'the highly symbolic census resistance', a key act in militants' 'creative dramas of exclusion and participation'.[26] Alongside were published many new suffrage biographies, among which Angela V. John's *Henry Nevinson* (2006) stands out here.[27]

Suffrage historians might now recognize the boycott as WFL-inspired; yet it remained the better-known WSPU which continued to shape public imagination. Information about what happened on census night could still be obtained only from autobiographies and secondary sources. It was still not yet known exactly who had boycotted and precisely what had been written on individual schedules. New biographies of the Pankhursts could do little more than repeat what their subjects – notably Emmeline Pankhurst – had claimed: that the census 'campaign appealed to militants and constitutionalists alike'.[28]

Only the eventual release of the individual household schedules could offer the crucial primary evidence required to reassess suffrage historiography and the responses of Edwardian feminists to being persistently denied that crucial symbol of citizenship, the vote. So how long would researchers have to wait before these key documents became publicly accessible? Time to revisit census historiography which, as noted earlier, ran alongside, yet separate from, suffrage literature.

Just as earlier Reports of the 1911 census had made no mention (indeed, seemingly almost went out of their way to avoid mention) of the suffragette boycott, so subsequent census historians, not having access to the schedules either, have ignored it too. Rather, they posed a different set of questions. Scholarly 'histories of the census' have thus broadly offered analysis (often quantitative) of the evidence contained in the successive printed tabulations of 1911 census data. Since the 1980s, census historian Edward Higgs has provided definitive guides to reading and interpreting individual schedules – from their earliest 1801 variant, but especially from the 1841 transition to modern census-taking. A generation of local history students and family history enthusiasts have found his guidance clear and authoritative, as successive new editions testify.[29]

Also dating from the 1980s, demographic historians at Cambridge were granted privileged advance access to sample 'individual level' anonymized schedules. Their monumental study, *Changing Family Size in England and Wales* (2001), was significantly subtitled *Place, Class and Demography, 1891–1911*. It examined factors influencing family-building and child-bearing strategies, and concluded that location carried considerable weight; and that 'neighbourhood norms' significantly shaped the 'fertility transition' to reduced family size ('keeping down with the Joneses'). So one of their key arguments was that 'where' was more influential than 'who'. Indeed, the co-authors even went so far as to state that '"class" was geography'. This impressive study however ignores women's exclusion from citizenship, even in 1911. Nevertheless, their notion of 'communication communities' does offer an extremely useful approach to mapping patterns of suffrage-census arguments, which have helped shape the 'Places and spaces' section.[30]

The work of Higgs remains pre-eminent among census historians: his recent 'census and the state' studies having a direct bearing on the 'battle for the census'. In 'The Statistical Big Bang of 1911' (1996), he focuses on civil servants' technocratic innovations (notably electrically driven card-counting machinery), rather than on the political challenge to census compliance, making no reference to women's continued disenfranchisement. Five years later, Higgs's broader survey, 'The Rise of the Information State', tracked the development of state surveillance, arguing that the decennial census was less about social control, as conventionally thought, and more about creating welfare benefits and rights – including voting rights. Again, the argument is persuasively informed, and certainly the 1911 census was intimately linked to conveying social benefits. However, many Edwardian women, notably suffragettes, viewed the penetrating census questions not as hastening their citizenship claims, but rather as impertinent.[31]

Two separate and distinct literatures have been tracked over the last hundred years, from the immediate census aftermath right through to the current work. It is clear then demographic-census historians on the one hand and suffrage historians on the other each occupied different intellectual terrain, posing different sets of questions and creating their own distinct historiographies.

The 1911 schedules were expected to be made publicly accessible at New Year 2012 under the hundred year rule: to be reawakened, rather like Sleeping

Beauty, after a century had passed. So when eventually released, would they indicate who had a better grasp of the real significance of what took place on census night, 2 April 1911?

And where would this all leave the growing army of family historians? The release of the 1901 census in January 2002, with data electronically searchable for the very first time through the internet, had triggered such an insatiable popular appetite that, within hours of the launch, the National Archives' computers crashed for several months.[32] A genealogists' quaintly obsessive hobby was transformed into an insatiable quest for family histories and personal identities. This was further boosted in 2004 when BBC TV launched its immensely popular series, *Who Do You Think You Are?* with celebrity genealogists effortlessly tracing their ancestral roots. Since then, a veritable do-it-yourself family history industry has been spawned, with monthly magazines and fairs.

So it was certainly to be expected that large swathes of the public – suffrage and social historians, plus family history searchers – would eagerly await 2 January 1912. Research calendars had that date marked. However, during 2007–8 small tremors underfoot suggested some early earth-shifting movement at the National Archives. It looked as if it would be possible to discover three years early what exactly had taken place on census night 1911.

19

Sources and their analysis: vanishing for the vote?

While the previous chapter might have been written by any scholarly researcher tracking the historiography, these final pages necessarily adopt a more personal tone. Almost overnight, in January 2009 historians were faced with the immense richness of brand new archival evidence – and had to determine their own approach. To make sense of this vast documentation, it was necessary to select. Additionally, suffrage searches on the handwritten schedules needed to look for missing women, for absences. Such an ambitious project had not been previously attempted: personal research methods had to be carefully determined at the outset.

Earlier, I had electronically searched the 1891 and 1901 censuses for Yorkshire campaigners featured in *Rebel Girls* (2006), to track the ancestry of for instance Lilian Lenton, daughter of a Leicester carpenter. In winter 1911–12 Lilian had been so inspired by Emmeline Pankhurst's oratory that she determined on window-smashing and, from 1913, on burning empty buildings. Accused of attempted arson in Doncaster, Lilian appeared in court, later escaping from the Leeds police and remaining a particularly elusive suffragette.[1] In 2007 I searched for the Lentons c. 1911, then living in Bristol. I found that, armed with an exact address, I could order by post a copy of the family's 1911 schedule. It did indeed reveal Lilian as missing from home in Bristol – undoubtedly evading the enumerator. Later, under the 'Cat and Mouse' Act, Lilian was released from prison into the care of a Birmingham suffragette, and became a fugitive. Elizabeth Crawford's *The Women's Suffrage Movement: a reference guide* provided the exact address, and I ordered the schedule. It included a note: 'Suffragette – Information refused'. So already I had discovered my first evader and my first resister.[2]

I found these two discoveries compelling. The exorbitant fee was a major deterrent to further freelance searches, but I learnt that this early release of the 1911 census schedules sprang from a recent ruling under the Freedom of Information Act (FOI) 2000. Moreover, greater accessibility was promised: sounds coming from the National Archives (TNA) grew increasingly audible.

In November 2008 I contacted Elizabeth. We shared a fascination with how census schedules could illuminate campaigners' lives. She had recently written for TNA's *Ancestors* magazine on 'No votes for women, no information from women', illustrating some dramatic ways suffragettes boycotted the census. It now became apparent to both of us that not only was TNA bringing forward the release date by a full three years, but it was also making searches easier and affordable.[3]

Wise after its 2002 initial debacle, TNA now ensured reliable public access. On Tuesday 13 January 2009, selected counties of England overnight became searchable by the public. Excitement was palpable. By midnight, 3.4 million searches and 17.4 million pages had been viewed, mainly by family historians.[4] There was particularly wide interest in this 'lost generation', the last census before the First World War.

But it was suffragettes who grabbed the headlines. TNA's publicity photograph of Christabel Pankhurst and Annie Kenney holding a large 'Votes for Women' placard was widely reproduced.[5] The *Guardian* used this image to illustrate its report, 'Past Lives: 1911 census goes online' – as did *The Times* with its headline '1911 Census: the secret suffragettes who refused to be counted'. Only now, *The Times* added, nearly a century later, had the full extent of this 'mass protest by women campaigning to be allowed to vote ... finally come to public attention.' The BBC also covered the release, posing the question to which no ready answer was yet available: 'so how many women *did* boycott the census?'[6]

By now, our appetites were whetted: Elizabeth and I agreed to collaborate and met within three days of the census release. TNA's operation ran smoothly: gradually the remaining counties became available. We could now track evasion and resistance to the 1911 census across the length and breadth of England. So what did all these sparkling new resources, coupled with 'the statistical Big Bang of 1911', enable suffrage historians to discover?

We could now sharpen our research aims. These would be threefold. First, we would assess how widespread were suffragette evasions and resistance. This would offer a sense of the boycott's quantitative significance, suggesting at least a lower limit, even if the upper limit still remained speculative. It would also help clarify whether demographers were correct to ignore the boycott, or suffrage historians right to celebrate its significance. Second, we would map the boycott geographically across the English regions, cities and towns, urban and rural communities. We aimed to link these patterns with centres of most intense suffrage activity (usually the presence of a local organizer or energetic branch secretary), in other words, demographic historians' 'communication communities'. Third, we would examine individual suffrage allegiances (notably WSPU, WFL and NUWSS), plus look at occupations and family structure. Finally, we would evaluate the boycott's broader significance to historians.

Our main source for research was the official website, 1911census.co.uk. We were looking both for census evaders, likely to be nigh impossible to track; and for resisters, their schedules accompanied by their rebellious statement. For individual electronic searches to be effective, we needed to know the subject's name, ideally their address for 1911 and date of birth. We had to start somewhere. So we decided our initial searches would be the 319 names listed in Elizabeth's *Reference Guide* and resident in England during the census. We created a database summarizing information on each schedule – name, age and address; whether they were present on census night, any defiant statement, and to this we added their suffrage organization. We could then sort our database by column, particularly useful for grouping local areas and suffrage affiliations. So, with *Reference Guide* in hand, we each began searching from our home computers. This method was efficient *if* we were reasonably certain the right woman had been found. The expense of obtaining schedules from home, however, ruled against taking too many chances. We needed to search at TNA where access to the 1911 census was free. We visited Kew in February 2009: TNA's infrastructure investment was immediately striking: carpet 'footsteps' guided visitors towards the special bank of 1911 computer terminals, with 'help' staff in blue census shirts.[7]

Working at Kew, we could experiment with speculative searches to locate 'missing' women, however nebulous the information: sometimes a subject's name had been mis-transcribed, or only her husband's name was recorded as she was absent. Then from summer, the enumerators' summary pages became available, listing individual houses by street, so we could now peer even more closely into neighbourhoods.[8] All this helped to confirm many women as actual evaders – with an enumerator's exasperated note sometimes appended. Often he wrote in the numbers estimated to be spending the night under a particular roof, even though none of the evaders would give him information.

So we began to view schedules completed by suffragettes and suffragists in their own hands ninety-eight years earlier. Some, such as Mary Howey, had boldly embellished their schedule with 'Votes for Women'; and under the 'Infirmity' column, she had added for herself and the female servant present, 'not enfranchised'.[9] Others had written 'No Vote No Census' right across, a rubric adopted by members of both the WFL and the WSPU. Yet while we were often able to tease out these resisters, searching for evaders proved extremely frustrating: one does not expect to find these elusive women easily. And we could only look for possible evaders where we knew at least their *name*. How could we identify those about whom we knew almost nothing? Like Donald Rumsfeld, we mused on the complexities of the 'unknown unknowns'.

Our profile of 319 names inevitably disproportionately privileged

London-based leaders. So we opened a second database, for local branch activists recorded in *Votes for Women* and *The Vote*.[10] However, often only a surname and an imprecise address was given; with such scant biographical details, our searches grew time-consuming and often frustrating. Elizabeth then added ingenious 'random' searches to locate 'missing' women: by keying either 'Miss' or 'Mrs', she uncovered women for whom the enumerator had been unable to elicit even a first name. (Thus a 'Mrs Lee' living in north London eventually turned out to be Mary Leigh, WSPU hunger striker.)[11] Such boycotters often popped up in surprising places, and we were particularly delighted to add in these fresh names. By December 2009 our 'Local' database contained 253 names; adding these to our 319 Main entries, we arrived at 572 names (plus the enumerators' figures, even if not the names, for mass evasions).

We could begin to analyse our data. Patterns began to emerge. It soon became apparent that virtually all NUWSS suffragists had complied. By contrast, among suffragettes, many had boycotted; married women were often absent that night from the marital home – the 'mysteriously missing wife'. Similarly, many boycotters were single women living in rented rooms or flats in London; it was very easy for such 'new' women to slip from the view of the census enumerator, and of suffrage historians a century later. These searches also threw up interesting and certainly unexpected cases. For instance Victor Prout, an illustrator of Palmer's Green in Middlesex, refused to fill in his schedule and had written across it:

> I wish to protest against the terrible treatment women have been recently subjected to as the result of the Liberal Government's method of repressing the agitation in favour of Women's Enfranchisement, and I refuse to fill this census form because women are claiming that until they are given the rights of Citizenship they shall not be counted, and I leave out the men as an act of sympathy with that claim.
>
> All this withheld information will be freely given as soon as Women's Enfranchisement Bill becomes law. Victor Prout.[12]

On Tuesday 4 April the enumerator reported to his registrar that he had read the Census Act to Mr Prout – who had responded most civilly, explaining that he did not wish to inconvenience the official but that he adhered to his decision. About a week later, the registrar received a Memorandum from Archer Bellingham himself, requesting he merely 'fill up a Schedule with the best information available, concerning Mr Prout and the other occupants [of the house] on census night'. Eventually a schedule *was* completed: the registrar had somehow managed to extract some information about Victor and his family. Standard memoranda like this were circulated to all registrars reporting difficulties with evaders or resisters. So, when John Burns made his statement as early as Wednesday 5 April, he must have trusted that such persistent boycotters were not numerically significant.

Our database could however only capture information on those boycotters whose identities we had uncovered. Without such serendipitous surprises as Victor Prout's correspondence, how could we estimate how many others women had boycotted the census? Better to focus on what we *did* know.

Our 572 names revealed distinct geographical patterns across England. Despite all our searches, there remained a far higher incidence of boycotters in the capital than across the rest of the country. To map this spatial patterning more accurately, we undertook a systematic study of two regions, necessarily selecting those areas with which we were closely familiar. For Elizabeth, this meant London, and for myself Yorkshire. Together, they represented one-quarter of England's 34 million population. Naturally, London's economic and social structure was distinctive. The three Yorkshire Ridings, however, encompassed industrial, commercial, agricultural and seaport communities, and so offered a more representative profile.[13] Immediately, dramatic differences became striking. For London, Elizabeth's database soon acquired 215 names. By contrast, I struggled woefully to reach seventy, names across Yorkshire, finding fewer boycotters.[14] Yet all our reading of suffrage literature had led us to believe that the boycott had spread widely across the country.

Armed with our 572 names, we then drafted our article. Our findings could only be provisional, but we found just under a hundred resisters. As it was infinitely easier to slip away in the dark of night (or, for the wealthier, to be away on holiday), we naturally found twice as many evaders – nearly two hundred. All the remaining names complied with the census, and of course represented many, many more campaigners; unsurprisingly, virtually all NUWSS suffragists complied. This evidence suggested fierce intellectual and political debate over the census, as Edwardians argued about women's citizenship and about tactics that would best achieve that, about the suffrage movement's demand for Votes for Women, and the Liberal government's reform agenda in the increasingly frenetic prewar years. Subtitled 'the battle for the 1911 census', our article was published in spring 2011 to coincide with the census centenary.[15]

By early 2010, Elizabeth had moved her research focus sideways. I however remained fascinated. I felt dissatisfied that our article could offer only a provisional survey, hedged around with cautious ('Preliminary') phrasing, with some questions left open. My curiosity was still razor sharp, intrigued by what could yet be uncovered. So I committed to produce a full-length account of the 'battle for the census'. Within this debate, I aimed to marry both quantitative data and qualitative evidence (notably personal memoirs), so the book could present the complex political arguments around the 1911 census. I therefore needed to shift to a new research and writing tack.

Four points became clear. First, rather than merely extending our original database, I decided to pursue a fresh strategy.[16] I would structure the research, not around individual names, but around households, the basic census unit.

After all, the further one peered into what individual boycotters got up to on census night, the more it emerged that their behaviour touched sisters and daughters, husbands (often sympathetic but not always), and, crucially, domestic servants – all living under that one roof. Rather than individual names, the Gazetteer therefore lists five hundred household schedules.

Second, instead of including all compliers, I determined to focus on just resisters and evaders. That, after all, was the point of this 1911 census story. So our Gazetteer summarizes the schedules of those who evaded or resisted, or whose compliance is surprising, as we would have expected them to boycott (e.g. Hannah Mitchell). Only a few significant NUWSS compliers have been included, those mentioned in the text (e.g. Pippa Strachey).

Third, I was forced to rethink my own suffrage landscape. I had found uncovering the discrepancy between London and Yorkshire boycotters personally unsettling. My earlier suffrage writing had focused on women across the north – first, the radical suffragists in Lancashire's cotton towns for *One Hand Tied Behind Us* (1978); later, on suffragettes across Yorkshire for *Rebel Girls: their fight for the Vote* (2006). I now discovered not only that the radical suffragists had complied, as might be expected; but also, and more surprisingly, that very few of the suffragettes active a couple of years earlier in Yorkshire's textile towns had boycotted either.[17] I confess that, as a suffrage historian, I had wanted (and certainly had expected) the primary evidence to go one way – yet it largely pointed in the opposite direction, towards broader census compliance. As a result, I found that my research centre of gravity shifted decisively from the Pennines about 120 miles further south down towards areas like Hampden's Buckinghamshire. And I acknowledged that research on the 'battle for the census' was emerging as more complex (and historically richer) than I had imagined, with geographical mapping a strong factor.

So fourth, following the sobering discovery of widespread census compliance, particularly away from London, I decided to put spatial patterning at the heart of the book. My starting point was 'communication communities' and even the provocative suggestion that 'class was geography'.[18] This focus was strengthened by current research on gender and community. Feminist work on neighbourhoods included 'history walking' and 'street work', looking for instance at how suffrage pioneers in Bloomsbury adapted their respectable private homes into political spaces. This new emphasis on proximity, facilitated for Edwardians by trams and trains linking outer suburbs to city centre, heightened my awareness of geographical space on census night 1911: the size of cities, their distance from London.[19] Turning back to Doreen Massey's *Space, Place and Gender* (1994) reminded me that 'geography matters to the construction of gender', for instance the difficulty of tracking women in the city who keep moving. It was almost as if the new generation of feminist geographers since the 1980s had in mind the 1911 census night, in cities like London and Manchester. I certainly retained my sense of excitement about mapping 'Spaces and places' as a central focus of this book.[20]

So, my focus became selected communities where the boycott was well organized, and where neglected threads of autobiographical evidence could vividly expand the bare census schedules. Such discoveries entailed travelling. My initial journeys in 2010 were modest in scope: walking the pavements of Hampstead, Kensington and Chelsea; in Battersea, striding John Burns's street to view his home, then down to Nine Elms searching (fruitlessly, owing to slum clearance) for Charlotte Despard's house. In Manchester I tracked down Denison House, ventured out to Sale, and then tried tracing the Eccles evaders' midnight cycle ride. Gradually places and their people assumed shape: the Nevinsons' Hampstead and the Housmans' Kensington, the Blathwayts' Bath and Jessie Stephenson's Manchester.

I began more ambitious journeys at Whitsun. I headed south to Hampden's Buckinghamshire, then further down to retrace the first WFL caravan route, and westwards towards Wiltshire tracking that elusive vanner, Lillian Dove-Willcox. Eventually I crossed into Somerset to read the intimate Housman correspondence lodged in Street Library; then down to Clemence's Swanage hidey-hole on the Dorset coast, and later on, admired the grandeur of the Bath evaders' site, plus Mary Blathwayt's Batheaston. I coursed the length and breadth of England.

Evidence was often dispersed. For instance, Jessie Stephenson's typescript is housed in the Museum of London, the postcard of Manchester's mass evasion was unearthed in a Birmingham museum outpost, while the originals of the 'Census Lodge' images were discovered only at the book's final draft stage, by tracking the photographer who had recently restored them.[21] Of perilous transmission stories, probably the most dramatic was that of Helen Watts, who emigrated to Canada; her manuscript material sailed across the Atlantic, then mysteriously surfaced at Bristol docks where it would have remained forgotten but for an enterprising local history teacher. Now it is back in Nottingham, to help bring to life this Midlands WSPU branch.[22]

As I followed the steps of boycotters a century earlier, digital camera in hand, I photographed their houses and mass evasion sites.[23] Then, by summer 2011 it was time to stop the criss-crossing journeys, and time to start writing. Finally, during 2012, Elizabeth and I worked collaboratively again to produce a Gazetteer. We deployed search techniques similar to those we had used in 2009, though now with more sophisticated understanding of the boycott's dimensions. Considerable gritty determination and patience was still required, particularly to locate elusive mass evasion schedules. At last we completed our Gazetteer with its five hundred schedules.[24] So what does it all tell us about Edwardian campaigners' responses on census night, their personal motivations, the thinking behind their action. In other words, what is it now possible to conclude?

Suffrage literature had strongly suggested the boycott engaged women of all societies; but our new evidence confirmed that this impression was distinctly misleading. There were still only a handful of boycotters among NUWSS members. Given how robustly their leadership had opposed the law-breaking tactic of boycotting, this was scarcely surprising: tens of thousands of suffragists had been bidden to comply – and did so, with a consistently high level of compliance among members. The handful who *did* boycott usually had an individual explanation, such as joint membership. Dr Ethel Williams in Newcastle evaded, and was also a WTRL member. Economic independence lent a few the confidence to defy the NUWSS leadership: a woman doctor in Devon; the O'Shea sisters near Portsmouth complying but adding a strong statement. However, these few stand out as rare exceptions.

Rather, boycotters are almost all members or supporters of the main militant organizations: WSPU, particularly in city centres and inner suburbs; WFL, especially in outer suburbs; the WTRL, mainly in London and the Home Counties; plus support groups like the Men's League. Without backing from larger organizations like the NUWSS or Women's Co-operative Guild, the boycott was indeed smaller-scale than suffragette propaganda had suggested.

Of the five hundred Gazetteer households, who – and where – were these resisters and evaders, what precisely did they do on census night, and *why*? First, where they lived made a very significant difference. The stark contrast found earlier between the London and Yorkshire regions is replicated right across country. In London and its suburbs, the Gazetteer confirms a far higher incidence of boycotters than in distant counties. The location of mass evasions (see pp. 243–4) makes this instantly clear; of the individuals recorded, about half (eight hundred) were in central London (mainly skating at the Aldwych); with others elsewhere in the capital (Kensington, Fulham), they comprise altogether about two-thirds of mass evaders. The other great mass evasions took place in large cities with well-developed suburbs, notably Manchester (296) and also Sheffield (57).

More generally, of individual boycotters, nearly two-thirds are found in London boroughs and Middlesex. Realizing this, I found my research centre of gravity dropped south once again, nearer north London The remaining boycotters either lived across the southern counties (below a rough line between the Wash and the Bristol Channel), or were in large cities and their suburbs in the Midlands and north. When breaking the law, there was safety in numbers – hence the higher numbers found in key London boroughs, the Home Counties and cities like Newcastle and Leicester. For instance, in the borough of Kensington, with a population of 172,000, the Gazetteer lists twenty-nine schedules where one or more occupants boycotted (including two mass evasions). By contrast, for Nottinghamshire, with a much larger population of 600,000, the Gazetteer lists just eight schedules where one or more people boycotted, predominantly just in the one city. And the form boycotting took was shaped by geography too:

in boroughs like Hampstead there were many truculent resisters; for them the enumerator just noted 'All information refused'. By contrast, in a county like Leicestershire, the Gazetteer includes only a couple of resisters, with local suffragettes preferring the relative safety of evading together at the WSPU Leicester offices.

Likewise, patterns of compliance were shaped by geography and local economic structures. Thus boycott enthusiasm was noticeably patchy in great ports like Hull and Southampton, and in coal-mining areas.[25] Across London itself, in working-class boroughs to the east like Shoreditch or Bethnal Green, it is also hard to identify boycotters. And distance from London remained a strong determining factor, with the WTRL, for instance, never making great inroads much further out. Indeed, unsurprisingly, the more remote from London was a community, the more sporadic was the scattering of boycotters. Rural counties revealed a similar pattern, even in southern England. In Dorset, Clemence Housman and her handful of like-minded women in Swanage had every reason to feel extremely isolated.

Second, the Gazetteer confirms that economic circumstance and individual occupation significantly shaped census night responses. Women who owned their own home (and so would be likely to benefit from a Conciliation Bill, however narrowly framed) had both a strong incentive to boycott, and would be less deterred by the fear of being fined. Financial self-confidence allowed women to cock their snook at the census. Examples are plentiful. In Sale, Mary Manning's widowed mother undoubtedly owned their house, which became the site of Mary's WFL mass evasion. In her spacious house in Cheltenham, Frances Stirling did fill in her schedule, but grudgingly added that 'This Form is Filled in through the Magnanimity of a Suffragette'. Single women like Mary Blathwayt, living on dividends from investments (plus a parental allowance), enjoyed some financial independence – and the confidence to evade. Certainly, the number living on 'private means' stand out among the boycotters, particularly those with military pensions, often from service in India (like Colonel Blathwayt), while Mrs Brackenbury was the widow of a general.

Women's own paid occupations also played a crucial role in shaping identities, and so motivations on census night. Many who felt sufficiently confident to boycott were professional women, notably women doctors – like tax resister Dr Elizabeth Knight (WFL) living by Hampstead Heath near the Brailsfords. In the Harley Street neighbourhood, hospital physician Dr Octavia Lewin resisted, as did Edith Mansell-Moullin, wife of a consulting surgeon. Doctors certainly represented a key occupation within the Tax Resistance League: in Hackney, Dr Elizabeth Wilks hosted a mass evasion of forty women. Even among women doctors, however, responses were not of course uniform. Some complied: Dr Ethel Bentham in north Kensington did, as did Dr Mary Murdoch in Hull. The point is, this elite professional group might be small, but it was committed, courageous and well-informed. Of the twenty-two women doctors listed in the Gazetteer, almost three-quarters boycotted. The others would have been very clear exactly why they decided to comply.

A more sizeable occupational group was teachers. Teaching had become a rapidly expanding field for women: over 125,000 were employed in local authority schools alone. Many teachers were active suffragettes; however their individual responses on census night were mixed. In the Middlesbrough WFL branch, sisters Charlotte and Amy Mahony both taught in county council schools; but, with the enumerator on the doorstep, a fully compliant schedule was handed over. Living near the Coates resisters, head-teacher Winifred Jones, who had chaired the Margaret Nevinson meeting, also complied. Yet in the Manchester region, teachers apparently felt more confident about boycotting; they included Agnes Hordern, probably evading in Denison House; and Janet Heyes of Eccles, possibly one of the midnight cyclists. It appears that local authority employers varied, with urban councils like Manchester more politically sympathetic than predominantly rural North Riding. In contrast, privately employed teachers in fee-paying schools and training colleges certainly felt less constrained about boycotting – especially if it was their own school. The Misses Thompson of Ilkley make that point.

One other significant occupational group was of course those working in the worlds of theatre or art – like Mary Howey, 'Artist and Suffragette' resister near Malvern; painter Mary Sargant Florence along the Thames valley; musician Ethel Smyth; and writer Laurence Housman, who complied himself, but naturally made his Kensington studio available to four female evaders. In Sale's mass evasion, among those hiding away were undoubtedly two local artists, Ada Hines and Lucy Fildes. Actors were of course particularly visible on census night: Decima Moore declaiming at the Aldwych skating rink, and down at Portsmouth's mass evasion, a theatrical company with its reading of Ibsen's *Ghosts*. Meanwhile, other women's newer occupations pop up surprisingly: market-gardeners in Berkshire, a masseuse in Paddington, even a ju-jitsu teacher in Islington, plus of course scientists like Hertha Ayrton.

Most women worked in the major paid occupations: domestic service, textile manufacture and the clothing trades. The Gazetteer confirms that not many boycotters can be identified among them. There were few to be found across the northern textile communities, for instance in Yorkshire among those appearing in *Rebel Girls*. In Huddersfield, of the names identified in the earlier WSPU minute book, those who had been active suffragettes now complied. Thus twenty-year-old weaver Dora Thewlis (who appeared on the book's cover) decided against boycotting the census, as did her fellow local textile workers.[26] Among tailoresses too it is hard to find many boycotters. One boldly vocal exception is Sybil Marsden, dressmaker of Kensington High Street, furious at having 'been taxed for the upkeep of no 10 Downing Street', not least because Mrs Asquith took her custom to Paris.[27] Rather more typical was Amy Scott, dressmaker in Exeter, who resisted more modestly.[28] But there are few such.

Of these three major employment groups, domestic service occupies a special place. The great majority of households listed in the Gazetteer included at least one live-in servant. In the politicization of homes on census night, they inhabited a crucial interior space at the heart of any boycott. How exactly did they respond? Frustratingly, it is extremely hard to know: servants' own experiences went largely unrecorded, other than through the pen of their employers – upon whom they were doubly dependent, for wages but also for a roof. The schedules themselves do however offer revealing glimpses of upstairs–downstairs relationships on census night.

In some evaders' households, servants remained at home, despite the disappearance of their mistress: in Batheaston, the Tollemaches' cook signed the schedule. In Manchester, Esther Roper and Eva Gore-Booth probably evaded, leaving behind their housekeeper and her family. There are also examples of the woman of the family evading and apparently 'taking' her servants with her: in their large house near Holland Park, Henrietta Lowy evaded – along with her four servants (plus husband and children). Near Cheltenham, Florence Earengey who evaded seems to have taken with her at least one servant (there were eleven rooms to keep clean).[29] In some evaders' households it was left to the enumerator to note that a servant had gone too: this was so in George Pratt's house in Ipswich, where they must all have gone to Constance Andrews's mass evasion.

What consultations took place with servants before census night? Again, there is tantalizingly little evidence. In Kensington, Stanley Mappin merely stated he would not provide any information for his five servants, with no indication of their views. In Middlesbrough, Charles Coates refused to provide details for his wife, daughter and two female servants, as 'they object'. It would be good to know if they did indeed all object. Of evidence about discussion between mistress and servant, the nearest is perhaps Clemence Housman's references to her maid Jane who seems to have been persuaded by Clem. But could a servant refuse? The heavy personal dependence on an employer militated against that. In the north Surrey suburbs, thirty-one year-old Lilian Beldon's occupation is given as lady's companion to a sixty-eight year-old widow of private means; Lilian was apparently a WSPU activist and yet she complied.[30] Presumably she just could not afford to jeopardize her position? Living-in female servants, the last to benefit from any Conciliation Bill provisions, remained meshed in dependency.[31]

Overall, the prospect of a £5 fine deterred many women. After all, such a fine represented four times the wages of, say, boot-maker George Baines. So often wives were dependent upon a husband's modest wage: in Wolverhampton WFL, Abigail Cresswell's husband was a pattern-turner, in West Hartlepool WFL, Minnie English's husband sold life insurance. Both households complied, though sadly in such households there is scant record of any marital conversations that lay behind their decisions.

With five hundred schedules, the Gazetteer is now sufficiently broad to suggest local examples of neighbourhood boycotting solidarity on census night. Near Hampstead Heath the enumerator's summary page included the homes of Jane Brailsford and Elizabeth Knight, both recorded as having 'refused to fill up Form'. In residential hotels clustered near Bloomsbury and Holborn, resisters were emboldened to refuse information. Similarly, in Rose Hyland's Manchester neighbourhood, fellow boycotters often lived within just a few minutes' walk of each other. In Sussex, boycotting seaside boarding-house landladies and teachers running their own schools were often near neighbours. Further down the coast at Torquay, it is surely no coincidence that two resisters lived right next door to each other on the seafront. In such neighbourhoods, the politicization of the domestic sphere on census night acted as the social glue of the suffrage movement.

There are however also some less congenial, rather eye-watering local conjunctions: in Belsize Park, the Stracheys lived just a few doors away from WSPU evader Daisy Koettgen, and almost cheek-by-jowl with the boycotting Nevinsons. And by Kensington High Street, all the Housmans' immediate neighbours apparently complied – though failing to dent Laurence's unquenchable optimism.

London exceptionalism remains striking; but what explains local clusters of census defiance elsewhere? The Gazetteer confirms that one crucial factor was the presence of an active suffragette organizer who could whip up local boycott support, hopefully for a mass evasion. This seems especially so for the WSPU: Mary Phillips in Bradford, the Archdale–Pankhurst household in Sheffield, Charlotte Marsh in Portsmouth. The further a community lay from London, the more this organizing role was vital.[32] In the absence of an organizer, a dynamic local branch secretary could be decisive, especially in or near London: for instance, in Hampstead Miss Lucas (WFL), and Lilian Hicks and Constance Collier (WSPU). Indeed, in certain communities the branch secretary *was* the boycott: at Pinner in Middlesex, Janie Terrero (WSPU) evaded, amid a sea of compliance. Boycotting in such areas required real bravery: secretary of Peckham WFL, Julia Pickering, wife of a milk vendor, was a rare evader across her corner of south-east London.[33]

One final correlation is with health inequalities in families, especially infant mortality. This, after all, was largely the point behind the government's new census columns – about a wife's current marriage, how many children born alive, how many had died.[34] These questions, although often resented at the time, confirm the prevalence of child deaths, even among upper-middle-class families. For his wife, Colonel Blathwayt recorded one child death on his schedule; Helen Watts had lost a brother; and four of May Sinclair's brothers had tragically died early. All these women complied on census night: were they swayed at all by a wish to provide accurate data? Among lower-middle- and working-class families, sadly fewer biographical detail survive. However, the schedules do make clear the prevalence of multiple infant mortality. Jennie Baines had lost two of her five children; three of the Mahonys' siblings had died. More broadly, in working-class neighbourhoods like north Kensington, infant mortality was so rife it prompted Ethel Bentham to found her pioneer baby clinic in late 1911 as a Women's Labour League memorial.[35]

It is difficult to tease out exactly what motivated individual women who might be expected to boycott but who in fact complied; but it does seems likely that health inequalities led some families to be persuaded by the 'sin against science' argument. Additionally, by 1911 many suffragettes themselves suffered very poor health. Imprisonment, hunger striking and forcible feeding had already taken their savage toll. Certainly, some of those who had experienced persistent ill-health – Hannah Mitchell, Jennie Baines, Helen Watts – did comply, rather than boycotting as might have been expected.[36] It remains tricky to unplait the subtle mix of motivations for each such complier. Other hunger strikers seem to have been galvanized by the brutality of their prison experiences, like Mary Leigh, Charlotte Marsh, Mabel Capper. More broadly, general health inequalities, and the factors behind them, apparently helped shape census responses, though individual thinking remains largely elusive and undocumented.

So, is it possible to judge from the five hundred Gazetteer schedules approximately how many boycotters there may have been on census night across England? Even rough estimates must still remain cautious. While we can be fairly certain of the resisters whose schedules we can read, evaders always remain more slippery to pin down, especially young women in cities. However, a rough calculation might be attempted of likely minimum and possible maximum numbers of boycotters. Of mass evaders, there are at least 1,700 listed; with others yet to be identified (eluding even our most persistent searches), perhaps there may have been as many as 2,500 mass evaders.[37] Of individual boycotters, a rough estimate of between 500 and 800 may be identified with some certainty; with perhaps a guess at an additional 300 to 1,000 elusive 'weak evaders' (i.e. where information remains insubstantial or searches have proved too tricky). This might suggest a minimum of perhaps 2,500, a possible maximum of 4,500. There were certainly well under ten thousand boycotters, and an estimate of about three to four thousand may be likely.[38]

Margaret Nevinson's *Suffrage Annual* estimate of 'thousands of women' missing does therefore seem reasonable. However, Agnes Metcalfe's claim of evaders running 'into six figures' (i.e. at least one hundred thousand), seems distinctly exaggerated; and Margaret Nevinson's subsequent upping her estimate to 'some hundreds of thousands' (minimum two hundred thousand) seems wildly optimistic. Laurence Housman's own autobiographical guess of 'many tens of thousands' quite possibly 'the hundred thousands', is again hard to substantiate.

So does John Burns's ministerial claim that the number evading enumeration in 1911 was 'altogether negligible' hold good? His statement on Wednesday 5 April would be based upon information from Archer Bellingham and Bernard Mallet: that enumerators and registrars helped by police had head-counted (even if not obtained details for) the great majority of boycotters.[39] They could probably feel reasonably confident that their overall population data was fairly reliable, even if individual names were missing and personal details patchy.[40] Should we then concur with demographic historians that the overall effect of the boycott was indeed statistically slight? Probably yes. After all, the census for England had to enumerate a population of no fewer than 34 million people, within which three to four thousand represented just a tiny fraction.

However, arithmetic is only one part of the larger story. Given the promise of National Insurance reforms, the boycott's opponents' stinging jibes about 'sin against science', plus the narrowness of the Conciliation Bill, it is surely highly surprising that any women had the *chutzpah* or indeed daring to evade, let alone to resist. For many, given all the arguments and pressures, it was indeed a close call on census night. Beyond those with confidence derived from an independent income (or carefree youth), especially outside London and major city centres, it demanded remarkable courage. Despite all the WSPU, WFL and WTRL propaganda and publicity – including postcards imagining evaders drifting sky-wards suspended beneath a balloon – prospective boycotters were right up against the Edwardian state, which had already rigorously pursued tax-resisters and forcibly fed suffragettes. We now know not a single boycotter was dragged through the courts. On census night, they did not. So that perhaps three to four thousand women were prepared to take this risk remains indeed remarkable.

Individual schedules contain tantalizing absences and silences, of boycotters' details, or surprise compliers' motivations. Yet the census continues to offer historians a unique and invaluable snapshot on census night 1911 of resisters, evaders and compliers, and of their suffrage organizations, both big and small. Their citizenship arguments touched distant branches, isolated communities and little-known individuals. This census turned the family home into a contested space, politicized acutely and dramatically one night, transforming the domestic and private into the public and political. Indeed, the 1911 census reflects a sharp collision of ideas. Some now felt wary about supporting such narrow enfranchisement proposals. Even among those who did agree on the Conciliation Bill, there was sharp tension over tactics: to remain constitutional or to break the law. And then there were also two rival concepts of citizenship: government 'by the people' stood in contrast to government 'for the people'. For one, democracy worked and offered vital welfare reforms; for the other, it denied full citizenship and did *not*. Many, like the Women's Co-operative Guildswomen or ILP members, found themselves caught in between – and opted for statistical accuracy to strengthen the Liberals' progressive agenda.

The lower than expected number of boycotters reflects the intensity of this 'battle for the census', rather than measuring the true strength of the suffrage movement in 1911. This clearly cannot be read directly from the census figures. Indeed, just weeks later, in the Coronation Procession on 17 June, forty thousand women marched together, constitutionalists and militants alike in a spirit of optimism and cooperation. This sense of firm determination and shared purpose was further strengthened in November, when Asquith's threat of manhood suffrage triggered outraged protest right across the movement. This included not only WSPU window-smashing (and later arson), but also the NUWSS's alliance with labour against Liberal by-election candidates. Therefore, if the census had been conducted in April 1912, the number of infuriated women prepared to boycott Asquith's requirements and to break the law would undeniably have been far, far higher. It would probably have extended to most suffrage campaigners (other than diehard Liberal loyalists), and have included women in the ILP and trade unions; and it would probably have spread far more broadly across regions and social classes, so that, in sprawling urban areas like east Bristol, Lilian Lenton would not have appeared a lone boycotter. Indeed, a boycott of a 1912 census might well have been as widespread as the 1991 census protest again the poll tax, with its estimated under-enumeration of one million.[41]

Moreover, to judge the 1911 census rebellion merely by its arithmetic is to miss the boycott's compelling symbolism and its historic significance – both for suffragettes then and for historians a century later. It was the first time women had been faced on census night with a political dilemma; and the first time a sizeable group of the disenfranchised had defied a government and refused to be counted – all without one single arrest. As Laurence Housman put it later: 'Honest John Burns … climbed down in a night, and … let the offenders off … The women had come off victors from the field', without any street violence or imprisonments. This climb down lent considerable confidence over the coming months to active civil disobedience – both Clemence Housman's quiet yet celebrated tax resistance in the autumn, and from November WSPU's escalated militancy.

So, in April 2011 for the census centenary, celebrations were held to mark the courageous stand these Edwardian women took over that fundamental of democratic citizenship: no government without the consent of the governed. The best-remembered evaders remain Emily Wilding Davison's sojourn in her parliamentary cupboard, the Aldwych skaters, Emmeline Pankhurst in her Holborn hotel and Jessie Stephenson's Manchester 'census lodge' sleepers. In the end

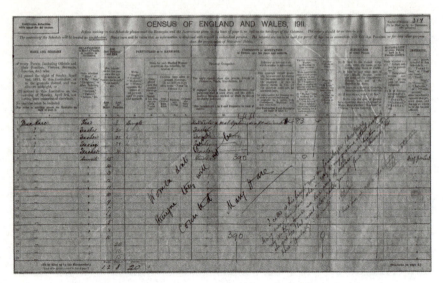

44 Census schedule, Mary Hare and her school, Hove, Sussex.

however, it is the little-known women, often extremely isolated in their midnight risk-taking, whose courage to 'vanish for the vote' retains its power to inspire.

For it is individual boycotters' own words that, over a century later, still strike home. So we end by highlighting one schedule. It was completed by Mary Hare, WFL co-secretary Brighton and Hove branch, not far from the route taken by the first caravan just three years earlier. Mary was head-teacher of an 'oral system deaf and dumb' school, and firmly inscribed her institutional schedule at a defiant angle: 'Women don't count therefore they will not be counted'.

Gazetteer of campaigners

compiled by
Elizabeth Crawford and Jill Liddington

Contents

Introduction

Each entry in the Gazetteer represents one **household schedule**, completed on census night 1911. A total of five hundred schedules are listed. They are arranged geographically across England: by region, county (or London borough), town or city, and by neighbourhood.

The information given here is just as it appears on the schedule, recording who was present on census night (usually family members, plus any visitors, boarders and servants). Individual suffrage affiliations for spring 1911 have been added, where they are known.

The entries fall under three headings: compliers and boycotters (i.e. both evaders and resisters). **Compliers** comprise those recorded as present on census night, for whom information is accurate. The Gazetteer is not of course at all a comprehensive listing of all who complied. From the vast number of names of compliers, selected here are:

(*a*) NUWSS members mentioned in the text e.g. Helena Swanwick in Cheshire;
(*b*) adult suffragists mentioned in the text e.g. Dr Ethel Bentham in Kensington;
(*c*) those whose compliance is surprising, given their suffragette (notably WSPU, WFL) affiliation e.g. Hannah Mitchell in Manchester; or because their compliance is significant in some other way. With so many such compliers, we have had to be highly selective.

Entries for compliers are usually straightforward, their schedules recording their household structure accurately.

Those who evaded the census may be subdivided into two groups: mass evaders and individual evaders. For **mass evasions**, the number of evaders present and their location is given, along with the name of the evasion host, where it is known. As groups were often determined not to be tracked, their schedules can be particularly hard to find, e.g. Laura Ainsworth in Kent. A table of mass evasions may be found on pp. 243–4, listed by the number of recorded evaders. There is naturally no firm distinction between mass evasions and larger home gatherings of friends or neighbours, which are not included here.

For those **individuals evading** the census on their own or in small household groups, the names and details of as many of those about whom we can be fairly certain are included. Evasion however remains a slippery category, and evaders are predictably those who did not *want* to be found – by the enumerator on the night, by the Registrar the following week, or by suffrage historians like ourselves a century later. They are those about whom it is still most tricky to be precise. Those nigh impossible to track down with certainty (often young single women in large cities) have had to be omitted. Where someone is highly likely to have evaded but has left no evidence, they have been noted briefly on their most likely schedule, either as absent at home or in their most probable location (e.g. Alice Hawkins, missing from the family schedule, was undoubtedly evading at Leicester's WSPU office). In a handful of cases, however, we *have* included evaders even though no schedule has been found, as their evasion is almost certain e.g. the Duvals in Wandsworth. Although some uncertainty or imprecision inevitably remains, the repetition of 'probable' and 'possible' has been kept to a minimum.

We aim to include as many known **census resisters** as possible, along with many of their statements of defiance. A formal note was often added by the enumerator or registrar, using fairly standard wording, and many of these are included too. For certain persistent boycotters, the registrar added in information, noting it was 'Inserted on authority of the Registrar General in letter dated [.] April', or similar wording. Where a resister's statement has already been quoted in the text (e.g. Mildred Mansel in Bath), the page reference is provided. Where certain words are missing or obscured, suggested wording is denoted in square brackets.

The distinction between those who evaded (i.e. eluded the enumerator) and those who resisted (i.e. confronted the enumeration system) is not always a clear one, especially in London. Numbers of resisters wrote on their schedules – and then proceeded to evade, often skating at the Aldwych; so here they are designated as 'resister/evader'. More generally, the term 'boycotters' is used as a clear umbrella designation for all those who refused to comply with the census.

Evidence from **other sources** has had to be adduced for some boycotters, especially evaders – notably the 1901 census taken a decade earlier. This supplementary data (e.g. campaigners' precise ages) is denoted by square brackets.

Additionally, each enumerator compiled a **summary book** for a neighbourhood, with one name and address per line. Where individual schedules either withhold key information or have proved impossible to trace, these summaries have proved invaluable.

Finally, the 1911 census required the head of household to record, for **each**

married woman under his roof, the number of children born alive, still living and who had died. Thus in Poplar, MP George Lansbury noted for his wife Elizabeth, twelve children were born, nine were living and three had died. His schedule also recorded those children present on census night: of Elizabeth Lansbury's children, just six were present. However, these new census questions prompted much confusion, a husband sometimes supplying information for himself rather than his wife. This has however allowed us occasionally to discover how many children a woman had – even though she is a mysteriously missing wife (e.g. in Hackney, Sarah Mustard evades; her husband notes three children, yet only two daughters are present, suggesting Sarah was accompanied by her eldest daughter).

The Gazetteer lists **five hundred schedules** here, and these form the basis for the estimations of the likely numbers of boycotters across England discussed in the final chapter.

Here, we aim to provide a good balance between accuracy and accessibility. Readers should easily find who they want by looking up the person's name in the book's index (page numbers in *italics*); or by noting their geographical location and then turning to that section of the Gazetteer. Thus readers will hopefully be able to find exactly whom they are searching for. If the name you want is *not* here, then the person probably:

(*a*) is not in England on census night (e.g. Sylvia Pankhurst); or
(*b*) may be an evader we have had to omit due to insufficient evidence; or
(*c*) is one of the many, many compliers not listed in this Gazetteer; or
(*d*) is a boycotter whose name is little known, as yet.

We hope that this Gazetteer will act as a spur to further research.

Abbreviations used in the Gazetteer

AFL   Actresses' Franchise League
ASL   Artists' Suffrage League
CathWS   Catholic Women's Suffrage Society
CLWS   Church League for Women's Suffrage
CUWFA   Conservative and Unionist Women's Franchise Association
FCLWS   Free Church League for Women's Suffrage
ILP   Independent Labour Party
LSWS   London Society for Women's Suffrage (NUWSS)
MPU   Men's Political Union for Women's Enfranchisement.
MLWS   Men's League for Women's Suffrage
NCSWS   New Constitutional Society for Women's Suffrage
NIPWSS   National Industrial and Professional Women's Suffrage Society
NUWSS   National Union of Women's Suffrage Societies
PSF   People's Suffrage Federation (adult suffrage)
Suff At   Suffrage Atelier
WCG   Women's Co-operative Guild
WLabL   Women's Labour League
WLibL   Women's Liberal Federation
WSPU   Women's Social & Political Union
WFL   Women's Freedom League
WWSL   Women Writers' Suffrage League

Aldwych   Aldwych Skating Rink
LCC   London County Council

Key mass evasions

Location	Host or venue	Total	Female, male	Suffrage organization
Westminster	Aldwych Skating Rink, Strand	570	500f, 70m	WSPU, WFL & others
Westminster	Gardenia Restaurant, Covent Garden.	230	200f, 30m	WSPU, WFL & others
Manchester	Stephenson, Jessie	208	156f, 52m	WSPU, WFL & others
Manchester	Hyland, Rose	88	77f, 11m	WSPU & others
Sheffield	Pankhurst/Archdale	57	54f, 3m	WSPU
Portsmouth	Marsh, Charlotte	52	39f, 13m	WSPU
Hackney	Wilks, Elizabeth	40	40f	WTRL
Paddington	Ayrton, Hertha	c.40	c.40f	WSPU
Gillingham	Ainsworth, Laura	40?	39f, 1m?	WSPU
Birkenhead	Ker, Alice	38	37f, 1m	WSPU
Bath	Mansel, Mildred	36	36f	WSPU
Kensington	Conder, Helen	36	35f, 1m	?
Newcastle	Williams, Annie	29	27f, 2m	WSPU
Kensington	Brackenbury, Marie	26	25f, 1m	WSPU
Ipswich	Andrews, Constance	21	16f, 5m	WFL (+ WSPU)
Sale	Manning, Mary E.	20	20f	WFL
Leicester	Hawkins, Alice?	c.20	c.20f	WSPU
Fulham	Anon.	17	9f, 8m	?
Anerley, Kent	Fennings, Misses	14–16	14–16f	WFL
Cheltenham	Flatman, Ada	13	12f, 1m	WSPU
Hendon, Msx	Wyatt, Mrs	13	9f, 4m	WSPU
Brighton	Turner, Minnie	12	12f	WTRL, WSPU
Lowestoft	Fairchild, Lottie	11	11f	?
Wandsworth	Marshall, Kitty	11	10f, 1m	WSPU
	(caravans on Putney Heath/Wimbledon Common)			
Fulham	Bessle, Miss	11	11f	?
Bradford	Phillips, Mary	10	10f	WSPU

King's Norton (Bhm)	Steen, Fanny	c.10	c.10f	WSPU
King's Norton (Bhm)	Impey, Edith	10	8f, 2m	?
Hampstead Garden Suburb	How-Martyn, Edith	8	7f, 1m	WFL
Hastings	Harrison, Mrs Darent	6	6f	WTRL
Wimbledon	Hellrich, Victor	–	'several' m & f	WSPU?
Bromley, Kent	Harvey, Kate	?	'suffragettes'	WFL, WTRL
Hampstead	Nevinson, Margaret	?	unknown number	WFL
Willesden, Msx	Penn Gaskell, Eleanor	?	unknown number	WSPU
Portsmouth	?Mottershall, Miss	?	unknown number	WFL
Bristol	Kenney, Annie	1	1f (recorded)	WSPU

Details of these schedules follow, listed by geographical location.

London boroughs and Middlesex

LONDON: population 4,500,000

CENTRAL

Westminster: population 160,000

In or near Palace of Westminster

Davison [miswritten as **'Davidson'**]**, Emily Wilding**, '35 years' [39 years].
Houses of Parliament.
'Found Hiding in Crypt' of Westminster Hall (enumerator's summary).
Census night: evader; schedule signed by Clerk of Works, Houses of Parliament.
Occupation: 'school teacher'.
Suffrage: WSPU.
See also: St Pancras (p. 261).

Chapman, Mrs Adeline, [64 years].
24 Buckingham Gate.
Census night: evader.
Family: husband, Cecil, metropolitan magistrate.
Household: 25 rooms, 5 servants.
Suffrage: NCSWS.

Boyle, Miss [Nina].
Flat 6, Block 1, 23 Victoria Street.
Census night: resister.
Statement: 'Flat filled with Census Resisters. No Votes, No Census. Votes for Women.'
Enumerator: 'Called at Mansions 7 April 1911. Had interview with the manager, who ascertained from the maid that 5 females slept here 2/4/11 – one of these, Miss Boyle's sister, objected to the proceedings and was by her own request enumerated with the staff by the manager.' Registrar signs.
Suffrage: WFL.

Forsyth, Mrs, and daughter, Jean, [32 years].
59 Carlisle Mansions, Carlisle Place.
Census night: evaders.
Household: 6 rooms.
Female caretaker: 'The family is away and consists only of women who do not count as citizens and therefore should not be counted in the census. The House of Lords lately decided that "Women are not Persons".'
Suffrage: NCSWS.

Aldwych

500 women, 70 men, all anonymous.
Aldwych Skating Rink, Aldwych.
Census night: evaders.
Statement: 'Report from the Census Office.'
Suffrage: WSPU, WFL, other societies (see Chapter 12).

[Pankhurst, Christabel, 31 years.
Census night: evader; no schedule, but was present at Aldwych.
Suffrage: WSPU.]

Tuke, Mrs Mabel, [40 years].
Census night: evader, no schedule, undoubtedly at Aldwych.
Occupation: WSPU honorary secretary.
Suffrage: WSPU.

Covent Garden

200 women, 30 men, all anonymous.
Gardenia Restaurant, 6 Catherine Street.
Census night: evaders.
Statement: 'Report from the Census Office.'
Suffrage: WSPU, WFL, other societies.

Craig, Edith, 41 years.
31 Bedford Street.
Census night: complies.
Occupation: actress and theatrical.
Household: 8 rooms.
Suffrage: AFL.

Miller, Irene Florence, 'abt 30' [31 years].
30 Long Acre.
Census night: resister.
Occupation: fashion designer.
Household: 2 rooms.
Statement: 'I refuse to assist in any census whilst women are unenfranchised! The above statement was written with the pen with which I earn my living.'
Suffrage: WFL?

Parkes, Mrs Margaret Kineton, [46 years].
10 Talbot House, 98 St Martin's Lane.
Census night: evader, doubtless at Aldwych.
Suffrage: WTRL.

East of Kingsway

Pethick-Lawrence, Mrs Emmeline, 'abt 50' [44 years].
4 Clement's Inn.
Census night: resister.
Statement: 'Until the government recognizes my position as a citizen of this country by according to me and other duly qualified women the right to take part in the election of representatives in Parliament, I have a conscientious objection to assisting the Government by furnishing them with information and I accordingly refuse to fill in the particulars requested.'
Suffrage: WSPU.

Pethick, Ethel Mary, '40 years',
4 Clement's Inn.
Census night: resister.
Statement: 'No Vote No Census.'
Suffrage: WSPU.

Mayfair area

McTurk, Agnes Nellie, [40 years].
8 Hanover Square.
Census night: resister (visitor).
Others: Emily Ridout (head) and her sister, milliners; their nephew.
Household: 9 rooms, 2 servants.
Statement: 'Suffragist. Refuses information.'

Simson, Mrs Lena [Ashwell], 39 years.
36 Grosvenor Street.
Census night: complies.
Occupation: actress.
Family: husband, doctor.
Household: 20 rooms, 6 servants, secretary.
Suffrage: AFL, WTRL.

Holborn: population 49,000

Pankhurst, Mrs Emmeline, [53 years] and **Wright, Ada**, [49 years].
Inns of Court Hotel, High Holborn.
Census night: evaders.
Statement: Registrar: 'I am of the opinion that at least one of the above viz Mrs Pankhurst was counted at the Aldwych Skating Rink. I find however that this lady returned to the Hotel at 5 am on the morning of the 3rd April 1911. Under the circumstances I have allowed her name to stand and be counted herein,' 15 Apr 1911.
Suffrage: WSPU.

Bloomsbury

Carwin, Sarah, 'abt 40 years' [48 years].
11 Tavistock Mansions, Tavistock Place.
Census night: resister.
Other: Miss Milligan ('abt 50'), LCC schoolteacher.
Enumerator: 'Information refused'.
Suffrage: WSPU.

Martel, Mrs Ellen [Nellie], 45 years.
8 Francis Street.
Census night: evader?
Household: 2 rooms, 2 visitors.
Enumerator signed schedule, noting Martel 'absent when [schedule] called for'.
Unclear who entered details.
Suffrage: WSPU.

Fawcett, Millicent, 63 years.
2 Gower Street.
Census night: complies.
Occupation: writer.
Family: sister, Agnes, retired house decorator; daughter Philippa (42), LCC
Education Department.
Household: 13 rooms, 3 servants.
Suffrage: NUWSS.

Wilson, Helen, 45 years.
Thackery Hotel, Great Russell Street.
Census night: complies.
Occupation: doctor, retired.
Household: other hotel guests.
Suffrage: NUWSS

West of Gower Street

Jones, Miss.
65 Bedford Court Mansions, Bedford Avenue.
Census night: resister.
Household: 1 female servant, also a resister.

Jethro-Robinson, Mrs Favoretta, [47 years].
Bedford Court Hotel, Bayley Street, Bedford Square.
Census night: evader.
Family: husband, hotel manager; 2 sons.
Others: many hotel guests.
Suffrage: WSPU, CLWS.

Guest, Mrs Hilda, [42 years].
14 Bedford Square.
Census night: evader.
Family: husband, 2 sons, 2 daughters.
Household: 15 rooms, 6 servants.
Suffrage: NCSWS?

MacArthur, Miss Ellen A., Davenport, Miss, and Jones, Rosalie.
15 & 16 White Hall, Bedford Place
Census night: resisters.
Others: fellow hotel guests etc.
Enumerator: 'Information declined – suffragette' (three times).

Wray, Miss.
Kingsley Hotel, Hart Street.
Census night: resister.
Others: fellow hotel guests etc.
Enumerator: similar to above.

Dallas, Hilda, [33 years] and sister **Irene**, [28 years].
36 St George's Mansions, Red Lion Square.
Census night: evaders.
Occupation: Hilda [artist].
Suffrage: WSPU.

Finsbury: population 87,923

Homer and Bourner, Misses, 'abt 27 yrs'.
31 Claremont Square.
Census night: resisters.
Statement: 'We are longing to write
Our names and our age,
And information too,
On this quaint yellow page.
But since we don't count
(Though our taxes we pay)
We'll forgoe [*sic*] this delight
Till some future day.'
Registrar: signs.

NORTH

Hampstead: population 85,495

Belsize Park

Nevinson, Margaret Wynne, [53 years] and **Henry**, 54 years.
4 Downside Crescent.
Census night: Margaret probably present, evading; Henry evading at Aldwych.
Occupation: MWN [author], HN journalist.
Family: son (21) art student.
Household: 11 rooms, 2 servants; an unspecified number of women.
Statement: see p.138.
Suffrage: Margaret: WFL, WWSL, CLWS, WTRL. Henry: MPU, MLWS.

Hicks, Mrs Lilian, [58 years], and probably daughter, **Amy** [33 years].
33 Downside Crescent.
Census night: resister/evader(s); no inhabitants recorded in enumerator's summary.
Household: 10 rooms.
Statement: 'As I am not regarded as a responsible citizen, I *refuse* to fill up this paper. Lilian M. Hicks. Occupier.'
Registrar: 'No information obtainable.'
Suffrage: WSPU, WTRL.

Davies, [Sarah] Emily, 80 years.
17 Glenmore Road.
Census night: complies.
Household: 8 rooms, 2 servants.
Suffrage: NUWSS.

Copsey, Helen, [22 years].
18 Glenloch Road.
Census night: evader.
Occupation: [artist].
Family: father, picture dealer; mother, brother.
Other: male boarder, accountant.
Household: 9 rooms.
Suffrage: Suff At.

Strachey, [Lady] Jane, 71 years.
57 Belsize Park Gardens.
Census night: complies.
Status: widow, 13 children, 10 still living, 3 have died.
Family: sons Ralph 42, Oliver 36, Lytton 31; daughters Philippa 38, and Pernel
35 (Figure 26, p. 143).
Household: 18 rooms, 5 servants.
Suffrage: NUWSS/LSWS.

Koettgen, Daisy, [34 years].
63 Belsize Park Gardens.
Census night: evader.
Family: father, merchant; sister.
Household: 14 rooms, 3 servants.
Suffrage: WSPU.

Harraden, Beatrice, [47 years].
3 Fitzjohns Mansions, Netherhall Gardens.
Census night: resister.
Occupation: [author].
Household: 1 servant.
Statement: 'No Vote No Information.'
Suffrage: WSPU, WWSL, NCSWS.

Styer, Mrs Louisa, [47 years]; and daughters **Catherine**, [26 years], **Dorothy**,
[24 years], **Vera**, [21 years].
12 Wedderburn Road.
Census night: resisters.
Family: husband, solicitor; son, articled clerk.
Household: 4 servants, 13 rooms.
Statement: 'refuse all information until the franchise is granted to women.'
Husband filled in names, and appears to be author of statement.

Phillips, Harford, and **Ellen?, Misses.**
37 Frognal.
Census night: resisters.
Occupations: cook (Phillips), housemaids.
Others: Wolf Levy (67), wife Mary (55), 2 daughters, 1 son, 1 female visitor.
Household: 16 rooms.
Statement: against servants' names Levy wrote: 'Refuse to give information
being suffragettes.'

Richmond, Mrs Ennis.
West Heath School, 25 & 27 Ferncroft Avenue.
Census night: resister.
Others: Boyd (male, 'manager of hostel'), Mr and Mrs Gayter ('gardener', 'cook'), resisters.
Household: 25 rooms.
Statement: Ennis Richmond: 'If others have slept in this house I have no clue to their names or identity.'
Enumerator: 'Section 2 of Act read to Mrs Gayter.'
Suffrage: WFL?, WTRL?

Holiday, Winifred, [45 years].
Oak Tree House, Branch Hill.
Census night: evader.
Family: father, artist; mother.
Household: 12 rooms, 3 servants.
Suffrage: NCSWS.

Black, Clementina, Miss, 57 years.
Pilgrims Place House, 56 Rosslyn Hill.
Census night: complies.
Occupation: author, journalist.
Family: sister, preparatory school mistress; niece, dramatic student.
Household: 3 rooms.
Suffrage: NUWSS.

Up Haverstock Hill, near Hampstead Heath

Brailsford, Mrs Jane, [37 years], and **Henry,** 37 years.
32 Well Walk.
Census night: resisters.
Family: journalist (Henry).
Household: 6 rooms.
Statement, Registrar and enumerator's summary (see p. 142).
Suffrage: WSPU, MLWS.

Lane, Mrs.
13 Christchurch Road.
Census night: resister.
Statement: 'No vote no census. You cannot expect me to fulfil a citizen's duties not having the rights of one.'

Knight, Elizabeth, [42 years].
7 Gainsborough Gardens.
Census night: resister.
Occupation: physician.
Enumerator's summary: 'Mrs [*sic*] Knight refused to fill up Form.'
Suffrage: WFL, WTRL.

Kennedy, Miss.
94 Heath Street.
Census night: resister.
Statement: (very faintly) 'Information refused'.
Enumerator: 'All information refused.'

Edwards, Annette, Miss.
62 Constantine Road.
Census night: resister.
Occupation: boarding-house keeper.
Household: 9 rooms; 1 female, 4 male boarders.
Statement: 'filled in without my consent – unenfranchised'.
Enumerator: 'complete information refused.'

Goodliffe, Misses.
62 High Street.
Census night: resisters, 2 sisters.
Statement: 'No Vote No Census.'

Lucas, Miss.
21 Gayton Road.
Census night: evader?
No schedule, nor mention in enumerator's summary.
Suffrage: WFL.

To West Hampstead

Thompson, Mary, [45 years], and **Margaret**, [47 years].
10 Stanley Gardens.
Census night: resisters.
Occupation: [teachers].
Household: 6 rooms; probably 1 female servant (resister).
Statement: 'No Vote No Census. As women are not persons in the eyes of the law, why count cyphers in the census. Mary Davies Thompson.'
Suffrage: WSPU.

Van Raalte, Mrs Jeanette, [42 years].
23 Pandora Road.
Census night: evader.
Family: husband, Leon, correspondence clerk; added '?' to his entry as 'Head';
son, daughter.
Household: 8 rooms.
Suffrage: WFL.

Solomon, Mrs Georgiana, [67 years], **and daughter, Daisy**, [29 years].
98 Sumatra Road.
Census night: evaders?
No schedule for the house (although son recorded here on 1911 electoral register).

Further south, towards Primrose Hill

Hall, Miss S. Elizabeth.
33 Canfield Gardens.
Census night: resister.
Statement: 'No vote no census return. Those who do not *count* in the nation
cannot be *counted*.'

Spong, Annie, 38 years.
66 Adelaide Road.
Census night: complies; no trace of mother, Frances (69), nor sister Florence,
both presumably evading.
Family: father, engineer.
Household: 9 rooms, 1 servant.
Suffrage: WSPU.

Hartley, Mrs Beatrice, [48 years].
168 Adelaide Road.
Census night: resister.
Status: widow.
Others: 2 females.
Enumerator's summary: 'information refused.'
Suffrage: NCSWS.

Bache, Margaret, [73 years].
2 College Road.
Census night: resister.
Household: 6 rooms.
Statement: 'No votes for women no information from women.'

Jansson, Mrs Edith, [54 years], and daughters, **Mary**, [26 years], **Gladys**, [23 years].
63 King Henry's Road.
Census night: absent, evaders.
Family: husband/father, Johan (59), son/brother (22).
Household: 8 rooms, 1 servant.
Suffrage: CLWS.

Collier, Constance, [57 years], **Florence**, [58 years].
119 King Henry's Road.
Census night: resisters.
Household: 1 servant
Statement: 'As I have no Parliamentary vote because women are not persons – I decline to fill in the census paper which is for the enumeration of the persons in the country. C. L. Collier.'
Suffrage: WSPU.

Sullivan, Frances
99 Fellows Road.
Census night: evader.
Others: female boarding-house keeper, 4 female, 5 male boarders.
Household: 13 rooms.

Estall, Alice, [52 years].
19 Steeles Road.
Census night: resister.
Occupation: [dressmaker].
Household: 10 rooms.
Statement: '*No Vote No Census* as a protest.'

Price, Mrs Louisa Thompson.
42 Parkhill Road.
Census night: resister.
Household: 11 rooms.
Statement: 'As I have no vote, I give no census information. The fundamental basis of democracy is Government *by consent of the governed*.'
Suffrage: WFL.

Marylebone: population 118,160

South of Marylebone Road

Bowker, Dorothy A., 'about 30 years'.
7 York Street.
Census night: resister.
Status: single, lodger.
Household: 1 room.
Statement: 'No Vote – No Census. I am Dumb politically Blind to the Census Deaf to Enumerators. Being classed with criminals lunatics and paupers I prefer to give no further particulars'.
Suffrage: WSPU.

Ede, Frances, 'about 50 years', and **6 female servants** [may have included Dr Amy Sheppard].
13 Upper Berkeley Street.
Census night: resisters.
Occupation: doctor.
Household: 12 rooms.
Statement: 'No Vote No Census'.
Suffrage: WSPU.

East of Baker Street

Moore, Decima [Mrs Frederick Guggisberg], 40 years.
132 Clarence Gate Gardens.
Census night: evader, performing at Aldwych.
House shown as uninhabited.
Suffrage: AFL

Troy, Miss, 'about 45 years'.
41 Beaumont Street.
Census night: resister.
Occupation: head of nursing home.
Others: 1 female, 1 male patient (resisters).
Household: 12 rooms, 5 servants (resisters).
Statement: 'No vote no information'.
'Particulars entered by enumerator.'

Lewin, Octavia, '30 years' [42 years].
25 Wimpole Street.
Census night: resister.
Occupation: assistant physician, London Homeopathic Hospital.
Family: 2 sisters (resisters).
Others: 3 visitors.
Household: 15 rooms, 4 female servants (all resisters).
Statement: 'No Vote No Census. I absolutely refuse to give any information.'
Suffrage: WSPU.

Mansell-Moullin, Mrs Edith, '50 years'.
69 Wimpole Street.
Census night: resisters.
Status: married.
Family: husband, Charles, consulting surgeon.
Others: 3 visitors (all resisters).
Household: 14 rooms, 4 servants (all resisters).
Statement: 'No Vote No Information.'
Suffrage: WSPU; Charles, MLWS.

Bentinck, Mrs Ruth Cavendish, 43 years.
78 Harley Street.
Census night: attempted resister (her details added by enumerator).
Status: married 23 years, 5 children, 4 living, 1 died.
Family: husband, barrister; daughter.
Household: 22 rooms, governess, 11 servants.
Suffrage: WSPU.

Garrett-Anderson, Louisa, '40 years' [38 years].
114a Harley Street.
Census night: resisters.
Status: single.
Occupation: doctor.
Household: 14 rooms, 4 female servants (all resisters).
Statement: Information refused.
Suffrage: WSPU.

Marks, Alfred, '53 years', **Marie**, 'about 40 years', **Bertram**, '19 years'.
7 Duchess Street.
Census night: resisters (Alfred signed, but all information filled in by enumerator).
Status: married, 1 son.
Occupation: Alfred, Stock Exchange; Marie, 'militant suffragette'.
Others: 3 visitors (all resisters).
Household: 11 rooms, 5 female servants (all resisters).
Enumerator: 'I have reason to believe a number of militant suffragettes were on the premises last night.'

St John's Wood

Sennett, Mrs Maud Arncliffe?
6 Wellington Road.
Census night: probably evading, with husband.
House recorded in enumerator's summary as uninhabited, then this is deleted.
Suffrage: WTRL, WSPU, WFL, AFL.

St Pancras: population 218,387

South of Euston Road

Lytton, Constance, 'over 60' [42 years].
15 Somerset Terrace.
Census night: absent? resister.
Occupation: 'Daughter and Sister of an Earl'.
Household: 4 rooms.
Statement: 'Filled in by Registrar. Information refused for political reasons'.
Suffrage: WSPU.

MacIrone, Edith, 'about 30', **Emily**, 'about 26'.
16 Somerset Terrace.
Census night: absent? resisters.
Occupation: independent means. [Emily: medical student].
Household: 4 rooms.
Statement: similar to Lytton.

Carter, Mrs, 'about 40'.
18 Somerset Terrace.
Census night: absent? resister.
Statement: same as Lytton.

Mackwall, Anne or Amelia [Mary Mack Wall], 'about 60'.
19 Somerset Terrace.
Census night: absent? resister.
Occupation: independent means.
Statement: similar to Lytton.

Neal, Mary, 'about 45' [51 years].
21 Somerset Terrace.
Census night: absent? resister.
Occupation: independent means.
Household: 4 rooms, 1 female servant (resister).
Statement: similar to Lytton.
Suffrage: WSPU sympathizer.

Bloomsbury

Stephen, Adeline Virginia, 29 years [Virginia Woolf].
29 Fitzroy Square.
Census night: complies.
Occupation: journalist.
Status: single.
Family: brother, Adrian, 27.
Household: 11 rooms, 3 servants.
Suffrage: PSF.

Brown, James S., 57 years.
28 Gordon Square.
Census night: complies, but resists on behalf of women of the household.
Occupation: Pensioned civil engineer (Indian railways).
Status: married.
Family: wife, daughter – both resisted.
Household: 6 rooms, 2 female servants, both resisted.
Statement: 'Decline to give information about women of my household in protest of the fact that Englishwomen are not granted the full rights of citizenship.'

Cutts, Miss, 'about 34'.
17 Upper Woburn Place.
Census night: resister.
Status: single, lodger.
Household: 17-room boarding house.
Enumerator: 'Suffragist. Information obtained from Head.'

Davison, Emily Wilding, 38 years.
31 Coram Street.
Census night: absent, evader.
Status: single.
Household: 2 rooms.
Statement: none surviving (see p. 129).
Information given by landlady.
Suffrage: WSPU.
See also: Westminster (p. 245).

Kerr, Harriet Roberta, 'over 40'; **May, Alice**, 'about 52'.
18 Doughty Street.
Census night: resisters.
Occupation: clerks in political office.
Status: single, widowed.
Household: 4 rooms.
Registrar: information from landlord, noting 'Information refused for political reasons'.
Suffrage: Kerr WSPU employee.

Lawson, Marie, 'over 30', **Ridler, Emily**, 'over 30'.
4 Guilford Street.
Census night: resisters.
Occupation: secretaries to suffragettes.
Status: single.
Household: 3 rooms.
Registrar: same as Kerr/May.
Suffrage: Lawson, WFL.

North of Euston Road

Wharry, Olive, [25 years].
7 Cambridge Gate.
Census night: doubtless evading.
Family: father, retired doctor.
Household: 18 rooms, 4 servants.
Suffrage: WSPU.

Hinscliff, Mrs Gertrude, [37 years].
11 St Mark's Crescent.
Census night: doubtless evading.
Family: husband Claude, clergyman, CLWS Secretary.
Household: 7 rooms, no servants listed. 1 male visitor.
Suffrage: CLWS.

Neilans, Alison, [37 years]; **Turner, Madge; Scott, Lily.**
Hampstead Road [outdoors, no location specified].
Census night: evaders.
Status: all single.
Occupation: Lily, coffee bar waitress.
Registrar: 'Homeless persons found by police', subject of police report.
Suffrage: Alison and Madge, WFL.

Pitfield, Ellen, '49'.
New Hospital for Women, Euston Road.
Census night: resister.
Occupation: patient.
Statement: 'Suffragette. Refused information.'
Suffrage: WSPU.

Lee [Leigh], **Mary**, '37'.
6 Houghton Place.
Census night: absent? resister.
Status: married.
Household: 2 rooms.
Enumerator: 'All other information unobtainable (Suffragette).'
Suffrage: WSPU.

Camden

Alder, M.
12 Wilmot Place.
Census night: resister.
Occupation: 'suffragette'.
Household: 1 room.
Note: completed by enumerator.

Bell, Florence.
29 Lady Somerset Road.
Census night: complies? (no ages recorded).
Family: husband, clerk.
Household: 3 rooms.
Suffrage: WLabL, adult suff.

To west

Hankinson, Frederick, 35 years.
60 Haverstock Hill.
Census night: complies.
Occupation: minister of religion (Unitarian).
Status: single.
Household: 5 rooms, 1 female servant ('housekeeper and suffragist').
Suffrage: WSPU, WFL.

Islington: population 327,203

North-east of borough

Long, Dr Constance, [36 years] and **Haslam, Dr Sarah Kate**, [34 years].
10 Warltersville Road, Upper Hornsey Rise.
Census night: resisters.
Family: Constance's father, Joseph (82) is only name entered.
Statement: 'No other "person", for women are not legally "persons".'
Enumerator: partially complete schedule, signing for Constance ('suffragette'),
as head of household; and adding for Sarah 'passive suffragist?'.
Suffrage: WTRL.

Hankinson, Mary, [43 years].
67 Shaftesbury Road, Hornsey Rise.
Census night: evader.
Enumerator: 'Did not sleep here (not suffragette).'
Suffrage: WFL.

Frost, Mrs.
65 Shaftesbury Road, Hornsey Rise.
Census night: evader.
Enumerator: 'Slept away did not return (not suffragette).'
[However, the proximity to Mary Hankinson suggests suffrage connection.]

Young, two Misses.
48 St John's Mansions, Pemberton Gardens, Holloway.
Census night: evaders.
Household: 2 rooms.
Statement: 'Suffragette[s].'
Enumerator: 'Believed to have passed the night away from the flat.'

Holloway Road area

Browne, Clare.
11 Gladsmuir Road.
Census night: evader.
Family: father, architectural surveyor; mother.
Suffrage: WSPU.

Bryer, Constance, [41 years].
49 Tufnell Park Road.
Census night: evader.
Family: father, mother, brother, 2 sisters.
Household: 11 rooms, 2 servants.
Suffrage: WSPU, CLWS.

Purdie, Mrs Ethel Ayres, [36 years].
13 Stock Orchard Crescent.
Census night: evader.
Occupation: [accountant].
Family: father, Henry Ayres (63); mother; husband, Frank Purdie (39), educational traveller.
Status: married 13 years.
Other: 1 male visitor.
Household: 9 rooms.
Suffrage: WTRL.

Garrud, Mrs Edith, 38 years.
61 Hartham Road, Holloway.
Census night: complies.
Status: married 18 years, 3 children.
Occupation: Ju-jitsu teacher.
Family: husband, ju-jitsu teacher; daughter (15), assisting in business.
Household: 3 rooms.
Suffrage: WSPU.

Franklin, Hugh, 21 years.
Her Majesty's Prison, Pentonville, Caledonian Road.
Census night: complies (no choice).
Suffrage: MPU.

Patch, Dr Winifred.
31 Highbury Place.
Census night: resister (apparently filled in only her name and occupation).
Occupation: doctor.
Household: 11 rooms, 1 female servant, resisted.
Suffrage: WTRL.

WEST

Kensington: population 172,000

South of High Street Kensington

Housman, Laurence, 48 years.
1 Pembroke Cottages, Pembroke Square.
Census night: complies for himself; resister, refusing information on females in house.
Occupation: author and dramatist.
Others: 4 female visitors [may include a servant].
Household: 8 rooms and detached studio.
Statement: 'All information refused by Women inmates as a protest against their exclusion from the Franchise.'
Enumerator inserted the figure '4' before the word 'Women'.
Suffrage: WFL, MPU, MLWS, Suff At.

Palliser, Edith, 57 years.
26 Pembroke Square.
Census night: complies.
Occupation: literary work.
Other: Dr Mabel Paine (joint occupier).
Household: 7 rooms, 2 servants.
Suffrage: NUWSS.

Rowe, Louisa Jopling, 67 years.
7 Pembroke Gardens.
Census night: complies.
Status: married.
Occupation: artist.
Household: 12 rooms, 3 servants.
Suffrage: WFL, NCSWS, Suff At.

Sinclair, May, 47 years.
4 Edwardes Square Studios.
Census night: complies.
Occupation: novelist, writer. No private means.
Household: 3 rooms.
Suffrage: WSPU, WFL, WWSL.

North, near Church Street

Marsden, S[ybil], 'about 37'.
69 Kensington Church Street.
Census night: resister.
Occupation: 'dressmaker'.
Statement: 'I, Mdme Mantalini [dressmaker's name in *Nicholas Nickleby*], a
municipal voter and tax payer, refuse to fill in this census paper, as I have no
intention of furnishing this government with information and thereby helping
them to legislate for women without obtaining their consent or first consulting
them ...'
Statement runs to 225 words (see Chapter 19, note 27).
Suffrage: WSPU.

Eaton, Gertude, [46 years].
3 Gloucester Walk.
Census night: evader.
Household: 9 rooms, parlourmaid.
Suffrage: WTRL.

Sharp, Evelyn, 'about 35' [42 years].
15 Mount Carmel Chambers, Dukes Lane.
Census night: resister, evader.
Statement: 'While fully realizing the seriousness of refusing to fill in this paper, still more deeply the grave damage of supplying information to be [used] as a basis for future legislation over which voteless women have [no] control. Furthermore the insult of being counted as a citizen when [the] Census is taken and ignored as a citizen when Governments are el[ected] is no longer to be borne by self-respecting women. Therefore, with [apologies] for the trouble I am causing to officials, who are not responsible [for] the Government for turning law-abiding women into rebels [I] must decline to supply any particulars either with regard [to] myself or to anyone else who passed the night on my p[remises]. Evelyn Sharp.'
Suffrage: WSPU, WWSL.

Conolan, Gertrude, [39 years].
23 Mount Carmel Chambers, Dukes Lane.
Census night: absent, evader.
No schedule; enumerator's summary lists flat as uninhabited.
Suffrage: WSPU, NCSWS.

Rendel, Frances Elinor, 26 years.
5 Hornton Street.
Census night: complies.
Family: father, former barrister and director of Indian railway companies; mother.
Household: 15 rooms, 4 servants.
Suffrage: NUWSS.

Murray, Flora, [41 years], and **Janet Campbell, Misses.**
86 Campden Hill Court, Campden Hill.
Census night: evader and resister.
[The enumerator got thoroughly confused. Originally the schedule said 'The Misses Campbell', altered to 'Miss Murray'. But in a note, he refers to 'Dr Janet Murray', thus conflating the two women (joint householders) and eliminating one. He decided that 'Dr Janet Murray' and 1 servant were absent on census night; presumably both householders were absent.]
Occupation: [Flora] medical doctor.
Household: 7 rooms, 2 servants.
Statement: 'I refuse to fill in this form as a protest against the action of the government which refuses to give Parliamentary Representation to Women Householders.'
Note attached dated 2/4/11: 'To the Enumerator. Please do not come to my door and worry my maid. Any questions wh[ich] you have to ask must be addressed to me as the occupier. If you wish to see me call on Wednesday at 11 am. F. Murray.'
Suffrage: WSPU.

Up Church Street, near Holland Park

Lowy, Mrs Henrietta, [45 years].
76 Holland Park.
Census night: evaders.
Family: husband, 2 daughters, 2 sons (all evaders)
Household: 18 rooms, 4 servants (evaders).
Enumerator: completed blank schedule 'From information obtained elsewhere'.
Suffrage: WSPU, MPU, WTRL.

Brackenbury, Mrs Hilda, [79 years], daughters, **Georgina,** [46], and **Marie,** [45].
2 Campden Hill Square.
Census night: present, resisters, host evasion.
Others: enumerator estimated 25 females, 1 male.
Statement: 'Miss Marie Brackenbury in charge takes this opportunity of registering her protest against the votelessness of the women of Great Britain by refusing to fill in this form'.
Suffrage: WSPU.

Conder, Helen Elizabeth, [46 years].
20 & 20a Campden Hill Gardens (studios).
Census night: evaders [no schedule].
Others: 1 male, 35 females [details from enumerator's summary].

Luxmoore, Myra, [46 years].
57 Bedford Gardens.
Census night: evader; enumerator marked her studio as uninhabited (but she is nowhere else).
Occupation: [artist].
Suffrage: CUFWA.

Smith, Emily, 27 years.
64 Bedford Gardens.
Census night: resister.
Occupation: cook.
Others: Bernard Jenkin, (married, head), his young daughter. Is his wife evading?
Household: 9 rooms, 2 other servants.
Note: 'Refuses to give information because women have not got the vote.'

North of Notting Hill Gate

Mort, Mrs Louise, [widow, 63 years].
1 Stanley Crescent.
Census night: resister
Household: 11 rooms, 3 female servants (all resisted).
Statement: 'No Vote No Census.'

Bentham, Dr Ethel, 50 years.
74 Lansdowne Road.
Census night: complies.
Status: single.
Occupation: doctor.
Others: Mary Longman, Marion Phillips (all joint householders).
Household: 5 rooms, 1 servant.
Suffrage: WLabL, adult suffrage.

Bensusan, Inez, [40 years].
8 Lansdowne Road
Census night: evading at Aldwych.
Occupation: [actress].
Household: 2 rooms, housekeeper.
Suffrage: AFL, WWSL.

Gray, Mrs P. Constance.
27 Ladbroke Square.
Census night: resister.
Household: 12 rooms; 3 female servants, 1 male (all resisters).
Statement: 'No Vote No Census.'

Wright, Mrs Mary, [56 years], daughters, **Alexandra,** [32 years], **Gladys,** [27 years].
27 Pembridge Crescent.
Census night: evaders.
Household: 18 rooms, 2 servants.
Suffrage: NCSWS.

Pine, Catherine Emily, [47 years].
9 Pembridge Gardens.
Census night: resister.
Occupation: [nurse].
Household: 3 patients, 1 nurse.
Statement: 'Above names at request. For the rest No Votes No Information.'
Suffrage: WSPU.

Woodward, Miss, and **Newland, Mrs** (servant).
14 Bonchurch Road.
Census night: resisters.
Household: '5 rooms – portion of house.'
Enumerator: 'Suffragettes – only information obtainable.'

Woodward, Alice Bolingbroke, 48 years.
13 Arundel Gardens.
Census night: complies.
Occupation: painter.
Family: father, retired civil servant; mother; 3 unmarried sisters (51, 46 and 43).
Household: 12 rooms; 3 servants.
Suffrage: ASL.

South of Notting Hill, east of Church Street

McKenzie, Miss E., '40'.
16 Palace Gardens Terrace.
Census night: resisters.
Household: 12 rooms, 3 female servants (all resisters).
Statement: 'No Vote No Census.'
'Disability' column: 'Every woman in the house is unenfranchised.'
Suffrage: WSPU.

Home, Mary, [25 years].
7 Palace Gardens Terrace.
Census night: evader.
Family: father, surgeon general retired; mother, sister,
Household: 10 rooms, 2 servants.
Suffrage: WSPU.

Jones, Mrs, and **Miss Chapman,** '25'.
Block B, 28 York House Mansions.
Census night: resisters.
Household: 10 rooms, 3 female servants (all resisters).
Statement: 'No Vote No Census. Violet Jones.'

South of High Street

Brinton, Mary, 19 years.
8 Queens Gate Terrace.
Census night: complies.
Occupation: London University student.
Family: father, doctor; mother.
Household: 18 rooms, 4 servants.
Suffrage: NUWSS.

Mappin, Stanley A., [38 years].
12 Albert Hall Mansions, Kensington Gore.
Census night: resisters.
Occupation: [silversmith].
Family: wife, daughter, both resisters.
Household: 9 rooms, 5 servants (all resisters).
Statement: 'As a protest against the attitude of the government in denying women the rights of citizenship I refuse to fill in or sign the paper. Stanley A. Mappin.'
Suffrage: WSPU?

South of Brompton Road

Williams, Mrs May G., '40'.
21 Ovington Square.
Census night: resister.
Household: 11 rooms, 3 servants (all resisters).
Statement: 'The occupier is away and I am in charge. Until women have the vote
I shall not fill in any census paper.'

Marshall, Catherine, 30 years.
38 Evelyn Gardens.
Census night: complies.
Family: father, retired schoolmaster; mother, brother.
Household: 11 rooms, 4 servants.
Suffrage: NUWSS.

Tite, Miss [Constance], [40 years?].
53 Drayton Gardens.
Census night: resisters.
Household: 2 servants, resisters.
Statement: 'No persons here only women!'
[Notices attached of the 'Census Meeting April 1st Trafalgar Square'.]

Massy, Mrs Rosamund, [41 years].
57 Drayton Gardens.
Census night: evader, probably with 18-year-old daughter
Others: husband.
Household: 6 rooms, 1 servant.
Suffrage: WSPU.

Woods, Eliza, 67 years.
4 Drayton Court, Drayton Gardens.
Census night: complies.
Occupation: vice-chairman CUWFA.
Others: Helen Dowding (44), hon. sec. CUWFA, complies.
Household: 8 rooms, 2 servants.

Sheppard, Miss C. S.
3a Seymour Place.
Census night: resister.
Occupation: [artist].
Household: studio.
Statement: 'No Vote No Information.'

Barry, Miss.
36 Seymour Place.
Census night: resister.
Household: 2 rooms.
Statement: 'No Vote No Census'.

Whately, Reginald Pepys, 50 years.
75 Harcourt Terrace.
Census night: complies, writing in all family members' names. He subsequently strikes out (initialling the alteration) the names of 3 of his daughters (Mary Monica, Angela and Catherine Cecilia), all of whom were evaders.
Occupation: retired army officer.
Household: 15 rooms, 3 servants
Suffrage: Monica, CathWSS.

'A suffragette who refuses all information about herself until she gets a vote.'
53 Redcliffe Square.
Census night: resister.
Others: Miss Fanny Fosberry (head); 2 female, 1 male visitor, all comply.
Household: 12 rooms, 2 servants.

Postlethwaite, Mary Emily, 'about 48' [56 years].
27 Warwick Chambers, Pater Street.
Census night: resister.
Household: 3 rooms.
Statement: 'Didn't count in the General Election so won't be counted now.'
Suffrage: WSPU.

Chelsea: population 66,386

In west, south of Fulham Road

Capron, Miss N. M.
20 Halsey Street.
Census night: resister.
Others: 2 female evaders.
Statement: 'Sorry that I cannot conscientiously give the information – Qualified for citizenship, except for being a woman, the Authorities deny me this priviledge [*sic*] while not scrupling to impose tasks & burdens upon me – I am therefore logical and justified, in common with many others, in refusing the information. Should the Conciliation Bill pass the House of Commons this Session, I will with pleasure give the required information at any later date. N. M.Capron.'

Goldstein, Miss Vida, [42 years].
22 Rawlings Street.
Census night: evader.
Enumerator: 'Particulars unobtainable. Suffragette stayed out all night.'
Suffrage: WSPU.

Moore, Eva [Mrs Henry Esmond], [43 years].
21 Whiteheads Grove.
Census night: absent, probably evading at Aldwych.
Occupation: actress.
Status: married, 1 daughter.
Family: husband, actor; daughter, 3.
Household: 9 rooms, 3 servants.
Suffrage: WTRL.

Napier, Misses.
13 Pond Place.
Census night: resisters.
Enumerator: '2 females all information refused.'

Graham, Miss.
6 Markham Square.
Census night: resister.
Household: 1 room.
Statement: 'No Vote No Census.'

Ellis, Miss.
4 Queens Elm Square
Census night: resister.
Others: 1 female visitor, also resister.
Household: 9 rooms, 2 servants.
Statement: 'I refuse to give any information.'
Registrar: 'Reported to Census Office.'

Lowndes, Mary, 54 years.
Brittany Studios, 259 King's Road.
Census night: complies.
Occupation: stained glass artist.
Other: Barbara Forbes, glass painter
Household: 8 rooms, 1 servant.
Suffrage: both ASL.

South of King's Road

Pertwee, Mrs Emily, [51 years].
4 Tite Street.
Census night: absent, probably evading at Aldwych.
Occupation: reciter.
Status: married, at least 2 sons.
Family: husband, 52, author and elocutionist; son, 28.
Household: 8 rooms, 2 servants.
Suffrage: AFL.

Downing, Edith, [54 years].
30 Tite Street.
Census night: evader.
Occupation: [sculptor].
[Flat marked as uninhabited; against her name in enumerator's summary is 'Report to Reg.'].
Suffrage: WSPU.

Monck-Mason, Mrs Alice, '70'.
93 Oakley Street.
Census night: resister.
Status: [widow].
Family: daughter, Winifred [Mayo]; '45'; sister, '74', all resisters. Winifred evading at Aldwych.
Household: 11 rooms, 2 servants (resisters).
Enumerator: 'Suffragettes refused all information and wrote across census form "No Vote No Census". Information obtained from neighbours.'
Suffrage: WSPU, AFL (Winifred).

Dreier, Katherine S., [34 years].
11 More's Gardens, Cheyne Walk.
Census night: resister.
Occupation: [artist].
Other: 1 female.
Household: 8 rooms.
Statement: 'No Vote No Census. I have joined the brave women of England in their dignified protest against the systematic blocking by the Government of the "Women's Conciliation".' [US citizen].

Joachim, Maud, [42 years].
118 Cheyne Walk.
Census night: resister.
Occupation: artist.
Household: about 11 rooms; 1 female servant (resister).
Enumerator: 'Suffragette information refused.'

Newcombe, Bertha, 54 years.
1 Cheyne Walk.
Census night: complies.
Occupation: 'private means' [artist].
Family: father, sister.
Household: 15 rooms, 4 servants.
Suffrage: ASL.

Wolfe, Miss [Lilian?].
139 Beaufort Street.
Census night: resister.
Occupation: [civil servant?].
Household: 3 rooms.
Enumerator: 'Suffragette.'

West along King's Road

Coates, Mrs Dora Meeson, 41 years.
10 Glebe Place.
Census night: complies.
Occupation: artist.
Status: married 8 years, no children.
Family: husband, artist.
Household: 2 rooms.
Suffrage: ASL.

Ford, Emily, 60 years.
44 Glebe Place.
Census night: complies.
Occupation: painter.
Household: 5 rooms, 1 female visitor (charwoman),1 servant.
Suffrage: ASL, NUWSS.

Hamilton, Cicely?
28 Glebe Place? [difficult to confirm address].
Census night: probably evading.
Other/s: sister perhaps also evading?
Occupation: [writer].
Suffrage: WFL, WWSL, AFL.

Fulham: population 153,284

Maund, Mrs Eleanora, 38 years.
8 Edith Road.
Census night: would-be resister.
Family: husband Edward, 60, company director; 2 sons, 1 daughter.
Status: married 21 years, 5 children.
Household: 13 rooms, 2 servants.
Husband's statement: see Chapter 13 (p. 152).

Marsden, Dora, 29 years.
21 Edith Road.
Census night: complies.
Others: Mrs Menzies, head; her 2 sisters, 2 visitors.
Household: 10 rooms.
Suffrage: recently resigned as WSPU organizer.

Ayrton, Phyllis, [27 years].
62 Edith Road.
Census night: absent, evader.
Family: aunt, head; 2 sisters.
Household: 10 rooms, 2 servants.
Suffrage: WSPU, Clerks' WSPU.

Thomson, Louisa.
18 Rockley Road.
Census night: complies, with protest.
Status: married 23 years, 3 children.
Family: 2 daughters.
Occupation: schoolmistress.
Statement: 'I fill up this form *under protest*, for if I am intelligent enough so to do, I am surely capable of putting my cross on a Parliamentary ballot paper.'

Cook, Miss.
9 Portland Mansions, Addison Bridge Place.
Census night: resister.
Occupation: 'Militant Suffragette.'
Household: 4 rooms.
Statement: 'Information refused.'

Anon.
40 Avonmore Gardens.
Census night: presumably suffrage resister?
Others: 9 female, 8 male visiting evaders?
Enumerator's summary: uninhabited.

Barons Court

Lomax, Mrs, Misses J. and **A.**
3 Perham Crescent.
Census night: resisters.
Household: 14 rooms, 2 female servants (resisters).
Statement: 'No Vote No Census. H. Lomax.'

Bouchier, Dr Helen, 'about 50'.
1 Livingstone Mansions, Queens Club Gardens.
Census night: resister.
Occupation: 'Doctor (believed to be medicine).'
Household: 3 rooms.
Statement: 'Votes for Women. No Census.'
Suffrage: WTRL, WFL.

Bessle, Miss.
2 Broomhouse Road.
Census night: resister.
Others: 5 visitors, totalling 11 evaders.
Registrar: Reg. Gen. 'Suffragettes'.

Canter (or Carter), Mrs, 'about 32'.
28 Ellerby Street.
Census night: resister.
Household: 6 rooms.
Enumerator: 'Mrs Canter is a Suffragist and refuses all information.'

Hammersmith: population 121,421

Willis, Miss [E.], 'about 35', **Joseph, Miss,** 'about 30'.
4 Stanlake Villas.
Census night: 'slept out', evaders.
Suffrage: Suff At.

Morrison, Mrs Evelyn Mary, about 40 years [widow, 51 years].
11 Addison Mansions, Blythe Road.
Census night: resister.
Others: 1 male; 1 female [possibly her daughter, Evelyn, 30 years].
Statement: 'As a voteless taxpayer I refuse all information until such time as women are enfranchised. "government rests upon the consent of the governed".'
Suffrage: WSPU.

By Thames

Sanderson, Mrs Annie Cobden, [58 years].
15 Upper Mall.
Census night: evader? [no trace of schedule].
Suffrage: WFL.

Rowe, Mrs Frances.
11 Hammersmith Terrace.
Census night: absent, evader?
Status: married, 27 years.
Family: husband, Louis Rowe, 55, solicitor.
Household: 9 rooms, 2 servants.
Suffrage: WSPU.

Paddington: population 142,551

Hyde Park

Dugdale, Una, [32 years], **Joan,** [29 years].
13 Stanhope Place.
Census night: evader[s].
Family: father, Navy (retired); mother, 'unpaid housekeeper'; brother; married
sister (23) 'unpaid housekeeper'.
Household: 16 rooms, 3 servants.
Suffrage: WSPU.

Hale, Beatrice, [28 years], sister, **Cicely,** [26 years].
3 Sussex Place.
Census night: comply (but see Chapter 18, p. 215, for probable mis-memory).
Occupation: Beatrice, artist; Cicely, 'Women's Suffrage sec'.
Suffrage: WSPU.

Paddington

Ayrton, Mrs Hertha, 'about 60' [56 years].
41 Norfolk Square.
Census night: resister.
Status: widow.
Household: 18 rooms, 2 female servants, also resisters.
Statement: 'How can I answer all these questions if I have not the intelligence to choose between two candidates for parliament? I will not supply these particulars until I have my rights as a citizen. Votes for Women.'
Enumerator apparently failed to record about 40 evaders given shelter on census night (see Chapter 18, p. 212).
Registrar: (7 April, to Census Office) 'I regret to report that Mrs Ayrton of 41 Norfolk Sq ... refuses to fill up or give any particulars for the census schedule. Mrs Ayrton and 2 female servants (at least) were in the house during the Sunday night also a number of ladies and gentlemen. I cannot obtain the least idea as to this number: Mrs Ayrton informs me that she has kept a careful record of all the persons and the particulars required for census purposes which she will be willing to send to you in May if certain promises are made. Wherever these parties have been held I am informed these records have been kept. Will you kindly let me know if the Enumerator is to make up a Schedule with Mrs Ayrton and 2 servants on it.'
Archer Bellingham: 'I am directed by the Registrar General ... to express his thanks for the trouble you have taken in regard to Mrs Ayrton. Please fill in a Schedule with the best particulars available, of the numbers etc of persons present on Census night, and hand it to the Enumerator concerned, with instructions to include the return in his Summary Book.'
Suffrage: WSPU.

Gibbes, Miss J. E. M.
78 Gloucester Terrace.
Census night: resister.
Statement: 'No Vote No Census. I have a conscientious objection to fulfilling citizen's duties until I am recognised as a citizen.'
Enumerator: 'in house on Sunday night Miss Gibbes, housemaid age 25 about, cook age 38 about and *some* lady friends.'

Ward-Higgs, Mrs [Haydee N.], [41 years].
23 Queensborough Terrace.
Census night: resister.
Status: married.
Family: 3 daughters, all resisters.
Household: 14 rooms; 4 female servants, all resisters.
Statement: 'My husband the occupier is temporarily away from London. I refuse to answer any Census questions until the parliamentary Vote is granted to women occupiers.'
Registrar: 'Mrs Ward-Higgs and her servants refused all information. The above particulars were obtained elsewhere.'

Maida Vale

Green, Jessie Georgina, about 50 years.
40 Warwick Crescent.
Census night: resister.
Household: 12 rooms, 2 female servants, both resisters.
Statement: 'I have conscientious objection to giving any information to any Government which legislates for women without their consent.'
Suffrage: NCSWS.

Gancia, Mrs.
7 Blomfield Court, Maida Vale.
Census night: resister/evader.
Statement: 'Deserted by women who want the Vote.'
Registrar: 'Not more than three or four occupants.'

Bourne, Adeline, [38 years].
6a Blomfield Road.
Census night: evader, at Aldwych.
Suffrage: AFL.

Leo, Mrs Isabelle, about 70 years, daughter **Rosa,** about 40 years.
45 Ashworth Mansions, Elgin Avenue.
Census night: resisters/evader; Rosa was at Aldwych.
Status: [widow].
Household: 7 rooms.
Statement: 'No Vote No Census. If I am intelligent enough to fill in this census form, I am surely intelligent enough to make a X on a ballot paper.'
Suffrage: WSPU, AFL (Rosa).

Rogers, Evan M., 57 years.
62b Portsdown Road.
Census night: complies (for himself).
Status: married 27 years, 2 children.
Occupation: general export merchant.
Family: wife, resister.
Household: 8 rooms, 1 female servant, resister.
Statement: 'I omit the women of this Household as a Protest against the persistent refusal of the Government to grant the Parliamentary Franchise to duly qualified women.'
Registrar: 'I utterly failed to persuade the occupier to give further particulars.'

Williams, Mrs Lilian, about 50 years.
36 Portsdown Road.
Census night: resister.
Status: widow.
Occupation: masseuse.
Household: 12 rooms, 1 female servant, resister.
Statement: 'I refuse to fill in this form as a protest against being called upon to perform a citizen's duties while denied a citizen's rights.'
Registrar: 'I failed to persuade Mrs Williams to give any particulars.'

Maguire, Cynthia, [21 years].
15 Carlton Vale.
Census night: evader/resister.
Occupation: commercial clerk.
Family: father (62) stock broker, mother; 3 younger brothers; sister (14).
Father wrote her in, then a line was put through her details. Comment in margin (heavily scored through) appears to note that Cynthia was not back until Monday.
Suffrage: WSPU.

Davis, Mrs Annie, about 50 years.
37 St Luke's Road.
Census night: resister.
Family: son (about 30) and daughter (about 28), resisters.
Household: 11 rooms, 1 female servant, resister.
Statement: 'No Vote No Census. Annie Davis.'
Registrar: 'Information obtained from next door.'

Further north and west, see Middlesex, p. 293

SOUTH OF THAMES

From west (Surrey border) to east (Kent border)

Wandsworth: population 311,360

Putney Heath

Marshall, Mr [Arthur].
Caravans on Putney Heath (but 'of Theydon Bois, Essex').
Census night: resister.
Schedule cover is filled in as 'Mrs Marshall and Suffragist Party'.
Family: Kitty Marshall (wife).
Others: '9 women' 'Suffragists'.
Enumerator's summary: 1 male, 10 females.
Suffrage: WSPU.
[For these Wimbledon vanners, see end Chapter 16 and start Chapter 17].

Wandsworth

Duval, Mrs Emily and family.
37 Park Road, Wandsworth Common.
Census night: evaders, no trace of entire family.
Suffrage: WSPU.

Chapman, Mrs Florence, 42 years.
57 Gorst Road, Wandsworth Common.
Census night: complies.
Family: husband, hosier manager; 2 sons.
Household: 7 rooms.
Suffrage: WSPU.

Burnham, Louisa, about 46 years.
192 Elms Road, Clapham.
Census night: resister.
Family: sister (about 48 years), resister.
Household: 5 rooms, 1 maid, resister.
Statement: 'No Vote No Census. If I am intelligent enough to fill in the Census
Form I can surely make a X on a Ballot Paper.'

Tyson, Mrs [Helen], about 64 years; 2 daughters (probably **Diana,** 41, **Leonora,** 27 years).
37 Drewstead Road, Streatham.
Census night: resister.
Household: 10 rooms.
Enumerator: completed schedule (left blank), 'Usual inhabitants of the house.'
Suffrage: WSPU.

Battersea: population 167,743

North-east

Despard, Mrs Charlotte, 'abt 70 yrs' [67 years].
2 Currie Street.
Census night: present, resister.
Status: widow.
Household: 10 rooms.
Enumerator: 'Refused further information – a suffragette.'
Suffrage: WFL.

By Battersea Park

Henderson, Marguerite.
115 Albert Palace Mansions, Lurline Road.
Census night: evader.
No schedule, flat shown as uninhabited.
Suffrage: WFL.

Sanders, Mrs Beatrice, 'abt 40 yrs' [37 years].
18 Brynmaer Road, Battersea Park.
Census night: present, resister.
Status: married 'abt 12 yrs'.
Suffrage: WSPU.

Ogston, Helen, 27 years.
70 Albany Mansions, Albert Bridge Road.
Census night: complies.
Occupation: Organizer for Woman Suffrage Society.
Other: Olive Lett (29), teacher of Swedish gymnastics.
Household: 5 rooms.
Suffrage: NCSWS.

Lieben (or Luben?), Miss.
28 Albany Mansions, Albert Bridge Road.
Census night: resister.
Enumerator: 'Suffragette – schedule returned to porter.'

Longley, Mrs.
75 Overstrand Mansions, Battersea Park.
Occupation: protesting suffragette.
Status: widow (visitor).
Others: she was visiting Harold Macmurdo, retired stockbroker, his wife, and 1 male visitor.
Household: 7 rooms, 1 female servant.
Enumerator: 'was out all night.'

South: Lavender Hill

Strong, Mrs Clara, 52 years.
84 Elspeth Road.
Census night: complies.
Occupation: milliner.
Status: married 32 years; 5 children, 3 living.
Family: husband (59), pensioner; 2 daughters (one is LCC teacher).
Household: 6 rooms.
Suffrage: WSPU?

Underwood, Florence.
31 Rush Hill Road.
Census night: evader.
Others: only one family is enumerated (occupying 4 rooms of this large house).
Suffrage: WFL.

Lambeth: population 298,058

North, near Waterloo

Parnall [?], Miss.
Waterloo Hotel, 2–14 York Road.
Census night: resister.
Statement: 'Particulars refused until I get a vote.'

Matters, Muriel, [34 years].
91 Fentiman Road.
Census night: resister.
Statement: see Chapter 16, Figure 41.
Suffrage: WFL.

Tillard, Violet, [37 years].
91 Fentiman Road.
Census night: resister.
Statement: 'No Vote No Census. Should women become persons in the eye of the law this session – full information will be forwarded.'
Suffrage: WFL.

Jewson, Margaret.
91 Fentiman Road.
Census night: resister.
Statement: 'No Vote No Census. I shall be pleased to supply all information when the Franchise Act is passed & I am recognized as a person. Margaret Jewson.'
Suffrage: WFL.

South

Tanner, Mrs Kathleen.
32 Wynne Road, Brixton.
Census night: evader.
Status: [married 24 years, 2 children].
Family: husband (49), LCC schoolteacher; son, (23) LGB clerk.
Household: 8 rooms, 1 female servant.
Suffrage: WSPU.

Southwark: population 191,907

North by Thames

Rotherhithe

A group of women, all making the same statement, probably all associated with the Bermondsey Settlement:

Martin, Miss Anna, [53 years].
63 Union Road, Rotherhithe.
Census night: resister.
Occupation: [social worker at Bermondsey Settlement].
Statement: 'Return refused as a protest against non-representative government.
No Vote No Census.'

Britten, Miss.
63 Union Road, Rotherhithe.
Census night: evader/resister; schedule is blank although enumerator indicated
on cover she was 'away'.
Statement on cover: '[I refuse] to fill up form as a protest against [a non-represe]n-
tative Government.'

Frank, Miss.
63 Union Road, Rotherhithe.
Census night: evader/resister.
Statement: same as Britten.

To South

Bowers, Miss
14 Gomm Road.
Census night: resister.
Statement: 'Not filled in as a protest against non-representative Government.'

Camberwell: population 261,328

Evans, Miss, 'abt 45 yrs'.
404 Old Kent Road [Nurses' Home].
Census night: resister.
Occupation: sick nurse.
Enumerator: 'Miss Evans refuses to fill in Schedule or to see Registrar.'
Suffrage: WSPU.

Christmas, Miss L.
106 Peckham Road.
Census night: evader.
Statement: 'Away aiding the Women's Suffrage Cause. L. Christmas. Votes for
Women.'

Pickering, Mrs Julia, [37 years].
23 Albert Road, Peckham.
Census night: evader.
Status: married 16 years, no children.
Family: husband, Herbert (38), milk vendor.
Household: 3 rooms.
Statement (husband): 'Wife's whereabouts unknown. Unable to state her age.'
Suffrage: WFL.

Dulwich

Moore, Mr, Mrs and Master.
86 Melbourne Grove.
Census night: evaders.
Enumerator: 'Suffragetts [*sic*] were away at night to avoid being enumerated.'

Hefford, Miss Annette, [33 years].
54 Barry Road.
Census night: evader.
Occupation: [school teacher].
Family: father, heating engineer; mother, 2 younger brothers, bank clerks.
Suffrage: WSPU.

Bartels, Mrs Marion, 50 [49 years], daughters **Margaret,** 24 [23 years], **Olive,** 21 [22 years], son, **Wilfred,** 16 [15 years].
23 Acacia Grove.
Census night: resisters.
Status: widow.
Enumerator: 'Prominent suffragettes. Schedule filled up by order of the Registrar General the ages etc are estimated and the information is all that is available at the moment.'

Lewisham: population 160,834

Billinghurst, May, [36 years].
7 Oakcroft Road.
Census night: evader.
Family: father, retired bank manager; mother.
Suffrage: WSPU.

Townsend, Hannah, [42 years], sister, **Caroline,** [40 years].
27 Murillo Road.
Census night: evaders.
Family: sister, Annie (47), LCC schoolteacher.
Suffrage: WSPU.

Llewhellin, Ethel, [28 years], **Olive,** [22 years].
114 Burnt Ash Hill.
Census night: evaders.
Family: mother, sister.
Household: 5 rooms.
Suffrage: WSPU.

Lambert, Clara, [36 years].
174 Glenfarg Road, Catford.
Census night: evader.
Family: 2 brothers and sister, all working in the family laundry. Possibly mother and other sisters also evading.
Household: 5 rooms.
Suffrage: WSPU.

Downing, Miss C. L.
286 Devonshire Road, Forest Hill.
Census night: resister.
Household: 7 rooms.
Enumerator: 'suffragette – information refused.'

Streatfield, Mrs Fanny, [60 years], daughter, **Maud,** [33 years].
28 Longton Avenue, Sydenham.
Census night: resisters/evaders (no schedule).
Enumerator's summary: 'Information refused (suffragettes).'
Suffrage: WSPU.

London: borders here on Kent

NORTH-EAST

Hackney: population 273,192

Brown, Mrs Myra Sadd.
34 Woodberry Down, Stoke Newington.
Census night: absent, as is husband, Ernest; evaders.
Family: niece, son, 2 daughters, sister-in-law.
Household: 13 rooms, 5 servants.
Suffrage: WFL, CLWS, WTRL.

Cunningham, Mrs A.
114 Holmleigh Road, Stamford Hill.
Census night: marked by enumerator as 'absent' – form blank: evader.
Suffrage: WFL.

Scriven, Miss R.
131 Holmleigh Road.
Census night: resister.
Household: 4 rooms.
Statement: 'No Vote No Census.'

Mustard, Mrs Sarah, [46 years].
49 Moresby Road.
Census night: absent; probably evading with eldest daughter, Nora.
Status: married 19 years, 3 children.
Family: husband, John, schoolmaster/lecturer; 2 younger daughters.
Household: 6 rooms.
Suffrage: WFL.

Wilks, Mark and Dr Elizabeth.
47 Upper Clapton Road.
Census night: Mark absent, Elizabeth evader.
Occupation: [Mark: teacher]
Family: Elizabeth was probably evading there with (enumerator estimated) 39 other females.
Household: 12 rooms.
Mark's statement: 'I was away from home on April 2–3. I have no knowledge who was in the house, beyond that there were a no. of Suffragists.'
Suffrage: WTRL.

Pierotti, Mrs Laura, [41 years].
31 Walsingham Road.
Census night: absent, evader.
Family: husband, post office sorter; 2 daughters.
Suffrage: WFL.

Cale, Miss M. [Minnie] L., 'about 40' [34 years].
11 Clarence Gardens, Lower Clapton.
Census night: resister.
Family: father, William, retired cab proprietor.
Household: 4 rooms.
Statement: 'No Vote No Census. I refuse to give any information regarding women while they are denied the rights of citizenship and I will not assist in providing statistics on which legislation affecting women is based, while women have no voice in the making of the laws.'

Poplar: population 162,449

Garnett, [Frances] Theresa, 22 years.
London Hospital Training School, Bow Road.
Census night: complies.
Occupation: trainee nurse.
Suffrage: ex-WSPU organizer.

Lansbury, George, 52 years.
101 & 103 St Stephens Road, Bow.
Census night: complies.
Occupation: timber merchant and MP.
Family: wife (50), married 30 years, 12 children, 9 still living, 3 have died; 4 daughters, 2 sons at home.
Household: 11 rooms.
Suffrage: WSPU, PSF.

Stepney: population 279,804

Sbarbaro, Mrs Jane, 69 years.
34 St George's House, Whitechapel.
Census night: complies.
Occupation: [either her hand or her husband's] 'Suffragette. 6 weeks in Holloway for wanting the Vote.' [In enumerator's hand] 'Office cleaner.'
Family: husband (78).
Household: 1 room.
Suffrage: WSPU.

Bennett, Mrs Florence, 39 years.
219 Rhodeswell Road, Limehouse.
Census night: complies.
Family: husband (55), general labourer; daughter (14).
Others: 1 visitor, 2 lodgers.
Suffrage: WSPU?

MIDDLESEX: population 1,126,465

From Tottenham area (bordering Essex) westwards, i.e. anti-clockwise

Thompson, L. M.
29 Marquis Road (on address page of schedule she has scored this through, substituting 1 Robert Street, WFL headquarters).
Statement: 'No Votes for Women No information from women.'
Enumerator: 'Suffragette refused information. Slept out of house.'
Suffrage: WFL.

Sims, Marie.
11 Elmhurst Road.
Census night: evader.
Other: family of John Selby, mining engineer's clerk, with whom she was probably lodger.
Household: 6 rooms, 1 female servant.
Suffrage: WFL.

Goulden, Mrs Laura, [43 years].
6 Radcliffe Road.
Census night: evader.
Family: husband; stepson (24); daughter (4).
Household: 9 rooms.
Suffrage: WSPU (Mrs Pankhurst's sister-in-law).

Palmers Green

Gargett, Florence, [31 years], **Hilda,** [25 years].
4 Stonard Road.
Census night: evaders.
Family: father (58); sister (27).
Suffrage: Hilda, WSPU.

Prout, Victor, 'about 50 years'.
6 Stonard Road.
Census night: resister.
Occupation: black and white artist.
Family: wife (about 50), 2 daughters (13 and 9).
Household: 6 rooms.
Enumerator: 'I have to report that Mr Victor Prout … refused to properly fill up
the form (notwithstanding I read the Census Act (sec 2) to him) …'
(See Chapter 19, p. 222).
Suffrage: WSPU?

Highgate

Jacobs, Mrs [Agnes] Charlotte, [53 years].
57 Talbot Road.
Census night: evader.
Family: husband, Herbert (47) complies.
Household: 10 rooms, 1 female servant.
Suffrage: Herbert, MLWS.

Hampstead Garden Suburb

How-Martin [-Martyn], Herbert, and **Mrs [Edith],** [36 years].
38 Hogarth Hill.
Census night: resisters/evaders, schedule completed by registrar.
Occupation: (Herbert) 'scientific man'.
Others: 6 females, all resisters.
Household: 5 rooms.
Statement: 'Legislation without Representation is slavery.' 'No Votes for Women
No Information from Women'. 'The occupier of this house is not a person only
a Woman – see decision of the House of Lords Scottish Graduates Case 1908.'
Registrar: 'Information received that this was an open house on census night.'
Suffrage: WFL.

Stockman, Mr and **Mrs [Margaret],** 'about 34 years'.
180 Willifield Way.
Census night: resisters.
Household: 6 rooms, 1 female servant, resister.
Statement: 'I refuse all information to a government which governs me with-
out my consent'. And 'In the absence of the legal occupier, a woman not a
person.'
Suffrage: (Margaret): WFL probably; Fabian Women's Group certainly.

Bondfield, Margaret, 38 years; **Ward, Marion,** 38 years.
8 Denman Drive.
Census night: both comply.
Occupation: (Ward) lecturer PSF; (Bondfield) lecturer Labour Party and ILP.
Household: 5 rooms.

Fairfield, Letitia, 'about 30 years'.
Fairlehope, Chatham Close.
Census night: resister.
Occupation: [doctor].
Others: 3 female resisters/evaders.
Household: 6 rooms; 1 female servant, resister.
Registrar: 'Enumerator informed by Miss Fairfield that she intended avoiding the census.'

Parley, Mrs Irene, [28 years].
Holmcroft, Hampstead Way.
Census night: evader.
Family; brother-in-law, mother-in-law, husband.
Household: 7 rooms.
Suffrage: WSPU.

Drysdale, Charles V., 'about 38 years', **Bessie,** 'about 35 years'.
49 Rotherwick Road.
Census night: resisters.
Occupation: Charles, 'scientific man'.
Family: daughter (6).
Household: 6 rooms, 1 female servant, resister.
Statement: 'As the Government refuses me a vote, and as I am therefore not recognized as a citizen, I refuse to perform the duties of one, in giving the information required by the Government. Signed: Bessie J. E. Drysdale (Member of the WFL).'
Suffrage: Bessie, WFL; Charles, MLWS.

Finchley

Bennett, Miss [Sarah Bennet], [61 years].
Norton, [24] Village Road.
Census night: resister/evader; blank schedule returned in envelope addressed to the 'Enumerator'.
Statement: 'I am denied the full rights of citizenship, so I will not perform the duties of a citizen. I will not help to supply with information a Government which classes me with criminals and lunatics and I refuse therefore to answer the Census questions.'
Suffrage: WTRL, NCSWS.

Owen, Mrs.
11 Manor Villas, Squire's Lane.
Census night: evader.
Family: husband (36).
Household: 8 rooms, 1 female servant.
Suffrage: WFL.

Barnet

Watt, Susan, [29 years].
13 Strafford Road.
Census night: evader.
Family: mother, sister.
Household: 6 rooms.
Suffrage: WSPU.

West to Hendon

Bower, Mrs and **daughter**.
2 Down Cottages, Parson Street.
Census night: resisters.
Registrar: 'Suffragettes.'

Next-door-but-one

Wyatt, Mrs, '50 years'.
Derby House, Parson Street.
Census night: resister/evader.
Family: about 4 daughters and 4 sons, all resisters.
Others: Vera Wentworth, 2 Misses Allman, 1 other female visitor, all resisters.
Household: about 14 rooms.
Enumerator: 'No-one slept here.'
Registrar (who filled in schedule): 'Inserted by instruction of the Registrar General, dated 7 April 1911.'
Suffrage: WSPU.

Growse, Emily, [52 years].
St Ursula's, Heriot Road.
Census night: evader.
Family: sister.
Household: 7 rooms, 1 female servant.
Suffrage: WSPU.

Keevil, Gladice, 26 years.
Clutterhouse Farm, Cricklewood.
Census night: complies.
Occupation: suffragette (speaker etc.) [but had been ill, probably not currently working].
Family: father, farmer; mother, sister.
Household: 8 rooms, 1 servant.
Suffrage: WSPU.

Terrero, Mrs Janie, [53 years].
Rockstone House, Pinner.
Census night: evader.
Family: husband, 'private means'.
Household: 12 rooms; no servants listed.
Suffrage: WSPU.

To south-west Middlesex

Huntsman, Mrs, 'about 40 years.'
61 Headstone Road, Harrow.
Census night: resister.
Other: 1 female (about 22 years).
Household: 8 rooms, 2 female servants – resisters.
Note: 'Suffragette. Information refused.'
Suffrage: WFL.

Penn Gaskell, Eleanor.
12 Nicoll Road, Willesden.
Census night: evader.
Family: husband George, barrister; no children.
Statement (George): 'A number of women suffragettes spent the night of 2nd
April in my h[ouse]. As members of a disenfranchised sex they object to giving
any particulars concerning themselves for the purpose of enumeration under a
Ce[nsus] in the framing of which their sex has had no voice. They base themselves upon the principle that government should rest upon the c[onsent] of the
governed, and as I myself uphold this democratic p[rinciple] I do not feel justified in filling up any particulars concern[ing] them against their will.'
Enumerator: 'I interviewed Mr Penn Gaskell in order to obtain the necessary
information, but was politely, but firmly, refused.' He records 2 people, adding
'with the exception of the Suffragists who were in the House'.
Suffrage: WSPU; George, MPU.

Cunningham, Mrs Marion, 'about 50 years'.
Oakdene, High Road, Hayes.
Census night: resister/evader.
Status: married, 1 daughter.
Other: 1 male boarder.
Note: 'The enumerator called four times to deliver Schedule and was unable
to do so. The enumerator called three times on Monday and three times on
Tuesday (no one at home).'
Suffrage: WFL, WTRL.

Fielden, Mrs.
Lynton, Dormers Wells Road, Southall.
Census night: evading (missing wife).
Family: Edward, 32, civil servant, 'head'; possibly other family also evading?
Household: 6 rooms.
Suffrage: WFL.

To Ealing and Acton

Finlay, Mrs.
35 Warwick Road.
Census night: evader;
Enumerator's summary lists her name, but house is shown as uninhabited.
Suffrage: WSPU.

Tritton, Mrs E. G.
1 Northcote Avenue.
Census night: evader.
Enumerator's summary shows flat as uninhabited.
Suffrage: WFL.

Wallace-Dunlop, Mrs [Lucy], [75 years].
16 Montpelier Road, Acton.
Census night: resister/evader, presumably with daughter, Marion [40 years].
Registrar: 'Two female servants passed the night at 16 Montpelier Road but the head of the house being a suffragette refused to fill up the schedule or to allow the two to give me any information.'
Suffrage: WSPU.

Arney, Mrs Alice, [34 years].
11 Willcott Road.
Census night: evader.
Family: husband, assistant teacher, 2 young daughters.
Other: female visitor (33).
Household: 7 rooms.
Suffrage: WFL.

South to Thames

Singh, Princess Sophia Duleep [about 34 years].
Faraday House, Hampton Court.
Census night: resister.
Statement: 'No Vote No Census. As women do not count they refuse to be counted, & I have a conscientious objection to filling up this form'.
Registrar: 'Best information obtainable.'
Suffrage: WSPU, WTRL.

Middlesex borders Buckinghamshire (to west) and Surrey (to south)

Southern England

SOUTH-EAST

Surrey: population 920,000

North-west Surrey, by River Thames

Kew

Clayton, Edwyn, [52 years].
Glengariff, Kew Road.
Census night: evades (though signs schedule).
Occupation: [chemist].
Family: wife Clara, daughter Hilda and probably servant/s evade too.
Household: 9 rooms.
Statement: 'This house was entirely shut up, and the family away, on the night and morning above-mentioned [Sun & Mon]: therefore –
   1) No one passed the night of Sunday, April 2nd 1911, in this dwelling; and
   2) no one arrived in this dwelling on the morning of Monday, April 3rd 1911. [The family left the house as a protest against the exclusion of women from the parliamentary franchise.]'
Suffrage: WSPU, CLWS; Edwyn, MLWS, MPU.

Casey, Eileen, [29 years].
25 West Park Road.
Census night: evades.
Family: father, surgeon, alone is recorded; although his wife is absent (probably evading), he noted marriage of 31 years, 4 children born, 1 has died.
Household: 8 rooms (probably servant also evaded).
Suffrage: WSPU.

Slade, Vera, 25 years.
4 Pagoda Avenue.
Census night: complies.
Family: father, retired timber merchant; mother, 3 sisters.
Household: 9 rooms, 1 servant.
Suffrage: WSPU.

Richmond and Barnes

Shelton, Ferdinanda Marie, 36 years.
30 Graemesdyke Avenue, East Sheen.
Census night: complies (reluctantly?)
Status: married 9 years, no children.
Family: husband, 34, LCC clerk; mother, 65 (French).
Household: 6 rooms.
Suffrage: WFL.

Beldon, Lilian, 31 years.
56 Castelnau.
Census night: complies.
Occupation: lady's companion.
Others: widow (68), her son; Lilian's sister (children's maid).
Household: 12 rooms, 2 servants.
Suffrage: WSPU.

Wimbledon

For caravans on Wimbledon Common, see Putney Heath, Wandsworth (p. 284).

Hellrich, Victor, 25 years.
9 Thornton Road.
Census night: complies (for himself).
Occupation: accountant (abroad).
Household: 7 rooms.
Statement: 'Several ladies and gentlemen in the house refused to give any particulars whatever, on the grounds "No Votes for Women No Census".'
[Sadly, no enumerator's summary appears available.]
Suffrage: WSPU?

Bremner, Christiana S., [about 54 years].
Holly Mount, Pepys Road.
Census night: resists.
Occupation: 'suffragette'.
Status: visitor, single.
Others: Herbert Morgan-Browne, barrister-at-law; his wife Agnes, and 2 daughters.
Household: 12 rooms, 5 servants.
Suffrage: long-standing suffragist.

Begbie, Edith M., 'abt 45' [45] years.
107 The Ridgeway.
Census night: resists; 'all Information refused'.
Family: husband, East India merchant; at least 3 children, all absent from schedule.

Lamartine Yates – *see* Kent (p. 306).

South-west

Rathbone, Nina, 'abt 48 or 50'.
Randalls Farm, Old Cobham.
Census night: resists; 'Information Refused.'
Occupation: 'Suffragist (Professed).'
Registrar (signs schedule): 'from the best information available … on the authority of the Registrar General'.

Woking area

Smyth, Ethel M. [recorded as Miss E. M.Smith], [54 years].
Coign [Cottage].
Census night: resists, and then evades in London (see pp. 156–7).
Occupation: private means.
Others: 2 servants apparently remain after Ethel departed.
Household: 'probably 8' rooms.
Statement: 'No vote no census'.
Registrar: signed schedule (and possibly added what little information there is).
Suffrage: WSPU.

Stables, Mrs Mary Elizabeth.
Deerstead House, St John's.
Census night: resists.
Occupation: private means.
Family: daughter, 2 female visitors.
Household: 10 rooms, 3 servants.
Statement: 'No vote no census. As Mrs Stables is deprived of her citizen's right of voting, she declines to make a census of either her visitors, family or servants in this year of 1911'. (However, she signs schedule.)
Registrar: Information on the 7 inhabitants is added in red, with note 'Entered as per Instructions.'
Suffrage: probably CUWFA.

Pethick-Lawrence, Frederick, 39 years.
Mascot, Holmwood.
Census night: complies for himself and male visitor.
Household: 12 rooms, 1 servant, unnamed (added in another hand, as is 'wife about 35' (though see also Westminster, i.e. Emmeline counted twice).
Statement: complies 'so far as males are concerned. The women in the house being suffragists have requested me not to include them & I have accordingly not done so.'
Suffrage: WSPU.

South of Guildford

Chance, Lady Julia C., 46 years.
Orchards, Godalming.
Census night: complies.
Family: husband, 57, baronet; cousin.
Household: 20 rooms, 6 servants.
Suffrage: CUWFA.

Campbell, Muriel, 36 years.
1 Golf Bungalow, Hindhead.
Census night: resists.
Household: Muriel & her young son are boarders.
Statement: 'Votes for Women' (written at defiant angle).

18 miles east

Redhill

Cather, Mrs John L.
Red Cottage, Cavendish Road.
Census night: evades.
Occupation: John, 30, lieutenant Royal Navy (retired), motor body builder.
Status: married 2 years, no children.
Household: 9 rooms; probably 'took' servant with her.
Statement: 'Conscientious scruples prevent me from rendering a return of the female occupants of this house for the purpose of assisting the preparation of statistical tables, which will be used as the basis of further vexat[ious] legislation affecting women, & in which they have no voice. Should the Conciliation Committee's bill be pa[ssed] into law this session the additional details required will be forthcoming.'
Enumerator: 'Two Females inserted in Summary B[oo]k figures by Registrar as the probable number.'
Suffrage: probably WSPU?

Richmond, Mrs.
Fengates House.
Census night: apparently evades.
Household: no schedule found yet (though one house on Fengates Road is apparently 'uninhabited').
Suffrage: WSPU.

8 miles north

Croydon area

Holmes, Marion, [43 years].
327 Brighton Road.
Census night: probably evading (with older daughter?).
Family: husband, 57, chemist & shopkeeper; daughter, 7 years.
Household: 7 rooms, 1 servant.
Suffrage: WFL.

Cameron-Swan, [Grace, 31 years].
79 Mayfield Road, Sanderstead.
Census night: evades.
Family: husband, Donald, managing director of engraving firm; two young sons.
Household: 8 rooms; probably servant evaded with Donald's myseriously missing wife?
Suffrage: WSPU; Donald MPU.

Neligan, Dorinda, [77 years].
Oakwood House, 5 Sydenham Road.
Census night: undoubtedly evades.
Others: Eleanor Megarry, lodger, 61, sole occupant, signs schedule.
Household: 3 rooms.
Suffrage: WSPU, WTRL.

Terry, Mrs Elizabeth, [46 years].
9 Morland Avenue.
Census night: evades.
Family: husband, accountant for county education committee; cousin; visitor.
Household: 8 rooms, 1 servant.
Suffrage: WFL.

Gliddon, Katie E., 27 years.
70 Croham Road.
Census night: complies.
Occupation: artist.
Family: father, investment broker; mother, sister, brother, grandmother.
Household: 12 rooms, 1 servant.
Suffrage: WSPU?

Kent: population 1,020,000

North-west Kent, bordering Surrey

Fennings, Ethel, [34 years], **Jessie,** [33], **Agnes,** [32] and **Muriel,** [25 years].
149 Croydon Road, Anerley.
Census night: hosted all-night party.
Occupations: no information.
Household: 11 rooms.
Enumerator (signs schedule): 'I heard from occupants of next house that from 10 to 12 other females slept in this house on the night of April 2nd 1911.'
Suffrage: WFL.

Towards east and south

Harvey, Mrs Kate.
Brackenhill, 47 Highland Road, Bromley.
Census night: resister/evader.
Enumerator: 'House filled with suffragettes who refuse information.'
Summary gives no figures.
Suffrage: WFL, WTRL.

Barnes, Elizabeth.
Hurstpierpoint, Amherts Road, Sevenoaks.
Census night: resists.
Statement: 'No vote no census.'

Rollinson, Alice R., 35 years.
Kismet, Pier Road, Northfleet, Gravesend.
Census night: complies.
Occupation: teacher in county council school.
Others: she is a boarder of another county council teacher, his wife and their three children.
Household: 6 rooms.
Suffrage: WFL.

Ainsworth, Laura.
32 Stuart Road, Gillingham (absent from her lodgings).
Census night: [organized mass evasion in Jezreel Hall, Canterbury Street, Gillingham].
Occupation: [WSPU organizer for Medway towns area].
Household: 39 female and 1 male evader [source: *Chatham Observer*].
No schedule found.
Suffrage: WSPU.

Yates, Rose Lamartine, 'about 40', and **Tom,** 'about 42'.
The Cottage, Preston Parade, Whistable-cum-Seasalter, near Blean (on holiday, normally Wimbledon).
Census night: resist.
Occupation: Tom, barrister-at-law.
Others: no record of young son Paul, or servant.
Household: 8 rooms.
Suffrage: WSPU, MPU.

Wightwick, Mrs, 'probably 60'.
3 The Drive, Barton Fields, Canterbury
Census night: resists.
Family: widowed; son, solicitor, & two daughters.
Household: 16 rooms, 3 servants.
Schedule partly completed, and signed, by registrar.

Along coast

Harraden, Gertrude, 'about ?30'.
Stoney Croft, The Bungalows, Walmer (Deal).
Census night: resists, hosts evasion.
Occupation: of independent means.
Others: 6 female visitors, names unknown.
Household: ?9 rooms, 2 servants, names unknown.
Note: 'See letter Census Office 4th April 11.'

Smart Suffragette, Mrs, '(about) 60' years.
30 Bouverie Road West, Folkestone.
Census night: resists.
Occupation: 'Boarding House Keeper'.
Others: 2 female visitors, both un-named and '(about) 40'; probably one is Florence Macaulay, WSPU organizer for Canterbury area.
Household: 1 servant.
Registrar (signs schedule): 'Mrs Smart refused to fill up a Schedule and the others refused information for the reason that they state women have no Vote. This schedule is filled up on the authority of the Reg[istra]r General.'
Suffrage: WSPU

Inland

Abbott [...] and Ferguson [...].
Rosemary, Crookham Hill, Edenbridge.
Census night: resist.
Occupations: private means.
Household: 2 servants.
Registrar (signed schedule, minimal information): 'on the Authority of the Registrar General'.

Lelacheur, Lydia J., 68 years.
The Wilderness, Tunbridge Wells.
Census night: complies?
Occupation: 'Treasurer, Tunbridge Wells WSS'.
Family: daughter, Mabel, 20.
Household: 18 rooms, 7 servants (who, unusually, are listed above the Lelacheurs; cook & nurse appear to have 'suffrage' written by their name).
Suffrage: NUWSS.

Sussex: population 667,000

East Sussex

Hastings

Darent, [Mrs] Harrison, 68 years?
1 St Paul's Place.
Census night: resists.
Status: widow.
Occupation: private means.
Others: 5 female visitors (anonymous)
Household: 'about 14 Rooms', 2 servants.
Statement: 'No Vote no Information.'
Registrar signs schedule; adds 'Note from Police' (presumably of number of occupants).
Suffrage: WTRL.

Davidson, F. E.
The Bungalow, Kite's Nest.
Census night: resists.
Occupation: private means.
Household: 9 rooms, 2 servants (no names).
Statement: 'No Parliamentary Vote No Information' (at oblique angle).
Registrar (signs schedule): 'The particulars are the best of my information.'

Eastbourne

Allen, Lillie J., 42 years.
18 Upperton Gardens.
Census night: complies.
Occupation: 'Wife, Mother, housekeeper, dressmaker, cook, teacher, laundress & Suffragist'.
Status: married 16 years, 2 children.
Family: husband, 54, solicitor; 2 sons, 3 daughters [probably she is his second wife].
Household: 11 rooms, 2 servants.
Suffrage: WFL.

Haldane/Hardane.
11 Grand Parade.
Census night: resists.
Household: 2 rooms, 1 servant (lady's maid, Emily Dumpère, signs schedule).
Enumerator: 'Suffragist'.

Jones, Mrs.
10 Southfields Road.
Census night: resists.
Enumerator's summary: 5 females, 'Suffragette Information refused'.

Brighton

Turner, Minnie, 40 years.
Sea View, 13 Victoria Road.
Census night: resists, hosts mass evasion.
Status: 'Rated Occupier (Head)'.
Others: 'probably 11 other females. Further information refused.'
Household: 10 rooms.
Enumerator signs schedule; his summary gives 12 females.
Suffrage: WTRL, WSPU.

Cozens, Mary, [about 54 years].
74 Stanford Avenue.
Census night: probably evader.
Family: Ellen Cozens, 89, widow, [mother?].
Household: 8 rooms, 2 servants.
Suffrage: WSPU?

Martindale, Louisa, 38 years.
10 Marlborough Place.
Census night: complies.
Occupation: medical practitioner.
Others: Ismay Fitzgerald, resident patient, 40, private means; 2 other patients (one 3½ weeks); nurse.
Household: 14 rooms, 2 servants.
Suffrage: NUWSS.

Hove

Hare, Mary, [about 51 years].
8 San Remo.
Census night: resists.
Occupation: head-teacher of oral system, deaf & dumb.
Others: 4 teachers, all anonymous.
Household: 12 female & 3 male pupils, aged 5–20 years.
Statement: 'Women don't count therefore they will not be counted Mary Hare.'
Enumerator: 'I called at this house & saw the housekeeper (Miss Hare being away from Hove) who, in reply to my questions, without [reveal]ing my identity, informed me there were 16 scholars – more boys than girls – one girl 20, but most others rather young, four mistresses, Miss Hare & (probably) 3 servants. I find this is not a charitable instit[ution].'
Enumerator's summary: number of females deleted, altered to 16, giving total of 28 people [suggesting Mary may have sheltered some local evaders].
Suffrage: WFL (See Figure 44, p. 234).

Budd, [Mrs], 35 years.
Nurnberg, Palmeira Avenue.
Census night: probably hosts evasion.
Family: husband, dentist, signs schedule; son; all others added faintly.
Others: 5 female visitors, aged 20–40, no names.
Household: 11 rooms, 2 servants, no names.

To north

Parks, Mrs [Elizabeth Robins].
[Backsettown, Henfield.]
Census night: resists? ['Parks' is her married name; no address or signature].
Occupation: author, journalism.
Household: 7 rooms, 2 servants.
Suffrage: WWSL, WSPU.

West Sussex

Zangwill, Edith, Mrs, [36 years].
[East Preston, nr Littlehampton].
Census night: resists.
Family: [Edith and 11-month-old daughter added in red ink, probably by registrar.]
Household: 8 rooms, 2 servants.
Statement: 'The rest of the household is not entered as we feel that until women have the political rights of citizens, they should not perform the duties of [citizens?]. Mr [Israel] Zangwill is not at home.'
Registrar: signs schedule, adding 'By instruction from Registrar General'.
Suffrage: Israel, MLWS; Edith, WSPU, NCSWS.

Inland

Beck, [Ellen and Edith].
Duncans Farm, Billingshurst.
Census night: evaders?
Family: brother, 62, private means.
Household: 18 rooms, 4 servants.
Suffrage: WSPU, (tax resisters).

West

de Fonblanque, Florence, [46 years].
Duncton, Petworth.
Census night: undoubtedly evaded.
Family: Robert (Comte de Fonblanque), 42, private means.
[After his name, there is a 3-line gap; Florence may have 'taken' 2 other servants with her.]
Household: 8 rooms, 1 servant.
Suffrage: WFL, CUFWA.

Cummin, Vinvela, ['estimated 40'], and Christobel, 36 years.
Easebourne Vicarage, near Midhurst.
Census night: Vinvela and Christobel evade.
Family: Joseph Cummin, father, 69, widower, Vicar, signs schedule.
Added by another hand: sisters, Elsie 34, and Mary 29, both apparently present.
Statement: 'Suffragettes wandering about all night.' [3 lines are blank, then a third hand writes in names of Vinvela and Christobel.]
Household: 11 rooms; possibly servants are evading too?
Suffrage: WFL.

North

Costelloe, Rachel [Ray, later Strachey], 22 years.
Vann Bridge, Fernhurst.
Census night: complies.
Occupation: engineering student.
Family: Bertrand Russell, 38, lecturer, uncle; wife Alys, 43 (signs schedule); sister Katherine, student; visitor, Goldsworthy Lowes Dickinson, lecturer.
Household: 9 rooms, 2 servants.
Suffrage: NUWSS.

Near Chichester

Binnie, A. M., 'about 45'.
West Wittering (by 'late coastguard station').
Census night: resists.
Family: 2 children, about 8 and 10.
Others: 2 female visitors (both Woodruff), plus unknown female (German).
Statement: 'No vote, no census – till women have the rights & privileges of citizenship, I for one decline to fulfil the duties.'
Note: 'Filled in by Registrar on best Information available, after careful Inquiries.'

Hampshire: population 920,000

Portsmouth: population 231,000

St James's Hall, 4 & 6 Charlotte St, Landport.
Census night: 'Suffragettes Meeting Held Here.'
Occupants: 13 males, 39 females, 52 people.
Enumerator's summary: hall, above 3 lock-up shops [no schedule].
Suffrage: WSPU organizer (see below).

Surry, Blanche W., 46 years.
22 Copnor Road.
Census night: complies.
Status: married 20 years, 1 child
Family: husband, 49, Naval Pensioner; son, Launcelot, 15, school.
Household: 6 rooms.
Suffrage: WSPU.

Portsmouth: Southsea

Marsh, Charlotte A. L., 23 years.
4 Pelham Road.
Census night: absent, resister.
Occupation: Organizing Secretary, Women's Suffrage League.
Status: single, lodger.
Household: 2 rooms.
Note: 'This person spent the night at St James Hall Landport & returned to 4 Pelham Road the next day. (Absolutely refuses to fill up paper.)'
Suffrage: WSPU.

Bullin, Catherine, 39 years.
Kent Lodge, Queen's Crescent.
Census night: complies.
Family: husband, furniture dealer; son.
Household: 10 rooms, 1 servant.
Suffrage: WSPU.

Peacock, Miss [Lilian?, 39 years].
7 Craneswater Avenue.
Census night: absent, undoubtedly evading (St James's Hall).
Occupation: [shorthand writer?].
Family: [mother, widow, 79; brother, 42].
Enumerator's summary: listed as uninhabited.
Suffrage: WSPU.

Whetton, Sarah.
64 Devonshire Avenue.
Census night: absent, evader [probably at Mottershall's].
Family: husband, civil servant; 2 sons.
Household: 6 rooms.
Suffrage: WFL.

Shaw, Beatrice [Mrs Donald Hay], 34 years.
4 Campden Villas, Saxe Weimar Road.
Census night: present, complies.
Occupation: author.
Status: married 5 years, 2 children.
Family: husband (Captain, Royal Marine Artillery); 2 children, 3 relatives.
Household: 1 servant, 11 rooms.
Suffrage: WFL.

Along Esplanade

Portsmouth: Old Portsmouth

Mottershall, Miss, [Mary E., 55 years].
6 Clarence View, Pembroke Road.
Census night: absent, undoubtedly evading; probably hosting mass evasion.
Other: George Pinkstone, Retired W[ar] O[office], India Service, 71 years, signs.
His statement: '9 rooms, which are let out to visitors in the Summer, but at present are empty.'
Suffrage: WFL.

Across Harbour

Portsmouth: Gosport

Turner, Ellen E., 45 years.
74 Whitworth Road.
Census night: complies.
Family: husband (shoe examiner, government); 5 children.
Household: 6 rooms
Suffrage: WFL.

To north

O'Shea, Norah, 46 years.
The Cottage, Cosham.
Census night: complies.
Occupation: private means.
Family: sister Margaret (51); joint occupiers.
Household: 14 rooms, 2 servants.
Statement: 'We have filled in this paper under protest because Women should vote for Members of Parliament, Margaret O'Shea, Norah O'Shea'.
Suffrage: NUWSS.

Isle of Wight

Gonne, Katherine.
Hygeia Nursing Home, Ventnor (patient).
Census night: resister.
Enumerator: 'Suffragette – refused to give information.'
Suffrage: sister of Captain Gonne, MLWS.

30 miles west

Bournemouth: population 79,000

Blackledge, Miss N.
Terra Firma/Dovedale, Slater Road, Christchurch.
Census night: resister.
Family: mother, 2 sisters, nephew.
Household: 9 rooms, 2 servants.
Enumerator (signs): 'Information refused.'
Suffrage: WSPU.

Hume, Mrs Alice Hutteman.
Longhtonhurst, West Cliff Gardens.
Census night: absent, evading?
Family: husband, James, 57, vegetarian boarding-house keeper (signs schedule);
daughter, 18, assistant.
Also: **Digby, Miss,** and **Harding, Edith,** boarders.
Census night: resisters.
Household: 42 rooms.
Suffrage: Alice, WFL, FCLWS.

BRISTOL AND THE SOUTH-WEST

Somerset: population 490,000

Bath: population 51,000

Mansel, Mildred, [42 years].
12 Lansdown Crescent.
Census night: present, organizes mass evasion, resister, signs schedule (giving
Bath WSPU address).
Others: 'and 35 other Ladies'.
Statement: 'No Vote No Census (*Cheers*!).' (See Figure 33, p. 164).
Suffrage: WSPU.

3 miles east

Batheaston

Blathwayt, Linley and Emily, 71 and 59 years.
Eagle House.
Census night: comply (daughter Mary, 32, evading in Bath).
Occupation: Lieutenant Colonel, Bengal Staff Corps, Retired.
Status: married 36 years, 3 children, 2 still living, 1 died.
Others: gardener's family.
Household: 21 rooms, 2 servants.
Suffrage: offer hospitality to WSPU.

Tollemache, Aethel and Grace, [29 years], and mother **Frances,** [61 years].
Batheaston Villa.
Census night: absent, entertaining mass evaders in Bath.
Household: 11 rooms, 3 servants (cook signs schedule).
Enumerator's summary: 'Mrs Tollemache away (servants).'
Suffrage: WSPU (Frances, WTRL).

12 miles south

Watts, Helen, 29 years.
?Bilucathra, Chilcompton.
Census night: complies.
Status: single, boarder.
Family: brother Nevile, 26 years, schoolmaster (Downville College).
Household: 6 rooms (station master and his wife).
Suffrage: WSPU lapsed?

20 miles south-west

Clark, Alice, [36 years].
Millfield, Street.
Census night: possibly evading (or abroad?). On line below her mother's name,
a name was added and then heavily blocked out; was this Alice?
Status: single.
Family: father, 72, boot manufacturer; mother, Helen, 70; cousin, visitor.
Household: 16 rooms, 4 servants.
Suffrage: tax resister, NUWSS.

Gloucestershire: population 670,000

Cheltenham: population 49,000.

Flatman, Ada, [about 35 years].
Bedford Lodge, College Road.
Census night: resister, organizes mass evasion.
Others: 1 male, 12 females evading.
Household: 8 rooms, 1 servant.
Suffrage: WSPU.

Angus, Mrs.
Lindley, College Road.
Census night: resists.
Family: 4 daughters, no names.
Household: 12 rooms, 3 servants and governess, no names.
Enumerator: 'Suffragettes.'

Stirling, Frances, 51 years.
30 Clarence Square.
Census night: complies, signs schedule.
Status: married 26 years, 7 children, 5 still alive, 2 died.
Occupation: 'private means. Suffragette.'
Family: 3 daughters, 14–24 years (Elvira, 24, 'Women's Suffrage').
Household: 10 (15?) rooms, 1 servant.
Statement: 'This Form is Filled in through the Magnanimity of a Suffragette.
Hoping that a more generous & just Legislation for Women will soon be forth-
coming from those in Power in Great Britain.'
Suffrage: WSPU.

Eamonson, Miss.
Lintray Villas [obtained from enumerator's summary].
Census night: resisting (at a Mrs Boult's house).
Household: 8 rooms, 1 servant.
Suffrage: WFL.

Bardsley, Miss.
Snowdon, Sydenham Villas.
Census night: resists.
Others: Mr and Mrs Wilkins, no information.
Household: 7 rooms, 1 servant.

Outside town

Earengey, Florence, [33 years].
Ashley Rise, Battledown, Charlton Kings.
Census night: absent, evading (probably with daughter [Lucy, 15] and servant).
Family: husband William (35), solicitor.
Household: 11 rooms.
Statement: see p. 165.
Suffrage: WFL; William, MLWS.

Godfrey, Mrs.
Whitcombe.
Census night: resists (signs, but provides limited information).
Family: 2 daughters, sister.
Household: 5 rooms.

Bristol: population 357,000

Kenney, Annie, [31 years].
9 Whatley Road, Clifton.
Census night: resister, organizes evasion?
Others: none recorded.
Household: 4 rooms.
Enumerator: see p. 166.
Suffrage: WSPU.

James, Misses.
Clifton Down House.
Census night: resisters, probably evading nearby.
Household: 'about 10' rooms, 1 servant.
Statement: 'Suffragettes' (see p. 167).
Suffrage: WSPU?

Rogers, Frederick William.
2 Kensington Villas, Royal Park, Clifton.
Census night: resister.
Family: wife [evading in Bath], 2 daughters,
Household: 11 rooms, 1 servant.
Statement: 'No one occupied this house during the times specified.'
Enumerator: 'Suffragettes. Information obtained here is from neighbour which I fully believe is correct.'

North

Priestman, Anna Maria and Mary, 83 and 80 years.
37 Durdham Park.
Census night: comply.
Status: single.
Family: niece.
Household: 12 rooms, 5 servants.
Suffrage: tax resisters, NUWSS.

Fowler, Mrs [Gertrude, 37 years].
19 Westbury Road.
Census night: probably evading.
Family: husband, smelting works manager; 2 young daughters.
Household: 11 rooms, 1 servant.
Suffrage: WSPU.

Right across city, in east Bristol

Lenton, Lilian, [20 years].
32 Pennywell Road.
Census night: undoubtedly evading, probably with mother.
Family: father, 44, foreman carpenter; 2 brothers and sister.
Household: 6 rooms.
Suffrage: WSPU.

Ayles, Bertha, 34 years.
12 Station Road.
Census night: complies.
Family: husband, ILP secretary.
Household: 6 rooms.
Suffrage: WLabL, ILP.

Wiltshire: population 280,000

Gramlick, Miss B.
Springfield, Trowbridge.
Census night: possibly evading?
Family: widowed father, 68 years; 5 sisters (23–34 years).
Household: at least 13 rooms, 5 servants (including butler).
Suffrage: WSPU.

Dove-Willcox, Lillian M., [35 years].
Trowbridge Town Hall [exact location of caravan is obscured on schedule, possibly Melksham].
Census night: evading in caravan in rural Wiltshire.
Status: widow.
Household: 2-roomed van.
Statement: see pp. 165–6.
Suffrage: WSPU.

Abraham, Katherine, 23 years.
2 Estcourt Street, Devizes.
Census night: probably evading (line drawn through her entry), perhaps with others.
Occupation: at home.
Family: widowed mother; brother, medical student.
Household: 7 rooms.
Suffrage: WSPU.

Dorset: population 220,000

Housman, Clemence.
Greycott, Linden Road, Swanage.
Census night: resister (refused to complete schedule, which is left blank).
Others: none recorded, but undoubtedly 3–4 other evaders.
Statement: 'No Vote No Census Clemence.'
Enumerator: 'Information refused.'
Enumerator's summary: inhabited house, number left blank. (See Figure 27, p. 149).
Suffrage: WTRL, Suff At.

Mills, Ernestine and Herbert, 37 and 41 years.
Briarbank, Studland.
Census night: comply.
Occupation: 'artist in silver & enamel'; Herbert, doctor.
Status: married 10 years, 1 child.
Family: daughter 8 years.
Household: 8 rooms, governess.
Suffrage: WSPU, Fabians.

Shaw, Louise.
Holly Lodge, Branksome Park, near Poole.
Census night: resists.
Family: husband 'private means', 2 sons.
Others: 3 visitors (Wakeman).
Household: 12 rooms, 5 servants.
Enumerator: 'Further information absolutely refused.'

Branson, Mrs C. M.
31a Westbury, Sherborne.
Census night: resister [address given in enumerator's summary].
Status: widow.
Family: 1 daughter.
Household: 9 rooms, 1 servant, 4 visitors (Mrs & 3 Misses Harvey).
Statement: 'Until I am acknowledged to be a citizen of Great Britain I refuse to carry out the duties of citizens. C. M Branson.'
Suffrage: independent, WSPU link.

Devon: population 702,000

North coast

Preston-Whyte, Mrs [Joanna].
The Bungalow, Instow, near Bideford.
Census night: resists.
Occupation: private means.
Family: daughter.
Others: visitors Miss and Mrs Anderson: 'No votes, so do not fill in this paper'.
Household: 20 rooms, 5 servants.
Statement: 'No votes no census.'
Note: 'Filled in by Registrar on the authority of Registrar General in letter dated 9 April 1911.'
Suffrage: NUWSS.

South coast

Scott, Amy, Mrs.
34 Fore Street, Heavitree, Exeter.
Census night: resists.
Occupation: dressmaker.
Family: daughter, 13; widowed mother.
Household: 7 rooms.
Statement: 'No vote No census. Since women do not count we refuse to be counted.'

Torquay

Duffin, Lara?
Livermead Hotel, Torbay Road.
Census night: resists.
Statement: 'No vote no census.'

Next door on seafront

Fausten, Mary.
Chalet La Rosaire, Livermead.
Census night: present, refuses to give age (American).
Occupation: 'Woman's Suffrage' (similarly, elder daughter).
Family: husband (German, retired engineer), another daughter.
Household: 12 rooms, 1 servant.
Suffrage: WSPU, Nat Lib L.

Ramsay, Mabel, 'about 35'.
4 Wentworth Villas, Plymouth.
Census night: resists, as seemingly do other occupants, 'Suffragettes'.
Occupation: doctor.
Family: widowed mother, 'about 60'.
Others: visitor, Nora Bridges, author.
Household: 10 rooms, 3 servants.
Registrar (completed schedule): 'See letter & authority from Registrar General.'
Suffrage: NUWSS.

Cornwall: population 325,000

Corbett, [Catherine].
The Bungalow, Falmouth.
Census night: evades/resists?
Family: husband, 48, private means.
Household: 7 rooms, a nurse, 2 servants.
Enumerator: 'These [servants] refused all information concerning themselves to Mr Corbett, & also to myself.'
Suffrage: WSPU.

THAMES VALLEY AND THE CHILTERNS

Oxfordshire: population 198,000

Richards, Mrs E. F.
209 Woodstock Road, Oxford.
Census night: evader.
Family: husband and daughter present.
Household: 12 rooms, 2 servants.
Suffrage: WSPU.

Down river, below Reading

Fife, Stella.
Wood Hill, Henley-on-Thames.
Census night: evades.
Family: mother, 2 sisters, visitor.
Household: 11 rooms, 2 servants.
Suffrage: WSPU.

Berkshire: population 303,000

Scott, Mrs.
Hurst Nurseries, Twyford.
Census night: evades (as do her mother-in-law and female visitor).
Family: husband (market gardener), signs, but also signs statement; 2 nephews;
baby son and niece.
Statement: 'All Adult females omitted as a protest against the Government's
Veto of the Women's Franchise Bill. WOMEN DON'T COUNT!'

Ashman, Fanny, 52 years.
Broad Street, Thatcham.
Census night: complies (though son signs).
Status: widow, 14 children, 11 still living, 3 died.
Family: 6 daughters, 2 sons.
Suffrage: WFL.

Buckinghamshire: population 194,000

Courtauld, Catherine, 32 years.
Bocken, Great Missenden.
Census night: complies.
Occupation: sculptor.
Family: brother, private means.
Household: 14 rooms, 2 servants, visitor.
Suffrage: Suff At [normally Hampstead].

South

Florence, Mary Sargant, 'about 45' [43 years].
Lords Wood, Marlow.
Census night: resists.
Family: widowed; son, daughter, female visitor.
Household: 'about 12' rooms, 2 servants.
Statement: 'No Vote No Census.'
Registrar: 'This schedule filled up in accordance with instructions from Registrar General. Vide his letter 7th April 1911.'
Suffrage: WTRL (WFL?).

Nearby

Lenten, Miss.
Bovington Green (from enumerator's summary).
Census night: resists.
Household: 6 rooms, 1 servant.
Registrar: 'This schedule filled up in accordance with instructions from Registrar General. Vide his letter 7th April 1911.'

Down river towards Windsor

Allen, Mary, [32 years].
Bowry House, Wraysbury.
Census night: evading?
Family: father, 70; mother, 10 children, 9 still living; daughter, granddaughter.
Household: 15 rooms, 2 servants.
Suffrage: WSPU.

Hertfordshire: population 287,000

Letchworth

Lee, Clara
2 Norton Way.
Census night: evades (though signs schedule, adding 'Occupier, Taxpayer, Voteless').
Household: 7 rooms, 1 servant (Laura Bell, married 10 years, 'husband's chattel & earning her own living').
Others: 2 visitors (Maxwell Kineton Parkes, 18, student; Cyril Bell, 5).
Statement: '[If women] are classed with lunatics, why [are they] asked to give information which will be used as a basis for legislation … Women occupier, whilst denied Citizenship by the Government, declines to give information for the Census preferring to spend the weekend on the Continent or elsewhere.' [*Further comment follows, not all legible.*]
Registrar: 'On enquiry I have ascertained that Miss Lee was not in Letchworth on Census night.'
Suffrage: WFL (WTRL?).

Parker, Signe Maria Cecilia, 27 years (Swedish).
102 Wilbury Road.
Census night: complies, reluctantly?
Family: married to artist; 2 young children.
Suffrage: WFL.

To south

White, Ethel Maud, 39 years.
Gravels, Radlett.
Census night: complies.
Occupation: indexer and classical coach.
Family: husband, 2 sons.
Household: 7 rooms, 2 servants.
Suffrage: WSPU.

Atherton, Mrs.
Chums, Heronsgate, Chorleywood.
Census night: resists.
Occupation: Society of Artists.
Family: sister.
Statement: 'No Vote No Census. When Women become citizens, they will fulfil the duties of citizens.'

Paw, Mathilde O.
Kimpton, near Hitchin.
Census night: resists, hosts evasion.
Others: 4 female visitors, no names.
Household: 8 rooms, 1 servant.
Statement: 'No Vote No Census.'

Bedfordshire: population 198,000

Billinghurst, Olive, 24 years.
45 Tavistock Street, Bedford.
Census night: complies.
Occupation: cookery teacher, county council.
Status: lodger in boarding house.
Suffrage: WSPU.

Stacy, Ethel M., 34 years.
34 Kimbolton Road, Bedford.
Census night: complies.
Occupation: doctor.
Family: parents, cousin.
Others: 2 nurses, 4 patients, 3 servants.
Suffrage: NUWSS.

Logan, Dorothy, 'about 45', and **Bracewell, Nora,** 'about 30' years.
Tempesford, near Biggleswade.
Census night: both resist, both 'Suffragette'.
Household: 6 rooms, Dorothy is head, Nora a visitor.
Statement: (Dorothy) 'Voteless'.

EAST ANGLIA

Starting at border with London, moving north-east

Essex: population 1,330,000

Baldock, Minnie, [about 47 years].
490 Barking Road, Plaistow.
Census night: absent, evading?
Family: husband, 46, driller; married 28 years; 2 sons.
Suffrage: WSPU.

Haslam, Ethel.
68 Cranbrook Road, Ilford.
Census night: evades.
Family: father (private means); mother and servant/s also evading?
Household: 10 rooms.
Suffrage: WSPU, CLWS.

Rock, Dorothea, 29 years.
[The Red House], Ingatstone.
Census night: resists.
Occupation: news vendor (for news agency).
Family: mother, 55; sister, Madeline, 25.
Household: 15 rooms, 3 servants (no names).
Statement: 'I, Dorothea Rock, in the absence of the male occupier, refuse to fill up this Census paper as, in the eyes of the Law, women do not count, neither shall they be counted.'
Enumerator: partly fills in schedule (signed by registrar).
Suffrage: WSPU.

Sky, Rosina, [52 years].
28 Cliff Town Road, Southend.
Census night: resists.
Occupation: [runs tobacconist and fancy goods shop].
Family: [widow, 3 children].
Statement (diagonally across): 'No votes for women, no information from women.'
Enumerator: 'From information received no one slept on these premises'.
Suffrage: WSPU, NCSWS, WTRL.

Frye, Kate Parry, 32 years.
73 High Street, Maldon.
Census night: present, but intended to evade.
Occupation: actress [NCSWS organizer].
Household: boarder with licensed victualler's family.
Suffrage: NCSWS.

Lilley, Kate, 37 years.
Holland House, Clacton.
Census night: complies.
Family: father, company director [Lilley & Skinner]; brother, 3 sisters.
Household: 6 servants.
Suffrage: WSPU.

Weaver-Baillie, Gertrude and Harold, [both '60?' years].
[West House, Widdington, Newport, near Saffron Waldon.]
Census night: resist.
Occupation: Harold, retired barrister; [Gertrude, novelist, aka Gertrude Colmore].
Household: 'probably about 10' rooms, 2 servants, unnamed.
Suffrage: Harold, MLWS; Gertrude WFL, possibly WWSL.

Marion, Kitty, [about 40 years].
10 Mensea Road, Colchester.
Census night: resister, 'refused information'.
Occupation: music hall artiste.
Household: boarder with dairyman's family.
Suffrage: AFL, WSPU.

Suffolk: population 383,000

Mordan, Clara, 66 years.
Sanatorium, Nayland, near Colchester.
Census night: complies (no choice).
Status: patient.
Suffrage: WSPU, CLWS.

Ipswich

Old Museum Rooms & Offices, Museum Street.
Census night: mass evasion, organized by Constance Andrews, WFL.
Enumerator's summary: 5 males, 16 female, 21 people, 'suffragettes'.
Suffrage: WFL, and WSPU (joint evasion). (See pp. 188–9).

Pratt, [Lilla].
160 Norwich Road.
Census night: evades.
Family: husband George, 47, music teacher; two teenage sons.
Household: 11 rooms.
Enumerator: 'There were two female Suffragists [Lilla and sister Constance Andrews] in this family who went to some place unknown for the night. The female servant went with them.'
Suffrage: WFL.

Hossack, Mrs [Marie].
49 Berner Street.
Census night: evading.
Family: husband, 42, surgeon; daughter and 2 sons.
Household: 12 rooms, 2 servants.
Suffrage: WFL.

Roe, Grace.
19/21 Silent Street?
Census night: absent; evading? [probably at joint evasion with WFL].
Household: lodger, with printer's family.
Occupation: [WSPU organizer].

8 miles west

Hadleigh

Bastian, Mrs Katherine, [63 years].
Fernbank, 19 Gallows Hill.
Census night: evading.
Family: husband, private means.
Household: 9 rooms, probably servant also evading.
Registrar (signs schedule): 'in accordance with instructions received from Census Office, Mr Bastian having declined to give any information'.
Suffrage: WFL.

Next door

Matthew, Miss [Dorothy?].
21 Fir Tree Terrace.
Census night: evades?
Family: widowed mother, 71; sister Ada, 39.
Suffrage: WFL.

10 miles north-west

Josling, Ellen, 53 years.
59 Lime Tree Place, Stowmarket.
Census night: complies.
Family: husband, labourer.
Household: 5 rooms, 3 boarders.
Suffrage: WCG, WFL.

On coast

Anderson, Elizabeth Garrett, [74 years].
Alde House, Aldeburgh.
Census night: evades; schedule completed by registrar.
Household: about 20 rooms, 4 servants.
Suffrage: WSPU.

Fairchild, Lottie, 47 years.
305 London Road, Lowestoft.
Census night: hosts mass evasion.
Occupation: boarding-house keeper.
Family: 3 sons, 2 daughters.
Household: 11 rooms, 2 servants.
Others: 10 female visitors: 3 named (Ponder, Worthington, a Mrs Drummond),
2 ladies from Harleston (16 miles east), and 5 ladies 'unknown'.
Enumerator: 'A schedule was left in the ordinary way with the occupier. On calling, it was handed me not filled up, but with the words "No Votes for Women – No information from Women" written across the schedule. Further information was refused & the servants and family instructed not to give any information whatsoever. The information now given has been gathered by me from the Husband (who was not living at Home on 2nd April) & other members of the family. I gathered that the several Ladies mentioned slept at this home intentionally to evade enumeration. This is the best information available, subject to above qualification.'

Norfolk: population 489,000

Willis, Edith, 35 years,
Carrow House, Norwich.
Census night: complies.
Occupation: hon. secretary, women's suffrage society.
Family: visiting her relations, the Colmans.
Household: 28 rooms, 6 servants.
Suffrage: NUWSS.

Cambridgeshire: population 215,000

Ward, Mary Anne, [about 60 years].
6 Selwyn Gardens, Cambridge.
Census night: evades.
Family: husband, 68, professor; daughter, 21.
Household: 12 rooms, so undoubtedly servant/s evading too.
Suffrage: NUWSS.

Midlands

EAST MIDLANDS

Nottinghamshire: population 604,000

Nottingham: population 260,000

City centre

Burgis, [May] Catherine Mary, Miss, [36 years].
21 Chaucer Street.
Census night: evader.
Occupation: [teacher]
Family: mother, widow, 62; sister, Kate, 27, teacher; brother, 19, student.
Household: 1 visitor, 1 servant, 9 rooms.
Suffrage: WSPU.

Wallis, Muriel, Miss, [29 years].
The Residence, Nottingham Castle.
Census night: evader.
Family: father, absent [director Nottingham Art Gallery & Museum], possibly also evaded with family.
Household: 2 servants, 8 rooms.
Suffrage: WSPU.

Beyond castle

Crocker, Ellen (Nellie), [38 years].
8 East Circus Street?
Census night: evader.
Others: boarding-house keeper's family; boarder.
Household: 12 rooms, 1 servant.
Suffrage: WSPU.

Hutchinson, Miss S.
5 Cavendish Crescent South, The Park.
Census night: absent, evader.
Family: mother and father absent, probably also evading.
Household: 3 servants, 12 rooms.
Suffrage: mother and daughter, WSPU.

Dowson, Helena, 44 years.
The Park, Nottingham.
Census night: complies.
Occupation: Secretary, Women's Suffrage Society.
Family: husband, lace manufacturer.
Household: 3 servants, 13 rooms.
Suffrage: NUWSS.

To west

Watts, Alice, 27 years.
Vicarage, 35 Church Street, Lenton.
Census night: complies.
Occupation: Secretary, Suffragist Society.
Family: father, Reverend Alan, 59; mother, Ethelinda, 57; 9 children, 8 still living, 1 died; sister, Ethelinda, 23, teacher; 2 brothers, school.
Household: 2 servants, 11 rooms.
Suffrage: NUWSS, CLWS.
For Helen Watts and brother Nevile, see Bath area (p. 317).

To north

Shaw, Leonora.
445 Mansfield Road.
Census night: evader.
Family: husband, Dr Philip, 45, science lecturer; mother and sister.
Household: 2 servants, 9 rooms.
Suffrage: WSPU.

Greenhall, Miss.
Red Hill, Mansfield Road.
Census night: resister/evader.
Household: 3 rooms.
Enumerator: 'Suffragette (No information) House Closed.'
Enumerator's summary lists it as inhabited.

30 miles north

Retford

Harmer, Nurse.
18 St John Street [undoubtedly WSPU shop, recorded as unoccupied but with her name on enumerator's summary].
Census night: evader?
Household: probably small-scale evasion.
Suffrage: WSPU.

Hutchinson, Anna.
Egmanton. [schedule not found yet].
Census night: [probably evading with Harmer].
Occupation: nurse, church worker.
Suffrage: WSPU, CLWS.

Lincolnshire: population 558,000

Rawle, Mary Anne, 32 years.
Hospital, Grantham.
Census night: complies (enforced?).
Status: patient.
Occupation: housewife.
Suffrage: WFL.

Cohen, Leonora, 38 years.
?Gortchew, Winthorpe, Skegness.
Census night: complies.
Family: husband, 44, importer and jewellery agent; son, 8; 1 child died.
Suffrage: WSPU.

Leicestershire: population 481,000

Leicester

'Suffragettes (about 20)', 'varying from 17 to 50' years.
Suffragette offices, 14 Bowling Green Road.
Census night: mass evasion.
Enumerator: 'Most of these were people of no occupation. A doctor's wife and daughter were amongst them.'
Registrar signs schedule.
Suffrage: WSPU.

Hawkins, Alice, [48 years].
2 Gaul Street.
Census night: evading (undoubtedly at WSPU offices).
Family: husband, Alfred, 53, invalid; 3 sons, 1 daughter.
Household: 6 rooms.
Suffrage: WSPU.

Carryer, Evelyn, [about 59 years].
Rough Close, St John's Road.
Census night: resists/evades?
Statement: 'No Vote No Census'; under infirmity, 'unenfranchised'.
Suffrage: NUWSS.

Taylor, Mary Ellen.
Smeeton, Leicester.
Census night: evading, with daughter Dorothea, and possibly servant.
Family: husband, 47, instrument manufacturer; son, 7.
Household: 11 rooms, 1 servant.
Statement: 'Women absent protesting. "No vote no census".'
Suffrage: WSPU.

Northamptonshire: population 364,000

Smith, [Mrs Jessie King] England.
Newstead, Hatton Park, Wellingborough.
Census night: evades.
Family: husband, 45, leather merchant.
Household: 9 rooms, 1 servant.
Suffrage: WFL.

Sharman, [Violet?].
Ivy Lodge, Wellingborough.
Census night: absent, evading?
Family: mother, 72, widowed, private means; her 2 grandsons; visitor.
Household: 20 rooms, 5 servants, lady's companion.
Suffrage: WFL.

WEST MIDLANDS

Warwickshire: population 1,024,000

Birmingham: population about 750,000

City centre: WSPU evasion likely (probably organized by Dorothy Evans), but schedule not yet found.

Edgbaston

Mannox, [Lizzie Greener?], 50 years.
287 Gillott Road, off Hagley Road.
Census night: resists. '(Suffragettes) refused information'.
Household: Henry Deakin (clerk) and wife; Charlotte Drake, boarder; perhaps Mannox also boarder?

Ryland, Bertha, [c. 29 years].
19 Hermitage Road, off Hagley Road.
Census night: evading.
Family: father, retired lawyer; mother Alice; sister Edith, 36; 2 brothers, photographer and fruit grower; 2 female visitors.
Household: 12 rooms, 3 servants.
Suffrage: WSPU (Bertha & Alice).

Parker, Alice.
11 Greenfield Crescent, Edgbaston.
Census night: resists.
Family: widow, two daughters.
Household: 12 rooms, 2 servants.
Statement: 'No Vote No Census. If I am intelligent enough to fill in this Census Form I can surely make a X on a Ballot Paper.'

Between Birmingham and Coventry

Floyd, Lettice Annie, [about 46 years].
Meriden [no address on schedule; no summary available].
Census night: evades? Sister Mary resists.
Family: Mary, private means; 6 female visitors: Hope Lupino (50, married, local); Mrs Bullock, 4 unknown.
Household: 15 rooms, 4 servants.
Suffrage: both sisters WSPU.

Dawson, Miss.
St Peter's Vicarage, Coventry?
Census night: absent, evades? [lodger?]
Household: parish priest and his son; Joseph Clayton, visitor, 42, journalist.
Suffrage: WSPU; Joseph, MLWS.

Wightwick, Ada Florence, 40 years.
16 Clarendon Square, Leamington.
Census night: complies, but adds statement.
Family: widowed, private means; niece.
Household: 15 rooms, 2 servants.
Statement: written round edges of schedule: 'Votes for Women!' (5 times), to which word 'No' has been pencilled in 3 times.
Ada signs, adding 'Non-militant suffragist (at present)'.

Worcestershire: population 562,000

Birmingham's southern suburbs:

Impey, Edith Adair.
Copthorne, Middleton Road, King's Norton.
Census night: resists, hosts local evaders.
Family: husband, son.
Household: 7 rooms; 1 servant, name withheld; 'and about 6 females'.
Registrar (signs schedule): 'Suffragette – information refused.'

Steen, Fanny.
61 Woodfield [College], King's Heath.
Census night: resists, hosts local evaders.
Household: 6 rooms; Fanny + 'about 9 other females'.
Registrar (signs schedule): 'Suffragette – information refused.'
Suffrage: WSPU.

Varley, Julia, 40 years.
42 Hay Green Lane, Selly Oak.
Census night: complies.
Occupation: trade union organizer.
Suffrage: was WSPU, now probably adult suffrage.

Further from Birmingham

Cottrell, Miss.
418 Stratford Road, Yardley.
Census night: resists [address in enumerator's summary].
Statement: 'Full particulars will be given when *all* ratepayers have a *vote*.'

Margesson, Lady Isabel Augusta, [about 48 years].
Barnet Green House, near Worcester.
Census night: absent, probably evading; daughter Catherine also absent, possibly evading.
Family: husband, Sir Mortimer, 50, private secretary; son; 2 visitors.
Household: 20 rooms, 4 servants, governess.
Suffrage: WSPU.

Herefordshire: population 113,000

Howey, Mary, 27 years.
Holly Lodge, Cradley, Bromyard, near Malvern.
Census night: resists.
Occupation: artist and suffragette.
Family: Mary describes herself as 'daughter'; but her mother, Gertrude, is not
listed and was probably evading, also Mary's sister Elsie?
Household: 10 rooms, 1 servant.
Statement: 'VOTES FOR WOMEN' inscribed boldly across schedule.
Suffrage: WSPU.

Staffordshire: population 1,360,000

North-west of Birmingham

Burkitt, [Evelyn] Hilda, [about 35 years].
214 Wellington Road, Hansworth.
Census night: absent, evading? (Possibly with servant/s?)
Family: widowed father, 64, company director, hardware merchant; two
brothers.
Suffrage: WSPU.

North to Black Country

Brockhouse, Mrs.
Lawnside, Hill Top, West Bromwich.
Census night: evades, possibly with eldest daughter?
Family: Henry (Harry), husband, 42, company secretary (coach spring axle and
ironwork); 4 young daughters, 1 son.
Household: 9 rooms, 2 servants.
Suffrage: WSPU. Henry: MLWS.

Thacker, Eveline, 30 years.
Buchanan Road, Walsall.
Census night: apparently complied.
Family: father, retired ironmonger; mother, 2 sisters.
Household: 9 rooms, 1 servant.
Suffrage: WSPU.

Wolverhampton

Sproson, Emma, 43 years.
Kelmscott, Horden Road.
Census night: apparently complies.
Family: married 15 years, 3 children; husband, Frank, 41, postman; sons (11, 4); daughter, 14.
Suffrage: WFL, WTRL.

Boswell, Helen.
117 Dunstall Road.
Census night: evading (possibly with sister/s).
Family: father, 62, credit draper; mother, 50, 10 children born, 8 living, 2 died; brother, 25, doctor; niece.
Household: 11 rooms, 1 servant.
Suffrage: WSPU.

Cresswell, Abigail, 43 years.
25 Rugby Street.
Census night: complies.
Family: husband, pattern-turner; 2 children.
Household: 6 rooms.
Suffrage: WFL.

30 miles north to Potteries

Pedley, Emily, 43 years.
18 Bower Street, Hanley.
Census night: complies.
Occupation: artist on pottery.
Family: Emily widowed (married 4 years, 2 children, 1 living, 1 died); son, 21, pottery draughtsman. Her widowed mother is head.
Household: 6 rooms.
Suffrage: WFL.

North to Cheshire

Northern England

MANCHESTER AND THE NORTH-WEST

The counties of Lancashire and Cheshire are here treated by adjoining neighbourhoods, out of geographical sequence, following the narrative in chapters 9 and 15.

Lancashire: population 4,800,000

Manchester: population 714,000

South of city centre, by Victoria Park

Stephenson, Miss S. J. (Jessie, Sara), 'about 40' years.
Denison House, Denison Rd.
Census night: present, resister, organizes mass evasion.
Occupation: Organizing Secretary WSPU.
Household: about 20 rooms.
Others: 156 females (including Flora Drummond, Mabel Capper), 52 males, 208 persons.
Registrar: (fills in and signs schedule) 'Suffragists here to avoid Census'.
Suffrage: WSPU.

Round corner

Hyland, Mrs (Rose), 'aged about 72'.
Holly Bank, Conyngham Road.
Census night: present, resister; hosts evasion;
Occupation: private means.
Status: widow.
Household: about 12 rooms, 2 servants.
Others: 74 females, 11 males, 88 persons,
Registrar: (as above) 'Suffragists here for evading Census.' Registrar signs schedule.
Suffrage: WSPU and others.

End of Denison Road

Roper, Esther, and Gore-Booth, Eva.
4 Park Crescent, Rusholme.
Census night: absent; probably evading at Denison House.
Others: visitor.
Household: 8 rooms; housekeeper and her family.
Suffrage: NCSWS, NIPWSS (anti-protective legislation).

Ratcliffe, Jane, 51 years.
19 Parkfield Street, Rusholme.
Census night: complies.
Status: married 26 years.
Family: none present.
Household: 8 rooms.
Enumerator: 'There are also 3 daughters at this house. Avoided Census last night
& I am told at Victoria Park, Rusholme' [undoubtedly Denison House].
Suffrage: WSPU.

Hordern, Agnes Ethel.
89 Clitheroe Road, Longsight.
Census night: evading in Hyland's house.
Occupation: [school teacher].
Household: 6 rooms; probably boarder, with married couple.
Suffrage: WFL.

Further south

Wallwork, Kate, 22 years.
20 Burlington Road, Withington.
Census night: probably absent, & evading in Denison House.
Occupation: shorthand typist.
Family: father, cloth manufacturing agent; mother; brother, salesman/clerk for
father; 3 sisters.
Household: 8 rooms.
Suffrage: WSPU.

Ashton, Margaret, 55 years.
8 Kinnaird Rd, Withington.
Census night: complies.
Occupation: private means.
Other: Ethel Snowden, 29, married, visitor.
Household: 9 rooms, 2 servants.
Suffrage: NUWSS.

Near city centre

Capper, Mabel H., [22 years].
21 Oxford Road.
Census night: evading in Denison House.
Family: father, William Bentley Capper, 58, self-employed dry stores; mother
Elizabeth, absent, probably evading with Mabel; possibly also brother William.
Suffrage: WSPU (Mabel, Elizabeth); MLWS (William). (See p. 178).

North of city

Barnes, Frederick Stanton, 30 years.
12 Deyne Avenue, Prestwich.
Census night: complies.
Occupation: railway assistant.
Family: wife, married 5 years, no children.
Household: 7 rooms, 1 servant.
Suffrage: MLWS.

Foot of Oldham Road

Robinson, Annot, [36 years].
73 Caroline Street, Ancoats.
Census night: absent, probably evading.
Family: husband, Samuel, 42, City Council Tramway clerk; daughter Catherine, 1 year.
Household: 4 rooms.
Suffrage: WLabL, ILP, NUWSS.

3 miles up Oldham Road

Mitchell, Hannah, 39 years.
18 Ingham St, Newton Heath.
Census night: apparently present, complies perhaps reluctantly.
Family: husband Gibbon, 42, Co-op tailoring manager; son, Frank, 14, school.
Occupation: Hannah, none.
Status: married 15 years.
Household: 5 rooms.
Suffrage: WFL, ILP.

4 miles further up: Oldham (see p. 348)

Beyond Salford: Eccles area

Heyes, Janet.
Newholme, Hazlehurst, Worsley.
Census night: evading (possibly midnight cycling).
Occupation: teacher?
Other: 1 servant (signs schedule).
Household: 6 rooms.
Suffrage: WFL.

Kipps, Miss.
16 Fitzwarren Street, Seedley.
Census night: absent, probably evader.
Occupation: elementary school teacher?
Others: family of 5 (probably boarder.)
Household: 11 rooms; 1 visitor, 1 boarder, 1 servant.
Suffrage: WFL.

5 miles south

Hudson, Muriel, [21 years].
Oakland Villas, Moorside Road, Flixton.
Census night: evading, probably one of 'Urmston walkers'.
Family: father, 62, elementary head teacher; wife Elizabeth absent, probably evading; 3 sons; possibly daughter [Ethel, 27] also evading.
Household: 8 rooms.
Suffrage: WFL.

Beanland, John, 42 years.
52 Princess Road, Urmston.
Census night: complies.
Occupation: foreign correspondent (export shipping).
Family: daughter, 17, student; wife [Emma, 45] absent, probably evading.
Household: 6 rooms.
Suffrage: MLWS, WFL?

Cook, John.
12 Lime Avenue, Flixton Road, Urmston.
Census night: absent, probably evading.
Family: wife, 47; 6 children, 5 living; 2 sons (clerks), 2 daughters (machinist, at school).
Household: 7 rooms, 1 visitor.
Suffrage: MLWS.

Cheshire: population 900,000

North Cheshire, southern suburbs of Manchester

Manning, Miss M. E. [Mary], [29 years].
Harper Hill, Derbyshire Road, Sale.
Census night: evader; organizes evasion; no schedule?
Others: 19 females.
Household: mother (Emma) and sisters, probably evading.
Enumerator's summary (no schedule): 'Suffragettes. Paper handed over to Registrar 4.4.11'.
Suffrage: WFL organizer.

Geiler, Miss [?Lucy], 29 years]
Thornlea, Wardle Road, Sale.
Census night: evader.
Family: father, Hermann, 57, machinery exporter; mother, [Anna, 50], and sister [Minnie, 27], both absent, probably evading; 2 other sisters, 32 and 20; 3 brothers.
Household: 20 rooms, 3 servants.
Suffrage: WFL.

Fildes, Lucy.
[Studio, Tatton Buildings, Sale.]
Census night: undoubtedly evading (schedule not yet found).
[Occupation: artist, with Hines.]
Suffrage: WFL.

Hines, Ada.
The Nook, Cecil Avenue, Ashton-upon-Mersey.
Census night: undoubtedly evading.
Occupation: [artist, with Fildes].
Family: father, 71, woollen agent; mother, Eliza B. Hines, 67; 5 children born, 2 living, 3 died.
Household: 10 rooms, 1 servant.
Statement: Alfred: 'E. B. Hines's name would *not* have been on this list had she been able to go from [i.e. leave] home.'
Suffrage: WFL.

8 miles east

Baines, Jennie, 44 years.
66 Chatham Street, Stockport.
Census night: complies.
Occupation: none.
Status: married 24 years; 5 children, 3 living, 2 died.
Family: husband, George, 47, boot-maker; sons, 14 and 12, school; daughter, 21, assistant housekeeper; son-in-law (cotton spinner unemployed), their baby.
Household: 6 rooms.
Suffrage: WSPU.

8 miles south of Sale

Swanwick, Helena, 46 years.
Annandale, Knutsford.
Census night: complies.
Occupation: newspaper editor [*Common Cause*]
Status: married 23 years, no children.
Family: husband, Frederick, 59 years, university lecturer.
Household: 8 rooms, 1 servant; visitor, Kathleen Courtney.
Suffrage: NUWSS.

Lancashire cotton towns

Lees, Sarah Anne, 68 years, and **Marjory,** 32 years.
Werneth Park, Oldham.
Census night: both present, comply.
Occupation: private means.
Others: 1 visitor.
Household: 18 rooms, 5 servants.
Suffrage: NUWSS.

North of Manchester

Chew, Ada Nield, 41 years.
3 Kilnerdeyne Terrace, Rochdale.
Census night: complies.
Occupation: assisting in business.
Family: husband, general dealer/shop; daughter Doris, 12, school.
Household: 8 rooms.
Suffrage: NUWSS.

Reddish, Sarah, 61 years.
9 Bertrand Road, Bolton.
Census night: complies.
Occupation: Organizer, Women's Trade Unions and Women's Suffrage Societies.
Status: single.
Others: housekeeper and husband (industrial school); boarder.
Household: 7 rooms.
Suffrage: NUWSS, WCG.

Farrington, Margaret.
118 Dorset Street, Bolton.
Census night: absent, evading?
Family: husband, 47, journalist; parents-in-law.
Household: 5 rooms, 1 visitor.
Suffrage: WSPU.

Cooper, Selina Jane, 43 years.
59 St Mary's Street, Nelson.
Census night: complies.
Occupation: NUWSS organizer and lecturer.
Status: married 14 years; 2 children, 1 died.
Family: husband, Robert, cotton weaver; daughter Mary, 11.
Household: 4 rooms.
Suffrage: NUWSS, ILP.

Rigby, Edith, [38 years].
28 Winckley Square, Preston.
Census night: evader.
Family: husband, physician and surgeon, 53; adopted son, 8.
Household: 9 rooms, a 'lady help'.
Suffrage: WSPU.

Waring, Lily, 34 years.
Penwortham House, near Preston.
Census night: complies (visitor).
Occupation: 'Women's Suffrage Agitator', NUWSS organizer.
Others: Beatrice Todd, husband and daughter.
Household: 12 rooms, 4 servants.
Suffrage: NUWSS.

Liverpool, Merseyside and rural Cheshire

Liverpool

Woodlock, Winifred Patricia, 36 years.
46 Nicander Road.
Census night: complies.
Family: father, artist; mother, sister, brother.
Household: 6 rooms, 1 boarder.
Suffrage: WSPU.

Evans, Mrs.
49 Kimberley Drive, Great Crosby.
Census night: absent, evading?
Status: married 13 years; 1 child, died.
Family: husband, 42, jobbing gardener; father, mother.
Household: 7 rooms.
Suffrage: WFL.

Merseyside

Barry, Florence, 25 years.
66 Park Road South, Birkenhead.
Census night: complies.
Occupation: private means.
Family: sister.
Household: 11 rooms, 1 visitor.
Suffrage: WSPU.

Ker, Alice, 'about 53' [57 years].
6 James Street, Birkenhead (rented house).
Census night: evader.
Occupation: doctor.
Others: Alice's 2 daughters; Alice Davies, 'lady organiser' WSPU; 32 other females; caretaker (John Freeland). Total: 38 people.
Household: 11 rooms, 1 servant.
Statement: 'No other "persons", only many women, Alice Davies.'
Registrar fills in details (other than caretaker) in red ink.
Suffrage: WSPU.

Abraham, Mrs Katherine
2 Kingsmead Road, Birkenhead.
Census night: evading, perhaps with daughters.
Status: married, 30 years, 6 children, 1 died.
Family: husband, manufacturing chemist; 2 sons, students; son-in-law, engineer.
Household: 11 rooms, 2 servants.
Suffrage: WSPU.

Rural Cheshire

Woodall, Miss E.
13 Abbey Square, Chester.
Census night: evader.
Enumerator's summary: house listed as uninhabited, and name deleted.
Suffrage: WFL.

Elmy, Elizabeth C. Wolstenholme, 77 years.
Buxton House, Buglawton, Congleton.
Census night: complies.
Status: widow.
Family: son, 36, assistant overseer/rate collector for local council.
Household: 10 rooms.
Suffrage: WSPU.

Cumberland

Marshall family, Keswick – *see* Kensington.

YORKSHIRE

West Riding: population 3,045,000

South

Sheffield

Crookesmoor suburb

Pankhurst, Adela, [25 years], and **Archdale, Helen,** [about 35 years].
45 Marlborough Road.
Census night: resist, host mass evasion.
Family: Helen's sons, 8 and 5, daughter, 3; Adela, boarder.
Household: 8 rooms, 2 servants, nurse.
Others: 1 male, 48 female visitors: total 57 people.
Registrar (signs schedule): 'From information Received'.
Suffrage: WSPU.

Round corner

Balbirnie, Rosa Catherine, and probably **Macdonald, Jessie**.
21 Harcourt Road.
Census night: Rosa evades (though signs); Jessie, if living there, undoubtedly also evades, possibly with female boarder/s and servant/s.
Household: 8 rooms, 2 male boarders.
Enumerator: 'Signatory away from house on the Census night, and only occupants as stated above.'
Suffrage: WFL, (CUFWA?).

Nearby

Barnett/Barnet, Miss.
[5 Victoria Flats, Glossop Road.]
Census night: Probably evading at Marlborough Road?
Enumerator's summary omits a fifth flat; no schedule found yet.
Suffrage: WFL.

Across city

Clarke, Gertrude, 33 years.
17 Bradford Street, Attercliffe.
Census night: complies.
Family: husband, labourer; 6 children born, 2 died, 4 living (2 daughters, 2 sons).
Household: 4 rooms; a boarder.
Suffrage: WSPU?

Higgins, Annie, [about 45 years].
72 Pearce Road, Darnall.
Census night: evades.
Family: husband, 42, steel cutlery maker; daughters, 11 and 13 years.
Household: 5 rooms.
Enumerator: 'Wife evading census.'
Suffrage: WFL.

Whitworth, Edith Clara, 39 years.
100 Haley Bank Road.
Census night: complies.
Family: husband, 42, postal telegraphist (government employee); 3 children born, 1 died, 2 living (son, daughter).
Household: 7 rooms.
Suffrage: WFL.

Wilson, Dr Helen – *see* Holborn hotel, London (p. 249).

To north-east

Slack, Mrs.
3 Highfields, Doncaster Road, Rotherham.
Census night: evading?
Enumerator's summary records house as uninhabited (no schedule found).
Suffrage: WSPU.

Gervis, Miss.
60 Albany Road, Balby, Doncaster.
Census night: evades?
Family: probably brother, 37, house painter; sister-in-law.
Household: 5 rooms.
Suffrage: WSPU.

Fisher, Ada, 49 years.
61 Albany Road, Balby, Doncaster.
Census night: complies.
Family: husband, railway inspector; daughter, 21; 2 grandchildren; widowed father.
Household: 6 rooms.
Suffrage: WSPU, ILP, Railway Women's Guild.

North

Huddersfield and district

Near town centre

Key, Edith A., 39 years.
68 Regent Place, Bradford Road.
Census night: complies (signs for blind husband).
Family: husband, Frederick, 38, musical instrument/sewing machine dealer; sons, 19 and 17.
Occupation: 'assisting in the business'.
Household: 5 rooms.
Suffrage: WSPU.

Thewlis, Dora, 20 years.
14 Bradley Street South.
Census night: complies.
Occupation: woollen weaver.
Family: sister, 25, woollen weaver.
Others: boarding-house keeper and daughter, charwoman; male boarder (professional music hall artiste); visitor.
Household: 5 rooms.
Suffrage: WSPU lapsed?

Lowenthal, Bertha, 47 years.
The Grange, Edgerton Road.
Census night: complies.
Occupation: private means.
Family: brother, wool merchant; sister.
Household: 14 rooms, 3 servants.
Suffrage: WSPU.

Colne Valley

Thewlis, Eliza, 50 years.
Oak View, Manchester Road, Linthwaite.
Census night: complies.
Family: husband, fancy worsted weaver; daughter 13; grandson, nephew.
Household: 5 rooms.
Suffrage: WSPU lapsed?

Pinnance, Elizabeth, 31 years.
13 Longwood Road, Milnsbridge.
Census night: complies.
Occupation: rag cloth weaver.
Family: husband, cloth presser; of her 3 children, 1 died; present are son 11 and daughter 9.
Household: 3 rooms.
Suffrage: WSPU lapsed?

8 miles north

Halifax

Jones, Dr. Helena
3 Rhodesia Avenue.
Census night: evades.
Household: 7 rooms, 1 servant (signs schedule).
Enumerator: 'Dr Helena Jones (Suffragette) did not pass the night of Sunday April 2nd 1911 in this dwelling and did not arrive in this dwelling on the morning of Monday 3rd April 1911.'
Suffrage: WSPU.

Saltonstall, Lavena, [29 years].
13 Park Place? King Cross.
Census night: undoubtedly evading.
Occupation: weaver?
Household: 4 rooms; slipper-maker family (Lavena a boarder?)
Suffrage: WSPU.

Taylor, Mary, [about 47 years].
32 Skircoat Green.
Census night: evades.
Family: husband, 46, blacksmith.
Household: 6 rooms.
Suffrage: WSPU, WLabL.

Willson, Laura, 33 years.
117 Beechwood Road, Illingworth.
Census night: complies.
Family: husband, machine tool-maker; son, daughter, mother-in-law.
Household: 7 rooms, 1 servant.
Suffrage: WSPU lapsed?

6 miles up Calder Valley

Berkley, Elizabeth, 27 years.
21 Bankside, Hebden Bridge.
Census night: complies.
Occupation: button-hole machinist.
Family: widowed mother, 52 years, 7 children born, 5 living, 2 died; Lizzie's 2 sisters, machinists.
Household: 4 rooms.
Suffrage: WSPU lapsed?

6 miles north-east

Bradford

Phillips, Mary, [about 31 years].
68 Manningham Lane.
Census night: hosts mass evasion.
Others: 9 other females, details not known.
Statement: 'NO VOTE NO CENSUS …' (see Chapter 16, p. 186).
Enumerator: 'I am unable to obtain any more definite information', adding 'This is a lock-up shop, with no Sleeping accommodation'.
Enumerator's summary, at the end of his book, recorded Mary Phillips, in a 'lock-up shop', total of female occupants 10 ('Suffragettes').
Suffrage: WSPU.

Beldon, Bertha, [47 years].
9 Walmer Villas, Manningham Lane.
Census night: evades.
Family: husband, 46, solicitor; 6 children born, 4 are present.
Household: 17 rooms, 3 servants.
Suffrage: WSPU.

8 miles north

Thompson, Misses Elizabeth, 54 years; **Rachel,** 52, **Sarah,** 50.
Heathfield, Westwood, Ilkley.
Census night: resist (information on the 8 adult females added in red ink by enumerator).
Occupations: Elizabeth, headmistress, girls' high school; Rachel and Sarah, assistant mistresses.
Others: 5 teachers (boarders); 21 female pupils (10–18), all boarders; 4 servants, giving total 33 females.
Statement: 'No Vote No Census. If you expect women to fulfil duties, give them the right to which, by the performance of their duties, they are entitled. Elizabeth Thompson.' 'With the exception of [first] eight places' (see above), she signs the schedule.
Registrar: 'Can't get any further information.'
Enumerator's summary (next line): another assistant mistress, provides some information (perhaps objecting to boycott).
Suffrage: WSPU?

10 miles east of Bradford

Leeds

Evasion at Clarion Institute: schedule not yet found.

Titterington, Mary, [about 54 years].
Calverley Lane, Horsforth.
Census night: evading.
Enumerator's summary: 'Suffragette not at home on Sunday night.'
Suffrage: WSPU.

Thomas, Mrs.
21 Burley Grove.
Census night: resists.
Household: 3 rooms.
Enumerator: 'Information Refused.'

Cohen, Leonora – *see* Skegness, Lincolnshire (p. 336).

East Riding: population 507,000 (including York)

Hull

Murdoch, Mary C., 46 years.
103 Beverley Road.
Census night: complies.
Occupation: physician/surgeon.
Others: Florence Stacey, 26, physician/surgeon; nurse.
Household: 11 rooms, 2 servants.
Suffrage: ex-NUWSS, WSPU sympathizer?

Harrison, Mabel, 39 years.
14 Welbeck Street.
Census night: complies.
Occupation: midwives inspector, Hull Corporation.
Family: sister.
Suffrage: WSPU lapsed?

Little, Charlotte, 48 years.
85 Park Street.
Census night: complies.
Occupation: superintendent, trained nurses.
Family: sister, assistant superintendent.
Others: patient, visitor.
Household: 10 rooms, servant.
Suffrage: WSPU sympathizer?

30 miles north-east

York

WSPU evasion (organized by Violet Key-Jones): schedule not yet found (see below).

Coultate, Annie.
33 Melbourne Street.
Census night: evader (though signs schedule).
Family: Henry, 29, grocer assistant (son?).
Household: 5 rooms.
Enumerator: 'The signature is that of a well-known suffragette. She was away from home during the night of the Census, but was most probably enumerated amongst a number of Suffragettes who passed the night in a room in Coney St, York, with the object of evading the Census.'
Suffrage: WSPU.

Pearson, Annie J., 33 years.
6?4 Heworth Green.
Census night: complies.
Family: husband, railway clerk; 2 sons, daughter.
Household: 9 rooms, servant.
Suffrage: WSPU.

North Riding: population 417,000

35 miles north-east

Scarborough

Mackenzie, Dr Marion.
Census night: undoubtedly evading, with others: schedule not found.
Suffrage: WSPU, tax resister.

35 miles north-west

Middlesbrough: population 168, 000

Schofield-Coates, Alice.
Wilstrop House, Roman Road, Linthorpe.
Census night: resists.
Family: husband Charles, 47, manager, coal exporting firm; young daughter, unnamed.
Household: 11 rooms, 2 servants, unnamed.
Statement (Charles): 'No information can be given of the female residents in this house on April 2nd as they object to give such information until women are enfranchised.' He signs, adding 'subject to the qualification respecting the females'.
Registrar: 'This information [of females] is added by me the undersigned in accordance with the letter from Census Office dated 7th April 1911.'
Suffrage: WFL.

Coates-Hanson, Marion.
North Gate, Roman Road, Linthorpe.
Census night: resists.
Family: husband Friedrich, 45, coal merchant and manager.
Household: 12 rooms, 2 servants, unnamed.
Statement (Friedrich): 'The females in this house refuse to supply any information whatever until they are granted the rights and privileges of citizenship. "No vote no census of women".' He signs, adding 'with exception of information of females'.
Registrar: As above.
Suffrage: WFL.

Jones, Winifred, 33 years.
4 Philips Avenue, Linthorpe.
Census night: complies.
Occupation: head-teacher, Middlesbrough borough council.
Family: father, accountant; mother, 5 children living, 1 died; 1 brother, 3 sisters (one is assistant teacher, Middlesbrough).
Household: 7 rooms.
Suffrage: WFL.

Mahony, Charlotte, 24 years, and **Amy**, 23 years.
27 Waterloo Road.
Census night: both comply (though Amy may have resisted slightly?)
Occupation: both school teachers in county schools.
Family: father, Co-operative hall keeper; mother, 51, 8 children, of whom 3 died and 5 living; 2 sisters, at school. (See Chapter 16, Figure 38.)
Household: 7 rooms, 1 servant.
Suffrage: WFL.

North over River Tees

NORTH-EAST

Durham: population 1,377,000

English, Minnie, 47 years.
23 Carlton Street, West Hartlepool.
Census night: complies.
Family: husband, self-employed life assurance agent; son, daughter.
Household: 6 rooms.
Suffrage: WFL.

15 miles up coast

Palliser, Barbara, 34 years.
10 Fox Street, Sunderland.
Census night: complies.
Family: husband, commercial traveller for flour miller.
Household: 7 rooms.
Suffrage: WFL.

Northumberland: population 697,000

Williams, Dr Ethel.
3 Osborne Terrace, Newcastle.
Census night: evader.
Others: Helen Moss, 31, doctor, locum, signs schedule 'for Dr Ethel Williams'; Clementina Gordon, 27, organizing secretary NUWSS.
Household: 16 room, 2 servants.
Suffrage: NUWSS, tax resister.

Williams, Annie.
77 Blackett Street, Newcastle.
Census night: co-ordinates mass evasion.
Others: 2 males, 26 female, total 29.
Registrar notes letter (3 April) from Chief Constable: '... the Police observed women going to the above named Club and kept observation on same till 9am today. Twenty seven women and two men were known to be in the rooms amongst them being Miss Williams, Organising Secretary to the Womens Social and Political Union. There was also a Miss Wilcox there, Sergeant Graham having heard her name mentioned ... They had all left the Rooms at 9am with the exception of seven who could be seen inside the rooms.'
Suffrage: WSPU.

20 miles west

Taylor, Mona [Maria], [about 59 years].
Chipchase Castle, Hexham.
Census night: evading.
Family: husband, 61, colliery owner; daughter, Violet, 23.
Household: 9 servants.
Suffrage: WSPU.

Scottish border: 30 miles north.

Notes

References and abbreviations used in the notes and select bibliography

BL	British Library
BMJ	*British Medical Journal*
CH	Clemence Housman
Comm	Committee
Conf	Conference
corr	correspondence
CPS	C. P. Scott
DNB	*Dictionary of National Biography*
EHM	Edith How-Martyn
Exec	Executive
FOI	Freedom of Information
GRO	General Register Office
HSJ	*Housman Society Journal*
HW	Helen Watts
HWJ	*History Workshop Journal*
JB	John Burns
LIG	Lloyd George
LSWS	London Society for Women's Suffrage
MG	*Manchester Guardian*
Mil Dept	Militant Department
mins	minutes
MoL	Musuem of London
MLWS	Men's League for Women's Suffrage
PEN	*Portsmouth Evening News*
TWL	The Women's Library
VfW	*Votes for Women*

WCG   Women's Co-operative Guild
WFr   *Women's Franchise*
WHN   Women's History Network
WHR   *Women's History Review*

Introduction

1 Here 'suffragettes' denotes those who deployed militant tactics, and 'suffragists' those using constitutional means. However, contemporary uses of this terminology were much less precise. Helpful here is Claire Eustance, 'Meanings of Militancy: the ideas and practice of political resistance in the Women's Freedom League, 1907–14', in Maroula Joannou and June Purvis (eds), *The Women's Suffrage Movement: new feminist perspectives*, Manchester University Press, 1998.

2 *Women's Franchise*, 2 Jul 1908, International Woman Suffrage Alliance [IWSA]; and IWSA history, 1929.

3 See Kathleen Canning and Sonya Rose, 'Gender, Citizenship and Subjectivity', *Gender & History*, 13:3, 2001.

4 A major example is Sylvia Pankhurst, *The Suffragette Movement: an intimate account of persons and ideals*, 1931 and 1977, plus numerous subsequent texts.

5 Notably, George Dangerfield, *The Strange Death of Liberal England 1910–1914*, 1935, has just two chapters.

6 For historiography, see Chapter 19. Broadcast in June 2013 just as this book was going to press, BBC Radio 4's excellent ten-part series '1913: The Year Before' is therefore a significant contribution. Presented by Michael Portillo, it included not only Elizabeth Crawford on 'Women's Rebellion' but also Ireland and industrial strikes – thus updating Dangerfield's 1935 panoramic sweep.

7 Elizabeth Crawford, *The Women's Suffrage Movement: a reference guide 1866–1928*, Routledge, 1999 and 2001.

8 We hope this study will encourage similar research on Wales and Scotland.

9 *History Workshop*, 71, spring 2011.

10 The Elizabeth Garrett Anderson UNISON Gallery in the former EGA Hospital building on Euston Road, London.

11 Liddington and Crawford, 'Battle for the 1911 Census', pp. 116, 119 and note 82. The conclusions reached here do not contradict this earlier article, but can now be more authoritative and include the Gazetteer.

12 Liddington, *Rebel Girls: their fight for the vote*, Virago Press, 2006.

13 Jill Liddington and Jill Norris, *One Hand Tied Behind Us: the rise of the women's suffrage movement*, Virago Press 1978 and 1984, Rivers Oram Press 2000.

14 See Liddington, *Rebel Girls*, 'Suffrage detective: tracking the evidence', pp. xi and 335. For the analytical framework that emerged, see Chapter 19.

15 There are signs this is changing; see *History Workshop*, 71, 2011, editorial, 'Digital sources, access and "History of a Nation"?' Also, BBC Radio 4, Lisa Jardine, 'A Point of View: a convert to family history', 2 Dec 2011.

16 Helpful here is Laura E. Nym Mayhall, *The Militant Suffrage Movement: citizenship and resistance in Britain, 1860–1930*, Oxford University Press, New York, 2003.

17 Though note George Barnsby, *Votes for Women: the struggle for the vote in the Black Country 1900–1918*, Wolverhampton, 1995, booklet, p. 31. Also Elizabeth Crawford, *The Women's Suffrage Movement in Britain and Ireland: a regional survey*, Routledge, Abingdon, 2006, p. 125.

18 Obviously, it is impossible to be precise about the number (probably few) who did escape this head-count; what *is* often missing for boycotters is personal information on age, occupation etc.

19 This structure is influenced by my *Female Fortune: the Anne Lister diaries 1833–36*, Rivers Oram, 1998, 'Note on Text', pp. 77–80; despite such contrasting source material, the shared need for selection criteria has guided my thinking here. More generally by *Rebel Girls* (2006); and by Sandra Holton, *Suffrage Days: stories from the women's suffrage movement*, Routledge, 1996.

20 Other diaries noting the census boycott include Dr Alice Ker, Birkenhead; and Kate Frye, East Anglia, see www.womanandhersphere.com.

21 The cut-off point of five hundred schedules was largely determined by the book length, and will hopefully inspire local historians and others to continue further research, both in England and more widely.

22 For a helpful introduction to the literature, see Kathryne Beebe, Angela Davis and Kathryn Gleadle, 'Space, Place and Gendered Identities: feminist history and the spatial turn', *Women's History Review*, 21:4, 2012.

1 Charlotte Despard and John Burns, the Colossus of Battersea

1 Andro Linklater, *An Unhusbanded Life: Charlotte Despard: suffragette, socialist and Sein Feiner*, Hutchinson, 1980, pp. 43–50. This remains an invaluable biography, though exasperatingly lacks references.

2 Linklater, *Despard*, pp. 44 and 62.

3 Linklater, *Despard*, pp. 83.

4 Margaret Bondfield, *A Life's Work*, Hutchinson, [1949], p. 75.

5 Crawford, *Reference*, p. 166, quoting Elizabeth Wolstenholme Elmy.

6 Linklater, *Despard*, pp. 106–7.

7 Kenneth Brown, *John Burns*, Royal Historical Society, 1977, p. 7; this is more scholarly than the earlier biography, William Kent, *John Burns: Labour's lost leader*, Williams & Norgate, 1950. Kent however talked to Burns before he died.
   Also, The Rt Hon John Burns MP, 'Careers in Pictures', *The Strand* magazine, Mar 1911.

8 Brown, *Burns*, pp. 8–9 and 12. He had also travelled widely.

9 Brown, *Burns*, pp. 58–9.

10 Kent, *Burns*, pp. 152–4 and 161.

11 John Burns's Diary, British Library, Add MS 46260 and Add MS 46281: minor punctuation added.

12 *British Medical Journal* (*BMJ*), 16 Jun 1906. George Newman, *The Health of the State*, 1907, p. 123. Newman was Medical Officer of Health for Finsbury.

13 Brown, 'Burns', *DNB*.

14 1911 census; its definition of a 'room' included kitchen but not scullery, bathroom etc.

15 Historians are not helped because, as becomes clear, Despard did not fill in her 1911 census schedule.
16 Burns's Diary, Sat 9 Oct and Sun 14 Nov 1909.
17 *The Vote*, 19 Mar 1910.
18 Linklater, *Despard*, pp. 113–15.
19 For other interpretations, see for instance June Purvis, *Emmeline Pankhurst: a biography*, Routledge, 2002, pp. 93 and 97.
20 *WFr*, 28 Nov 1908. Mrs Duval was Battersea branch secretary.
21 Quoted in Linklater, *Despard*, pp. 125–6.
22 A. J. R., *The Suffrage Annual and Women's Who's Who*, Stanley Paul, 1913, p. 363; Emma Sproson Papers, Wolverhampton Record Office, p. 49.
23 Linklater, *Despard*, pp. 127 and 131.
24 NUWSS patterns varied across England; see *One Hand Tied Behind Us* for Lancashire.
25 *WFr*, 2 Jan 1908.
26 *The Times*, 31 Jan 1908; Alison Neilans and Irene Miller were among those arrested. Possibly as many as ten from the WFL were imprisoned.
27 Stella Newsome, *Women's Freedom League 1907–1957*, Woman's Freedom League, [1960] p. 4; the exact occasion is unclear.

2 Muriel Matters goes vanning it with Asquith: campaigning cross country

1 H. C. G. Matthew, 'Herbert Henry Asquith' *DNB*.
2 Quoted in Andrew Rosen, *Rise Up, Women! The militant campaign of the Women's Social and Political Union 1903–14*, Routledge & Kegan Paul, 1974, p. 97, HC Debates, 17 Apr 1892. Letter, 1920, quoted in Crawford, *Regional Survey*, p. 280; while obviously written twelve years later, it encapsulates Asquith's fears of the female.
3 Quoted in Rosen, *Rise Up!*, p. 98.
4 *The Times*, 31 Jan 1908.
5 Martin Pugh, *The March of the Women: a revisionist analysis of the campaign for Women's Suffrage, 1866–1914*, Oxford University Press, Oxford, 2000, p. 153.
6 *WFr*, 12 and 19 Mar 1908.
7 Churchill then stood successfully in Dundee, so retaining his ministerial post.
8 Muriel Matters Society, *Why Muriel Matters: a centenary celebration*, Adelaide, 2010.
9 *The Vote*, 'Concerning Muriel Matters', 19 Feb 1910.
10 1911 population figures. WFL had just a branch in Croydon, and another in Bromley.
11 Walt Whitman, *Leaves of Grass*. As Crawford notes, he was very much the suffragettes' poet.
12 *WFr*, 21 May 1908.
13 *WFr*, 21 May 1908.
14 *Guildford Free Press*, 23 May 1908; *WFr*, 4 June 1908.
15 *WFr*, 4 Jun 1908.
16 *The Vote*, 14 May 1910.
17 *WFr*, 11 Jun 1908.
18 *WFr*, 25 Jun and 16 July 1908.

19 Museum of London, 1930. Matters married, Oct 1914; Tillard died in 1922 in Russia.
20 *W Fr*, 27 Aug 1908 (Hythe).
21 Margaret W. Nevinson, *Life's Fitful Fever: A Volume of Memories*, A. & C. Black, 1926, pp. 214–15; *WFr*, 24 Sep 1908.
22 *WFr*, 27 Aug 1908.
23 *WFr*, 11 Jun 1908. Also, Lisa Tickner, *The Spectacle of Women: imagery of the suffrage campaign 1907–14*, Chatto & Windus, 1987.
24 Barbara Caine, *Bombay to Bloomsbury: a biography of the Strachey family*, Oxford University Press, 2005, p. 121.
25 Caine, *Strachey*, pp. 307–12.
26 Newnham College Club Letter 1908, quoted in Crawford, *Reference*, 'Caravans'.
27 Ray Costelloe, 3, 2 and 10 July 1908, TWL; *WFr*, 23 Jul 1908; *Oxford Chronicle*, 31 Jul 1908.
28 *WFr*, 20 Aug 1908; for Yorkshire tour, see *Rebel Girls*, pp. 205–10.
29 Mayhall, *Resistance*, pp. 46–9 ff.
30 *Illustrated London News*, 7 Nov 1908.
31 Nevinson, *Fitful*, p. 208.
32 WFL Organizing Committee, 23 Nov 1908 and 2–15 Jun 1909 and ff. *Vote*, 23 July, 20 and 27 Aug 1910.

3 Propaganda culture: Clemence and Laurence Housman

1 Thanks to Tara Morton for discussion.
2 Though both grew quickly impatient with MLWS.
3 See Jill Liddington and Tara Morton, 'Walking with Women's Suffrage in Kensington and Chelsea', *Herstoria*, spring 2011; also three talented Woodward sisters, linked to the NUWSS and WSPU, designing for ASL.
4 Angela V. John, *Evelyn Sharp: rebel woman, 1869–1955*, Manchester University Press, 2009, pp. 57–9. Suffrage enamellist Ernestine Mill also lived nearby.
5 *VfW*, 1 Sep 1911.
6 Tickner, *Spectacle*, p. 19. Bertha Newcombe's *The Apple Seller* (1910) depicts John Stuart Mill MP with the first women's suffrage petition. Emily Ford designed posters: her 'Factory Acts' decorated the NUWSS caravan.
7 Letter, 1933, quoted in A. E. Housman, *DNB*.
8 Elizabeth Oakley, *Inseparable Siblings: a portrait of Clemence & Laurence Housman*, Brewin Books, 2009 is particularly informative. Also note Ann Born, 'Clemence Housman 1861–1955', typescript, 1978, Housman mss.
9 Laurence Housman, *Unexpected Years*, Jonathan Cape, 1937, pp. 82–3. Linda Hart, 'Laurence Housman: a subject in search of a biographer', *HSJ*, 31, 2005, pp. 15–17, is incisive.
10 Jo Hunt, 'Laurence Housman – the Younger Brother', *HSJ*, 16, 1990, pp. 7–8. Oakley, *Siblings*, p. viii, notes AEH's family tree (1908) detailing achievements of all seven Housman siblings – apart from LH and CH, about whom he recorded nothing, other than date of birth.

11 Housman, *Unexpected*, pp. 170–1.

12 Now fairly unreadable and mawkish; however, Jonathan Wild reviews 'the publishing sensation of 1900', *Times Literary Supplement*, 2 Nov 2012.

13 Housman, *Unexpected*, pp. 194–5. *DNB* and Hunt say they moved in 1903; the blue plaque says Rothenstein lived there to 1902.

14 Housman, *An Englishwoman's Love Letters*, John Murray, 1900, p. 25.

15 Rodney Engen, *Laurence Housman*, Catalpa, 1983, p. 28; Hart, 'Biographer', p. 27; Housman papers, 1912 letter.

16 Quoted in Hart, 'Biographer', p. 21; LH's views here are complex.

17 Letter dated 8 May 1916, when LH was about to sail to New York; but although heightened by wartime, this doubtless represents LH's relationship; many thanks to Elizabeth Oakley on this.

18 Housman, *Unexpected Years*, pp. 190 and 264–5. Stephen Housman, 'The Housman Banners', *HSJ*, 1992, p. 41.

19 Undated letter, 33B, Housman mss; probably Mar 1911.

20 In Housman, *Articles of Faith in the Freedom of Women*, Fifield, 1910, p. 7.

21 Housman, *Unexpected*, p. 190.

22 Tickner, *Spectacle*, p. 94 and note 129, citing *Ashbee Journals*. Also Housman, 'Banners', pp. 40–2.

23 Housman, 'Banners', pp. 42–3.

24 LH to Sarah Clark, 6 Dec [1912?], quoted in Tickner, *Spectacle*, note 61, p. 291. Also, Oakley, *Siblings*, p. 77; *VfW*, 23 Jul 1909.

25 LH elected to MLWS Committee and Literature Sub-Committee in April 1909.

26 Discussed in Holton, *Suffrage Days*, pp. 144ff.

27 See Hilary Frances, '"Pay the Piper, call the tune!" the Women's Tax Resistance League', in Joannou and Purvis, eds, *Perspectives*, p. 66; also Quaker Alice Clark resisted payment of taxes, 1907.

28 *WFr*, 19 Dec 1907, 16 Jan 1908; Mrs Sargant Florence was active, see Chapter 6.

29 *WFr*, 14 May 1908.

30 *WFr*, 3 Jun 1909.

31 *Vote*, 12 Feb 1910.

32 WFL Organizing Comm, [1 Feb] 1909. Muriel Matters's flight was immortalized on film, and in a BBC broadcast, Feb 1939, describing her exhilarating flight and how the airship was blown off course, landing in Coulsdon, Surrey.

4 Parallel politics: Lloyd George plus Midlands suffragettes

1 On historiography, biographies of Lloyd George scarcely mention hunger striking or forcible feeding; while most suffragette accounts make scant reference to the Finance Bill. However, note C. J. Bearman, 'An Army Without Discipline? Suffragette militancy and the budget crisis of 1909', *Historical Journal*, 50: 4, 2007; yet this detailed research is marred by anti-WSPU axe-grinding.

2 Pat Thane, *Foundations of the Welfare State*, Longman, 1982 and 1996, p. 77.

3 Kenneth Morgan, '"Rare and Refreshing Fruit": Lloyd George's People's Budget', *Public Policy Research*, 16: 1, Mar–May 2009; *DNB* quoting *Hansard*.

4 Bentley B. Gilbert, *David Lloyd George: a political life: the architect of change 1863–1912*, Batsford, 1987, pp. 385–6.

5 *WFr*, 6 May 1909.

6 *VfW*, 7 May 1909.

7 HW, 'Speech at Welcome Supper, March 1909', typescript, pp. 2–3, Helen Watts mss, Nottingham.

8 *Evening News*, 28 Jul 1908.

9 There are suggestions of two hundred members, including lace workers and dressmakers, but there is little evidence of their activity in the branch.

10 Speech given by HW, Birmingham, 18 May,1909, typescript, HW mss; HW was also involved in the Girls' Realm Guild.

11 HW, 'Welcome Supper, March 1909', pp. 3–4. Helpful is Hilda Kean, 'Searching for the Past in Present Defeat: construction of historical and political identity in British feminism in the 1920s & 1930s', *WHR*, 3:1, 1994.

12 HW to Mother, Father and all, 24 Feb 1909, HW mss.

13 Mother to daughter, 25 Feb 1909, HW mss.

14 No date [mid-Mar?] MB to HW, HW mss.

15 'Welcome Supper', March 1909.

16 *VfW*, 2 Jul and 17 Sept 1909; Bearman, 'Army', p. 875.

17 'Copy of talk given at Morley's Café, Nottingham, 17 Sept 1909', HW mss.

18 *VfW*, 10 Sept 1909; Richard Whitmore, *Alice Hawkins and the Suffragette Movement in Edwardian Leicester*, Breedon Books, 2007, pp. 88–9.

19 'Morley's Café', 17 Sept 1909.

20 'Morley's Café', 17 Sept 1909; *VfW*, 17 Sep 1909.

21 Caprina Fahey, 17 Sept 1909, Hendon.

22 'Morley's Café', 17 Sept 1909.

23 Warwickshire 1911 figures: had been 500,000; but after the census Birmingham was extended (into Staffordshire and Worcestershire), increasing the city's population by about half.

24 Elizabeth Crawford, *From Frederick Street to Winson Green: the Women's Suffrage Movement in Birmingham 1866–1918*, 2000, pp. 11–14.

25 Purvis, *Emmeline*, p. 133; Bearman, 'Budget crisis', p. 877; there are minor reporting differences in the accounts.

26 Winson Green Visiting Committee minutes, 24 and 25 Sep 1909.

27 Visiting Comm mins, 28 Sept 1909. Those forcibly fed included Mabel Capper (Manchester) and Charlotte Marsh (see Chapters 15 and 16).

28 Angela V. John, *War, Journalism and the Shaping of the Twentieth Century: the life and times of Henry W. Nevinson*, I. B. Tauris, 2006, pp. 80–2 and 101.

29 Quoted by Gilbert, *Lloyd George*, p. 395; Hattersley, *Outsider*, p. 258; Morgan, 'Fruit', p. 32.

30 *Evening News*, 26 Jul 1910, and *Lenton Times*, No. 10, HW mss. HW spoke at Midsomer Norton (near Bath) 27 Nov 1909; her speech, however, bogged down in detail about women's sweated work, lacked the clarity of earlier speeches. She was also arrested in Nottingham Jan 1910, but her case was dismissed, and this appears to be HW's final act of militancy.

31 Bearman, 'Budget crisis', p. 881, says most newspapers refused to condemn forcible feeding, and only the *Manchester Guardian* stood out.

5 Plotting across central London: census and tax resistance

1 Burns, diary, e.g. 8 and 18 Sep 1909.
2 Brown, *Burns*, pp. 149–51; Thane, *Welfare*, pp. 89–90.
3 Edward Higgs, 'Sir Bernard Mallet', www.histpop.org; Mallet obituary, *The Times*, 29 Oct 1932.
4 S. R. S. Szreter, 'Thomas Stevenson', *DNB*; Higgs, 'Stevenson', www.histpop.org.
5 A helpful overview is Edward Higgs, *Life, Death and Statistics: civil registration, censuses and the work of the General Register Office, 1836–1952*, Local Population Studies, 2004, chap. 5, 'The evidence of statistical revival'. Also Audrey Collins, 'Sorting out the Census', *Ancestors*, 2009.
6 Committee on the Census 1911, RG19/48B, 20 and 22 Oct 1909, TNA; Edgar Harper (LCC) also present. Archer Bellingham's earlier 'Summary of Suggestions', Jul 1908, had noted staff increases needed etc.
7 Comm Census, 27 Oct 1909, Stevenson not present.
8 See Higgs, *Life, Death*, chap. 5, for the complexity of these concerns; Anna Davin, 'Imperialism and Motherhood', *HWJ*, 5, 1978; also Szreter, 'Stevenson', *DNB*. 1911 census, Stevenson, Barnet, Middlesex; Archer Bellingham, Wimbledon, Surrey.
9 Eustance, 'Militancy', p. 56; Linklater, *Unhusbanded*, pp. 141–2; Mayhall, *Militant*, p. 37; Frances, 'Pay the Piper, call the tune!', pp. 66–8.
10 Quoting Crawford, *Reference*.
11 Nevinson, *Fitful Fever*, p. 211.
12 WFL Organizing Comm, 9 and 30 Apr 1908, also 21 Dec 1908 when her suggestion that WFL form a Tax Resistance department was agreed.
13 Crawford, *Reference*; her husband remained in Leek, Staffordshire.
14 How-Martyn proposed it remain under WFL auspices; voting was 6 for, 9 against. WFL Nat Exec mins, 20 Nov 1909.
15 *Vote*, 11 Nov 1909.
16 WTRL, mins 8 Nov 1909.
17 *Vote*, 11 Nov 1909.
18 S. Housman, 'Banners',1992, p. 44, identifies it as now 13 Linden Road. Oakley, *Siblings*, pp. 81–2 and 94; CH often stayed with Kate and her family in Bath.
19 Housman correspondence, Street collection, 44c, n.d.; Oakley, *Siblings*, pp. 97–8.
20 WTRL, 17 Dec 1909, 4 and 25 Feb 1910.
21 Frances, 'Piper', pp. 70–1; however, many of her examples are c. 1912 i.e. post-census.
22 WTRL, 6 May, 10 and 24 Jun 1910. Also, Housman, 'Banners', pp. 44–5, on statue etc.

6 The battle for John Burns's Battersea revisited

1 Nevinson, *Fitful*, p. 203; Linklater, *Despard*, pp. 134–5.
2 *VfW*, 29 Oct 1909.

3 *Vote*, 4 Nov 1909.
4 WFL Org Comm, 12 Oct and 2 Nov 1909 (thirteen letters objecting received). *Vote*, 4 Nov 1909 (Alison Neilans and Mrs Chapin). Eustance, 'Militancy', p. 55.
5 Asquith and Birrell were older; however Lloyd George, Churchill and others were younger.
6 Diary, 22 Sep and 1 Dec 1909, quoted, Brown, *Burns*, p. 154.
7 *Strand Magazine*, Mar 1911, Battersea Library collection.
8 *Vote*, 23 Dec 1909, notes mainly: Scotland (Asquith, Churchill), Wales (Lloyd George), north England (Grey) and west (Birrell).
9 *VfW*, 10 Dec 1909. Kent, *Burns*, p. 200, 'Jessie Kennedy'; Kenney was organizing in Walthamstow.
10 Batt Liby, cuttings book, Dec 1909; Brown, *Burns*, p. 155. Also *Punch* cartoon, 15 Dec 1909, Burns astride Battersea.
11 WFL Org Comm mins, 9 Nov 1909; WFL Nat Exec mins, 13 Dec [1909].
12 *Vote*, 30 Dec 1909.
13 Cuttings scrapbook, Battersea Library.
14 Kent, *Burns*, 205–6; *Daily Graphic*, Sat 8 Jan 1910, cuttings scrapbook, Battersea Library.
15 Batt Liby, cuttings book, e.g. *Globe* [1 Jan 1910].
16 *Vote*, 8 Jan 1910; Kent, *Burns*, p. 206, says WSPU also denied all knowledge.
17 See Crawford, 'A Rich Network of Association: Bloomsbury and Women's Suffrage', *The Charleston Magazine*, 1999, pp. 17–19, note 18 on her biographer incorrectly placing her in NUWSS.
18 Burns, diary, 17 Jan 1910; Kent, *Burns*, p. 207.
19 Burns, diary, 25 Feb 1910.
20 Quoted in Linklater, *Despard*, p. 137; *VfW*, 28 Jan 1910.
21 *Vote*, 5 Feb 1910. Internal 5th Ann Conf typed mins reveal far more dissension among branches, often small communities far from London.
22 *Vote*, 19 Feb 1910, 'White Flag of Truce'.
23 E.g. Lady Strachey, in Caine, *Bloomsbury*, pp. 300–1.
24 Sandra Holton, *Feminism and Democracy: women's suffrage and reform politics in Britain 1900–1918*, Cambridge University Press, 1986, pp. 69–70.

7 The Census Bill and the boycott plan

1 Census Comm mins, 18 and 22 Feb 1910.
2 The 'Memorandum upon the possible utilisation of Census records of duration of [each] marriage and number of children born to marriages'; a double negative has been deleted to enhance clarity. Also Memorandum and proposal for table of fertility in marriage.
3 Census Comm, 24 Feb 1910, pp. 60–2. The Stevensons married when he was thirty, she twenty-nine years old.
4 Census Comm, 28 Feb 1910; on Herman Hollerith's tabulator, with fast hole-punching and reading of cards, powered by electric current, see Higgs, *Life, Death and Statistics*, chap 6.

5   See Documents relating to the preparation of 1911 census, LGB Memorandum, Feb 1910, p. 2.
6   Census Comm, 4 and 7 March and 11 April 1910.
7   *Hansard*: 4 March 1910, Census Bill, first reading, Herbert Lewis; Burns, Diary, 22 Mar 1910.
8   Census Comm, 18 Apr 1910.
9   Census (Great Britain) Act, 1910, 4 (1) c, 3 Aug 1910.
10 Census Comm, 28 Jun 1910.
11 Higgs, 'The Rise of the Information State', *Journal of Historical Sociology*, 14:2, 2001; also Higgs, 'The Statistical Big Bang of 1911', 1996.
12 'Memorandum upon … children born to marriage'.
13 For contemporary debate on women's right to work, note Olive Schreiner, *Woman and Labour*, 1911, and Cicely Hamilton, *Marriage as a Trade*, 1909.
14 WFL Nat Exec Comm Mins, 20 June and 31 Oct 1910. At no minuted 1910 discussion of the census boycott was there any suggestion that WFL Executive was aware yet of the new questions to be put about married women.
15 WFL Mil Dept, 'Letters sent out' file, 20 Jun – 23 Jul 1910.
16 WFL Annual Report for 1911, p. 8, claimed that 'the scheme to resist the Census' was [first] discussed by the WFL executive in March 1909; and 'it was first announced publicly at a meeting in London immediately after the reading of the King's Speech in February, 1910'. Surely a clerical error?
17 WFL Exec Comm Mins, 20 Jun & 31 Oct 1910.
18 WFL Mil Dept, letters, 30 July [1910], (note mixing of 'suffragist' and 'suffragette').
19 WFL Mil Dept, letters, n.d., p. 43.
20 WFL Mil Dept, letters, Mil Report, 20 Jun–23 Jul 1910 ff; Alison Neilans, initialled by EHM.
21 Holton, *Democracy*, p. 70.
22 Rosen, *Rise Up*, p. 137.
23 WFL Mil Dept, letters, 29 July [1910], p. 44.

8   Lloyd George goes a-wooing versus Burns's 'vixens in velvet'

1   Addison, 1934, quoted in *DNB*.
2   See Thane, *Foundations*, pp. 78–81.
3   Gilbert, *Lloyd George*, pp. 418–19; Hattersley, *Outsider*, pp. 291–3.
4   WTRL mins, 4 Feb – 24 Jun 1910; Oct 7, WTRL deputation to WSPU satisfactory.
5   WTRL mins, 6 May, 10 and 24 Jun, 18 Jul 1910.
6   Frances, 'Piper', pp. 70–2, gives a more optimistic picture; but, as noted, most examples are post-census.
7   Lyme Regis, Dorset, *Vote*, 3 Sep 1910. Also Dr Knight near Folkestone. Dr Patch slips through history books (even 1913 directory and Crawford, *Regional*), until her wartime bankruptcy proceedings.
8   *Vote*, 10 Sep 1910.
9   WTRL mins, 19 Sep 1910; magistrate was Cecil Chapman.
10 *Vote*, 1 Oct 1910.

11 WTRL mins, 28 Oct and 4–14 Nov 1910 ff. It was agreed that League should consist of two groups: those willing to resist immediately, and those willing to resist if five hundred others also willing.
12 *Vote*, 10 and 24 Sep 1910; however, Pippa Strachey for LSWS remained decidedly less enthusiastic.
13 *Vote*, 24 Sep 1910; e.g. the case of Mark Wilks and his wife, a doctor.
14 WFL Mil Dept letters, 19 and 27 Sep and 22 Oct 1910; *Vote*, 24 Sep 1910.
15 Housman, *Unexpected*, pp. 286–7.
16 WFL Mil Dept letters, 27 Oct [1910].
17 WFL Mil Dept letters; also Men's Comm for Justice to Women etc.
18 WFL Mil Dept, report of Caxton Hall, 27 Oct [1910].
19 *VfW*, 7 Oct 1910.
20 E.g. 7 & 15 Nov [1910], WFL Mil Dept letters.
21 Fawcett to Lady Frances Balfour, 28 Nov 1910, and Hume, *National Union*, p. 92. Although Figure 17 was designed later, the distrust between Burns and the suffragettes had deep roots.
22 John Burns diary; minor punctuation added. 1 Dec: gets 5s for broken windows from police.
23 Burns diary; Brown, *Burns*, p. 160 notes four suffrage organizations worked to 'keep Burns out'.
24 Burns diary, 11 Dec [1910].
25 Gilbert, *Lloyd George*, p. 429.
26 Hume, *National Union*, p. 95.
27 10 Dec 1910, Mins, WFL Mil Dept letters file.
28 WFL Exec Comm Mins, 6–7 Jan and 30 Jan 1911.
29 *Vote*, 4 Feb 1911, with others from Scotland etc; internal WFL tensions included the resignation of TBG, conspicuous by her absence.
30 WTRL, mins, 30 Jan 1911.
31 'Race Suicide', Mrs Edward Francis, NEC, address, Caxton Hall, *Vote*, 21 Jan 1911.

9 The King's Speech: Jessie Stephenson parachutes into Manchester

1 Katherine Chorley, *Manchester Made Them*, Faber and Faber, 1950, pp. 114 and 149.
2 For other groups, see *One Hand Tied Behind Us*.
3 Helena Swanwick, *I Have Been Young*, Gollancz, 1935, pp. 166 and 181–2.
4 The Papers of C. P. Scott, 1846–1932, Handlist of Correspondence.
5 LlG to CPS, 17 Jan 1911.
6 HNB to CPS, 19 Jan 1911, from Hampstead on CC notepaper. Brailsford wrote at least two dozen letters to Scott.
7 EP to CPS, 9 Jan 1911 (part missing); also see Purvis, *Emmeline*, pp. 122–3 and 154–6.
8 Quoted in Crawford *Reference*.
9 Stephenson, 'No Other Way', pp. 228–9.
10 Stephenson, 'No Other Way', p. 234; Cowman, *Right Spirit*, pp. 21–3.
11 E.g. *VfW*, 3 Feb 1911, 'Campaign throughout the Country', listing organizers but

not branch secretaries for the towns outside London includes Brighton, Portsmouth, Birmingham, Leicester, Bath, Bristol and Cheltenham.

12 Mary Gawthorpe, after long sick leave, retired from her WSPU post; Cowman, *Spirit*, pp. 161–2 notes complications about Dora Marsden.

13 Stephenson, *No Other*, pp. 236–8.

14 Stephenson, *No Other*, pp. 241–2; undoubtedly 10 Mar 1911.

15 Stephenson, *No Other*, p. 238.

16 CPS, *The Political Diaries of C. P. Scott 1911–1928*, 1970, pp. 35–7, 2 Feb 1911.

17 Stephenson, *No Other*, p. 238–41.

18 *Vote*, 18 Feb 1911.

19 *Vote*, 11 Feb 1911.

20 *Vote*, 11 Feb 1911; also *VfW*, 24 Feb 1911 ff.

21 WTRL mins, 10–24 Feb 1911.

22 *VfW*, 17 Feb 1911, acknowledging WFL and LH.

23 *VfW*, 24 Feb 1911,

24 *The Times*, 13 Feb 1911.

25 Scott, Handlist, notes just one early letter from Sadler; once Sadler arrived in Manchester there was presumably less need to write.

26 *DNB*, Sadler aged forty-nine, lived in Weybridge, Surrey.

27 *The Times*, 14 Feb 1911.

28 *MGn*, 7 Feb 1911 ff.

29 *The Times*, 16 Feb 1911; ARCS: Associate of the Royal Chemical Society; *Vote*, 18 and 25 Feb 1911.

10 Battleground for democracy: census versus women's citizenship

1 Census Comm mins, gap between 18 Nov 1910 (p. 185) and 26 Apr 1911 (p. 186).

2 Thane, *Foundations*, p. 79; Gilbert, *Lloyd George*, pp. 432–4.

3 Hume, *National Union*, pp. 100–1; Pugh, *March*, pp. 140–1. This second Bill devised by the Conciliation Committee modified the 1910 bill, by dropping the proposal to enfranchise women possessing a ten pound occupation qualification; this tightening aimed to allay fears of 'faggot voting' (i.e. endowment of small pieces of property on women, for extra votes).

4 *VfW*, 24 Mar 1911; *Dundee Evening Telegraph*.

5 *VfW*, 17 and 24 Mar 1911, *Daily Sketch* image.

6 *VfW*, 3 Mar 1911; also, measures 'to escape inclusion' (i.e. evade). *VfW*, 10 Mar 1911; and Census Ditty (Bath).

7 *VfW*, 24 Mar 1911; and 'Census Song'.

8 *VfW*, 31 Mar 1911.

9 *Vote*, 18 Feb 1911.

10 *Vote*, 4–18 Mar and 25 Feb 1911.

11 *Sheffield Daily Telegraph*, 14 Mar 1911.

12 *Vote*, 4 Mar 1911; WFL Nat Exec Comm mins, 24–5 Mar 1911.

13 *Vote*, 18 and 25 Mar 1911.

14 *Vote*, 18 and 25 Mar 1911.

15 WTRL mins, 20 and 24 Feb 1911; and 'Census Dept', 10 and 24 Mar 1911.

16 WCG Annual Reports, May 1910–May 1912.

17 *Co-op News*, Jan – 8 Apr 1911; a nasty dispute over the resolution wording between adult suffragist Marian Maud A. Ward (who shared a house with Margaret Bondfield), and women's suffragist Annot E. Robinson, Manchester.

18 Membership figures, Hume, *National Union*, pp. 229–30; Fawcett corr, 28 and 29 Sept 1910, MCRL.

19 NUWSS Exec Comm mins (unconfirmed), 5 Jan 1911; *Common Cause*, 16 Mar 1911.

20 Strachey mss, EHM to Lady Strachey, 17 Feb 1911, and undated draft reply.

21 LSWS lobbied by Kineton Parkes (WTRL), P. Strachey file, 19–24 Feb 1911.

22 LSWS, lobbied by WFL (E. How-Martyn), 20–1 Feb 1911 and 15 Mar 1911.

23 Previously North of England Society for Women's Suffrage. The Manchester & District Federation included East Lancashire, Cheshire and Derbyshire High Peak. Highly organized, its secretary was Kate Courtney (to early 1911); Swanwick resigned as honorary secretary, to edit *CC* in London.

24 Manchester & District Federation, First Ann Rep, 28 Oct 1911; it also worked with local WFL.

25 *Halifax Evening Chronicle*, 31 Mar 1911; also *Halifax Guardian*, 1 Apr 1911; he was Rev. W. L. Schroeder; minor punctuation added.

26 *Sheff Daily Independent* and *Sheffield Daily Telegraph*, 8 Feb 1911; speaker was Alison Neilans.

27 *Sheff Daily Tel*, 18 Feb 1911; WTRL speaker was Kineton Parkes.

28 *Sheff Daily Tel*, 14 Mar 1911, which remained very hostile. However, the sympathetic *Sheffield Daily Independent* took a 'flashlight photo' of Lawrence, Adela and a dozen suffragettes.

29 *Rebel Girls*, pp. 221–2. *Common Cause*, 9 Mar 1911; *Sheff Daily Tel*, 20 Mar 1911.

30 *Sheff Daily Tel*, 21–4 and 27 Mar 1911; undoubtedly suffragette Elsa Schuster.

31 *MG*, 3 Apr 1911, Evelyn Sharp and Maud Joachim; next day, Scott accused suffragettes of a grave 'offence against knowledge and civilization'.

32 WTRL mins, 10 Feb – 24 Mar 1911. Clem's absences from WTRL meetings suggest she was spending more time down in Swanage; I am most grateful to Elizabeth Oakley on this. LH spoke at least thirteen meetings (Dundee, Ipswich etc) in twenty-one days (e.g. his visit to Ilkley and Tomlinson sisters, likely to be c. 10–13 Mar). Like Clem, he often dated his letters in only the most peremptory fashion.

33 Stephenson, 'No Other Way', p. 237. Purvis, *Emmeline*, p. 54.

34 WTRL mins, 24 Feb 1911; *Vote*, 18 and 25 Mar 1911.

35 Stephenson, 'No Other Way', pp. 252–3; minor punctuation added.

36 Burns often 'cheered up' despondent officials.

37 *Sheff Daily Tel*, 30 Mar 1911.

38 *Daily Mirror*, 28 Mar 1911; *The Times*, 1 Apr 1911; Maud Arncliffe Sennett coll, BL.

11 Emily Wilding Davison's Westminster – and beyond

1 *VfW*, 6 Jan 1911, 'Closed Door'; also, Mary Lowndes, 'Justice at the Door', NUWSS, 1912.

2 Gertrude Colmore, 'The Life', in *Emily Davison* Liz Stanley with Ann Morley, *The Life and Death of Emily Wilding Davison: a biographical detective story*, with Gertrude Colmore's 'The Life of Emily Davidson' [1913], The Women's Press, 1988, pp. 12–21.

3 *VfW*, 11 Jun 1909 and n.d., quoted in Crawford, *Reference*.

4 Colmore, 'The Life', pp. 33–40.

5 See Stanley and Morley, pp. 186–7.

6 *The Suffrage Annual and Women's Who's Who*, 1913, p. 221. For debate on EWD as an unreliable maverick, see Stanley and Morley, pp. 92–3, 115–21 and 186–7; Cowman, *Spirit*, pp. 139 and 157–8.

7 *VfW*, 7 Apr 1911.

8 JB's diary, 31 Mar – 2 Apr 1911. Rather endearingly, Burns was among the many husbands who filled in their schedule wrongly, entering marriage/children details for himself, rather than for his wife. Churchill did likewise; Asquith began similarly, and then deleted; Lloyd George completed his correctly however.

9 At 1 Marie Place, St George.

10 43 Cadogan Gardens, Chelsea. His wife Marie is not present, perhaps having gone on holiday during the census, with their two sons.

11 Asquith's first wife died in 1891, and he remarried in 1894. That Asquith records his own adult children shows what headaches the census faced with second marriages.

12 *VfW*, 7 Apr 1911.

13 Giving this Westminster building as just a single room was somewhat of an understatement. Presumably EWD refused to give her age, and 'school teacher' occupation was possibly copied from elsewhere.

14 *VfW*, 7 Apr 1911; repeated by Gertrude Colmore, see Stanley and Morley, p. 40. There are other examples of retrospective talking-up of census night bravery.

15 *VfW*, 7 Apr 1911.

16 *VfW*, 7 April, 1911; Frederick Iredale. A note on the hotel schedule says 'see letters attached'; these probably related to Mrs Pankhurst, but unfortunately no longer appear present.

17 Smyth, *Female Pipings in Eden*, 1933, p. 194, quoted in Purvis, *Emmeline*, pp. 159–60, who notes this includes some discrepancies.

18 Her name is mistakenly given as 'Miss W M Smith', plus two servants; schedule was signed by the Registrar himself; summary page confirm address as Ethel's home, Coign.

12 The Nevinsons' Hampstead – and central London entertainments

1 Woolf, *Night and Day*, 1919, pp. 281–2; they married in 1912.

2 Woolf, *Night and Day*, pp. 55 and 277. Crawford, 'A Rich Network of Associations: Bloomsbury and women's suffrage', *Charleston Magazine*, 19, 1999, pp. 17–18.

3 The WSPU headquarters by LSE is sadly demolished.

4 *Vote*, 4 and 11 Mar 1911; *VfW*, 3–31 Mar 1911.

5 *Ham & High*, 4 Mar 1911.

6 *Ham & High*, Sat 11 and 18 Mar 1911; see Chapter 10 for M. A. Ward in *Co-op News*.

7 Both joined the Men's League, but Brailsford, impatient at its lack of radicalism, left in 1910 to help form the Men's Political Union.

8　Angela V. John, 'A Family at War: the Nevinson family', in Michael Walsh (ed.), *A Dilemma of English Modernism*, University of Delaware, 2007, is helpful.

9　John, *Nevinson*, pp. 93, 96 and 100–1.

10　John, *Nevinson*, pp. 3 and 83, on reworking of masculinity etc.; also pp. 94 and 87 (1901).

11　See John, *Nevinson*, p. 93; e.g. *Vote*, 14 May 1909.

12　Nevinson, *Life's Fitful*, pp. 21 and 224; later dramatized, directed by Edith Craig; also *Vote*, 27 Aug 10.

13　Nevinson, *Fitful*, pp. 229–30.

14　Henry Nevinson diaries, Bodleian Libraries, MS. Eng.misc.e.613/3, folio 33–4. Also *Ham & High*, 25 Mar 1911.

15　Henry Nevinson diaries, MS. Eng.misc.e.613/3, folio 34–5.

16　Nevinson diaries, MS. Eng.misc.e.613/3, folio 35–6. John, *Sharp*, pp. 48–50, for the Saturday Walking Club.

17　Nevinson diaries, MS. Eng.misc.e.613/3, folio 36–7. The Lowy family live at 76 Holland Park, see Gazetteer.

18　*VfW*, 24 Mar 1911.

19　Nevinson diaries, MS. Eng.misc.e.613/3, folio 38–9. For Trafalgar Square, see *Vote*, 25 Mar 11, Nevinson is not listed among speakers; also Kineton Parkes, Mrs Nevinson, Laurence Housman.

20　Very confusingly, it is transcribed as 'Mevinson' in findmypast.

21　Nevinson, *Fitful*, p. 230. Evaders may have included Amy and Lilian Hicks, and Daisy Koettegen.

22　Original presumably had his signature? Perhaps, a cowed enumerator made a mess and re-did it?

23　*VfW*, 7 April 1911.

24　Nevinson diaries, MS. Eng.misc.e.613/3, folio 39.

25　*VfW*, 7 Apr 1911.

26　*VfW*, 14 Apr 1911; also *Daily Sketch* 4 Apr 1911.

27　*VfW*, 7 Apr 1911.

28　See Gazetteer, p. 246.

29　Nevinson diaries, MS. Eng.misc.e.613/3, folio 39–40.

30　Brian Harrison tape, 8SUF/B/024, interview recorded Nov 1974, TWL. Marie Lawson was moving away from WFL and in 1910 joined WTRL, then moving towards WSPU.

31　Nevinson diaries, MS. Eng.misc.e.613/3, folio 39–40. 'The model' reference remains unexplained.

32　*Vote*, 8 Apr 1911.

33　The enumerator noted: 'stated to have returned home shortly after midnight Sunday and removed on Monday morning'.

13　Laurence Housman's Kensington, with Clemence in Dorset

1　Lara Marks, *Metropolitan Maternity*, Rolopi, 1996, p. 53; 1911 census, 365 Portobello Road.

2　Marks, *Metropolitan*, figure 8:1, p. 271, pp. 66 and 139–40.

3　Including ILP member Marion Phillips.

4 Writer Cicely Hamilton was secretary of WFL Chelsea branch; Zoe Proctor, *Life and Yesterday*, pp. 95–7.

5 Lynne Walker, 'Locating the Global / Rethinking the Local: suffrage politics, architecture, and space', *Women's Studies Quarterly*, 34:1 & 2, 2006, p. 182.

6 Jill Liddington and Tara Morton, 'Walking with Women's Suffrage in Kensington and Chelsea', *Herstoria*, 2011.

7 Housman, *Unexpected*, pp. 286–7.

8 I am most grateful to Elizabeth Oakley for H. S. Housman's unpublished typescript.

9 Undated letter, probably 5 Apr 1911.

10 Undated letter, probably 3 Apr 1911. H. S. Housman suggests then Miss Wilson, a Mrs Calthrop, a Mrs Stratton and Jane were invited by Clem to evade with her; probable, though no corroborative evidence. It remains unclear whether 'Miss Wilson' is indeed 'Gertrude'.

11 Housman, *Unexpected*, pp. 287–8.

12 Undated, presumably 3 Apr 1911.

13 Probably 5 April 1911; again, 'in-wardness' suggests familiarity, even spirituality, in Clem's romantic medieval vocabulary.

14 Thus Clem became more a resister than an evader. Did the Registrar know that this inconspicuous-looking middle-aged woman had influential friends – and brothers? *See* Gazetteer for Dorset, p. 321.

15 Or was she persuaded to comply remembering her two children born to her earlier marriage, both of whom had died?

16 Possibly she remembered the early deaths of her four brothers.

17 *BMJ*, 19 Jul 1947, and *Lancet*, 12 Jul 1947; thanks to Irene Cockroft for these references. After Black Friday, her possibly reservations about militancy? Clemence appears not to know of Ernestine's proximity, though surely they were well acquainted.

18 With close (soon even closer) links to Strachey clan.

19 They put their feminism into domestic practice, employing just one servant, thirty-four-year-old Sarah Chapman. Four of Sarah's five children had died, leaving just one still living. And below 'married 12 years' Bentham had written in brackets 'deserted 6 [years]' (this addition was deleted, presumably by the enumerator).

20 Wolfe, 1875–1974, member of the Civil Service Socialist Society; later, *Freedom Press*.

21 I am most grateful to Dave Annal, late of TNA, for this discovery. *DNB* for E. A. Maund.

22 Phyllis Ayrton; *see* Gazetteer, pp. 277–8.

23 Housman, *Unexpected*, pp. 286–7.

14 Annie Kenney's Bristol and Mary Blathwayt's Bath

1 Kenney, *Memories*, p. 123; Crawford, *Regional*, p. 133.

2 Bristol (1888 Act) was deemed to be in counties of both Gloucestershire and Somerset (on its border); but the 1911 census, for convenience, shows it in Gloucestershire. See Gazetteer, pp. 319–20.

3 Oakley, *Siblings*, p. 94.

4 OS maps, Clifton Down, 1902 and Bristol (NW) Clifton, 1901. Only Bristol West, which included Clifton, was Conservative.

5 Jane Marcus (ed.), *The Young Rebecca*, p. 149 (written 1913).

6 Quoted in Crawford, *Reference*, p. 314. Indeed, one of Annie's brothers went on to edit the *Daily Herald*, while two sisters trained as Montessori teachers, later opening their own school near New York.

7 Mary Richardson, *Laugh a Defiance*, Weidenfeld and Nicolson, 1953, pp. 110–11; it overlooked the Wye Valley.

8 June Hannam, 'Blathwayt Diaries', in Claire Eustance, Joan Ryan and Laura Ugolini (eds), *A Suffrage Readers: charting directions in British suffrage history*, Leicester University Press, 2000, pp. 53–5. The Blathwayts also had a newly acquired gramophone.

9 Ex-NUWSS. Cowman, *Spirit*, pp. 30–1 and 51–3.

10 Hannam, 'Blathwayt', p. 56; possibly hypothyroidism. Crawford, *Reference*, p. 317.

11 Mary Blathwayt's diary [MB], Gloucestershire Archives.

12 Cowman, *Spirit*, pp. 82–4; Emily Blathwayt's diary [EB], 21 Mar 1911.

13 MB and EB diaries, 18 Mar 1911; EB, 13 Apr 1911. The details of Helen's move away from Nottingham remain unclear.

14 EB's and MB's diaries, 14 Mar 1911.

15 *VfW*, 10 and 24 Feb 1911.

16 *Vote*, 25 Mar 1911. *Cheltenham Chronicle* and *Gloucestershire Echo*, 31 Mar, 1 and 3 Apr 1911; the issue was about reaching fifty thousand population total, so that Cheltenham could gain county borough status.

17 *VfW*, 24 Mar 1911; Antonia Raeburn, *The Militant Suffragettes*, p. 176, for local 'Census Ditty'.

18 *VfW*, 17, 10 and 31 Mar 1911.

19 Oakley, *Siblings*, p. 88; *Bristol Times & Mirror*, 30 Mar and 1 Apr 1911.

20 Kenney, *Memories*, p. 168.

21 LB's diary, 31 Mar 1911.

22 MB's diary, 23 Mar 1911; MB's pocket diary, 31 Mar 1911; she then wrote up these jottings into her more formal diary.

23 EB's diary, pp. 188–9.

24 The schedule records that one of Emily's three children had died young; this death was much earlier, and Emily's diary does not mention it.

25 Mrs Rogers was wife of F. W. Rogers, Clifton, MLWS.

26 The address given on the schedule is that of the WSPU offices.
Helen Watts, twenty-nine, boarder with her brother (twenty-six, schoolmaster), Chilcompton, complies.

27 *Gloucs Echo*, 3 Apr 1911; *Cheltenham Chron*, 8 Apr 1911 for more laconic report.

28 Ada Flatman's schedule could be a copy of the original, with her statement omitted. The enumerator's summary page offers just the population totals for Bedford Lodge, College Road.

29 It almost looks like three hands: AK's, enumerator's and a third person. On foot of the summary page is added a note: 'See Form Enclosed', but this is seemingly no longer available.

30 *Bristol Times & Mirror*, 4 Apr 1911.

31 For Lilian and her mother Mahalah, see Liddington, *Rebel Girls*, pp. 267–8. Of Bristol's labour movement figures, the Gazetteer includes the example of Bertha Ayles (WLabL, ILP).

32 *Bristol Times & Mirror*, 4 Apr 1911.

33 Crawford, *Regional*, p. 132, notes that a second NUWSS branch was formed in industrial East Bristol, led by two ILP members.

15 Jessie Stephenson's Manchester and Hannah Mitchell's Oldham Road

1 Less well represented was WTRL (also Actresses, Writers, Artists). Swanwick's autobiography shows her very busy, up and down, rationalist and bitterly exasperated with WSPU.

2 *VfW*, 17 Mar 1911.

3 Stephenson, 'No Other Way', pp. 249–50.

4 *VfW*, 24 and 31 Mar 1911.

5 Mitchell, *The Hard Way Up*, 1968 [out of print], quoted in *One Hand*, p. 23.

6 Mitchell, *Hard Way*, quoted in *One Hand*, p. 223. Including Colne Valley, see *Rebel Girls*, pp. 148–9.

7 Mitchell, *Hard Way*, pp. 170–5.

8 Manchester Central Branch ILP, minutes, 7 Mar 1911 (Kemp re Poor Law) and 16 May 1911 (Sam Robinson proposes Mitchells as new members, so they had probably attended a few months before that).

9 Mitchell, *Hard Way*, pp. 175–7.

10 *Vote*, 25 Nov 1909 ff. *DNB* for John Manning and Ruth Manning-Saunders. House demolished, only the gateposts surviving.

11 *Vote*, 25 Feb 1911.

12 *Vote*, 11 Mar 1011; chairs crowded on to stairs outside, and Russian toffee sold.

13 *Vote*, 4–25 Mar 1911. Sadly, the minutes of the Manchester branch of the Men's League start in Aug 1912; however, they includes a useful list of officers' names and addresses.

14 *Vote*, 25 Mar and 1 Apr 1911.

15 Stephenson, 'No Other Way', pp. 254–5. Here and generally, minor punctuation additions.

16 Stephenson, 'No Other Way', p. 253.

17 Stephenson, 'No Other Way', p. 254. Birrell visited Manchester, guarded by detectives and police, one woman was arrested, *VfW*, 31 Mar 1911

18 Stephenson, 'No Other Way', p. 255; an early sleeping bag prototype?

19 Stephenson, 'No Other Way', pp. 255–6.

20 Is the woman in glasses (bottom left) Eva Gore-Booth? What are the two banners, and is it a Votes for Women box?

21 Stephenson, 'No Other Way', p. 256, and handwritten addendum, p. 255.

22 *MG*, 3 Apr 1911.

23 *MG*, 3 Apr 1911.

24 *MG*, 3 Apr 1911.

25 *Daily Sketch*, 4 Apr 1911, claiming its photographer took it; Maud Arncliffe Sennett cuttings coll., BL. In fact, this image is taken from the original photograph, among the family papers of John Brock's late father, which were originally the property of his cousin, Mabel Capper.

26 Stephenson, 'No Other Way', pp. 260–2. One reporter, surely *Guardian*, and Robert Banks were apparently were still present. A demand for 7s 6d for 'Census Lodge' as occupied.

27 Postcard, Nellie Hall papers, on loan to Birmingham Museums Trust.

28 *Vote*, 15 Apr 1911.

29 *MG*, 3 Mar 1911.

30 *Vote*, 15 Apr 1911.

31 *Vote*, 15 Apr 1911; route entailed crossing the Mersey.

32 See Gazetteer for Annot Robinson (at foot of Oldham Road), probably evading; and at top, the Lees of Werneth Park (NUWSS).

33 CP to JB, 19 Sep 1909 (JB mss), quoted in Cowman, *Spirit*, p. 29.

34 Cowman, *Spirit*, pp. 54, 57 and 131. E.g. her handbill on 'The Labour of Married Women: a working woman's reply to Mr John Burns'.

35 Sadly, the letters from London to JB end in Dec 1909; see Judith Smart, 'Jennie Baines: an Australian connection', in June Purvis and Sandra H. Holton (eds), *Votes for Women*, Routledge, 2000, pp. 251, a most useful discussion. Indeed, JB seems virtually to disappear from mid-1910 to mid-1912.

36 A public meeting was advertised as not only non-party but also non-militant: *Stockport Express*, 23 Mar 1911. Also Stockport Labour Church, 'Merrie England' Bazaar 1907, Official Handbook, lists Mr G. Baines among those running the Men's Stall. It is unlikely that George, with wife away or ill, was able to be more active.

16 English journey: sweeping back down from Teesside to Thames

1 NUWSS branch minutes do survive, but have omitted here.

2 Mbro WFL mins, 8 Dec 1910 and 23 Jan 1911.

3 Mbro WFL mins, 10 Jan and 17 Feb 1911, Alison Neilans; Miss Hawkins: appointed agent.

4 *North Eastern Daily Gazette*, 29 Mar 1911.

5 WFL member Elsie Hayton was an LEA teacher, and her father was local Registrar.

6 *Bradford Telegraph & Argus*, 3 Apr 1911. 'No hint is given of the number of suff'gettes who resisted, save that it is said to be large'. Ilkley link = Laurence H's 5 Misses Thompsons?

7 There were also local campaigns around health inequalities, led by Alderman Broadbent.

8 In nearby Halifax, where Emmeline had spoken, there were more boycotters.

9 *Sheff Daily Tel*, 3 Apr 1911.

10 *Nottingham Evening News*, 3 Apr 1911.

11 Barnsby, *Black Country*, p. 31.

12 *Suffrage Annual*, 1913, p. 363: '5 years a member of [WFL] Executive' (c. 1908–13).

13 Emma Sproson, handwritten memoirs, Wolverhampton, pp. 49–50; minor punctuation added.

14 Helen Boswell evades, a few minutes' walk away, large house. For evasions in Leicester, see Jess Jenkins, *The Burning Question: the struggle for women's suffrage in Leicestershire* (Leicester, 2012), chap 10. The Leicester registrar was particularly conscientious.

15 *Suffolk Chronicle*, 7 Apr 1911, plus other local papers; with thanks to Joy Bounds.

16 *Portsmouth Evening News* [*PEN*], 3 Apr 1911; Launcelot Surry more carping in his soured reminiscences. Dobbie, *Nest*, p. 46.

17 *VfW*, 3, 10 Feb 1911, and Hugh Franklin. CM earlier lodged with the Peacocks; Lilian Peacock was a key activist.

18 Sarah Peacock, *Votes for Women: the women's fight in Portsmouth*, City of Portsmouth 1983, pp. 8–9.

19 *Vote*, 11 and 18 Feb and 4, 11 and 25 Mar 1911.

20 *PEN*, 22 Mar 1911.

21 *VfW*, 31 Mar 1911; *PEN*, 25 and 27 Mar and 4 Apr 1911.

22 It was probably Number 14, sandwiched between Albert Buick's restaurant and Walter Gleave's fancy draper's, opposite Mills's booksellers. The arcade has much changed, and St James's Hall is in a heavily redeveloped area.

23 *PEN*, 29 and 30 Mar 1911. Play-reading by Leigh Lovel, Octavia Kenmore, *Vote*, 1 Apr 1911.

24 *PEN*, 3 Apr 2012. Again, police alerted to 'bogus enumerators', and close watch kept all day.

25 Undoubtedly Lilian Peacock; see Gazetteer.

26 *Vote*, 15 Apr 1911.

27 Also MAL coll, 'Midnight Supper Party on Wimbledon Common: Vanloads of Women'. Kitty Marshall's schedule records ten females, one male (Mr Marshall), Putney Heath. For details of prosecution of the drivers, see www.womanandher sphere.

28 The white strip over the Disability column is retained here, an as example of how schedules initially looked in 2009.

17 After census night: Clemence's resistance, Asquith's betrayal

1 Most of these press pages are taken from Maud Arncliffe Sennett's cutting books, BL.

2 *The Times*, 3 and 4 Apr 1911.

3 Burns's diary, BL.

4 Randolph S. Churchill, *Winston S. Churchill*, vol ii, 'Companion', part 3, 1911–14, 1069, p. 1471. See Chapter 10, note 36 above for diary reference.

5 *Hansard*, 5 Apr 1911, p. 2194, Oral Answers; Malcolm MP, Unionist, Croydon.

6 *Hansard*, 5 April 1911, Oral Answers, pp. 2194–5; also 30 June 1911, Written Answers, pp. 774–5; *MG*, 6 Apr 1911 (for cheers etc).

7 *VfW*, 7 Apr 1911, quoting *Pall Mall Gazette*.

8 *VfW*, 14 and 21 Apr 1911; and Laurence Housman at Queen's Hall, 10 April.

9 *Vote*, 8 and 15 Apr 1911.

10 Hume, *National Union*, pp. 104–6, quoting HNB to Fawcett, 7 May 1911.

11 *Vote*, 17 June 1911; no trace apparently remains of this Census banner.

12 Tickner, *Spectacle*, pp. 122–31: 'the largest and most triumphant, the most harmonious' of all demonstrations.

13 For Bellingham-Prout corr, see Chapter 18; also Gazetteer, p. 294.

14 Census Comm Mins, 26 and 27 Apr 1911.

15 Burns's diary, BL.

16 'Census of England and Wales, 1911', 'Preliminary Report with Tables of the Population', pp. iii–xiv, Jun 1911; figures for England and Wales.

17 Reports can be accessed at www.histpop.org, including lucid introductory essays by Edward Higgs.

18 *Hansard*, Written Answers, 30 Jun 1911, pp. 774–5.

19 Burns's diary, BL.

20 *Vote*, 15 Apr and 20 May 1911; also Dr Winifred Patch (Highgate) and Francis (Brighton). WTRL mins, 7 Apr – 26 May, 9 Jun and 21 Jul 1911.

21 *Evening Star*, 26 May 1911.

22 Interview, c. 1983, Betty Boyd-Brown aged about ninety-three, recorded by Nan Tuckey. Thanks to Joy Bounds.

23 *Vote*, 3 Jun 1911. This is little known to suffrage historians; however, 1913 *Suffrage Annual* claims that Constance was the first woman to go to prison for tax. Robert Ratcliffe, 'History of the Working Class Movement in Ipswich 1900–1918', thesis, pp. 73–5.

24 *Suffrage Annual* 1913, p. 363. Barnsby, *Black Country*, pp. 14–15. WTRL mins, 21 Jul 1911. Crawford, *Reference*, notes the dog was shot by police.

25 WTRL mins, 26 May 1911.

26 Housman, *Unexpected*, pp. 283–4. *VfW*, 29 Sep 1911.

27 Housman, *Alice in Ganderland: a one-act play*, Women's Press, pp. 3–4.

28 WTRL mins, 29 Sep 1911.

29 TWL image is slightly different from that in Oakley, *Siblings*, p. XIX (*Standard*, 30 Sep 1911) including Kineton Parkes; pp. 84–5, and quotes *The Times*, 30 Sep 1911.

30 Housman, *Unexpected*, p. 285.

31 HO/44/1169/214572, 2 and 3 Oct 1911.

32 Housman, *Unexpected*, p. 285; Oakley, *Siblings*, pp. 85–6.

33 Quoted in Holton, *Suffrage Days*, p. 174, which notes suffrage leadership reservations about tax resistance as a tactic.

34 *VfW*, 13 Oct 1911; Stephen Housman, 'Banners', p. 45.

35 Reproduced in Oakley, *Siblings*, p. XX.

36 Pugh, *The March*, pp. 140–1 and 199–200, on Liberal misgivings.

37 Purvis, *Emmeline*, pp. 259–60 and cover image.

38 'Census of England and Wales, 1911', Vol. I, 'Administrative Areas: Counties, Urban and Rural Districts etc', [Jul] 1912, pp. xxvi–xxvii, noting regional variations, and suggesting various factors, though not the boycott. (Table 4 gave figures just for England as 34 million, of whom 17.6 million were female, a ratio of 1,073 females to 1,000 males.)

39 'General Report, with Appendices', 1917.

18 Telling the story: suffrage and census historiographies

1 The following section owes much to Elizabeth Crawford's research for our *HWJ* article, 2011; see Chapter 19.

2 *The Suffrage Annual and Women's Who's Who*, ed. by A. J. R. [...], Stanley Paul & Co, 1913, pp. 112, 114–15.

3 A. E. Metcalfe, *Woman's Effort: a chronicle of British women's fifty years' struggle for citizenship 1865–1914*, B. H. Blackwell, 1917, pp. 170–1.

4 Both long out of print; reference copies of *Suffrage Annual* and *The Woman's Effort* read in Women's Library and British Library respectively.

5 G. Colmore, *The Life of Emily Davison: an outline*, Woman's Press, 1913, p. 40.

6 E. Pankhurst, *My Own Story*, 1914, US and Eveleigh Nash UK, pp. 190–1 and 193–4, Virago 1979 edition; Jill Craigie, 1978, Introduction; Emmeline's dictation began the first day of journey to New York.

7 E.g. Rosen, *Rise Up, Women!*, p. 167. In the circumstances, Emmeline's memory was understandably somewhat hazy.

8 1911 Census, Vol XII, 'Fertility of Marriage', Part II, 1923, p. vi.

9 A. Kenney, *Memories of a Militant*, E. Arnold, 1924, p. 168. Annie had reason for her census memory to be overlain; in 1920 she married, had a son, and led a secluded domestic life.

10 E. Sharp, *Hertha Ayrton, 1854–1923, a memoir*, E. Arnold, 1926, p. 231. Again, copies of this are rare, sometimes being catalogued under physics. For her census statement, see Gazetteer, p. 281.

11 Ray Strachey, '*The Cause': a short history of the women's movement in Great Britain*, Bell, 1928 and Virago 1978, p. 310.

12 Sylvia Pankhurst, *The Suffragette Movement*, Longmans, 1931, Virago 1977; there is little mention of WFL either.

13 Nor was the census boycott mentioned in Christabel Pankhurst's memoir of the suffrage campaign, *Unshackled*, Hutchinson, 1959, apparently written at this time but published only posthumously.

14 Nevinson, *Life's Fitful Fever*, pp. 229–30; with cover illustration by C. R. W. Nevinson. Copies are now virtually unobtainable.

15 John, *Nevinson*, pp. 197–8; she died in 1932.

16 Housman, *The Unexpected Years*, pp. 286–290. Afterwards, Frederick Pethick-Lawrence commented: 'I'm glad you forced our hand'.

17 Mayhall notes the commemorative role of the Suffragette Fellowship (see note 22). Note however R. Fulford, *Votes for Women*, Faber, 1957, p. 240, a brief account of the boycott, attributing it to the WFL. However he suggests just 'a few hundreds', making it sound a bit of a jolly jape.

18 Antonia Raeburn, *The Militant Suffragettes*, Michael Joseph, 1973, and 1974 edition pp. 7–9 and 176–7.

19 Harrison coll, 8SUF/B/021, Nov 1974. Among the oral collection's perilous transmission story, this tape had been listed as 'missing', yet the catalogue summary tantalizingly noted that it included the census protest; I am grateful to TWL staff for

locating it so I could at last listen, in Mar 2012. However, see Gazetteer, Paddington; Cicely in fact complied, so this is probably a mis-memory,

20 See the *Radio Times* Special (1974). Midge Mackenzie, *Shoulder to Shoulder: A Documentary*, Penguin 1975, pp. 172–3, quotes Emmeline's *My Own Story*, and has interior photo of Manchester boycott, but with no detail provided.

21 Virago reissued *Suffragette Movement* in 1977, and *My Own Story* in 1979. Linklater's *Despard* was published in 1980 and Dobbie's *A Nest of Suffragettes* on the Blathwayts in 1979.

22 L. Mayhall, 'Creating the "Suffragette Spirit": British feminism and the historical imagination', *WHR*, 4:3, 1995. Also Hilda Kean, 'Searching for the Past', *WHR*, 3:1, 1994.

23 Holton, *Suffrage Days*, pp. 173–4; includes a photograph of Housman speaking in Trafalgar Square on the boycott. Also Angela V. John and Claire Eustance, (eds), *The Men's Share? masculinities, male support and women's suffrage in Britain, 1890–1920*, Routledge, 1997, on the Men's League etc.

24 Eustance, 'Meanings of Militancy', in Joannou and Purvis (eds), *Women's Suffrage Movement*, 1998, pp. 58–9; also Frances, 'Pay the Piper, call the tune!', on WTRL, in the same collection.

25 Crawford, *The Women's Suffrage Movement*, UCL Press, 1999 and Routledge 2001, p. 721; she used the 1841–1891 census returns for biographical clues about women otherwise little known.

26 Mayhall, *The Militant Suffrage Movement*, Oxford University Press, 2003, pp. 8, 34, 44, 61

27 John, *War, Journalism and the Shaping of the Twentieth Century*.

28 Notably, Purvis, *Emmeline Pankhurst: a biography*, Routledge, 2002, p. 159, quoting Ethel Smyth. Also Cowman's meticulously researched *Women of the Right Spirit*, 2007, citing organizers' little-known memoirs.

29 For instance, Edward Higgs, *A Clearer Sense of the Census; the Victorian censuses and historical research*, HMSO, 1996.

30 E. Garrett, A. Reid, K. Schurer and S. Szreter, *Changing Family Size in England and Wales: place, class and demography, 1891–1911*, Cambridge University Press, 2001 and 2006; pp. 9, 20, 105, 321–2ff and 435; the Cambridge Group for the History of Population and Social Structure. However, their choice of eleven local studies across England (pp. 25–30) excluded large cities: unhelpfully there is no Bristol or Birmingham, no Leeds or Liverpool – exactly the urban centres where the suffrage movement was particularly strong.

31 Higgs, 'The Statistical Big Bang of 1911: ideology, technological innovation and the production of medical statistics', *Social History of Medicine*, 1996, pp. 413, 417–18. Higgs, 'The Rise of the Information State: the development of central state surveillance of the citizen in England, 1500–2000', *Journal of Historical Sociology*, 14:2 2001, pp. 183 and 192. More recently, his *Life, Death and Statistics*, Local Population Studies, 2004, offers a valuable historical overview of the GRO.

32 Peter Christian and David Annal, *Census: the expert guide*, The National Archives (TNA), 2008, p. 1.

19 Sources and their analysis: vanishing for the vote?

1 *Rebel Girls*, pp. 33–4 and 267ff.

2 First ordered 21 Dec 2007; received with a letter explaining the FOI ruling Dec 2006; Impey schedule, Birmingham.

3 Email correspondence, Nov 2008. Crawford, *Ancestors*, special 1911 census issue, 2009. The hundred years rule not was not introduced till the 1920 Census Act, thus making 1911 census early access unique.

4 Using an independent website operator, notably Findmypast. http://news.bbc.co.uk/1/hi/magazine, statement by findmypast.com commercial director.

5 This WSPU image probably predates the census boycott and is unrelated to it.

6 *Guardian* and *The Times*, 13 Jan 2009. Elizabeth Crawford interviewed on BBC Radio 5 Live.

7 By summer 2009, this was scaled down.

8 See Figure 29 for a sample summary page (Swanage).

9 As noted for Figure 41 (Muriel Matters), schedules initially had details in the 'Infirmity' column covered up; so Howey's 'not enfranchised' disability became apparent only very recently. See back cover.

10 Also Crawford, *The Women's Suffrage Movement in Britain and Ireland: a regional survey*, Routledge, 2006. Our MAIN Excel database revealed that very few NUWSS members had evaded or resisted; so for our LOCAL database, we did not search them rigorously.

11 Also, keying in the year '1811' eventually identified suffragettes who had refused to give information; or the word 'suffrage' turned up committed campaigners.

12 Prout's name was previously unknown to us; grateful thanks to Dave Annal at TNA for alerting us to this correspondence. Prout lived next door to the local Bowes Park WSPU secretary.

13 Populations: London, 4,522,000; Yorkshire 3,980,000; England, 34,000,000. Familiarity with the area was essential, for searches required knowledge of local boundaries and place names. Identifying representative sample regions of course remained always problematic.

14 About three-quarters of London WSPU names apparently boycotted, while across Yorkshire under half of those with some WSPU connection did so. And WFL was not strong outside Middlesbrough and Sheffield.

15 '"Women do not count, neither shall they be counted"', *HWJ*, spring 2011. It was based upon our joint paper presented at Women's History Network conference, Oxford, Sep 2009; see below.

16 The shift was also because searches for additional local names had become increasingly laborious and often fruitless.

17 Other than in Bradford, the boycott was more widespread in non-textile Yorkshire cities, notably Sheffield and York.

18 For the focus on four communities, see Introduction.

19 WHN conference (Sep 2009) on Women, Gender & Political Spaces: Historical Perspectives. Also discussion at Warwick University conference, Feb 2010, on my

paper, 'Communication Communities: Neighbourhood networks in the Evasion of the 1911 census', on forging 'shared bonds of identity'.

See also Walker, 'Locating the Global', 2006.

20 Doreen Massey's *Space, Place and Gender* (1994), pp. 2, 11, 169; chapter, 'A place called home?' The literature is clearly summarized in Beebe, Davis and Gleadle, 'Introduction: Space, Place and Gendered Identities: feminist history and the spatial turn', *WHR*, 21:4, Sep 2012.

I also drew upon other interdisciplinary work, notably Manchester University, Sociology Department, Neighbourhood Networks seminar, Oct 2010; Leeds University, POLIS seminars on radical social protest (e.g. Occupy movement); and Geography seminars on Citizenship & Belonging. Finally, recent discussion of new mapping technologies (GIS) at the IHR/RHS conference 'Locating the Past: history & geography', Feb 2012.

21 Mabel Capper postcard; also Manchester University Library for C. P. Scott mss.

22 Copies in Nottingham Archives; interview with Barry Edwards.

23 Some of these suffrage house images had to be omitted at final draft stage, but these and others may be seen by going to www.jliddington.org.uk

24 We moved between both Findmypast and Ancestry search engines, from our home computers, regretting we did not have more powerful broadband connections. Elizabeth compiled London boroughs and Middlesex, I all other counties.

25 See also Bristol and Liverpool.

26 Sadly, this minute book ended in Feb 1909 (see Chapter 16, note 7). By 1911, it is difficult to estimate the extent of active local membership. Some seemingly were lapsed WSPU members, or merely sympathetic supporters. Of the Huddersfield names, only a selection are included in Gazetteer, and so far no boycotters identified.

27 For her lengthy statement and story, see www.womanandhersphere.com

28 See Gazetteer for Devon, p. 322.

29 Other examples: Cameron-Swan household, Croydon, mysteriously missing wife and probably servant. In West Sussex, Florence de Fontblanque undoubtedly evaded, 'taking' two servants with her, leaving one behind with her husband.

30 Confusingly, Miss Beldon, secretary to Barnes WSPU branch, lived at Bishops Mansions, Fulham.

31 Possible exceptions include Emily Smith, cook (Kensington); and cook and housemaids who refused information 'being suffragettes' (Hampstead); see Gazetteer, pp. 269, 252. The growing literature notes how thinking about servants helps explore the home as workplace.

32 Also Laura Ainsworth in Gillingham; however no schedule identified yet, despite best efforts of both compilers, plus Medway towns' historian. The presence of a dynamic organizer (here, Dr Helena Jones) helps explain why there were more evaders in Halifax, say, than in neighbouring Huddersfield.

33 It seems WSPU branch structures remained more resilient in London area. For WSPU organizers, Cowman, *'Right Spirit'*; there is yet no study of WFL organizers.

34 Of course, it also aimed to link infant mortality and women's fertility with age on marriage and mothers' occupations.

35 Memorial to friends, Margaret MacDonald and Mary Middleton, who had both died

earlier in 1911. Additionally, of course, there remained adult suffrage criticisms of the Conciliation Bill.

36 Poignantly, in Sale sixty-seven-year-old Eliza Hines's schedule states that only ill-health prevented her from evading.

37 Mass evasions for which schedules have not yet been found include York, Birmingham, Leeds and Halifax. Since we completed the Gazetteer, we have discovered additional boycotters (e.g. a mass evasion near Birmingham) and we hope to include these in a subsequent edition.

38 The problem of double-counting (i.e. 'counting' an evader *both* as missing from home and as present at a local mass evasion) is recognized. However, this is arguably balanced by the unknown number of so many elusive 'weak' evaders.

39 Examples of conscientious registrars making 'careful Inquiries' for an individual schedule include Binnie, West Wittering. The mass evasion in Newcastle is an instance of co-operation between the registrar and chief constable.

40 In this sense, using the boycott as a vehicle to gain publicity rather than an attempt to invalidate the totals appears in retrospect to be the more effective – though of course this was not apparent at the time. Note from last chapter the slight revising of sex ratios.

41 The extent of under-enumeration in the 1991 census, the time of the poll tax, was estimated at over 1 million, especially of young city-centre men. See Daniel Dorling and Steve Simpson, 'Those Missing Millions: implications for Social Statistics of Undercount in the 1991 Census', *Radical Statistics*, 1993; thanks to David Lawrence for this reference. Outside Britain, examples of census resistance include Germany, United States and Bhutan; factors disengaging sections of the population from census compliance are less gender, and more often nationality, race and statelessness.

Select bibliography

Place of publication is London unless noted otherwise.

Primary sources

Archival collections: personal papers
Blathwayt Diaries, Gloucester Record Office.
John Burns Diaries, British Library.
Cuttings Book, Battersea Library.
Nellie Hall Papers, Birmingham Museums.
Housman Papers, Street Library.
H. Nevinson Diaries, Bodleian Library.
C. P. Scott Papers, Manchester University Library.
Maud Arncliffe Sennett Papers, British Library.
Emma Sproson Papers, Wolverhampton Record Office.
Stephenson, Jessie, 'No Other Way', unpublished typescript, [1932], Museum of London [MoL].
Strachey Papers, the Women's Library [TWL].
Suffragette Fellowship Papers, MoL.
Helen Watts Papers, Nottinghamshire Record Office.

Archival collections: organizations
Census Committee minutes, National Archives [TNA].
Home Office Papers, TNA.
Independent Labour Party [ILP], Manchester Central branch, minutes, Manchester Reference Library.
Men's League for Women's Suffrage, Manchester branch, minutes, John Rylands University Library of Manchester.
National Union of Women's Suffrage Societies, Executive Committee minutes, TWL.
Women's Freedom League, National Executive minutes, TWL.

Women's Freedom League, Middlesbrough branch, minutes, TWL.
Women's Freedom League, Militant Department, letters, TWL.
Women's Freedom League, Organizing Committee, minutes, TWL.
Women's Tax Resistance League, minutes, TWL.
Visiting Committee minutes, HM Prison [Winson Green], Birmingham Record Office.

Annual reports
Manchester and District Federation, NUWSS.
North of England [later, Manchester] Society for Women's Suffrage.
Women's Co-operative Guild.
Women's Freedom League (WFL).
Women's Social and Political Union (WSPU).

Newspapers and periodicals
British Medical Journal.
Common Cause.
Co-operative News.
Daily Mirror.
Daily Sketch.
Daily Telegraph.
Hansard.
Manchester Guardian.
Punch.
The Strand Magazine.
The Times.
The Vote.
Votes for Women.
Women's Franchise.

Local newspapers
Bradford Telegraph & Argus.
Bristol Times & Mirror.
Cheltenham Chronicle.
Gloucestershire Echo.
Guildford Free Press.
Halifax Evening Chronicle.
Halifax Guardian.
Lenton Times.
Nottingham Evening News.
North Eastern Daily Gazette.
Portsmouth Evening News.
Sheffield Daily Independent.
Sheffield Daily Telegraph.

Books

Autobiographies
Housman, Laurence, *The Unexpected Years*, Jonathan Cape, 1937.
Kenney, Annie, *Memories of a Militant*, Edward Arnold, 1924.
Mitchell, Hannah, *The Hard Way Up*, Faber 1968, & Virago 1977.
Nevinson, Margaret W., *Life's Fitful Fever: a volume of memories*, A. & C. Black, 1926.
Pankhurst, Emmeline, *My Own Story*, 1914, US & Eveleigh Nash UK, Virago 1979.
Smyth, Ethel, *Female Pipings in Eden*, Peter Davies, 1933.
Swanwick, Helena, *I Have Been Young*, Gollancz, 1935.

Novels, poetry and plays
Housman, Laurence, *An Englishwoman's Love Letters*, John Murray, 1900.
Housman, Laurence, *Articles of Faith in the Freedom of Women*, Fifield, 1910
Housman, Laurence, *Alice in Ganderland*, The Women's Press, 1911.
Watts, H. K. and N. H., *Poems by a Brother and Sister*, Saxton, Nottingham, 1906.
Whitman, Walt, *Leaves of Grass*, 1855 & Signet, New York, 1954.
Woolf, Virginia, *Night and Day*, Duckworth, 1919 & 1992.

Histories written by participants
Metcalfe, A. E., *Woman's Effort: a chronicle of British women's fifty years' struggle for citizenship 1865–1914*, Blackwell, Oxford, 1917.
Pankhurst, E. Sylvia, *The Suffragette Movement: an intimate account of persons and ideals*, 1931 & Virago, 1977.
Strachey, Ray, *'The Cause': a short history of the women's movement in Great Britain*, Bell, 1928 and Virago 1978.

Oral testimony
Cicely Hale, interview 6 Nov 1974, recorded by Brian Harrison, TWL.
Marie Lawson, interview 14 and 20 Nov 1974, recorded by Brian Harrison, TWL.
Betty Boyd-Brown, interview c. 1983, recorded by Nan Tuckey, Ipswich.
Muriel Matters, interview broadcast 1939.

Secondary sources

Reference
Crawford, Elizabeth, *The Women's Suffrage Movement: a reference guide 1866–1928*, Routledge, 1999 and 2001.
Crawford, Elizabeth, *The Women's Suffrage Movement in Britain and Ireland: a regional survey*, Routledge, Abingdon, 2006.
Dictionary of National Biography, Oxford University Press, 2004.
Pelling, Henry, *Social Geography of British Elections 1885–1910*, Macmillan, 1967.
R., A. J. (ed.), *The Suffrage Annual and Women's Who's Who*, Stanley Paul, 1913.
Saunders, Ann (ed.), *The A to Z of Edwardian London*, Harry Margary, 2007.

Biographies

Born, Anne, 'Clemence Housman 1861–1955', typescript, 1978, Street Library.

Brown, Kenneth, *John Burns*, Royal Historical Society, 1977.

Caine, Barbara, *Bombay to Bloomsbury: a biography of the Strachey family*, Oxford University Press, Oxford, 2005.

Colmore, Gertrude, *The Life of Emily Davison: an outline*, Woman's Press, 1913.

Engen, Rodney, *Laurence Housman*, Catalpa, Stroud, 1983.

Gilbert, Bentley B., *David Lloyd George: a political life: the architect of change 1863–1912*, Batsford, 1987.

Hattersley, Roy, *David Lloyd George: the great outsider*, Little, Brown, 2010.

John, Angela V., *War, Journalism and the Shaping of the Twentieth Century: the life and times of Henry W. Nevinson*, I. B. Tauris, 2006.

John, Angela V., *Evelyn Sharp: rebel woman, 1869–1955*, Manchester University Press, Manchester, 2009.

Kent, William, *John Burns: Labour's lost leader*, Williams & Norgate, 1950.

Linklater, Andro, *An Unhusbanded Life: Charlotte Despard: suffragette, socialist and Sinn Feiner*, Hutchinson, 1980.

The Muriel Matters Society, *Why Muriel Matters: a centenary commemoration celebration*, Adelaide, booklet, [2010]

Oakley, Elizabeth, *Inseparable Siblings: a portrait of Clemence & Laurence Housman*, Brewin Books, Studley, 2009.

Purvis, June, *Emmeline Pankhurst: a biography*, Routledge, 2002.

Sharp, Evelyn, *Hertha Ayrton, 1854–1923, a memoir*, E. Arnold, 1926.

Stanley, Liz with Morley, Ann, *The Life and Death of Emily Wilding Davison: a biographical detective story*, with Gertrude Colman, *The life of Emily Davison* [1913], Women's Press, 1988.

Histories

Barnsby, George, *Votes for Women: the struggle for the vote in the Black Country 1900–1918*, Wolverhampton [booklet], 1995.

Christian, Peter and Annal, David, *Census: the expert guide*, TNA, 2008.

Cowman, Krista, *Women of the Right Spirit: paid organisers of the Women's Social and Political Union (WSPU) 1904–18*, Manchester University Press, Manchester, 2007.

Crawford, Elizabeth, 'From Frederick Street to Winson Green': the women's suffrage movement in Birmingham 1866–1918 [booklet], 2000.

Dangerfield, George, *The Strange Death of Liberal England 1910–1914*, 1935 and Perigee, New York, 1980.

Dobbie, B. M. Willmott, *A Nest of Suffragettes in Somerset: Eagle House, Batheston*, Batheaston Society [booklet], 1979.

Eustance, Claire, Ryan, Joan, and Ugolini, Laura (eds), *A Suffrage Reader: charting directions in British suffrage history*, Leicester University Press, 2000.

Fulford, Roger, *Votes for Women*, Faber, 1957.

Garrett, Eilidh, Reid, Alice, Schurer, Kevin, and Szreter, Simon, *Changing Family Size in England and Wales: place, class and demography, 1891–1911*, Cambridge University Press, Cambridge, 2001 and 2006.

Higgs, Edward, *Life, Death and Statistics: civil registration, censuses and the work of the General Register Office, 1836–1952*, Local Population Studies, Hatfield, 2004.

Higgs, Edward, *Making Sense of the Census Revisited: census records of England & Wales, 1801–1901*, Institute of Historical Research, 2005.

Holton, Sandra, *Feminism and Democracy: women's suffrage and reform politics in Britain 1900–1918*, Cambridge University Press, Cambridge, 1986.

Holton, Sandra, *Suffrage Days: stories from the women's suffrage movement*, Routledge, 1996.

Hume, Leslie, *The National Union of Women's Suffrage Societies*, Garland, New York, 1982.

Joannou, Maroula and Purvis, June (eds), *The Women's Suffrage Movement: new feminist perspectives*, Manchester University Press, Manchester, 1998.

John, Angela V. and Eustance, Claire (eds), *The Men's Share? masculinities, male support and women's suffrage in Britain, 1890–1920*, Routledge, 1997.

Liddington, Jill, *Rebel Girls: their fight for the vote*, Virago Press, 2006.

Liddington, Jill and Norris, Jill, *One Hand Tied Behind Us: the rise of the women's suffrage movement*, Virago Press, 1978, 1984, Rivers Oram Press, 2000.

Mackenzie, Midge, *Shoulder to Shoulder: a documentary*, Penguin 1975.

Marks, Lara, *Metropolitan Maternity: maternal and infant welfare services in early twentieth century London*, Rodopi, Amsterdam, 1996.

Massey, Doreen, *Space, Place and Gender*, Polity, Cambridge, 1994.

Mayhall, Laura E. Nym, *The Militant Suffrage Movement: citizenship and resistance in Britain, 1860–1930*, Oxford University Press, New York, 2003.

Newsome, Stella, *Women's Freedom League 1907–1957*, Women's Freedom League [booklet], [1960].

Peacock, Sarah, *Votes for Women: the women's fight in Portsmouth*, City of Portsmouth [booklet], 1983.

Pugh, Martin, *The March of the Women: a revisionist analysis of the campaign for women's suffrage, 1866–1914*, Oxford University Press, Oxford, 2000.

Purvis, June and Holton, Sandra H. (eds), *Votes for Women*, Routledge, 2000.

Raeburn, Antonia, *The Militant Suffragettes*, Michael Joseph, 1973 and NEL, 1974.

Rosen, Andrew, *Rise Up, Women! The militant campaign of the Women's Social and Political Union 1903–1914*, Routledge, 1974.

Thane, Pat, *Foundations of the Welfare State*, Longman, 1982 and 1996.

Tickner, Lisa, *The Spectacle of Women: imagery of the suffrage campaign 1907–14*, Chatto & Windus, 1987.

Whitmore, Richard, *Alice Hawkins and the Suffragette Movement in Edwardian Leicester*, Breedon Books, Derby, 2007.

Journal articles

Bearman, C. J., 'An Army Without Discipline? Suffragette militancy and the budget crisis of 1909', *Historical Journal*, 50:4, 2007.

Beebe, Kathryne, Davis, Angela, and Gleadle, Kathryn, 'Space, Place and Gendered Identities: feminist history and the spatial turn', *WHR*, 21:4, 2012.

Canning, Kathleen and Rose, Sonya, 'Gender, Citizenship and Subjectivity', *Gender & History*, 13:3, 2001.

Collins, Audrey, 'Sorting out the Census', *Ancestors*, 2009.

Crawford, Elizabeth, 'A Rich Network of Associations: Bloomsbury and women's suffrage', *The Charleston Magazine*, 19, 1999.

Crawford, Elizabeth, 'No Votes for Women, No Information from Women', *Ancestors*, 2009.

Davin, Anna, 'Imperialism and Motherhood', *HWJ*, 5, 1978.

Hart, Linda, 'Laurence Housman: a subject in search of a biographer', *HSJ*, 31, 2005

Higgs, Edward, 'The Statistical Big Bang of 1911: ideology, technological innovation and the production of medical statistics', *Social History of Medicine*, 1996.

Higgs, Edward, 'The Rise of the Information State: the development of central state surveillance of the citizen in England, 1500–2000', *Journal of Historical Sociology*, 14:2, 2001.

Holton, Sandra, 'The Suffragist and the "Average Woman"', *WHN*, 1:1, 1992.

Housman, Stephen, 'The Housman Banners', *HSJ*, 1992.

Hunt, Jo, 'Laurence Housman – the Younger Brother', *HSJ*, 16, 1990.

Kean, Hilda, 'Searching for the Past in Present Defeat: construction of historical and political identity in British feminism in the 1920s & 1930s', *WHR*, 3:1, 1994.

Liddington, Jill and Crawford, Elizabeth, '"Women do not count: neither shall they be counted": suffrage, citizenship and the battle for the 1911 census', *HWJ*, 71 (2011).

Liddington, Jill and Morton, Tara, 'Walking with Women's Suffrage in Kensington and Chelsea', *Herstoria*, 2011.

Mayhall, Laura E. Nym, 'Creating the "Suffragette Spirit": British feminism and the historical imagination', *Women's History Review*, 4:3, 1995.

Morgan, Kenneth, '"Rare and Refreshing Fruit", Lloyd George's People's Budget', *Public Policy Research*, 16:1, 2009.

Morton, Tara, 'Changing Spaces: art, politics, and identity in the home studios of the Suffrage Atelier', *WHR*, 21:4, 2012.

Walker, Lynne, 'Locating the Global / Rethinking the Local: suffrage politics, architecture, and space', *Women's Studies Quarterly*, 34:1 & 2, 2006.

Websites

www.histpop.org – for 1911 census data.

www.womanandhersphere.com – for further details of the boycott.

www.jliddington.org.uk – for suffrage house images and other boycott information.

Theses

Ratcliffe, Robert, 'History of the Working Class Movement in Ipswich 1900–1918'.

Eustance, Claire, '"Daring to be Free": the evolution of women's political identities in the Women's Freedom League 1907–1930', University of York, D.Phil., 1993.

Index

Page numbers in *italics* refer to the Gazetteer.